— SHAMMAH BALISONG —

the one year®
THROUGH
the BIBLE
devotional

Shammah Balisong   *February 1.2011*

With devotionals by David R. Veerman

Shammah Praise V. Balisong

TYNDALE HOUSE PUBLISHERS, INC.
CAROL STREAM, ILLINOIS

Visit Tyndale's exciting Web site at www.tyndale.com

TYNDALE and Tyndale's quill logo are registered trademarks of Tyndale House Publishers, Inc.

The One Year is a registered trademark of Tyndale House Publishers, Inc.

The One Year through the Bible Devotional

Designed by Erik Peterson

Edited by S. Harrison

Previously published in 2000 as One Year through the Bible by Tyndale House Publishers under ISBN-13: 978-0-8423-3553-9 and ISBN-10: 0-8423-3553-6.

The One Year through the Bible Devotional first published in 2007.

The Library of Congress has cataloged the first edition as follows:

Veerman, David
    One Year through the Bible : with devotionals / by David R. Veerman and Daryl J. Lucas.
    p. cm.
    ISBN 0-8423-3553-6 (pbk.)
    1. Bible—Reading. 2. Bible—Devotional literature. 3. Devotional calendars. I. Lucas, Daryl.
II. Title.
BS617.V44 2000
242'.2—dc21   00-044704

ISBN 978-1-4143-1299-6

Printed in the United States of America

13 12 11 10 09
7   6   5   4   3

INTRODUCTION

CENTURIES AGO, THE APOSTLE PAUL wrote to his young protégé, Timothy: "All Scripture is inspired by God and is useful to teach us what is true and to make us realize what is wrong in our lives" (2 Timothy 3:16). Note that Paul said "*all* Scripture"—not a part or some, but all. *All* means all of the Bible, every part and every type of literature—law, history, poetry, prophecy, Gospel, epistle, and apocalypse.

That short passage in Paul's letter also emphasizes what Scripture does: "It corrects us when we are wrong and teaches us to do what is right. God uses it to prepare and equip his people to do every good work" (2 Timothy 3:16-17). In other words, the Bible tells us how to live by showing us what God wants. As we read Scripture, we need to think about what God is revealing about himself and what he is telling us to do—what actions to take and what changes to make.

This book helps you do just that—read and apply the Bible. Here's how it works:

— Each day features a daily reading, highlighted in the middle of the page. If you read all these passages from your Bible, you will read the entire Bible in a year.

— From each of the daily reading passages, we have selected a short excerpt, which is included on the same page. If you read only those smaller passages each day, you will get a sampling of the whole Bible, hitting the highlighted stories and teachings.

— Each selected Scripture passage also ties to a daily devotional reading, which is designed to help you understand the passage and apply it to your life.

I pray that God will use this book to impact your life, giving you a deeper appreciation and understanding of "all Scripture."

DAVE VEERMAN

Diets can be maddening because they make it so difficult to stick to your convictions. The plan looks great, with a limit on calories or grams of fat per day and a list of prohibited or acceptable edibles. But when offered a piece of pie, you give in to the temptation, forgetting your diet and your resolution to lose weight. This struggle is real. It's war.

This passage right at the beginning of the Bible tells all about the origin of the world, life, people, and work. It also covers husband-wife relationships. Closest to home, it explains how a perfect world went wrong and why human beings have struggled since then against all sorts of evil. It tells about temptation.

Read Genesis 1:1–3:24

Everyone struggles with temptation. We are tempted to lie, to cheat, to steal, and to indulge ourselves in countless ways that God has forbidden. We give in because of Satan (Genesis 3:1-6). Temptation is Satan's invitation to live his kind of life and give up on God's. Satan tempted Eve and succeeded in getting her to sin; soon after, Adam yielded to the pull of Satan's tempting offer. So sin entered the world, and every person since has been born a sinner. Today, Satan is busy trying to get us to give in to his temptations.

Eve and Adam could have resisted temptation by remembering what God had commanded them. We must realize that being tempted is not sin. We have not sinned until we give in to the temptation. To resist temptation, we must (1) pray for strength to resist (see Matthew 6:13), (2) say no when confronted with what we know is wrong (see James 4:7), and (3) run away from the temptation, sometimes literally (see Genesis 39:12). James 1:12 tells of the blessings and rewards for those who don't give in when tempted.

As you read about the tragic fall of our perfect ancestors, watch the progression of temptation and sin. Then determine to obey God rather than believe Satan's lies. Resist Satan and his temptations, and live.

¹The serpent was the shrewdest of all the wild animals the LORD God had made. One day he asked the woman, "Did God really say you must not eat the fruit from any of the trees in the garden?" ²"Of course we may eat fruit from the trees in the garden," the woman replied. ³"It's only the fruit from the tree in the middle of the garden that we are not allowed to eat. God said, 'You must not eat it or even touch it; if you do, you will die.'" ⁴"You won't die!" the serpent replied to the woman. ⁵"God knows that your eyes will be opened as soon as you eat it, and you will be like God, knowing both good and evil." ⁶The woman . . . saw that the tree was beautiful and its fruit looked delicious. . . . So she took some of the fruit and ate it. Then she gave some to her husband, who was with her, and he ate it, too.

GENESIS 3:1-6

³When it was time for the harvest, Cain presented some of his crops as a gift to the LORD. ⁴Abel also brought a gift—the best of the firstborn lambs from his flock. The LORD accepted Abel and his gift, ⁵but he did not accept Cain and his gift. This made Cain very angry, and he looked dejected. ⁶"Why are you so angry?" the LORD asked Cain. . . . ⁷"You will be accepted if you do what is right. But if you refuse to do what is right, then watch out! Sin is crouching at the door, eager to control you. But you must subdue it and be its master." ⁸One day Cain suggested to his brother, "Let's go out into the fields." And while they were in the field, Cain attacked his brother, Abel, and killed him. ⁹Afterward the LORD asked Cain, "Where is your brother? Where is Abel?" "I don't know," Cain responded. "Am I my brother's guardian?"

GENESIS 4:3-9

How do you react when someone suggests that you have done something wrong? Do you move to correct the mistake, or do you deny that you have a problem or need to do anything? What about when the critic is someone in your family?

This reading describes Adam and Eve's immediate family. It focuses mostly on Cain, the first son—his choices and what God thought of them. Don't read too fast or you will miss important details—but it's all there, including the most horrifying fact of all: Cain killed his brother, Abel. Our experiences today mirror what occurred between these two brothers, however horrifying, because theirs is the story of what can happen when anger and jealousy rule.

Tangles in the ties that bind—reacting to criticism, jealousy, sibling rivalry—all appear in this passage. The lessons bear remembering, so you'd better go slow.

Read Genesis 4:1–5:32

Cain's failures hinged on his reaction to God's rebuke (Genesis 4:6-7). We don't know why God rejected Cain's sacrifice. But instead of listening to God, learning, and changing his ways, he reacted impulsively. Cain was wrong, yet he would not accept responsibility for or deal with it. He countered God's correction with anger and denial.

After Cain's sacrifice was rejected, God gave him the chance to right his wrong and try again. God even encouraged him to do so, but Cain proudly refused. The rest of Cain's life is a startling example of what happens to those who refuse to admit their mistakes. It also shows what happens when we blame others for our problems and allow anger to build.

As you read this passage, learn from Cain's mistakes. Then the next time someone suggests you are wrong, especially God, take an honest look at yourself, and make the necessary changes.

The end of the world is always near, according to somebody. This person's placard states that we had better change our ways—or die. That group proclaims that the Lord will return one hundred days after the next presidential election. Each week brings numerous alarms from environmental and nutritional activists or religious and political zealots. Most people stopped listening long ago to the warnings of these "kooks" or "extremists," as they are labeled.

That's probably how people responded to Noah. This passage tells the story of the Flood, how Noah and his family built an ark in obedience to God, in response to his warning that the earth would be destroyed. Only a few generations had passed since Adam and Eve, yet Noah was the only righteous person living. The Bible doesn't state that people mocked Noah, but it certainly shows that no one listened to him or to God. This familiar story pictures God's mercy and the consequences when people forget (or stop caring) about their Creator.

The story also gives a snapshot of patience (living in an ark for more than a year); doing what is right in the face of criticism and ridicule ("Why would you build an ark now and here?"); and gratitude (for God's mercy).

Read Genesis 6:1–8:22

⁹This is the account of Noah and his family. Noah was a righteous man, the only blameless person living on earth at the time, and he walked in close fellowship with God. ¹⁰Noah was the father of three sons: Shem, Ham, and Japheth. ¹¹Now God saw that the earth had become corrupt and was filled with violence. ¹²God observed all this corruption in the world, for everyone on earth was corrupt. ¹³So God said to Noah, "I have decided to destroy all living creatures, for they have filled the earth with violence. Yes, I will wipe them all out along with the earth! ¹⁴Build a large boat from cypress wood and waterproof it with tar, inside and out. Then construct decks and stalls throughout its interior. . . ." ²²So Noah did everything exactly as God had commanded him.

GENESIS 6:9-14, 22

Noah got right to work when God told him to build the ark (Genesis 6:22). It seems that other people had been warned about the coming disaster (see 1 Peter 3:20) but, apparently, did not expect it to happen. This is how people today often react to warnings, even warnings from God. Each day, thousands are told of God's inevitable judgment, yet most don't really believe it will occur. Don't expect people to welcome or accept your message of God's coming judgment on sin. Those who don't believe in God will scoff at his judgment and try to get you to deny God as well.

As you read this passage, note God's covenant with Noah to keep him safe and God's promise to the world. Then determine to do what God tells you to do, despite the opposition, trusting him to bring you through the flood.

¹At one time all the people of the world spoke the same language and used the same words. ²As the people migrated to the east, they found a plain in the land of Babylonia and settled there. ³They began saying to each other, "Let's make bricks and harden them with fire." . . . ⁴Then they said, "Come, let's build a great city for ourselves with a tower that reaches into the sky. This will make us famous and keep us from being scattered all over the world." ⁵But the LORD came down to look at the city and the tower the people were building. ⁶"Look!" he said. "The people are united, and they all speak the same language. After this, nothing they set out to do will be impossible for them! ⁷Come, let's go down and confuse the people with different languages. Then they won't be able to understand each other."

GENESIS 11:1-7

We build monuments to great moments and great people. "Lest we forget" is etched on the bronze plates of more than one statue. But monuments are more than just memory aids; in building them we want, above all, to glorify something. We want to honor a person or idealize an event.

Shortly after the Flood, God made a covenant (or agreement) with Noah and his descendants. But soon the people forgot God, his goodness, his deliverance, his judgment, and his promise. And they became impressed with themselves, so much so that they decided to erect a monument—to themselves. They built their tower to glorify their greatness; it became, instead, a memorial to their (and our) greatest foolishness—human arrogance.

We can learn several lessons in this passage: (1) God is good and merciful to us. (2) God is greater than we are. (3) All humans are connected by sin.

Read Genesis 9:1–11:32

The people in this story built the Tower of Babel for the whole world to see (Genesis 11:3-4). This tower was most likely a *ziggurat*, a common structure in Babylonia at the time. Usually built as temples, ziggurats looked like pyramids with steps or ramps leading up the sides. Standing as high as three hundred feet and often just as wide, a ziggurat would stand out as the focal point of a city.

Today, people may not build statues, temples, or pyramids, but they still erect monuments (achievements, expensive clothes, big houses, fancy cars, important jobs) to call attention to themselves. When used to give personal identity and self-worth, these otherwise worthy pursuits take God's place. God gives us freedom to develop in many areas, but not the freedom to replace him.

As you read, check out the attitudes of the builders in the story, and consider any "towers" that you may be building. Tear down anything that stands in God's place.

No close relationship can function without trust. Like a huge diamond, hope is the largest, most precious, most irreplaceable component of every relationship. It is so difficult to get and yet so easy to lose.

This passage opens with one of the most significant events in the Bible—Abram receiving God's call. Abram's calling established the covenant (or agreement) by which God created the nation of Israel, his chosen people. Abram's move to Canaan and the challenges he faced living there with his nephew Lot stretched his faith the way life's challenges often stretch ours. With this calling God posed the question to Abram: Do you trust me?

This story also includes lessons about selfishness; generosity; helping out family; taking risks; and honoring God.

Read Genesis 12:1–14:24

God promised to bless Abram and to make him great. There was one condition to this promise, however: Abram had to do what God wanted him to do (Genesis 12:2). This meant leaving his home and friends and traveling to a new land, where God promised to build a great nation from Abram's family. Abram obeyed, walking away from his home, his comfort zone, accepting God's promise of even greater blessings in the future. Abram believed God, and he demonstrated his trust through his actions.

It's difficult to step out in faith. We know the past and can feel secure in the present. The future, though, is unknown and risky. But when God leads, we can follow, confident that his way is best.

¹The Lord had said to Abram, "Leave your native country, your relatives, and your father's family, and go to the land that I will show you. ²I will make you into a great nation. I will bless you and make you famous, and you will be a blessing to others. ³I will bless those who bless you and curse those who treat you with contempt. All the families on earth will be blessed through you." ⁴So Abram departed as the Lord had instructed, and Lot went with him. Abram was seventy-five years old when he left Haran. ⁵He took his wife, Sarai, his nephew Lot, and all his wealth—his livestock and all the people he had taken into his household at Haran—and headed for the land of Canaan. When they arrived in Canaan, ⁶Abram traveled through the land as far as Shechem.

GENESIS 12:1-6

As you read this passage, watch Abram live by faith. And think of where God may be trying to lead you to better serve him. Don't let the comfort and security of your present position make you miss God's plan for you. Be flexible and willing to change.

¹⁵Then God said to Abraham, "Regarding Sarai, your wife—her name will no longer be Sarai. From now on her name will be Sarah. ¹⁶And I will bless her and give you a son from her! Yes, I will bless her richly, and she will become the mother of many nations. Kings of nations will be among her descendants." ¹⁷Then Abraham bowed down to the ground, but he laughed to himself in disbelief. "How could I become a father at the age of 100?" he thought. "And how can Sarah have a baby when she is ninety years old?" ¹⁸So Abraham said to God, "May Ishmael live under your special blessing!" ¹⁹But God replied, "No—Sarah, your wife, will give birth to a son for you. You will name him Isaac, and I will confirm my covenant with him and his descendants as an everlasting covenant."

GENESIS 17:15-19

Right turns on red, your keyboard's escape key, and speeding tickets all testify to our hatred for waiting. More often than not, when we hear "Please wait," we want to say, "No, thank you." We are often asked to wait, and are often not good at complying.

It's a small wonder, then, that Abram and Sarai stopped waiting for God. We see their faith weaken and fail when Sarai and Abram agree to bring Hagar into the process of starting a family. As a result, Ishmael is born. Despite Abram and Sarai's impulsive decision, God reaffirms his promise and establishes the covenant of circumcision—a permanent sign of his relationship with Abram's descendants.

As you read, watch for other lessons on patience; trusting God to do what he promises; and not taking matters into your own hands.

Read Genesis 15:1–17:27

Abram and Sarai had trouble believing God's promise and began thinking up creative ways to manipulate events and have a child (Genesis 16:1-3). A married woman who could not have children was shamed by her peers and was often required to give a female servant to her husband in order to produce an heir. The children born to the servant woman were considered the children of the wife.

When Sarai gave Hagar to Abram, they were acting in line with the custom of the day, but this action revealed their lack of faith that God would fulfill his promise. Consequently, a series of problems arose. This invariably happens when we take over for God and try to fulfill his promises through efforts that are not in line with his specific directions. In this case, time provided the greatest test of Abram and Sarai's faith and their willingness to let God work in their lives. Sometimes, we, too, must simply wait. When we ask God for something and have to wait, we are tempted to take matters into our own hands and interfere with God's plans.

Do your continual prayers seem to go unanswered? Do you feel yourself getting impatient with God as you wait for him to fulfill his promise and meet your need? Consider what God might be teaching you in the process. Obey God, and trust him for the outcome.

When was the last time you heard "It's not fair!"? Perhaps that familiar phrase was uttered two minutes ago by a child, or maybe you can remember saying it yourself not long ago. Most people have a keen sensitivity to how the scales are tipped, especially when we think that we are being treated unfairly.

This reading shows us three kinds of belief and unbelief. Abraham and Sarah struggled to believe as three angels repeated another of God's specific promises. In contrast, the unbelief of Sodom and Gomorrah was so absolute that the entire population was destroyed. In between stood Lot, a man who seemed to think mainly of himself and who stretched the meaning of the term *righteous*. Notice how God dealt differently with each one.

Look for other lessons as you read: hospitality; not compromising with the world around you; and the dangers of desperation.

Read Genesis 18:1–20:18

Was God being unfair to the people of Sodom and Gomorrah (Genesis 19:27-28)? Actually, God's fairness stands out: (1) he agreed to spare them if only ten righteous people lived there (18:32); (2) he showed great mercy toward Lot, apparently the only man in either city who had any kind of relationship with him (19:12); and (3) he showed great patience with Lot, almost forcing him to leave Sodom before destroying the wicked city (19:16).

²⁴Then the LORD rained down fire and burning sulfur from the sky on Sodom and Gomorrah. ²⁵He utterly destroyed them, along with the other cities and villages of the plain, wiping out all the people and every bit of vegetation. ²⁶But Lot's wife looked back as she was following behind him, and she turned into a pillar of salt. ²⁷Abraham got up early that morning and hurried out to the place where he had stood in the LORD's presence. ²⁸He looked out across the plain toward Sodom and Gomorrah and watched as columns of smoke rose from the cities like smoke from a furnace. ²⁹But God had listened to Abraham's request and kept Lot safe, removing him from the disaster that engulfed the cities on the plain.

GENESIS 19:24-29

Remember God's patience when you are tempted to think he is unfair. All people, even the most godly, deserve his justice. We should be glad that God doesn't direct his justice toward us as he did toward Sodom and Gomorrah. As we grow spiritually, we should find ourselves developing a deeper respect for God because of his anger toward sin, and a deeper love for God because of his patience when we sin.

Take time today to recount God's acts of mercy and love for you. Thank him for *not* giving you what you deserve, and instead giving you what you don't deserve—forgiveness and eternal life through Christ. It certainly isn't "fair"—but isn't that great?

⁹When they arrived at the place where God had told him to go, Abraham built an altar and arranged the wood on it. Then he tied his son, Isaac, and laid him on the altar on top of the wood. ¹⁰And Abraham picked up the knife to kill his son as a sacrifice. ¹¹At that moment the angel of the LORD called to him from heaven, "Abraham! Abraham!" "Yes," Abraham replied. "Here I am!" ¹²"Don't lay a hand on the boy!" the angel said. "Do not hurt him in any way, for now I know that you truly fear God. You have not withheld from me even your son, your only son." ¹³Then Abraham looked up and saw a ram caught by its horns in a thicket. So he took the ram and sacrificed it as a burnt offering in place of his son.

GENESIS 22:9-13

What comes to mind when you hear the word *children*? Small children can take everything out of us, yet they can also brighten our lives with a cute action, a smile, or a loving word.

After years of waiting and several tests of faith, at last Sarah conceives and has a baby—Isaac, or "Laughter"—the promised son. But Abraham's faith must undergo one more test.

Tests of faith share the spotlight in this passage with other important lessons. As you read, note also what Abraham and others learn about the seriousness of sin; the importance of mourning; and the effect of a good reputation.

Read Genesis 21:1–23:20

Through the years, Abraham had learned many tough lessons about the importance of obeying God—when he was called out of Ur, when he went to Egypt, and when he had to wait for Isaac's birth. Initially, Abraham did not always show that he trusted or believed God; but through each test, he saw God's willingness and ability to keep his promises, even if it took a miracle.

That is why God asked Abraham to sacrifice Isaac (Genesis 22:1-2), to kill his beloved, only son—his miracle child—on an altar. God did not want Isaac to die, but he wanted Abraham to sacrifice Isaac in his heart so that he could learn to trust God completely (see Hebrews 11:19). Imagine what Abraham must have felt as he walked with Isaac up the mountain, each torturous step leading him painfully closer to unspeakable grief. Yet Abraham obeyed, and God honored his faith.

Obeying God may often be quite a struggle because it may mean giving up something that we truly want. We should not expect our obedience to God to be easy or to come naturally. Just as fire refines ore to extract precious metals, God refines us through difficult circumstances. When tested, we can complain or we can obey, trusting God as we try to see how he is teaching us. In what ways might God be testing your faith? What steps of faith do you need to take today to obey him?

Have you ever let a salesperson talk you into a dumb purchase? Have you ever given away a valuable possession and later wished you hadn't? Looking back on those experiences, you probably realize that you made the decision under pressure. In such moments of weakness, it's easy to make a decision that we later regret. Similarly, sudden crises test our convictions.

Just ask Esau. In this reading, Isaac grows up and gets married; soon thereafter, he and his wife, Rebekah, have twins, Esau and Jacob. God had told Abraham that he would become a great nation, and here we see the promise continuing to unfold. But the age-old stain of sin remains: within this chosen family of four are one shortsighted hothead and two skilled liars. Keep your eye on Esau's "moments of weakness."

There are many lessons in this passage—about being a servant; working hard; seeking God's guidance; staying faithful to our tasks; and resisting the temptation to scheme.

Read Genesis 24:1–28:9

A birthright was a special honor given to the firstborn son (Genesis 25:31). It included a double portion of the family inheritance, along with the honor of one day becoming the family's leader. Birthrights were priceless. In Isaac's family, the birthright belonged to Esau as the firstborn twin. But because of his shortsightedness, he did not hold on to it. When he was hungry and Jacob had some food, Esau could not see beyond his exaggerated sense of need. "Look, I'm dying of starvation!" he said (25:32). That was probably not true; it merely reflected how he felt. Esau acted on impulse, without pausing to consider the long-range consequences of what he was about to do. He did not need to eat the meal he so desperately wanted, but the pressure of the moment distorted his perspective and made the decision seem urgent.

What pressures do you face? You can avoid making Esau's mistake by comparing the long-range consequences of an action to its short-term satisfaction before you act. Getting through that initial, pressure-filled moment is often the most difficult—and most important—part of overcoming a temptation.

²⁹One day when Jacob was cooking some stew, Esau arrived home from the wilderness exhausted and hungry. ³⁰Esau said to Jacob, "I'm starved! Give me some of that red stew!" (This is how Esau got his other name, Edom, which means "red.") ³¹"All right," Jacob replied, "but trade me your rights as the firstborn son." ³²"Look, I'm dying of starvation!" said Esau. "What good is my birthright to me now?" ³³But Jacob said, "First you must swear that your birthright is mine." So Esau swore an oath, thereby selling all his rights as the firstborn to his brother, Jacob. ³⁴Then Jacob gave Esau some bread and lentil stew. Esau ate the meal, then got up and left. He showed contempt for his rights as the firstborn.

GENESIS 25:29-34

¹⁶Now Laban had two daughters. The older daughter was named Leah, and the younger one was Rachel. . . . ¹⁸Since Jacob was in love with Rachel, he told her father, "I'll work for you for seven years if you'll give me Rachel, your younger daughter, as my wife." ¹⁹"Agreed!" Laban replied. "I'd rather give her to you than to anyone else. . . ." ²⁰So Jacob worked seven years to pay for Rachel. . . . ²¹Finally, the time came for him to marry her. "I have fulfilled my agreement," Jacob said to Laban. "Now give me my wife so I can marry her." ²²So Laban . . . prepared a wedding feast. ²³But that night, when it was dark, Laban took Leah to Jacob, and he slept with her. . . . ²⁵When Jacob woke up in the morning—it was Leah! "What have you done to me?" Jacob raged at Laban. "I worked seven years for Rachel! Why have you tricked me?"

GENESIS 29:16, 18-23, 25

Have you ever had a bad choice come back to haunt you? Who hasn't? No medicine goes down more bitterly than your own.

Here begins the story of Jacob, two generations after Abraham. Through no merit of Jacob's, God renews his covenant with Abraham's descendants to him in a dream, and Jacob heads for his uncle Laban's home. This is a forced move, one that he has brought on himself. Jacob is shrewd, and he has proved it. Now he has to prove that he's resourceful as well.

As you read, look for these themes: personalizing faith; being patient; dealing with injustice; struggling with childlessness; resolving sibling rivalry; and taking matters into your own hands.

Read Genesis 28:10–30:43

Laban could scheme just like Jacob. It was the custom of the day for a man to present a dowry, or substantial gift, to the family of his future wife (Genesis 29:18-27). Jacob's dowry was not a material possession, for he had none to offer. Instead, he agreed to work seven years for Laban. But there was another custom of the land that Laban did not tell Jacob: the older daughter had to be married first. By giving Jacob Leah and not Rachel, Laban tricked him into promising another seven years of hard work.

Jacob was enraged when he learned that Laban had tricked him (29:23-25). The one who had deceived Esau was now deceived himself. We quickly become upset at an injustice done to us, yet we excuse, justify, or ignore the injustices that we do to others. Be careful how you treat others, because poor choices have a way of coming back to haunt you.

Think of a recent time when you felt cheated. How would God have you respond to the person who cheated you? And think of how you might have acted unjustly toward someone else. What should you do to make that situation right?

Next week's family reunion has you wrestling with a couple of conflicting emotions. You'll love seeing Erica—it seems that no matter how long it's been, you just pick up where you left off. But it's just the opposite with Cousin Dale. He's still bitter. Has he forgiven you? Or will it be awkward . . . again?

This is the last part of Jacob's story, and much has changed. Having fled *to* Laban, Jacob now flees *from* him. Having exploited Esau, Jacob now seeks to be reconciled. Having left home single and poor, he now returns with a family and wealth. The only constant from the past is his uncertainty: Jacob wonders what Esau will do—whether he still harbors anger and will seek revenge. But Jacob has learned to trust in God.

This story has much to say about everyday life and relationships. Look for lessons on dealing with jealousy; working hard; releasing children; letting go of bitterness; reconciling; and forgiving.

Read Genesis 31:1–36:43

When the two brothers meet again, the bitterness over losing his birthright and blessing (Genesis 25:29-34, 27:1-40) seems to have been forgotten by Esau. He greets his brother, Jacob, with a great hug (33:1-11). Imagine how difficult this must have been for a man who once had actually plotted to kill his brother (27:41). Instead of being consumed by thoughts of vengeance, however, Esau is content with what he has and is eager to reconcile. Time away from Jacob has allowed Esau's bitter wounds to heal. Jacob even exclaims how great it is to see his brother, obviously pleased with him (33:10).

[1]Then Jacob looked up and saw Esau coming with his 400 men. So he divided the children among Leah, Rachel, and his two servant wives. [2]He put the servant wives and their children at the front, Leah and her children next, and Rachel and Joseph last. [3]Then Jacob went on ahead. As he approached his brother, he bowed to the ground seven times before him. [4]Then Esau ran to meet him and embraced him, threw his arms around his neck, and kissed him. And they both wept. [5]Then Esau looked at the women and children and asked, "Who are these people with you?" "These are the children God has graciously given to me, your servant," Jacob replied.

GENESIS 33:1-5

Life can bring struggle and pain; we may even feel cheated, as Esau did. But we don't have to hold on to the past and remain bitter. We can remove our bitterness by honestly expressing our feelings to God, forgiving those who have wronged us, and being content with what we have.

What grudges have you been nursing? Whom are you refusing to forgive? What revengeful scenarios have you been imagining? Confess your thoughts and feelings to God and allow him to heal your memories. Be *better*, not *bitter*.

[19]Potiphar was furious when he heard his wife's story about how Joseph had treated her. [20]So he took Joseph and threw him into the prison where the king's prisoners were held, and there he remained. [21]But the LORD was with Joseph in the prison and showed him his faithful love. And the LORD made Joseph a favorite with the prison warden. [22]Before long, the warden put Joseph in charge of all the other prisoners and over everything that happened in the prison. [23]The warden had no more worries, because Joseph took care of everything. The LORD was with him and caused everything he did to succeed.

GENESIS 39:19-23

What are some of your most menial chores? No matter which ones you select (or how long the list), you doubtless have responsibilities that you would not miss if you never did them again.

Joseph, son of Jacob, dreams of being ruler of all, but is sold into slavery and is put in prison. Then he interprets the pharaoh's dreams and rises to power in Egypt. We see (as Joseph learns) that God rules over every circumstance, even the menial ones.

Sibling rivalry, lust, shame, despair, shattered hopes, and sudden success all play a part in this piece of Joseph's drama. As you read, look for lessons in each of these themes.

Read Genesis 37:1–41:57

As a prisoner and slave, Joseph could have seen his situation as hopeless (Genesis 39:20). Prisons were grim places with vile conditions. They were used to house convicted criminals, forced laborers, or, like Joseph, the accused who were awaiting trial. Prisoners were guilty until proven innocent and had no right to a speedy trial. In addition, Joseph's accuser was a very prominent member of society who would certainly be believed sooner than Joseph, a slave, would be. Joseph had every reason to despair.

Instead, Joseph did his best with each small task given him. His diligence and positive attitude were soon noticed by the warden, who promoted him to prison administrator (39:21-22). And even during these dark prison days, Joseph faithfully served his Lord. Eventually, Joseph rose to the top—from prison cell to Pharaoh's palace (41:39-40).

What predicament at work, at home, or at school seems at best, daunting, and at worst, hopeless? Follow Joseph's example by taking each small task and doing your best. Whatever your situation, no matter how undesirable, consider it part of your training for serving the Lord. Remember how God turned Joseph's situation around. Be assured that God sees your efforts, and remember that he can reverse desperate predicaments and overcome overwhelming odds.

High school reunions can be eye-opening experiences. The guy who was voted "most likely to succeed"—did he make it? The girl who was homecoming queen—what became of her? What about others? Have any of them turned out as expected? People change dramatically, and the changes catch us by surprise.

In this part of Joseph's story, his dreams come true, literally. Joseph discovers that his brothers (especially Judah) have changed—and so has he.

Don't miss the implications in this story for family relationships: mistakes don't have to be permanent. There's peace in this once-volatile family, and it's all in spite of, and *because of,* mistakes and tragic events.

Read Genesis 42:1–45:28

Joseph wanted to see if his brothers' attitudes had changed for the better, so he tested the way they treated each other (Genesis 44:16-34). When Judah was younger, he had shown no regard for his brother Joseph or for his father, Jacob. First, Judah convinced his brothers to sell Joseph as a slave (37:27); then he joined his brothers in lying to his father about Joseph's fate (37:32). But what a change had taken place in this man! Having promised Jacob that he would guarantee young Benjamin's safety (43:9), Judah now had a chance to keep that promise. Becoming a slave was a terrible fate, but Judah was determined to keep his word to his father. The man who had sold one favored little brother into slavery now offered to become a slave to save another favored little brother.

[14]Joseph was still in his palace when Judah and his brothers arrived, and they fell to the ground before him. [15]"What have you done?" Joseph demanded. . . . [16]Judah answered, "Oh, my lord, what can we say to you? How can we explain this? How can we prove our innocence? God is punishing us for our sins. My lord, we have all returned to be your slaves—all of us, not just our brother who had your cup in his sack." [17]"No," Joseph said. "I would never do such a thing! Only the man who stole the cup will be my slave. The rest of you may go back to your father in peace." [18]Then Judah stepped forward and said, "Please, my lord, let your servant say just one word to you. . . . [33]Please, my lord, let me stay here as a slave instead of the boy, and let the boy return with his brothers."

GENESIS 44:14-18, 33

When you are ready to give up hope on yourself or others, remember that God can work a complete change in even the most selfish personality. Think of the self-centered people in your life. Pray for them to understand and experience God's love and power. Think also about your own self-centeredness, and ask God to forgive and change you as well. God changes lives!

¹⁵Now that their father was dead, Joseph's brothers became fearful. "Now Joseph will show his anger and pay us back for all the wrong we did to him," they said. ¹⁶So they sent this message to Joseph: "Before your father died, he instructed us ¹⁷to say to you: 'Please forgive your brothers for the great wrong they did to you—for their sin in treating you so cruelly.' So we, the servants of the God of your father, beg you to forgive our sin." When Joseph received the message, he broke down and wept. ¹⁸Then his brothers came and threw themselves down before Joseph. "Look, we are your slaves!" they said. ¹⁹But Joseph replied, "Don't be afraid of me. Am I God, that I can punish you? ²⁰You intended to harm me, but God intended it all for good."

GENESIS 50:15-20

Bad news never comes at a good time. Whether it's a flat tire or the death of a close relative, negative and tragic experiences happen all too often. Can anything good come of these events?

The final events of Jacob's life play out in this section of Scripture. We learn of his family's move to Egypt. The famine in Egypt continues. Joseph's sons, Manasseh and Ephraim, become Jacob's, and Jacob blesses them. The passage of time has proven Joseph right. Now what?

As you read this story's ending, note the lessons available to each of the key people: to Joseph (choosing forgiveness instead of revenge, knowing that God is in control, and finding blessing in tragedy); to Jacob (seeing God keep his promises, depending on God); and even to Pharaoh (learning that God is great). And imagine how Manasseh, Ephraim, and Judah must have felt.

Read Genesis 46:1–50:26

When Joseph became a slave, Jacob thought he was dead and wept in despair (Genesis 37:33-35). Eventually God's plan allowed Jacob to regain not only his son, but his grandchildren as well. Circumstances are never so bad that they are beyond God's help. Jacob regained his son. Job got a new family (see Job 42:10-17). Mary regained her brother Lazarus (see John 11:1-44). We need never despair, because we belong to a loving God. We never know what good he will bring out of a seemingly hopeless situation.

God brought good from many bad circumstances in Joseph's life—his brothers' evil deed, Potiphar's wife's false accusation, the cup bearer's neglect, and seven years of famine. The experiences in Joseph's life taught him that God brings good from evil for those who trust him.

What difficult circumstances are you enduring? Do you trust God enough to wait patiently for him to bring good out of bad situations? You can trust him because, as Joseph learned, God can overrule people's evil intentions to bring about his intended results.

Don't you just hate it when people make excuses? Excuses mean that somebody is trying to avoid responsibility—some job or task that rightly belongs to that person but what he or she considers too inconvenient to do. On the surface the excuse looks right, but closer examination reveals major flaws in the argument.

This reading begins a new chapter in Israel's history. The small, privileged family of Joseph has become a large nation of oppressed Hebrew slaves. Moses will be their deliverer. After fleeing to Midian, Moses meets God at the burning bush, is given his assignment, and returns to Egypt. Moses is not qualified for the job.

Look for other lessons, including the dual excuse-busters *be courageous* (the Hebrew midwives) and *don't run from your problems* (Moses).

iiiiiiiiiiiiiiiiiiiiiiiiiiiiiiiiiiiiiiiiiiiiiiiiiiiiiiiiiiiiiii **Read Exodus 1:1–4:31**

¹⁰Moses pleaded with the LORD, "O LORD, I'm not very good with words. I never have been, and I'm not now, even though you have spoken to me. I get tongue-tied, and my words get tangled." ¹¹Then the LORD asked Moses, "Who makes a person's mouth? Who decides whether people speak or do not speak, hear or do not hear, see or do not see? Is it not I, the LORD? ¹²Now go! I will be with you as you speak, and I will instruct you in what to say." ¹³But Moses again pleaded, "Lord, please! Send anyone else."

EXODUS 4:10-13

Moses made excuses because he felt inadequate for the job that God asked him to do (Exodus 3:10–4:17). It was natural for him to feel that way, because he *was* inadequate all by himself. But God wasn't asking Moses to work alone. He offered other resources to help (God himself, Aaron, and the ability to do miracles). God often calls us to perform tasks that seem too difficult, but he doesn't ask us to do them alone. God offers us his resources, just as he did to Moses. We should not hide behind our inadequacies, as Moses did, but look beyond ourselves to God's great available resources. Then we can allow him to empower our unique contributions.

What has God asked you to do? What excuses are you using to avoid this responsibility and work? Obey God by stepping out in faith. He will give you the resources to do his work.

¹⁷Pharaoh shouted, . . . ¹⁸"Get back to work! No straw will be given to you, but you must still produce the full quota of bricks." ¹⁹The Israelite foremen could see that they were in serious trouble when they were told, "You must not reduce the number of bricks you make each day." ²⁰As they left Pharaoh's court, they confronted Moses and Aaron, who were waiting outside for them. ²¹The foremen said to them, "May the LORD judge and punish you for making us stink before Pharaoh and his officials. . . ." ²²Then Moses went back to the LORD and protested, "Why have you brought all this trouble on your own people, LORD? Why did you send me? ²³Ever since I came to Pharaoh as your spokesman, he has been even more brutal to your people. And you have done nothing to rescue them!"

EXODUS 5:17-23

If you've ever had to learn something you didn't want to learn, you know how much discipline it takes. No matter what the subject, you have to do some digging and some hard work. Learning isn't a downhill ride; it's more of a mountain climb. It takes *work*.

In this part of the story of the Exodus, God sends Moses to confront Pharaoh. Pharaoh's response is to make the Hebrews work even harder. Moses complains, God promises deliverance, and a showdown begins. Here we see the grand effects of feeble steps of faith (a tough lesson for anyone to learn).

Here's the lesson: Enduring rejection for our faith and trusting God when he seems to be ignoring our prayers are part of God's curriculum for us. As you read this passage, learn, with Moses, God's profound lessons.

Read Exodus 5:1–7:13

Moses did not like God's methods. Despite God's message—indeed, because of it—Pharaoh increased the Hebrews' workload. Moses protested that God was not rescuing his people (Exodus 5:22-23). Moses expected faster results and fewer problems. When God is at work, suffering, setbacks, and hardship may still occur. We can be sure, however, that each hardship has a purpose—to teach, discipline, punish, or accomplish another work of God. In James 1:2-4, we are encouraged to be joyful when difficulties come our way. Problems teach us to (1) trust God to do what is best for us; (2) look for ways to honor God in our present situation; (3) remember that God will not abandon us; and (4) watch for God's plan for us.

What tough lesson is God teaching you today? Think of what you can do to honor him through your attitude, words, and actions.

Perhaps you have heard people joke about "the terrible twos." In case you're not a parent or haven't heard before, they're speaking of how tenacious and stubborn two-year-old children can be. Mules have nothing on these determined individuals. Their displays of *stubbornness*—often culminating in a temper tantrum—test the resolve and endurance of the saintliest parents.

In this part of the story of the Exodus, God strikes Egypt with ten plagues: blood, frogs, gnats, flies, sick livestock, boils, hail, locusts, darkness, and (finally) the death of Egypt's firstborn sons. Each is a message to Pharaoh (and the world) that God rules. Unfortunately for Pharaoh, he doesn't get the point until it costs him his son. Stubbornness can be fatal.

These crucial chapters contain many other lessons. As we watch God free his people, we also learn about (1) not compromising with God; (2) persisting in doing right; (3) paying attention to God's message; and (4) being thankful for God's grace.

Read Exodus 7:14–12:30

Although he received many warnings, Pharaoh refused to obey God (Exodus 7:22; 8:15, 19, 32; 9:7, 12, 35; 10:20, 27). Before the ten plagues began, Moses and Aaron announced what God would do if Pharaoh didn't let the people go. But Pharaoh refused to listen and hardened his heart. Through the first six plagues, Pharaoh dug in a little more each time. Pharaoh wouldn't change, so God confirmed Pharaoh's arrogant decision, hardening his heart permanently (11:10) and setting the painful consequences of his actions in motion. This brought suffering upon Pharaoh and on his entire country.

¹Then the Lord said to Moses, "I will strike Pharaoh and the land of Egypt with one more blow. After that, Pharaoh will let you leave this country. . . ." ⁴Moses had announced to Pharaoh, "This is what the Lord says: At midnight tonight I will pass through the heart of Egypt. ⁵All the firstborn sons will die in every family in Egypt, from the oldest son of Pharaoh, who sits on his throne, to the oldest son of his lowliest servant girl who grinds the flour. Even the firstborn of all the livestock will die. . . ." ⁹Now the Lord had told Moses earlier, "Pharaoh will not listen to you, but then I will do even more mighty miracles in the land of Egypt." ¹⁰Moses and Aaron performed these miracles in Pharaoh's presence, but the Lord hardened Pharaoh's heart, and he wouldn't let the Israelites leave the country.

EXODUS 11:1, 4-5, 9-10

God gave Pharaoh every opportunity to change his mind; it was Pharaoh's stubbornness that prevented it from changing. Stubbornness against God leads to disobedience. When you stop stubbornly insisting on your own way and begin submitting to God, you may be surprised by the work he will do in your life.

²The whole community of Israel complained about Moses and Aaron. ³"If only the LORD had killed us back in Egypt," they moaned. "There we sat around pots filled with meat and ate all the bread we wanted. But now you have brought us into this wilderness to starve us all to death." . . . ⁶So Moses and Aaron said to all the people of Israel, "By evening you will realize it was the LORD who brought you out of the land of Egypt. ⁷In the morning you will see the glory of the LORD, because he has heard your complaints, which are against him, not against us. What have we done that you should complain about us?" ⁸Then Moses added, "The LORD will give you meat to eat in the evening and bread to satisfy you in the morning, for he has heard all your complaints against him."

EXODUS 16:2-3, 6-8

When you were a child, what foods did your family serve that you absolutely refused to eat? You know, the foods that you *hated*—foods you would go to war over, feed to the dog, or otherwise reject. It seems that everybody has one of these despised foods in his or her past. Food can evoke such emotion!

In this part of the story of the Exodus, the Israelites finally leave Egypt. Moses and Miriam celebrate with a song. The people complain about lack of food and water, but God provides. Enemies attack, but the Israelites defeat them. Moses and his father-in-law have a reunion. Finally, God's people worship in peace. Everything happens just as God had predicted. Did the Israelites understand and appreciate that fact?

In this passage, we also learn that celebration is good; that God keeps his promises; provides what we need; and always vindicates his people.

Read Exodus 12:31–18:27

As the Israelites encountered dangers, shortages, and inconveniences, they complained bitterly and whined about going back to Egypt. This happened often, but God still provided for them. They forgot, or did not believe, that God had promised to meet their needs if they would obey his instructions. These hardships were a test of faith; their complaining proved they were failing the test.

Difficult circumstances often lead to stress, and complaining is a natural response. But these circumstances are also a test of our faith. The question is this: Can we trust God to meet our needs in his own time and in his own way? The Israelites didn't really want to be back in Egypt—they just wanted life to be easier. In the pressure of the moment, they did not focus on trusting God; they could only think about escaping their circumstances.

When pressure comes your way, resist the temptation to complain or to seek an immediate escape. Instead, focus on God's power and wisdom to help you deal with the cause of your stress. Don't be a problem; be a solution.

What sorts of rules do you have in your house? They don't have to be written down—many firm rules never make it to paper or poster board, though sometimes they feel more official that way. Parents usually start with "Mom and Dad are in charge," and go on from there. Whenever two or more people gather together, there can be chaos; rules help us get organized.

This is the story of when God's people are given God's laws, including the Ten Commandments. The laws cover worship, servants, personal injuries, property, social responsibility, justice, the Sabbath, and three annual festivals. Israel encamps at Mt. Sinai for a year, giving them time to soak in God's commands.

These chapters also highlight the importance of keeping commitments; preparing for worship; honoring God above all else; being fair to others; making restitution; and being kind to the poor. Is there any area of your life that the list doesn't touch?

Read Exodus 19:1–24:18

Why did God give the Ten Commandments (Exodus 20:1-17)? Israel was God's people, and the commandments gave them a blueprint for a life of practical holiness, life as a people belonging to God. In these laws, the people could see God's nature and his plan for how they should live. The commands and guidelines were intended to direct the community to meet the needs of each individual in a loving and responsible manner. If we love God, we will love his will. We show our love by responding obediently to what God wants. The Ten Commandments tell us what God wants.

2"I am the LORD your God, who rescued you from the land of Egypt, the place of your slavery. 3You must not have any other god but me. 4You must not make for yourself an idol of any kind. . . . 7You must not misuse the name of the LORD your God. . . . 8Remember to observe the Sabbath day by keeping it holy. . . . 12Honor your father and mother. . . . 13You must not murder. 14You must not commit adultery. 15You must not steal. 16You must not testify falsely against your neighbor. 17You must not covet your neighbor's house . . . or anything else that belongs to your neighbor."

EXODUS 20:2-4, 7-8, 12-17

Take a fresh look at these familiar commandments; look at them from the positive side. For example, the commandment against adultery really means that you should honor the sanctity of marriage. And the commandment against murder means that you should respect all human beings as valuable creations of our loving God. Which commandments cause you the most difficulty? Does anything compete for God's place in your life? Do you show honor and respect to others?

30"Set up this Tabernacle according to the pattern you were shown on the mountain. 31For the inside of the Tabernacle, make a special curtain of finely woven linen. Decorate it with blue, purple, and scarlet thread and with skillfully embroidered cherubim. 32Hang this curtain on gold hooks attached to four posts of acacia wood. Overlay the posts with gold, and set them in four silver bases. 33Hang the inner curtain from clasps, and put the Ark of the Covenant in the room behind it. This curtain will separate the Holy Place from the Most Holy Place. 34Then put the Ark's cover—the place of atonement—on top of the Ark of the Covenant inside the Most Holy Place."

EXODUS 26:30-34

Does someone you know seem distant? It's amazing how two people can be in the same room physically and yet be miles apart relationally. It's one thing to be together in the same room; it's quite another to be together in mind and spirit.

Do you feel close to God? It's possible to be together in the same room and yet not together with him in mind and spirit. We come close to him through worship.

Some of the laws that God gave Israel regulated their worship. This passage records God's directions for building the Tabernacle—the tent and surrounding structures that would house God's place of worship during Israel's time in the wilderness. These detailed instructions leave little doubt about the importance that God places on our worship.

Other lessons in this section include the importance of respecting God's appointed teachers; God's holiness; and our need for holy rest. Take this passage in small bites, and chew slowly.

Read Exodus 25:1–31:18

One of the Tabernacle curtains separated two sacred rooms—the Holy Place and the Most Holy Place (Exodus 26:31-33). A priest would enter the Holy Place each day to commune with God and tend to the altar of incense, the lampstand, and the table with the Bread of the Presence. The Most Holy Place was where God himself resided, his presence resting on the atonement cover covering the ark of the covenant. Only the high priest could enter the Most Holy Place. Even he could do so only on the Day of Atonement, once a year, to make atonement for the sins of the whole nation. Without these vivid reminders, it is easy for us to forget the vast gulf between us and God's perfect holiness. Because of Christ, this barrier has been torn down forever. Now we can approach God's throne with confidence that he sympathizes with our weaknesses (see Hebrews 4:16). What a privilege!

Make worship a holy celebration of your relationship with your loving Lord. God, the Holy One of Israel, invites you to come close.

Bill is a Hindu. Sandy is a Muslim. You're a Christian. Your friend Rich says you're all pretty much the same. "You're all religious," he says. "You all believe in God." Is he right, or does it make a difference what a person believes—in *whom* a person believes?

Israel is still at Sinai after receiving many of God's laws on holy living and worship. Moses periodically brings God's words to them from the mountain. But the Israelites tire of waiting for Moses, so they sculpt and worship a golden calf instead. Here is a perfect example of the human tendency to remake God into something other than who he is.

Also watch for two other lessons in this passage: from the people, we learn that it's never too late to seek God's forgiveness; from Aaron, we learn that leading with integrity really does matter.

Read Exodus 32:1–34:35

Even though the Israelites had seen the invisible God in action, they still wanted gods they could see and shape into whatever image they desired (Exodus 32:1-10). Two popular Egyptian gods, Hapi (Apis) and Hathor, were thought of as a bull and a heifer (32:4-5). The Canaanites around them worshiped Baal, pictured as a bull. No doubt the Israelites, fresh from Egypt, found it quite natural to make a golden calf to represent the God that had just delivered them from their oppressors. They were weary of a God without a face. But they were ignoring the command God had just given them: "You must not make for yourself an idol of any kind or an image of anything in the heavens or on the earth or in the sea" (20:4). How much like the Israelites we are—wanting to shape God to our liking and make him into a thing for which we merely perform rituals, while we live as we please. Yet we, too, know that there is only one God, and he alone deserves to be worshiped. The gods we create blind us to reality and to the love that God wants to shower on us. God cannot work in us when we elevate anyone or anything above him.

[1]When the people saw how long it was taking Moses to come back down the mountain, they gathered around Aaron. "Come on," they said, "make us some gods who can lead us. We don't know what happened to this fellow Moses, who brought us here from the land of Egypt." [2]So Aaron said, "Take the gold rings from the ears of your wives and sons and daughters, and bring them to me." [3]All the people took the gold rings from their ears and brought them to Aaron. [4]Then Aaron took the gold, melted it down, and molded it into the shape of a calf. When the people saw it, they exclaimed, "O Israel, these are the gods who brought you out of the land of Egypt!" [5]Aaron saw how excited the people were, so he built an altar in front of the calf. Then he announced, "Tomorrow will be a festival to the LORD!"

EXODUS 32:1-5

³⁰Then Moses told the people of Israel, "The LORD has specifically chosen Bezalel son of Uri, grandson of Hur, of the tribe of Judah. ³¹The LORD has filled Bezalel with the Spirit of God, giving him great wisdom, ability, and expertise in all kinds of crafts. ³²He is a master craftsman, expert in working with gold, silver, and bronze. ³³He is skilled in engraving and mounting gemstones and in carving wood. He is a master at every craft. ³⁴And the LORD has given both him and Oholiab son of Ahisamach, of the tribe of Dan, the ability to teach their skills to others. ³⁵The LORD has given them special skills as engravers, designers, embroiderers in blue, purple, and scarlet thread on fine linen cloth, and weavers. . . . . ³⁶:¹Let them construct and furnish the Tabernacle, just as the LORD has commanded."

EXODUS 35:30–36:1

I can (check all that apply) paint; talk to people; make something out of cloth, paper, wood, metal, or plastic; mow grass; cut hair; grocery shop; hammer nails; vacuum; pick up trash; rearrange tables and chairs; read aloud. If you checked even one of those abilities, you can serve God in the church.

This section of Scripture tells how the Israelites carried out God's instructions for building the Tabernacle, God's mobile house of worship. The passage includes some Sabbath regulations, descriptions of materials used for the Tabernacle, and many miscellaneous anecdotes. Everyone pitches in.

As you read, you will learn about giving freely and generously, being helpful, and delegating responsibilities to others—a whole host of practical advice for ordinary believers who are ready to use their skills for God.

Read Exodus 35:1–40:38

Moses asked people with various abilities to help with the Tabernacle (Exodus 35:10-19). Those who could spin cloth made an important contribution—cloth. Bezalel and Oholiab, men with artistic skills, lent their expertise in cutting jewels, carving wood, and other areas (36:1-2). Moses laid out the steps, while Ithamar served as scribe for the project. God didn't ask Moses to build the Tabernacle alone, but to motivate others to do it. Once the Tabernacle was built, its physical care required a long list of important tasks (40:17-33).

Every one of God's people has been given special talents and gifts. We are responsible to develop these abilities—even those not considered religious—and use them for God's glory. This principle is important to remember today, when God's house is not a building but a body of people—the *real* church. Many seemingly unimportant tasks must be done to keep your local church functioning. Washing dishes, painting walls, or printing bulletins may not seem very spiritual, but these tasks are vital to the ministry of the church and have an important role in worship.

Surely everyone has uttered the words, "I can't afford it." Some things are just too expensive. You simply can't pay for them. You can save up or borrow enough for some items, but others will always command a higher price than you can pay.

The first verse of Leviticus 1 says, "The LORD called to Moses from the Tabernacle." The next seven chapters contain what God said, including the first set of instructions for worship and rules regarding sacrifices and offerings. It's quite clear from reading Leviticus that sin carries a very steep price.

Read Leviticus 1:1–7:38

Since Creation, God has made it clear that sin separates people from him, and that those who sin deserve to die. But because everyone has sinned (see Romans 3:23), God designed sacrifice as a way to seek forgiveness and restore a relationship with him. Because God is filled with love and mercy, he decided from the very beginning that he would send his Son into the world to die to pay sin's penalty (death). In the meantime, before God made the ultimate sacrifice of his Son, he instructed people to kill animals as sacrifices for sin. That's why when God taught his people to worship him, he placed great emphasis on sacrifices (Leviticus 1:2). They were God's Old Testament way for people to ask forgiveness for their sins.

Animal sacrifice accomplished two purposes: (1) the animal symbolically took the sinner's place and paid the penalty for sin; and (2) the animal's death represented one life given so that another life could be saved. This method, picturing what Jesus would do on the cross, continued throughout Old Testament times. It was effective in teaching and guiding the people and bringing them back to God. In New Testament times, however, Christ's death became the last sacrifice needed. He took the punishment once and for all for those who trust in him. Animal sacrifice is no longer required. Now, all people can be freed from the penalty of sin by turning away from their sin, trusting in Jesus, and accepting the forgiveness he offers.

Thank God for sacrificing his only Son for you. Then tell someone the Good News about God and his salvation.

27"If any of the common people sin by violating one of the LORD's commands, but they don't realize it, they are still guilty. 28When they become aware of their sin, they must bring as an offering for their sin a female goat with no defects. 29They must lay a hand on the head of the sin offering and slaughter it at the place where burnt offerings are slaughtered. 30Then the priest will dip his finger in the blood and put it on the horns of the altar for burnt offerings. He will pour out the rest of the blood at the base of the altar. 31Then he must remove all the goat's fat, just as he does with the fat of the peace offering. He will burn the fat on the altar, and it will be a pleasing aroma to the LORD. Through this process, the priest will purify the people, making them right with the LORD, and they will be forgiven."

LEVITICUS 4:27-31

¹Then the Lᴏʀᴅ said to Moses, ²"Bring Aaron and his sons, along with their sacred garments, the anointing oil, the bull for the sin offering, the two rams, and the basket of bread made without yeast, ³and call the entire community of Israel together at the entrance of the Tabernacle." ⁴So . . . the whole community assembled at the Tabernacle entrance. ⁵Moses announced to them, "This is what the Lᴏʀᴅ has commanded us to do!" ⁶Then he presented Aaron and his sons and washed them with water. ⁷He put the official tunic on Aaron and tied the sash around his waist. He dressed him in the robe, placed the ephod on him, and attached the ephod securely with its decorative sash. . . . ¹²Then he poured some of the anointing oil on Aaron's head, anointing him and making him holy for his work.

LEVITICUS 8:1-7, 12

Have you ever seen a one-year-old eat? It's amazing how much indifference a young child can show toward the location of his or her food. The child will tolerate food on the face and hands, inside the clothes, on the hair, anywhere. Cleanliness? What's that? Thankfully, most of us outgrow this form of apathy.

This section continues the instructions for worshiping God, with rules for the priests. It details the ordination of Aaron and his sons, the beginning of the priests' ministry, and the death of the priests Nadab and Abihu when they disregarded God's instructions. They paid for their apathy toward God. The story vividly reminds us that approaching God is serious business.

You may not be a priest, but these chapters are for you, too. In fact, they have much to say to anyone interested in approaching God; obeying God in everyday routines; staying close to the truth when teaching; and avoiding drunkenness.

Read Leviticus 8:1–10:20

God required that Aaron and his sons be cleansed and set apart for their duties as priests (Leviticus 8:1–9:24). Although all the men from the tribe of Levi were dedicated for service to God, only Aaron's descendants could be priests. They alone had the honor and responsibility of performing the sacrifices. These priests had to cleanse and dedicate themselves before they could help the people do the same.

Leviticus chapters 8 and 9 describe the priests' ordination ceremony. It showed that holiness came from God alone, not from the priestly role. Similarly, we are not spiritually cleansed just because we have a religious position or come from a religious family. Spiritual cleansing comes only from God. No matter how high our position or how long we have held it, we must depend on God for forgiveness and a relationship with him.

Don't take your relationship with God for granted and slip into apathy or mindless routine. Stay close to the Father; he wants to be close to you.

How much do you understand about the inner workings of your television? How about your car? your municipal government? your spouse? your kids? A wonderful fact of life is that we can enjoy many things without understanding how they work. We may satisfy our curiosity by understanding them, but we don't have to.

This is the final section of instructions for worshiping God (Leviticus 1:1–17:16). It includes instructions about food, childbirth, infectious skin diseases, mildew, bodily discharges, the Day of Atonement, and handling blood. There is more to this set of instructions than rules about eating, treating wounds, and personal hygiene. In them we see God's love and care for his people.

That's a good reason to study the other rules in this section, too—preparing for worship, practicing good health and hygiene, and keeping sex pure. What evidence of God's love and care do you see in these areas? Read on.

Read Leviticus 11:1–17:16

God wanted his people to be holy (set apart, different, unique), just as he is holy. That is why he designed laws to separate them—both socially and spiritually—from the wicked pagan nations they would encounter in Canaan.

These laws also had an immediate practical benefit. God told the Israelites how to diagnose infectious skin diseases and mildew so that they could avoid and treat them (Leviticus 13:1–14:57). These laws helped the Israelites avoid diseases that were serious threats in that time and place. Although the people would not have understood the medical reasons for some of these laws, their obedience to them made them healthier. Many of God's laws must have seemed strange to the Israelites. His laws, however, helped them avoid not only physical contamination, but also moral and spiritual infection.

We do not always understand why God commands us to do this or to avoid that. But his expressed will is for our good, even when we don't understand exactly how.

[2]The following instructions are for those seeking ceremonial purification from a skin disease. Those who have been healed must be brought to the priest, [3]who will examine them at a place outside the camp. If the priest finds that someone has been healed of a serious skin disease, [4]he will perform a purification ceremony.... [8]The persons being purified must then wash their clothes, shave off all their hair, and bathe themselves in water. Then they will be ceremonially clean and may return to the camp. However, they must remain outside their tents for seven days. [9]On the seventh day they must again shave all the hair from their heads, including the hair of the beard and eyebrows. They must also wash their clothes and bathe themselves in water. Then they will be ceremonially clean.

LEVITICUS 14:2-4, 8-9

²⁵"Because the entire land has become defiled, I am punishing the people who live there. I will cause the land to vomit them out. ²⁶You must obey all my decrees and regulations. You must not commit any of these detestable sins. This applies both to native-born Israelites and to the foreigners living among you. ²⁷All these detestable activities are practiced by the people of the land where I am taking you, and this is how the land has become defiled. ²⁸So do not defile the land and give it a reason to vomit you out, as it will vomit out the people who live there now. ²⁹Whoever commits any of these detestable sins will be cut off from the community of Israel. ³⁰So obey my instructions, and do not defile yourselves by committing any of these detestable practices that were committed by the people who lived in the land before you."

LEVITICUS 18:25-30

Where would we be without maps? We can't see too far ahead, we can't see too far behind, and we certainly can't see around the corner. Maps come to the rescue when our two-dimensional perspective of the road keeps us from being able to see where we are going. If we ignore maps in these situations, we will be lost.

This section of Scripture begins a set of instructions for everyday life—some for the people and some for the priests. It covers sexual relations, punishments for sin, rules for priests, and unacceptable sacrifices. These are God's expressed desires for his people—his map for our life's travels.

The landscape includes several highways: resisting the negative influence and immorality of the culture around us; showing mercy to those in need; avoiding occult practices; and giving our best efforts and gifts to God.

Read Leviticus 18:1–22:33

God gave many rules to his people, each for a reason. He did not withhold good from them; he prohibited those acts that would bring them to ruin and commanded those acts that would benefit them. All of us can see God's physical laws of nature. Jumping off a ten-story building will result in grave injuries or death because of the law of gravity. Eating healthy foods means fueling the body with what it needs. But some of us don't understand how God's spiritual laws work. God forbids us to do certain things because he wants to keep us from self-destruction. He commands us to do other acts because he knows what we need to flourish.

The next time you are drawn to a forbidden physical activity or emotional response, remember that it may lead to suffering and separation from the God who is trying to help you. The next time a good act seems unpleasant or inconvenient, remember that God has only the best planned for you.

What is your favorite holiday or time of year? What do you do to prepare for it? What are some of the ways that you observe it? How do you feel after the holiday has passed?

Here, through Moses, God provides more instructions for everyday life through the establishment of feasts, seasons, and festivals. There are seven annual "holidays" plus the Sabbath year and the Year of Jubilee. God also presents rules for honoring him in the Tabernacle and for maintaining justice. God says that observing these holidays will make a big difference.

We can learn other, more specific lessons from these chapters as well: giving God the "firstfruits" of our labors; not using God's name in vain; and having mercy on others (Jubilee). Consider all this a priority check.

Read Leviticus 23:1–25:55

Feasts played a major role in God's plan for Israel (Leviticus 23:1–44). These feasts were different from those of any other nation, because being ordained by God, they were times of celebrating with him, not times of moral depravity, drunkenness, or indulgence. God wanted to set aside special days for the people to come together for rest and refreshment, and to remember with thanksgiving all he had done for them. They celebrated God's goodness.

Much can be learned about people by observing what and how they celebrate. Consider your holidays and the traditions you observe. What do they say about your values? How do you celebrate? When do you take time to rest, refresh yourself, and remember God? Include in your calendar feasts and traditions that celebrate God's goodness, rejoice in your fellowship with other believers, and honor the Lord.

¹The Lord said to Moses, ²"Give the following instructions to the people of Israel. These are the Lord's appointed festivals, which you are to proclaim as official days for holy assembly. ³You have six days each week for your ordinary work, but the seventh day is a Sabbath day of complete rest, an official day for holy assembly. It is the Lord's Sabbath day. . . . ⁴In addition to the Sabbath, these are the Lord's appointed festivals, the official days for holy assembly that are to be celebrated at their proper times each year. ⁵The Lord's Passover begins at sundown on the fourteenth day of the first month. ⁶On the next day, the fifteenth day of the month, you must begin celebrating the Festival of Unleavened Bread. This festival to the Lord continues for seven days."

LEVITICUS 23:1-6

9"I will look favorably upon you, making you fertile and multiplying your people. And I will fulfill my covenant with you. 10You will have such a surplus of crops that you will need to clear out the old grain to make room for the new harvest! 11I will live among you, and I will not despise you. 12I will walk among you; I will be your God, and you will be my people. 13I am the LORD your God, who brought you out of the land of Egypt so you would no longer be their slaves. I broke the yoke of slavery from your neck so you can walk with your heads held high. 14However, if you do not listen to me or obey all these commands, 15and if you break my covenant by rejecting my decrees, treating my regulations with contempt, and refusing to obey my commands, 16I will punish you."

LEVITICUS 26:9-16

Parents issue a lot of warnings. To observers these warnings can seem harsh. Sometimes they seem harsh to the children as well, but loving parents issue them anyway. They know that the world's dangers are real.

This reading completes God's instructions for Israel's everyday living by summarizing the rewards for obedience to God, the consequences of disobedience, and by telling how to dedicate something to the Lord. It's a clear statement of why we should obey God.

The point: There is only one true and living God, so it doesn't make sense to live for money, possessions, or other idols. Not only that, but such living is dangerous.

Read Leviticus 26:1–27:34

Some people think that the Old Testament portrays God as harsh, pointing to passages like Leviticus 26:14-39 as an example. But this passage shows what God really wanted to accomplish with such warnings, and also what God meant when he said that he is slow to anger (see Exodus 34:6). God warned his people of sin's consequences for the same reason parents warn their children of danger—to protect and provide for them out of love. God wanted his people to prosper through their compliance to his design for life. And he wanted it so much that he promised to reward them if they obeyed (Leviticus 26:3-13). Even if the Israelites chose to disobey God and were scattered among their enemies, God would still give them the opportunity to repent and return to him (26:40-45). God did not want to destroy the Israelites; he wanted to help them grow. That is the purpose of his harsh warnings.

Our day-to-day experiences and hardships can sometimes seem overwhelming. God allows these events to happen to help us grow, not to curse us. We need to see that God's purpose is to help us live as he designed and to bring about continual growth in us. Jeremiah 29:11 puts it this way: "'For I know the plans I have for you,' says the LORD. 'They are plans for good and not for disaster, to give you a future and a hope.'" To retain hope while suffering shows that we understand God's merciful ways of relating to his people.

What are you struggling with these days? What stresses and problems are you facing? Endure hardship as God's teaching tool; ask God to teach you through every difficulty.

"You're not old enough!" or, "Sorry, you don't have enough experience." Either response can be disheartening, even when it's true. It means you will have to go through a frustrating, perhaps tiresome, time of growing up or acquiring experience.

The Israelites know what this is like. After the Lord delivered them out of Egypt, he led them to Mount Sinai. Here they've been encamped for more than a year, receiving God's laws and learning how to relate to him. But at the beginning of Numbers things begin to change. God isn't just giving the Israelites laws to live by anymore. In fact, the instructions he gives to Moses in the first two chapters seem a bit strange. But God always has a good reason for everything he does, and the instructions he gives here are for the Israelites' benefit.

Read Numbers 1:1–4:49

The Israelites were at a transition point in their journey, and taking a census was an important task (Numbers 1:2-15). The fighting men had to be counted to determine Israel's military strength before entering the Promised Land, and the tribes had to be organized to determine the amount of land each would need and to provide genealogical records. Without such a census, the task of conquering and organizing the Promised Land would have been more difficult.

At every transition point in life it is important to take inventory of our resources and count the cost of each alternative (see Proverbs 13:16). We will serve more effectively if, before plunging in, we set aside time to take stock of all we have—possessions, relationships, spiritual condition, time, goals, and so forth. While God does not want us to trust in our material resources, he does want us to use well what we have.

Before your next move or major decision, analyze your resources and count the cost. Then use what God has given you for his glory.

[1]A year after Israel's departure from Egypt, the LORD spoke to Moses in the Tabernacle in the wilderness of Sinai. On the first day of the second month of that year he said, [2]"From the whole community of Israel, record the names of all the warriors by their clans and families. List all the men [3]twenty years old or older who are able to go to war. You and Aaron must register the troops, [4]and you will be assisted by one family leader from each tribe. . . ." [17]So Moses and Aaron called together these chosen leaders, [18]and they assembled the whole community of Israel on that very day. All the people were registered according to their ancestry by their clans and families. The men of Israel who were twenty years old or older were listed one by one, [19]just as the LORD had commanded Moses.

NUMBERS 1:1-4, 17-19

²²The Lᴏʀᴅ said to Moses, ²³"Tell Aaron and his sons to bless the people of Israel with this special blessing: ²⁴'May the Lᴏʀᴅ bless you and protect you. ²⁵May the Lᴏʀᴅ smile on you and be gracious to you. ²⁶May the Lᴏʀᴅ show you his favor and give you his peace.' ²⁷Whenever Aaron and his sons bless the people of Israel in my name, I myself will bless them."

⁷:¹On the day Moses set up the Tabernacle, he anointed it and set it apart as holy. He also anointed and set apart all its furnishings and the altar with its utensils. ²Then the leaders of Israel—the tribal leaders who had registered the troops—came and brought their offerings. ³Together they brought six large wagons and twelve oxen. There was a wagon for every two leaders and an ox for each leader. They presented these to the Lᴏʀᴅ in front of the Tabernacle.

NUMBERS 6:22–7:3

Preparing for a vacation can be more stressful than actually going on the trip, but there's no escaping it. Without preparation, the trip will probably not go smoothly—or worse, it may not happen at all.

In this reading, the Israelites continue their preparations for entering the Promised Land. God gives them numerous instructions. Moses and Aaron bless them. The people dedicate the Tabernacle and celebrate Passover. Then God provides guidance for the journey. As you read, learn that especially at the onset of great plans, a right relationship with God comes first.

In this passage, you will find these lessons as well: making restitution; dealing with suspicion in marriage; avoiding foolish vows; pitching in to help; and doing what is right when compromise is necessary.

Read Numbers 5:1–10:10

As part of Israel's preparation for entering the Promised Land, Moses instructed Aaron to bless the people. A blessing was one way of asking for God's divine favor to rest upon others, and that's what Aaron and his sons did for the people of Israel here (Numbers 6:24-26). This blessing's five parts conveyed hope that God would (1) bless and protect them; (2) smile upon them (be pleased); (3) be gracious (merciful and compassionate); (4) show them his favor (give his approval); and (5) give peace.

When you ask God to bless others or yourself, you are asking him to grant these five requests. The blessing you offer will not only help the ones receiving it, but it will also demonstrate love, encourage them, and provide a model of caring for them. You can bless others through prayer and in person, face-to-face. Who can you bless in this way today?

What do you miss most about the past? What, for you, are "the good old days"? Is there a time of life you wish you could revisit? Is there a period of time that you remember as full of joy and wonder?

The Israelites find themselves doing this shortly after they leave Mount Sinai—only they take it too far. This is the story of Israel's first approach to the land God wanted to give them, and it's a disaster. From the food, to the leadership, to the Promised Land itself, the people cannot seem to find enough to complain about—despite God's faithfulness—and want to go back to the "good life" in Egypt!

There are too many lessons here to list, but here are a few key concepts to grasp in this passage: the Lord will provide for our needs; it's not wise to put the Lord to the test; and the Lord hears the cries of the faithful and answers their prayers.

Read Numbers 10:11–14:45

God became angry with the Israelites because they complained (Numbers 11:1-3, 10). They were grumbling because they didn't seem to notice what God was doing for them—setting them free, making them a nation, giving them a new land—because they were so wrapped up in what God *wasn't* doing for them (11:4-6). They could think of nothing but the delicious Egyptian food that they had left behind. Somehow they forgot that the price of that food was the brutal whip of Egyptian slavery.

Before we judge the Israelites too harshly, it's helpful to think about what occupies our attention most of the time. Dissatisfaction comes when our attention shifts from what we have to what we don't have.

⁴Then the foreign rabble who were traveling with the Israelites began to crave the good things of Egypt. And the people of Israel also began to complain. "Oh, for some meat!" they exclaimed. ⁵"We remember the fish we used to eat for free in Egypt. And we had all the cucumbers, melons, leeks, onions, and garlic we wanted. ⁶But now our appetites are gone. All we ever see is this manna!" ⁷The manna looked like small coriander seeds, and it was pale yellow like gum resin. ⁸The people would go out and gather it from the ground. They made flour by grinding it with hand mills or pounding it in mortars. Then they boiled it in a pot and made it into flat cakes. These cakes tasted like pastries baked with olive oil. ⁹The manna came down on the camp with the dew during the night.

NUMBERS 11:4-9

Are you grateful for what God has given you, or are you always thinking about what you would like to have? Don't allow your unfulfilled desires to cause you to forget God's gifts of life, food, health, work, and friends.

²There was no water for the people to drink at that place, so they rebelled against Moses and Aaron. ³The people blamed Moses and said, "If only we had died in the LORD's presence with our brothers! ⁴Why have you brought the congregation of the LORD's people into this wilderness to die, along with all our livestock? ⁵Why did you make us leave Egypt and bring us here to this terrible place? This land has no grain, no figs, no grapes, no pomegranates, and no water to drink!"

NUMBERS 20:2-5

The most negative person you know is probably not your favorite person. We are so averse to negative people that we have a small arsenal of verbal flyswatters devoted to shooing them away: "One bad apple spoils the whole bunch." "Don't rain on my parade." "Don't be a party pooper." "Don't be a stick in the mud." "You're such a wet blanket."

Many of the Israelites in this reading are "wet blankets." They struggle with bad attitudes that eventually lead to drastic and devastating consequences. Here you can see the enormous damage that negative attitudes can do.

There are other lessons in this passage on (1) ambition (good or bad?); (2) tithing; and (3) recognizing when we ourselves are at fault.

Read Numbers 15:1–21:35

After witnessing spectacular miracles and experiencing the actual presence of God, the Israelites still grumbled and rebelled against the Lord (Numbers 14:1–10; 20:2-5). We may wonder how they could be so blind and ignorant, yet aren't we just like them? Despite centuries of evidence, scores of Bible translations, and the convincing results of archaeological and historical studies, people today continue to grumble against God and go their own way.

Rebellion against God begins with dissatisfaction and skepticism, with grumbling about God and present circumstances. Then follows bitterness and resentment, and lastly, open hostility and rebellion.

If you are often dissatisfied, skeptical, complaining, or bitter—beware! These attitudes color your perspective and bias you against God. You can escape this trap by choosing a better attitude. Has God guided and protected you? Has he answered your prayers? Do you know people who have experienced remarkable blessings and healings? Do you know Bible stories about the way God has led his people? Focus your thoughts on what God has done.

Most people have mixed reactions around animals. But no one—even those who *love* animals—would say that animals should run our lives.

After wandering in the desert for disobeying God's command to enter Canaan, a new generation of Israelites has grown up. Now they are poised to enter the land, but the Moabites stand in the way. Their king, Balak, tries to get Balaam, a sorcerer, to stop them. Can he do it? Well, yes and no—Balaam's donkey has it right.

This section of Scripture is brimming with wisdom found by seeing what *not* to do.

Read Numbers 22:1–25:18

Balaam was a sorcerer, a person called upon to place curses on others (Numbers 22:4-6). The king of Moab wanted Balaam to use his powers with the God of Israel to place a curse on Israel—hoping that, by magic, God would turn against his people. Neither Balaam nor Balak had any idea whom they were dealing with!

Why would God speak through a sorcerer like Balaam (22:9)? God wanted to give a message to the Moabites, who had already chosen to employ Balaam. So Balaam was available for God to use. Balaam's devotion and motives were mixed. He had some knowledge of God, but not enough to quit his magic and turn wholeheartedly to God. Later passages in the Bible show that Balaam couldn't resist the tempting pull of money and idolatry (see 2 Peter 2:15; Jude 11).

²¹The next morning Balaam got up, saddled his donkey, and started off with the Moabite officials. ²²But God was angry that Balaam was going, so he sent the angel of the LORD to stand in the road to block his way. As Balaam and two servants were riding along, ²³Balaam's donkey saw the angel of the LORD standing in the road with a drawn sword in his hand. The donkey bolted off the road into a field, but Balaam beat it and turned it back onto the road. ²⁴Then the angel of the LORD stood at a place where the road narrowed between two vineyard walls. ²⁵When the donkey saw the angel of the LORD, it tried to squeeze by and crushed Balaam's foot against the wall. So Balaam beat the donkey again. ²⁶Then the angel of the LORD moved farther down the road and stood in a place too narrow for the donkey to get by at all.

NUMBERS 22:21-26

Do not take good feelings and apparent positive results as a sign of God's blessing on your life. A popular following, a track record of success, a speech about respecting God—Balaam had all of these, yet he still lacked a relationship with God. God was not blessing Balaam but using him in spite of his duplicitous heart.

What will it take to give your whole heart to God? Get rid of anything that would distract you from him.

having an undevided heart, not being a luke warm Christian —

¹⁵Then Moses said to the LORD, ¹⁶"O LORD, you are the God who gives breath to all creatures. Please appoint a new man as leader for the community. ¹⁷Give them someone who will guide them wherever they go and will lead them into battle, so the community of the LORD will not be like sheep without a shepherd." ¹⁸The LORD replied, "Take Joshua son of Nun, who has the Spirit in him, and lay your hands on him. ¹⁹Present him to Eleazar the priest before the whole community, and publicly commission him to lead the people. . . ." ²²So Moses did as the LORD commanded. He presented Joshua to Eleazar the priest and the whole community. ²³Moses laid his hands on him and commissioned him to lead the people, just as the LORD had commanded through Moses.

NUMBERS 27:15-19, 22-23

If you ever played kickball at recess, you know what a difference having the right team captain can make. If you end up on the wrong team, it can be a long game.

Leaders who continually make bad decisions cause anxiety and anguish for those they lead. That's why it's important to choose leaders carefully.

Moses knew the value of good leadership. In this reading, he asks God to appoint a successor to lead the Israelites. But Moses doesn't ask for just anyone, he asks the Lord for someone who will care for the Israelites. As you read this passage, notice whom God appoints as Moses' successor.

Also look for lessons on preparing for worship; taking holidays; and safeguarding against making foolish vows.

Read Numbers 26:1–31:54

Moses asked God to appoint a leader, one who could lead the people in battle but who would also care for their needs. The Lord responded by appointing Joshua, a man "who has the Spirit in him" (Numbers 27:18). Moses then presented Joshua to the people and commissioned him to serve as God had commanded. Moses also clearly told the people that Joshua had the authority and the ability to lead the nation.

Most of us are in the position of developing and choosing leaders. Leaders are important, and the kind of people we choose and the way we choose them matters a great deal. Whenever we see a change in leadership coming or we influence the choice of a leader, we should do as Moses did—first, ask God for a person who is both able and compassionate; then, commission and support the person in his or her new position.

In what ways are you developing leaders at home? at work? at church? in the community? What can you do to influence them to lead God's way?

how Do I Support my leaders??

`Prayer' ???

How easy it is to assume we know what others are thinking. We easily come up with our own reasons for why people do this or that. When we feel unsure about others' motives, we tend to assume the worst of them.

The Israelites are no different. Having finally entered the land of God's promise—the part that lies east of the Jordan River—a misunderstanding arises between Moses and three of the tribes of Israel. That leads to the age-old squabble over fairness. As you read, look for a lesson about communication and the problem with making wrong assumptions.

Other gems lie hidden in these chapters: a technique for avoiding past mistakes, and knowing when to be harsh.

Read Numbers 32:1–34:29

Three tribes (Reuben, Gad, and half of Manasseh) told Moses that they wanted to live on the land that was east of the Jordan River (Numbers 32:1-5). This land had already been conquered; the hard work had been done by all of the tribes together. When Moses heard the request of the three tribes, he immediately assumed that they had selfish motives and were trying to avoid helping the others fight for the land across the river (32:6-15). Moses jumped to the wrong conclusion. These tribes fully intended to continue the fight and promised to keep working with the others until everyone's land was conquered (32:16-19).

Don't automatically assume that others have wrong motives, even if their plans sound suspicious. With any person, take time to let the facts surface before making up your mind.

¹The tribes of Reuben and Gad owned vast numbers of livestock. So when they saw that the lands of Jazer and Gilead were ideally suited for their flocks and herds, ²they came to Moses, Eleazar the priest, and the other leaders of the community. They said, . . . ⁴"The LORD has conquered this whole area for the community of Israel, and it is ideally suited for all our livestock. ⁵If we have found favor with you, please let us have this land as our property instead of giving us land across the Jordan River." ⁶"Do you intend to stay here while your brothers go across and do all the fighting?" Moses asked the men of Gad and Reuben. ⁷"Why do you want to discourage the rest of the people of Israel from going across to the land the LORD has given them?"

NUMBERS 32:1-2, 4-7

¹⁰"Give the following instructions to the people of Israel. When you cross the Jordan into the land of Canaan, ¹¹designate cities of refuge to which people can flee if they have killed someone accidentally. ¹²These cities will be places of protection from a dead person's relatives who want to avenge the death. The slayer must not be put to death before being tried by the community. ¹³Designate six cities of refuge for yourselves, ¹⁴three on the east side of the Jordan River and three on the west in the land of Canaan. ¹⁵These cities are for the protection of Israelites, foreigners living among you, and traveling merchants. Anyone who accidentally kills someone may flee there for safety. ¹⁶But if someone strikes and kills another person with a piece of iron, it is murder, and the murderer must be executed."

NUMBERS 35:10-16

Suppose you were accused of murder. Wouldn't *you* want an impartial jury and a fair trial?

This reading concludes the story of Israel's campaign to take the land east of the Jordan River. Having defeated the Midianites and divided the land, all that remains is to give some towns to the Levites. Six of these are designated cities of refuge to serve as important safeguards on personal revenge and hotheaded lynch mobs. Doing justice isn't easy, as the anecdote about discrimination shows at the very end.

Also in this passage, look for lessons on the value of human life; a humane system of justice; and the importance of family.

Read Numbers 35:1–36:13

Of the forty-eight cities given to the Levites, six were cities of refuge (Numbers 35:6). Such cities were needed because the ancient customs of justice called for revenge in the event of any death, accidental or otherwise, by the hand of another person (see, for example, 2 Samuel 14:7). The Levites would hold a preliminary hearing outside the gates while the accused person was kept in the city until the time of his or her trial. If the killing was judged to be accidental, the person would stay in the city until the death of the high priest. At that time, he or she would be allowed to go free and could start a new life without worrying about revenge. If it was not accidental, the person would be handed over to the slain person's avengers for execution.

This shows how important God considers both justice and mercy. God wanted the people to be intolerant of the sin, yet impartial so the accused could have a fair trial.

It is unjust both to overlook wrongdoing and to jump to conclusions about guilt. When someone is accused of wrongdoing, stand up for justice, protect those not yet proven guilty, and listen carefully to all sides of the story.

If you were to give a slide show reviewing the last twenty years of your life, what would you highlight? The fun times? The disasters? The family outings? The struggles and pain? The brushes with greatness?

The book of Deuteronomy is where Israel gets to sit down for a little reminiscing—both good and bad. Moses highlights God's laws and how well (or poorly) Israel obeyed those laws along the way.

As you relive the history of Moses and the Israelites, watch for other important insights for God's people: understanding the qualities of good leaders; knowing when not to fight; and overcoming insurmountable obstacles.

Read Deuteronomy 1:1–5:33

God gave Israel many laws, and he commanded that the people remember those laws and then teach them to their children (Deuteronomy 4:8-9). Do these laws apply to Christians today? God designed his laws to guide his people in honoring and worshiping him and to help them see their sin and the proper way to deal with that sin. God's law is the perfect expression of who God is and how he wants his people to live.

God's laws always have a purpose, but in some cases the purpose has been finished. For example, God told Israel to practice animal sacrifice in worship to receive forgiveness and to express thanks. But Christ made the ultimate, final sacrifice for sin—we must now come to him for forgiveness. The principle (coming to God for forgiveness and thanking him), not the form (animal sacrifice), still applies.

¹"And now, Israel, listen carefully to these decrees and regulations that I am about to teach you. Obey them so that you may live, so you may enter and occupy the land that the LORD, the God of your ancestors, is giving you. ²Do not add to or subtract from these commands I am giving you. Just obey the commands of the LORD your God that I am giving you. ³You saw for yourself what the LORD did to you at Baal-peor. There the LORD your God destroyed everyone who had worshiped Baal, the god of Peor. ⁴But all of you who were faithful to the LORD your God are still alive today—every one of you. ⁵Look, I now teach you these decrees and regulations just as the LORD my God commanded me, so that you may obey them in the land you are about to enter and occupy."

DEUTERONOMY 4:1-5

Whenever you come upon a law directed specifically to Israel in its own time, look for the principle behind it. Look for ways to obey God; don't search for loopholes in his commandments.

¹"Be careful to obey all the commands I am giving you today. Then you will live and multiply, and you will enter and occupy the land the LORD swore to give your ancestors. ²Remember how the LORD your God led you through the wilderness for these forty years, humbling you and testing you to prove your character, and to find out whether or not you would obey his commands. ³Yes, he humbled you by letting you go hungry and then feeding you with manna, a food previously unknown to you and your ancestors. He did it to teach you that [we] do not live by bread alone; rather, we live by every word that comes from the mouth of the LORD. ⁴For all these forty years your clothes didn't wear out, and your feet didn't blister or swell. ⁵Think about it: . . . The LORD your God disciplines you for your own good."

DEUTERONOMY 8:1-5

"I'm starving!" we often say in deliberate exaggeration. It's just a signal to those nearby that we're *really* hungry and open to devoting great energy to getting access to food as soon as possible.

In this reminiscence by Moses, God reminds the Israelites that he allowed them to experience hunger for a purpose, to help them learn something about finding satisfaction. As you read, look for the lesson on where to find *spiritual* nourishment.

There's plenty more to learn in this passage: seeing God's place in everyday experiences; responding whenever success strikes; heeding warnings; and reading God's Word.

Read Deuteronomy 6:1–11:32

Jesus quoted Deuteronomy 8:3 when the devil tempted him to turn stones into bread (see Matthew 4:4). God's Word is the ultimate source of nourishment, and we should be much more concerned about feeding our spirits than feeding our bodies.

Many people think that life consists of satisfying physical appetites and indulging their desires. If they can earn enough money to dress, eat, and play in high style, they think they are living the good life. But indulging such desires does not satisfy a person's deepest longings. Instead, satisfaction comes from total commitment to God, the one who created life itself. This means relying on God and feeding on his Word. It requires discipline, sacrifice, and hard work—which is why most people never find it.

Be careful not to equate *indulgence* with *satisfaction*. When are you tempted to place your physical desires above your spiritual needs? Keep your focus on the Lord, and find your satisfaction in him.

New math. New philosophy. A new theory. New and improved. It seems as if everyone has something to sell, and they have to make it "new and improved" to make the sale. This approach is used in selling religion, too—false gods and phony worship can be packaged as brightly and promoted as aggressively as soap and cereal.

This may be one reason why God warns his people about false prophets and teachers. Moses explains how God's people can approach God. Many of these instructions have much to say to *all* worshipers who care about worshiping God properly.

As you read, be on the lookout for other areas that affect your worship: resisting temptations that lure you away from God; worshiping together as a family; giving to God's work; and helping the poor.

Read Deuteronomy 12:1–15:23

Moses warned the Israelites against false prophets who encouraged worship of other gods (Deuteronomy 13:1-3). New ideas from inspiring people may sound good, but we must judge them by whether or not they are consistent with God's Word. Some people speak the truth while directing people toward God, but others speak persuasively while directing followers toward themselves. It is even possible to say the right words but still lead people in the wrong direction. False prophets are still around today. The wise person will carefully test ideas against the truth of God's Word.

1"Suppose there are prophets among you or those who dream dreams about the future, and they promise you signs or miracles, 2and the predicted signs or miracles occur. If they then say, 'Come, let us worship other gods'—gods you have not known before—3do not listen to them. The LORD your God is testing you to see if you truly love him with all your heart and soul. 4Serve only the LORD your God and fear him alone. Obey his commands, listen to his voice, and cling to him. 5The false prophets or visionaries who try to lead you astray must be put to death, for they encourage rebellion against the LORD your God, who redeemed you from slavery and brought you out of the land of Egypt."

DEUTERONOMY 13:1-5

When people claim to speak for God today, check them in these areas: Are they telling the truth? Is their focus on God? Are their words consistent with what you already know to be true? When you hear a new, attractive idea, examine it carefully before getting too excited.

⁹"When you enter the land the LORD your God is giving you, be very careful not to imitate the detestable customs of the nations living there. ¹⁰For example, never sacrifice your son or daughter as a burnt offering. And do not let your people practice fortune-telling, or use sorcery, or interpret omens, or engage in witchcraft, ¹¹or cast spells, or function as mediums or psychics, or call forth the spirits of the dead. ¹²Anyone who does these things is detestable to the LORD. It is because the other nations have done these detestable things that the LORD your God will drive them out ahead of you. ¹³But you must be blameless before the LORD your God. ¹⁴The nations you are about to displace consult sorcerers and fortune-tellers, but the LORD your God forbids you to do such things."

DEUTERONOMY 18:9-14

People want to know the future. Most newspapers carry horoscopes and predictions by self-proclaimed future-tellers. There are even "psychic hotlines" to call. These people make a living because there's a market.

This section of Scripture highlights laws for ruling the nation of Israel. It covers the usual civil regulations, such as instructions on judges, the courts, and the king. But right smack in the middle are guidelines about the occult.

All citizens will find something here: responsibility to vote; responsibility of leaders; and balancing justice with mercy.

Read Deuteronomy 16:1–20:20

The Israelites were naturally curious about the occult practices of the Canaanite religions. They may have thought, *What's wrong with checking it out?* or *It won't hurt to dabble in it just a little.* But Satan is behind the occult, and God flatly forbade Israel to have anything to do with it (Deuteronomy 18:9-14).

Today, people are still fascinated by horoscopes, fortune-telling, Ouija boards, witchcraft, and even satanic cults. Often their interest arises from a desire to know and control the future. *What's the harm?* they may think. But Satan is no less dangerous today than he was in Moses' time. God tells us all we need to know about what is going to happen. We don't need to turn to occult sources for faulty information; instead we should seek the trustworthy guidance of the Holy Spirit through the Bible and the church.

It's called the world's oldest profession because it's been around for a long, long time indeed. Many people reason, therefore, that if prostitution is so persistent, that if it has survived this long, what's wrong with it?

The answer is here, among many other laws that God gives to his people at this crucial time in their history. They are receiving God's laws on human relationships, and one of the top areas of God's concern is the sexual one. It's too important to ignore.

Other laws in this section cover community responsibility; practical benefits in God's laws; kindness to the poor; discipline; and remembering what God has done.

Read Deuteronomy 21:1–26:19

Prostitution was not overlooked in God's law—it was strictly forbidden (Deuteronomy 23:17-18). Almost every other religion known to the Israelites included prostitution as a part of its worship services. But prostitution makes a mockery of God's original idea for sex, treating it as an isolated physical experience rather than an act of commitment to another person. Outside of marriage, sex destroys relationships. Within marriage, if approached with the right attitude, it can be a relationship builder. God frequently had to warn the people against the practice of extramarital sex. Today we still need to hear his warnings; young people need to be reminded about the dangers of premarital sex, and adults need to be reminded about the importance of sexual fidelity.

17"No Israelite, whether man or woman, may become a temple prostitute. 18When you are bringing an offering to fulfill a vow, you must not bring to the house of the Lord your God any offering from the earnings of a prostitute, whether a man or a woman, for both are detestable to the Lord your God. . . . 21When you make a vow to the Lord your God, be prompt in fulfilling whatever you promised him. For the Lord your God demands that you promptly fulfill all your vows, or you will be guilty of sin. 22However, it is not a sin to refrain from making a vow. 23But once you have voluntarily made a vow, be careful to fulfill your promise to the Lord your God."

DEUTERONOMY 23:17-18, 21-23

Don't be taken in by the cheapening of sex through self-indulgent, recreational sexual encounters portrayed in television shows, movies, books, music, and magazines. Sex was God's idea. He created it for procreation, for expressing love, and for enjoyment *within marriage*. Celebrate your sexuality God's way!

[16]"'Cursed is anyone who dishonors father or mother.' And all the people will reply, 'Amen.' [17]'Cursed is anyone who steals property from a neighbor by moving a boundary marker.' And all the people will reply, 'Amen.' [18]'Cursed is anyone who leads a blind person astray on the road.' And all the people will reply, 'Amen.' [19]'Cursed is anyone who denies justice to foreigners, orphans, or widows.' And all the people will reply, 'Amen.' . . . [24]'Cursed is anyone who attacks a neighbor in secret.' And all the people will reply, 'Amen.' [25]'Cursed is anyone who accepts payment to kill an innocent person.' And all the people will reply, 'Amen.' [26]'Cursed is anyone who does not affirm and obey the terms of these instructions.' And all the people will reply, 'Amen.'"

DEUTERONOMY 27:16-19, 24-26

Picture this: You're driving along at fifty miles per hour on a cloudy day. The road ahead is suddenly narrow, with deep, unforgiving ditches on both sides. But the two endless lines of fluorescent orange cones that line the road on either side keep you out of trouble.

If you think of the curses in this reading as fluorescent orange cones, you come pretty close to their meaning. If you understand that those cones are really doing you a favor, you can't help but be happy about them. The cones help everyone. The other chapters in this section of Deuteronomy are proof enough of that.

There are other road signs in today's reading: something to remember when it looks as if the world is falling apart; seeking God with all your heart, soul, and strength; and following a plan of action no matter how badly you've sinned.

Read Deuteronomy 27:1–30:20

The curses God wanted his people to remember were a series of oaths, spoken by the priests and affirmed by those listening, in which the people promised to stay away from wrong actions (Deuteronomy 27:15-26). Those saying *Amen*, "So be it," were taking responsibility for their actions.

Sometimes looking at a list of curses like this gives us the idea that God has a bad temper and is out to crush anyone who steps out of line. But we need to see these restrictions not as threats but as loving warnings about the plain facts of life. Wrongdoing toward others or God has tragic consequences, and God is merciful enough to tell us this truth plainly. His strong words help us avoid the serious consequences that result from neglecting God or wronging others. Just as we warn children to stay away from hot stoves and busy streets, God warns us to stay away from dangerous actions.

Books can entertain, educate, edify, and enrage. Well-written books draw us along, page by page, till the end. What memories do you have of books? What feelings do you have toward books?

This section constitutes Moses' last words of advice, and includes several points about reading (even singing) God's Book aloud. This isn't mere formality; it's a necessity.

Changes in leadership are sensitive times. Don't miss what happens here because it's Moses' last opportunity to impart God's word.

This passage touches on at least two additional topics to be aware of: music as a part of life with God, and differences in God's blessings to different people.

Read Deuteronomy 31:1–34:12

Moses commanded the Israelites to read God's laws to the whole assembly so that everyone, including the children, could hear them (Deuteronomy 31:10-13). Every seven years the entire nation would gather together and listen as a priest read the law to them. There were no books or Bibles to pass around, so the people had to rely on word of mouth and an accurate memory. Memorization was an important part of worship, because if everyone knew the law, ignorance would be no excuse for breaking the law.

To fulfill God's purpose and will in our lives, we need the content and substance of his Word in our hearts and minds. For the Hebrews, this process began in childhood.

⁹So Moses wrote this entire body of instruction in a book and gave it to the priests, who carried the Ark of the Lord's Covenant, and to the elders of Israel. ¹⁰Then Moses gave them this command: "At the end of every seventh year, the Year of Release, during the Festival of Shelters, ¹¹you must read this Book of Instruction to all the people of Israel when they assemble before the Lord your God at the place he chooses. ¹²Call them all together—men, women, children, and the foreigners living in your towns—so they may hear this Book of Instruction and learn to fear the Lord your God and carefully obey all the terms of these instructions. ¹³Do this so that your children who have not known these instructions will hear them and will learn to fear the Lord your God. Do this as long as you live in the land you are crossing the Jordan to occupy."

DEUTERONOMY 31:9-13

If you are resistant or feel awkward about leading family devotions, simply read the Bible to your children. There are Bibles available in English for all ages—storybooks for the youngest children, simple translations for early readers, and Bibles designed especially for young people and teenagers. Teaching your children (and new believers) should be one of your top priorities.

¹²Then Joshua called together the tribes of Reuben, Gad, and the half-tribe of Manasseh. He told them, ¹³"Remember what Moses, the servant of the LORD, commanded you: 'The LORD your God is giving you a place of rest. He has given you this land.' ¹⁴Your wives, children, and livestock may remain here in the land Moses assigned to you on the east side of the Jordan River. But your strong warriors, fully armed, must lead the other tribes across the Jordan to help them conquer their territory. Stay with them ¹⁵until the LORD gives them rest, as he has given you rest, and until they, too, possess the land the LORD your God is giving them. Only then may you return and settle here on the east side of the Jordan River in the land that Moses, the servant of the LORD, assigned to you."

JOSHUA 1:12-15

Think back to your first day on the job. Like most people, you probably felt a little overwhelmed by all the challenges ahead of you: new names and faces to learn, responsibilities, procedures, and high hopes.

The book of Joshua opens with the anticipation of a new job for Joshua, the new leader of Israel. No sooner does he get the job than he must deal with an unpleasant situation—calling upon the tribes of Gad, Reuben, and Manasseh to keep the promise they made to Moses. In addition, Joshua must follow God's orders and carry out a painful and possibly humiliating task. But he is capable and willing to do what the Lord desires of him as the leader of Israel.

This portion of the book of Joshua helps answer several other questions: (1) Is it ever right to lie? (2) How important is a pure heart? (3) What should a person do in the face of great opposition?

Read Joshua 1:1–5:12

Joshua's new job responsibilities included leading more than two million people into a strange new land and conquering it. What a challenge—even for a man of Joshua's caliber!

Every new job is a challenge. Without God it can be frightening. With God it can be a great adventure. Just as God was with Joshua, he is with us as we face our new challenges.

You may not conquer nations, but every day you face tough situations, difficult people, and strong temptations. However, God promises that he will never abandon you or fail to help you (see Deuteronomy 4:31). Ask God to direct your ways, and you will be able to conquer many of life's challenges.

There's something beautiful about a well-executed military strategy. Think of the Trojan Horse or Operation Desert Storm. The operation totally surprises the enemy and leaves hardly any casualties on your side. The victory is swift and sure. Generals who design these plans earn the reputation as geniuses because clean victories are so difficult to achieve.

It's good that the Israelites had God as their general because this passage is one long string of military engagements. The people find out who the real genius is. Fortunately, Joshua goes along with God's program too.

In this passage, we also learn about the possible negative effects of sin and about the responsibilities of family members.

Read Joshua 5:13–8:35

Why did God give Joshua so many complicated instructions for the battle (Joshua 6:3-5)? First, God was making it clear that the battle would depend on him and not on Israel's weapons and expertise. This is why priests, not soldiers, carrying the Ark led the Israelites into battle. Second, God's method of taking the city accentuated the terror already felt in Jericho (2:9). Finally, this strange military maneuver was a test of the Israelites' faith and their willingness to follow God completely.

It must have seemed strange to the Israelites that, instead of going directly to battle, they would march around the city for a week (6:3-20). But that was God's plan, and the Israelites had a guaranteed victory if they would follow it (6:2). As strange as the plan sounded, it worked.

¹Now the gates of Jericho were tightly shut because the people were afraid of the Israelites. No one was allowed to go out or in. ²But the LORD said to Joshua, "I have given you Jericho, its king, and all its strong warriors. ³You and your fighting men should march around the town once a day for six days. ⁴Seven priests will walk ahead of the Ark, each carrying a ram's horn. On the seventh day you are to march around the town seven times, with the priests blowing the horns. ⁵When you hear the priests give one long blast on the rams' horns, have all the people shout as loud as they can. Then the walls of the town will collapse, and the people can charge straight into the town."

JOSHUA 6:1-5

God's instructions may require you to take actions that don't make sense at first. Even as you follow him, you may wonder how things can possibly work out. Like the Israelites, take one day at a time and follow step-by-step. You may not see the logic of God's plan until after you have obeyed.

³But when the people of Gibeon heard what Joshua had done to Jericho and Ai, ⁴they resorted to deception to save themselves. They sent ambassadors to Joshua, loading their donkeys with weathered saddlebags and old, patched wineskins. ⁵They put on worn-out, patched sandals and ragged clothes. And the bread they took with them was dry and moldy. . . . ¹⁴So the Israelites examined their food, but they did not consult the LORD. ¹⁵Then Joshua made a peace treaty with them and guaranteed their safety, and the leaders of the community ratified their agreement with a binding oath. ¹⁶Three days after making the treaty, they learned that these people actually lived nearby!

JOSHUA 9:3-5, 14-16

To be an American is to be a connoisseur of sales pitches. We can't go to the store or even answer the telephone without someone trying to sell us something. They keep coming because they know we're vulnerable—many people cave in to the salesperson's pressure.

Shortly into their campaign to take over Canaan, Israel falls prey to something very similar. The sales pitch that does them in comes knocking door-to-door, the old-fashioned way. Observe their folly and learn from it.

You'll find other lessons here, too, on keeping your word and overcoming overwhelming odds.

Read Joshua 9:1–12:24

Israel's leaders got fooled (Joshua 9:3-17). When they sampled these men's provisions, they saw that the bread was dry and moldy, the wineskins cracked, and the clothes and sandals worn-out. But they did not see through the deception. After the promise had been made and the treaty ratified, the facts came out—Israel's leaders had been deceived. God had told Israel to make no treaties with the inhabitants of Canaan (see Exodus 23:32; 34:12; Numbers 33:55; Deuteronomy 7:2; 20:17-18). As a strategist, Joshua knew enough to talk to God before leading his troops into battle. But the peace treaty seemed innocent enough, so Joshua and the leaders made this decision on their own. By failing to seek God's guidance and wisdom and rushing ahead with their own plans, they had to deal with angry people and an awkward alliance.

Take the time, and have the courage, to consult God before making important decisions—especially when those decisions affect others. Read the Bible daily so that you will know what God wants.

If you could change one thing about the world, what would you change? Don't worry about how it would happen, whether it's realistic, or whether anyone would ever go for it—just dream. Imagine that it *could* happen. What would you change?

This period of time in Israel's history is their opportunity to change their world. Much of what God wants done is theirs to do, and their list of tasks lies before them like an agenda for change. But it means setting priorities.

In this passage, also look for the lessons about the rewards of faith in God, when to break with tradition, and hazards along the path of least resistance.

Read Joshua 13:1–19:51

Much of the Promised Land was unconquered at this point, but God's plan was to go ahead and include it in the divisions among the tribes (Joshua 13:7). God's desire was that it would eventually be conquered by the Israelites.

God knows the future, and as he leads us, he already knows about the victories that lie ahead. Just as the Israelites still had to go to battle and fight, so we must still face the trials and fight the battles of our unconquered land.

What are our unconquered lands? They may be overseas missionary territories, new languages in which to translate the Bible, new missionary areas in our neighborhoods, interest groups or institutions that need to change, unchallenged public problems or ethical issues, unconfessed sin in our lives, or underdeveloped talents and resources.

¹When Joshua was an old man, the LORD said to him, "You are growing old, and much land remains to be conquered. . . . ²All the regions of the Philistines and the Geshurites, ³and the larger territory of the Canaanites, . . . northward to the boundary of Ekron. It includes the territory of the five Philistine rulers of Gaza, Ashdod, Ashkelon, Gath, and Ekron. . . . ⁴In the north, the following area has not yet been conquered: all the land of the Canaanites, . . . stretching northward to Aphek on the border of the Amorites; ⁵the land of the Gebalites and all of the Lebanon mountain area to the east, . . . ⁶and all the hill country from Lebanon to Misrephoth-maim, . . . I myself will drive these people out of the land ahead of the Israelites. So be sure to give this land to Israel as a special possession, just as I have commanded you."

JOSHUA 13:1-6

What territory has God given you to conquer? This territory is *your* promised land. Trust God and take the land. Your inheritance will be a new heaven and a new earth (see Revelation 21:1).

¹Then Joshua summoned all the tribes of Israel to Shechem, including their elders, leaders, judges, and officers. So they came and presented themselves to God. ²Joshua said to the people, . . . ¹⁴"Fear the LORD and serve him wholeheartedly. Put away forever the idols your ancestors worshiped when they lived beyond the Euphrates River and in Egypt. Serve the LORD alone. ¹⁵But if you refuse to serve the LORD, then choose today whom you will serve. Would you prefer the gods your ancestors served beyond the Euphrates? Or will it be the gods of the Amorites in whose land you now live? But as for me and my family, we will serve the LORD."

JOSHUA 24:1-2, 14-15

You don't have to be old to forget something of great importance. It happens to people all the time. It's happened to you, hasn't it? Or can't you remember?

Israel is quite forgetful throughout this time in their history. "Now what was that God we were serving? Oh bother, I can't remember quite why I've got this book of the Law in my hands"—or something like that.

In this section, you will see the Israelites forgetting their heritage and lessons learned in the past, and you will see God reminding them.

Don't forget to note some of the other lessons: following through on your promises and responsibilities; knowing your weaknesses; and realizing the truth of the maxim, "Talk is cheap."

Read Joshua 20:1–24:33

The covenant between Israel and God was that the people would worship and obey the Lord alone. Their purpose was to become a holy nation that would influence the rest of the world for God. The conquest of Canaan was a means to achieve this purpose, but Israel became preoccupied with the land and lost sight of the Lord God.

The same can happen in our lives. We can spend so much time on the means or methods that we forget the end—to glorify God. Churches may make this mistake as well. For example, the congregation may pour all of its energies into a new facility, only to become self-satisfied or fearful of letting certain groups use it. If this happens, they have focused on the building and lost sight of its purpose—to bring others to God.

What is your purpose at work? at home? Make your actions there a part of fulfilling God's highest purposes. Remember what God has called you to do and your promises to him.

Pest control is a multibillion dollar national industry. Is this due to an irrational obsession with bugs? Not at all. Termites and carpenter ants can do serious damage to a home. Rats and many insects carry diseases. Bee stings can be life threatening to people who are allergic to them.

Did the Israelites understand this? In this reading, evidence mounts that they did not. But their pests bring a different kind of threat than to house and health; this time, compassion and convenience go too far, and it costs God's people dearly.

As you read this passage, you will also find other lessons: conditions on claiming God's promises, peer pressure, and the value of obstacles and problems.

Read Judges 1:1–3:6

God's people failed to drive the evil Canaanites from their land (Judges 1:21, 27-36). Why didn't they follow through and completely obey God's commands? First, they had been fighting for a long time and were tired. Although the goal was in sight, they lacked the discipline and energy to reach it. Second, they were afraid the enemy was too strong—the iron chariots seemed invincible. Third, since Joshua's death, power and authority had been decentralized to the tribal leaders, and the tribes were no longer unified in purpose. Fourth, spiritual decay had infected them from within. They thought they could handle the temptation of doing business with the Canaanites.

Don't coddle sin. Know that God has given you the means to do what he commands—whether you are tired, apathetic, confused, or just lazy. Victory comes from pressing on to do God's will today. Drive out those pesky sins!

⁷The Israelites served the Lord throughout the lifetime of Joshua and the leaders who outlived him—those who had seen all the great things the Lord had done for Israel. ⁸Joshua son of Nun, the servant of the Lord, died at the age of 110. ⁹They buried him in the land he had been allocated, at Timnath-serah in the hill country of Ephraim, north of Mount Gaash. ¹⁰After that generation died, another generation grew up who did not acknowledge the Lord or remember the mighty things he had done for Israel. ¹¹The Israelites did evil in the Lord's sight and served the images of Baal. ¹²They abandoned the Lord, the God of their ancestors, who had brought them out of Egypt. They went after other gods, worshiping the gods of the people around them. And they angered the Lord. ¹³They abandoned the Lord to serve Baal and the images of Ashtoreth.

JUDGES 2:7-13

I claim victory upon my life & my family

¹The Israelites did evil in the Lᴏʀᴅ's sight. So the Lᴏʀᴅ handed them over to the Midianites for seven years. ²The Midianites were so cruel that the Israelites made hiding places for themselves in the mountains, caves, and strongholds. ³Whenever the Israelites planted their crops, marauders from Midian, Amalek, and the people of the east would attack Israel, ⁴camping in the land and destroying crops as far away as Gaza. They left the Israelites with nothing to eat, taking all the sheep, goats, cattle, and donkeys. ⁵These enemy hordes, coming with their livestock and tents, were as thick as locusts; they arrived on droves of camels too numerous to count. And they stayed until the land was stripped bare. ⁶So Israel was reduced to starvation by the Midianites. Then the Israelites cried out to the Lᴏʀᴅ for help.

JUDGES 6:1-6

What provisions for emergencies have you made in your home? Syrup of ipecac, fire extinguishers, smoke alarms, emergency phone numbers by the phone, a planned escape route in case of fire—do any of these sound familiar?

This time of the judges is full of emergencies and chaos, brought on by Eglon, king of Moab; Jabin, king of Canaan; the Midianites; and the ever annoying Philistines. Read this passage to see if the Israelites learn anything from all this chaos.

Don't miss other lessons about God's use of "handicaps": leadership; when to take risks; finding courage; and some thoughts on jewelry.

Read Judges 3:7–8:35

The Israelites had a habit of hitting rock bottom and staying there, then trying to dig out of the hole by themselves. In one case, they endured twenty years of being oppressed by the Canaanites before crying to God for help (Judges 4:3). You would think one such emergency would teach them, but it didn't. The formula the Israelites applied was this: When in deep trouble, call on God as a last resort.

God should be the *first* place we turn when we are facing struggles or dilemmas. How much suffering the Israelites could have avoided if they had turned to God right away!

We, too, often try to control our own lives without God's help. When struggles come our way, God wants us to come to him first, seeking his strength and guidance.

Turn to God first for help each day, not as a last resort. Then turn to others for help as God directs. About what problem or struggle should you talk to God right now?

We do an awful lot of waiting, don't we? There's waiting at the doctor's office, at traffic lights, and at home. And then we wait for rides, for kids to come home, for kids to leave, and for the weekend. Waiting can be frustrating.

This passage contains a particularly poignant story about waiting. Jotham has to do it. Ask yourself whether you think *he* enjoys it, because his experience is much like everybody else's in some ways.

While you're pondering that, also read about when to call on God; making (and keeping) promises; and how *not* to respond when you feel left out.

Read Judges 9:1–12:15

Abimelech was the opposite of what God wanted in a judge, but it was three years before God moved against him, fulfilling Jotham's parable (Judges 9:22-24). Those three years must have seemed like forever to Jotham. And he must have wondered why Abimelech wasn't punished sooner for his evil ways.

We are not alone when we wonder why evil seems to prevail—many others have also wondered (see Job 10:3; Job 21:1-18; Jeremiah 12:1; Habakkuk 1:2-4, 12-17). God promises to deal with sin, but in his time, not ours. Actually, it is good that God doesn't punish us immediately, because we, too, deserve God's punishment for our sins. When we demand that God punish evil *now*, we are demanding that he punish us, too, and he's more merciful than that. In his mercy, God often spares us from immediate punishment and allows us time to turn from our sins and turn to him in repentance.

¹One day Gideon's son Abimelech went to Shechem to visit his uncles. . . . He said to them and to the rest of his mother's family, ²"Ask the leading citizens of Shechem whether they want to be ruled by all seventy of Gideon's sons or by one man. And remember that I am your own flesh and blood!" . . . ³After listening to this proposal, the people of Shechem decided in favor of Abimelech because he was their relative. ⁴They gave him seventy silver coins from the temple of Baal-berith, which he used to hire some reckless troublemakers who agreed to follow him. ⁵He went to his father's home at Ophrah, and . . . killed all seventy of his half brothers, the sons of Gideon. But the youngest brother, Jotham, escaped and hid. ⁶Then all the leading citizens of Shechem and Beth-millo . . . made Abimelech their king.

JUDGES 9:1-6

Understand that trusting God for justice means waiting for his timing. First, you must recognize your own sins, turn from them, and ask for God's forgiveness. You may face a difficult time of waiting for the wicked to be punished, but know that in God's time, all evil will be destroyed.

⁴Some time later Samson fell in love with a woman named Delilah, who lived in the valley of Sorek. ⁵The rulers of the Philistines went to her and said, "Entice Samson to tell you what makes him so strong and how he can be overpowered and tied up securely. Then each of us will give you 1,100 pieces of silver." ⁶So Delilah said to Samson, "Please tell me what makes you so strong and what it would take to tie you up securely." . . . ¹⁵Then Delilah pouted, "How can you tell me, 'I love you,' when you don't share your secrets with me? . . . You still haven't told me what makes you so strong!" ¹⁶She tormented him with her nagging day after day until he was sick to death of it. ¹⁷Finally, Samson shared his secret with her.

JUDGES 16:4-6, 15-17

Do you remember your first crush? At the time, you thought there was no one else quite like that special person. You daydreamed, you wished, and you hoped.

Samson is experienced with crushes. Despite his many opportunities, he never quite learns. Or does he?

As you read, see what you can learn about relationships with the opposite sex and about keeping your focus on God.

In this section of Scripture, there are also lessons on the kinds of people God uses; on how to use God's gifts; and on taking revenge. All courtesy of Samson.

Read Judges 13:1–16:31

Samson was deceived because Delilah flattered him and indulged his sexual appetite (Judges 16:15-19). Although Samson could strangle a lion, he could not smother his burning lust or his vanity. As a result, Delilah took advantage of him again and again. If Samson didn't realize what was happening after the first or second incident, surely he should have understood the situation by the fourth time! Yet his sexual appetite and weakness controlled him.

How can you keep your desire for love and sexual pleasure from deceiving you? First, decide what kind of a person you will love *before* passion takes over. Determine whether a person's character and faith in God are as desirable as his or her physical appearance. Second, look for what is truly important in a potential husband or wife. Because most of the time you spend with your spouse will *not* involve sex, your companion's personality, temperament, and commitment to solve problems must be as gratifying as his or her kisses. Third, you should be patient. Time often reveals what is beneath a pleasant appearance and attentive touch.

If you have ever ridden in an airplane, you know how much depends on workers' actions. Suppose the flight attendants decided to watch the movie instead of serve the meals? Or the copilot counteracted every move the captain made? Or the captain ignored the air traffic controllers?

Life in Israel at this time of the judges looks a lot like a trip on just such an airplane. They make idols, make war, and make points with cruel and violent visual aids (all against the rules). And why? Look for the very, very strong hint near the end of the story.

Read Judges 17:1–21:25

During the time of the judges, the people of Israel experienced great trouble because everyone became their own authority and acted on their own opinions of right and wrong (Judges 21:25). If they didn't like God's rules, they simply disregarded them.

Our world is similar. Individuals, groups, and societies have made themselves the final authorities without reference to God.

Some of the judges whom God sent to rescue Israel were little better. Men like Gideon, Jephthah, and Samson are known for their heroism in battle; but in their personal lives, they lacked deep commitment to obeying the God for whom they fought.

To be truly heroic, we must go into battle each day in our home, job, church, and society to make God's kingdom a reality. Our weapons are the standards and convictions we receive from God's Word. We need to do what is right in his eyes, not ours.

⁵Micah set up a shrine . . . and he made a sacred ephod and some household idols. Then he installed one of his sons as his personal priest. . . . ¹⁸:¹Now in those days . . . the tribe of Dan was trying to find a place where they could settle, for they had not yet moved into the land assigned to them when the land was divided among the tribes of Israel. . . . ¹¹So 600 men from the tribe of Dan, armed with weapons of war, set out from Zorah and Eshtaol . . . ¹³and came to the house of Micah. . . . ¹⁶As the 600 armed warriors . . . stood at the entrance of the gate, . . . ¹⁷five scouts entered the shrine and removed the carved image, the sacred ephod, the household idols, and the cast idol. . . . ¹⁸When the priest saw the men carrying all the sacred objects out of Micah's shrine, he said, "What are you doing?"

JUDGES 17:5; 18:1, 11,13, 16-18

[13]So Boaz took Ruth into his home, and she became his wife. . . . The Lord enabled her to become pregnant, and she gave birth to a son. [14]Then the women of the town said to Naomi, "Praise the Lord, who has now provided a redeemer for your family! May this child be famous in Israel. [15]May he restore your youth and care for you in your old age. For he is the son of your daughter-in-law who loves you and has been better to you than seven sons!" [16]Naomi took the baby and cuddled him to her breast. And she cared for him as if he were her own. [17]The neighbor women said, "Now at last Naomi has a son again!" And they named him Obed. He became the father of Jesse and the grandfather of David.

RUTH 4:13-17

When you're immersed in a problem, it can be difficult to see exactly what to do. But afterward, when you look back on the situation, you can see it all perfectly, and the solution seems obvious. You can see what you couldn't see before. As the saying goes, hindsight is 20/20.

The book of Ruth has that rare quality of showing us how the past has affected today. How could Naomi have seen, while feeling the pain of her bitter losses, that her future would hold more than ten times the good? She couldn't—she could only trust God—and that's a crucial lesson to learn.

You will find many other lessons in this book: self-lessness; praying honestly; gaining a good reputation (Ruth knows the secret); taking advice; and trusting God to bring good out of tragedy.

Read Ruth 1:1–4:22

To some people, the book of Ruth appears to be little more than a nice story about a fortunate young woman. This small book, however, records the birth of a man named Obed (Ruth 4:16-17). His birth and the other events recorded in Ruth were part of God's preparation for the births of David and Jesus. Ruth could not have guessed that her actions would lead to such a glorious future event—just as we, today, have no idea how our lives will affect others years from now.

It's easy to make decisions based totally on our present, limited perspective. Instead, we should consider God's eternal values as we make our choices. Although Ruth's perspective was limited, she faithfully obeyed God—and she left a significant legacy.

Live in faithfulness to God, knowing that the significance of your life will extend beyond your lifetime. God's rewards will outweigh any sacrifice you make.

It's frustrating to talk to someone who only pretends to listen. You want to shout, "I'm talking, but you're not listening!" You may be talking about something very important to you, but the person seems to be daydreaming or appears distracted. People can be close—even talking—and yet not communicate.

That problem characterized Israel for many years. God would speak, but Israel wouldn't listen. The birth of Samuel opens a new chapter in Israel's history. Decades have passed since a prophet of God has spoken; Samuel will reopen the lines of communication. As you read, learn about what it means to listen carefully to God.

This piece of Israel's grand story has other lessons as well: bringing the right kinds of gifts to God; praising God for his gifts to us; and knowing when to stop others from doing evil.

Read 1 Samuel 1:1–3:21

God had spoken directly and audibly with Moses and Joshua, but his word had become rare during the three centuries of rule by the judges. During this time, no prophets were speaking God's messages to Israel (1 Samuel 3:1). The attitude of Eli's sons provides the reason for the silence. They refused to listen to God, and they allowed greed to block their communication with him. Instead of listening to God, Israel had turned to other sources of wisdom. But when God spoke to Samuel, the young boy responded, "Speak, your servant is listening" (3:10).

¹Meanwhile, the boy Samuel served the LORD by assisting Eli. Now in those days messages from the LORD were very rare, and visions were quite uncommon. ²One night Eli, who was almost blind by now, had gone to bed. ³The lamp of God had not yet gone out, and Samuel was sleeping in the Tabernacle near the Ark of God. ⁴Suddenly the LORD called out, "Samuel!" "Yes?" Samuel replied. "What is it?" ⁵He got up and ran to Eli. "Here I am. Did you call me?" "I didn't call you," Eli replied. "Go back to bed." So he did. ⁶Then the LORD called out again, "Samuel!" Again Samuel got up and went to Eli. "Here I am. Did you call me?" "I didn't call you, my son," Eli said. "Go back to bed." ⁷Samuel did not yet know the LORD because he had never had a message from the LORD before.

1 SAMUEL 3:1-7

God does not always use the sound of a human voice, but he always speaks clearly through his Word. To receive his messages, we must be ready to listen and to act upon what he tells us. We must be open to God if we are going to hear and understand him. We must make a conscious choice to read his Word, to respond with prayer, and to be open to the prompting of his Spirit. Listening and responding are vital in a relationship with God.

Have you heard God lately? He's speaking to you. Like Samuel, be ready to say, "Here I am," when God gives you a message.

¹The men of Kiriath-jearim came to get the Ark of the Lord. They took it to the hillside home of Abinadab and ordained Eleazar, his son, to be in charge of it. ²The Ark remained in Kiriath-jearim for a long time—twenty years in all. During that time all Israel mourned because it seemed the Lord had abandoned them. ³Then Samuel said to all the people of Israel, "If you are really serious about wanting to return to the Lord, get rid of your foreign gods and your images of Ashtoreth. Determine to obey only the Lord; then he will rescue you from the Philistines." ⁴So the Israelites got rid of their images of Baal and Ashtoreth and worshiped only the Lord. ⁵Then Samuel told them, "Gather all of Israel to Mizpah, and I will pray to the Lord for you."

1 SAMUEL 7:1-5

Tourists and travelers purchase memorable souvenirs from the places they visit. What are your favorites? Souvenirs connect us to a place and an experience; they become hooks for our memories. Souvenirs also prove that we've been to a specific place, and they can be excellent discussion starters.

This reading highlights a bit of souvenir collecting—the Philistines grab a priceless Israelite treasure, and the Israelites build a collection of choice Canaanite items. In neither case are the souvenirs harmless, as you'll soon see. The Israelites took their collectibles from the inhabitants that they were to have driven from Canaan, clearly violating God's command. As you read, look for God's lesson about collecting the wrong kind of souvenirs.

This passage also has a lesson about listening to God, and it contains reminders about God's power.

Read 1 Samuel 4:1–7:17

As the Israelites began to inhabit Canaan, they were supposed to destroy all the idols they found. Instead, many people collected the idols, brought them home, and included them in their worship. They were clearly disobeying God because he had warned them to avoid idols (see Exodus 20:4). Samuel saw the Israelites' sin and urged them to get rid of their foreign gods (1 Samuel 7:3).

Today's idols don't look like the ancient gods of wood and stone, but they endanger us just as much. Whatever holds first place in a person's life is, in fact, that person's god. Money, success, material goods, pride, or anything else can be an idol if it takes God's place.

The Lord alone is worthy of our service and worship, and we must let nothing rival him. If we have "foreign gods," we need to dethrone them, giving the true God his rightful place.

What idols vie for control of your life? What should you do to keep God in first place?

Insecurities – wanting affection from others –

Many people take steps to fit in with the people around them—they say the right phrases, socialize at known establishments, walk a special way, show off important possessions, or are seen in the right places. Being accepted and fitting in matter a great deal.

In this reading, Israel finally gets a king—Saul. Remember, the nation has been in the process of conquering the land of Canaan, as God had commanded them. But they haven't felt comfortable with the unique identity they have in contrast to their neighbors. They want to fit in. By having a king, now they do—at least they think so. As you read this story, learn a lesson about what is more important than fitting in.

This passage, and the example of Saul, have much to teach us about seeing God's purposes in every circumstance; handling feelings of inadequacy; and channeling anger to constructive uses.

Read 1 Samuel 8:1–12:25

Israel wanted a king for several reasons (1 Samuel 8:4-9): (1) Samuel's sons were not fit to lead Israel. (2) The twelve tribes of Israel had continual problems working together because each tribe had its own leader and territory; they hoped that a king would unite the tribes. (3) The people wanted to be like the neighboring nations. This last reason, especially, was exactly what God didn't want. Having a king would make it easy for Israel to forget that God was their real leader. It was not wrong for Israel to want a king; God had mentioned the possibility (see Deuteronomy 17:14-20). What they really wanted, however, was to be just like all the other nations around them (1 Samuel 8:19-20). This was in total opposition to God's original intent for them. In reality, the people were rejecting God as their leader.

Often we let others' values and actions dictate our attitudes and behavior. Have you ever made a wrong choice because you wanted to be like everyone else? Be careful that the values of your friends or heroes don't pull you away from what God says is right. Trying to be like unbelievers is a recipe for spiritual disaster.

¹As Samuel grew old, he appointed his sons to be judges over Israel. ²Joel and Abijah, his oldest sons, held court in Beersheba. ³But they were not like their father, for they were greedy for money. They accepted bribes and perverted justice. ⁴Finally, all the elders of Israel met at Ramah to discuss the matter with Samuel. ⁵"Look," they told him, "you are now old, and your sons are not like you. Give us a king to judge us like all the other nations have." ⁶Samuel was displeased with their request and went to the Lord for guidance. ⁷"Do everything they say to you," the Lord replied, "for it is me they are rejecting, not you. They don't want me to be their king any longer. ⁸Ever since I brought them from Egypt they have continually abandoned me and followed other gods. And now they are giving you the same treatment."

1 SAMUEL 8:1-8

¹⁶Then Samuel said to Saul, . . . ¹⁹"Why haven't you obeyed the LORD? Why did you rush for the plunder and do what was evil in the LORD's sight?" ²⁰"But I did obey the LORD," Saul insisted. "I carried out the mission he gave me. I brought back King Agag, but I destroyed everyone else. ²¹Then my troops brought in the best of the sheep, goats, cattle, and plunder to sacrifice to the LORD your God in Gilgal." ²²But Samuel replied, "What is more pleasing to the LORD: your burnt offerings and sacrifices or your obedience to his voice? Listen! Obedience is better than sacrifice, and submission is better than offering the fat of rams. ²³Rebellion is as sinful as witchcraft, and stubbornness as bad as worshiping idols. So because you have rejected the command of the LORD, he has rejected you as king."

1 SAMUEL 15:16, 19-23

Joe can tell that Susan and Steve are Christians. They go to church, wear crosses and other religious jewelry, give to charity, and even serve on a committee at church. All the outward signs are there—they are Christians, all right.

Saul thought that outward appearances made all the difference. In fact, in this account he's got the outward signs covered. He's religious—you can tell just by looking (or so he thinks). As you read, note the difference between external religious signs and true, internal spirituality.

Other lessons in this section include taking (and giving) credit where it is due; doing God's work when you don't have the tools; and knowing how not to lead (hint: watch Saul).

Read 1 Samuel 13:1–15:35

This is the first of numerous places in the Bible that states the theme "Obedience is far better than sacrifice" (1 Samuel 15:22-23; see also Psalm 40:6-8; 51:16-17; Proverbs 21:3; Isaiah 1:11-17; Jeremiah 7:21-23; Hosea 6:6; Micah 6:6-8; Matthew 12:7; Mark 12:33; Hebrews 10:8-9). Samuel wasn't saying that sacrifice was not important; he was urging Saul to look at his *reasons* for making the sacrifice. A sacrifice involved giving to God a special gift, usually a lamb or a dove. It was a ritual exchange between a person and God that demonstrated the relationship between them. If the sacrificing person's heart was not truly repentant, or if he or she did not in fact love God, the sacrifice had no meaning.

Religious ceremonies mean nothing unless we perform them with a desire to love and obey God. He isn't impressed with the external signs of religion—going to church, displaying a bumper sticker, wearing a cross or witness T-shirt, serving on a committee, giving to charity, and so forth. What God wants are actions flowing out of devotion and obedience to him.

Do a spiritual inventory. You may look good on the outside, like Saul, but it's what's on the inside that counts with God. Determine to be *his* kind of person.

The world loves beautiful people. Teachers are more likely to call on attractive students in class and more likely to give them positive feedback. Employers are more likely to promote handsome or pretty employees. And people are more likely to like good-looking *anybodies,* to want their friendship, and even to envy them. They say that "Beauty is only skin deep," but that's as deep as most people seem to go.

This section of Scripture records a very significant event, the choosing of Israel's second king. It raises the beauty question directly. At first, Samuel gets it wrong, but then God shows him a better way. As you read, learn how God looks at people.

This passage is home to other great lessons, too—when to put plans on hold, and fighting "giants."

|||||||||||||||||||||||||||||||||||||||||||||| **Read 1 Samuel 16:1–17:58**

Saul was tall and handsome; he was an impressive-looking man. Samuel may have been trying to find someone who looked like Saul to be Israel's next king, but God warned him against judging by appearance alone (1 Samuel 16:7). God judges by faith and character, not appearances. And because only God can see on the inside, only he can accurately judge people. When people judge by outward appearances, they may overlook quality individuals who lack the particular physical characteristics that society admires. Appearance doesn't reveal what people are really like, or what their true value is.

Most people spend hours each week maintaining their outward appearances. There's nothing wrong with trying to look your best, but do you do as much to develop your inner character? While everyone can see your face, only your character determines how you will live and work and enjoy life. What steps can you take to improve your character?

¹Now the LORD said to Samuel, . . . "Fill your flask with olive oil and go to Bethlehem. Find a man named Jesse who lives there, for I have selected one of his sons to be my king." . . . ⁴So Samuel did as the LORD instructed. When he arrived at Bethlehem, . . . ¹⁰all seven of Jesse's sons were presented to Samuel. But Samuel said to Jesse, "The LORD has not chosen any of these." ¹¹Then Samuel asked, "Are these all the sons you have?" "There is still the youngest," Jesse replied. . . . "Send for him at once," Samuel said. . . . ¹²So Jesse sent for him. He was dark and handsome, with beautiful eyes. And the LORD said, "This is the one; anoint him." ¹³So as David stood there among his brothers, Samuel took the flask of olive oil . . . and anointed David with the oil. And the Spirit of the LORD came powerfully upon David from that day on.

1 SAMUEL 16:1, 4, 10-13

¹After David had finished talking with Saul, he met Jonathan, the king's son. There was an immediate bond between them, for Jonathan loved David. ²From that day on Saul kept David with him and wouldn't let him return home. ³And Jonathan made a solemn pact with David, because he loved him as he loved himself. ⁴Jonathan sealed the pact by taking off his robe and giving it to David, together with his tunic, sword, bow, and belt. ⁵Whatever Saul asked David to do, David did it successfully. So Saul made him a commander over the men of war, an appointment that was welcomed by the people and Saul's officers alike.

1 SAMUEL 18:1-5

Do you have any close friends? That's a tough question for many people. Everyone has *acquaintances.* Most have *friends*, too. But many cannot say that they have a *close* friend, someone who will sacrifice for them. Such friends don't come along every day.

In this reading, the young and popular warrior David meets young prince Jonathan, and they immediately become close friends. This friendship is good for them and for Israel, but it quickly becomes tested, as most friendships do. As you read, look for what makes a quality friendship.

In addition, each main character in this passage illustrates something else: how to handle popularity (David); obedience to parents (Jonathan); and the futility of trying to resist God's will (Saul).

Read 1 Samuel 18:1–20:42

When David and Jonathan met, they became close friends right away (18:1-4). Jonathan, the prince of Israel, later realized that David, and not he, would be the next king (23:17). But that did not weaken his love for David. Jonathan would much rather lose the throne of Israel than lose his closest friend. They stayed loyal to each other throughout their lives.

Their friendship is one of the deepest and closest recorded in the Bible: (1) they based their friendship on commitment to God, not just each other; (2) they let nothing come between them, not even career or family problems; (3) they drew closer together when their friendship was tested; and (4) they remained friends to the end.

What can you do to be that kind of friend to another?

Finding fault with the government is a national pastime. Some say the government controls us too little, others say it controls us too much. Everybody thinks it spends too little on this and not enough on that. Standard rules of etiquette say you shouldn't discuss politics in polite company—and for good reason.

This portion of Scripture shows us David still running for his life from Saul. We can plainly see that David has more reasons than most to find fault with his government. His example for dealing with these gripes has something to say to us all.

Along the way, David also teaches us several other valuable lessons, such as applying God's laws with compassion; suffering and its source (evil people); marks of true friendship; being fair to those who help us; having courage; and showing mercy.

Read 1 Samuel 21:1–26:25

David showed respect for Saul, despite the fact that Saul was trying to kill him (1 Samuel 24:5-6). Although Saul was sinning and rebelling against God, David still respected the position he held as God's appointed authority. David knew that one day he would be king; he also knew it was not right to strike down the man whom God had placed on the throne. By assassinating Saul, David would be setting a precedent for his opponents to remove *him* someday.

Romans 13:1-7 teaches that God has placed the government and its leaders in power. We may not know why, but like David, we are to respect the positions and roles of those to whom God has given authority. There is one exception, however—because God is our highest authority, we should never allow any earthly leader to pressure us to violate God's law.

Do you respect your political leaders? What can you do to be a better citizen?

¹²David took the spear and jug of water that were near Saul's head. Then he and Abishai got away without anyone seeing them or even waking up, because the Lord had put Saul's men into a deep sleep. ¹³David climbed the hill opposite the camp until he was at a safe distance. ¹⁴Then he shouted down to the soldiers and to Abner son of Ner, "Wake up, Abner!"

"Who is it?" Abner demanded.

¹⁵"Well, Abner, you're a great man, aren't you?" David taunted. "Where in all Israel is there anyone as mighty? So why haven't you guarded your master the king when someone came to kill him? ¹⁶This isn't good at all! I swear by the Lord that you and your men deserve to die, because you failed to protect your master, the Lord's anointed! Look around! Where are the king's spear and the jug of water that were beside his head?"

1 SAMUEL 26:12-16

¹Now the Philistines attacked Israel, and the men of Israel fled before them. Many were slaughtered on the slopes of Mount Gilboa. ²The Philistines closed in on Saul and his sons, and they killed three of his sons—Jonathan, Abinadab, and Malkishua. ³The fighting grew very fierce around Saul, and the Philistine archers caught up with him and wounded him severely. ⁴Saul groaned to his armor bearer, "Take your sword and kill me before these pagan Philistines come to run me through and taunt and torture me." But his armor bearer was afraid and would not do it. So Saul took his own sword and fell on it. ⁵When his armor bearer realized that Saul was dead, he fell on his own sword and died beside the king. ⁶So Saul, his three sons, his armor bearer, and his troops all died together that same day.

1 SAMUEL 31:1-6

Most American heroes wear the label "rugged individualist." These macho types set a sort of standard—an American ideal. And though we may argue about the details, most of us would agree that these heroes live by three rules: they blaze their own trail; they don't take orders (they give them); and they apologize to no one.

This is the story of Saul's death, and it's a dark time in Israel's history. Saul has tried to be a rugged individualist, and this portion of the Scriptures passes judgment on that experiment in living. Given the similarities to the way we're urged to live today, we'd do well to pay attention.

As you read, you'll find these other lessons: being patient; avoiding the occult; and remembering that those who do unglamorous, behind-the-scenes jobs to support the efforts of others are important too.

Read 1 Samuel 27:1–31:13

In Saul's death (1 Samuel 31:4-13) an ideal also died. Israel could no longer believe that having a king like the other nations would solve all their troubles. The real problem was not the form of government, but the sinful king. Saul tried to please God with spurts of religiosity; real spirituality takes a lifetime of consistent obedience. Saul didn't have it; he really was a "rugged individualist."

Heroic spiritual lives take a different approach. They are built by stacking days of obedience, one on top of the other. Like a brick, each obedient act is small in itself, but in time the acts pile up, and a huge wall of strong character results—a great defense against temptation. This strategy doesn't concern itself with trailblazing, calling the shots, or never saying, "Oops!" Rather, it concerns itself with striving for consistent obedience to God—doing it *his* way—each day.

Which kind of hero are *you* trying to be?

Kids of playground age can make merciless fun of a boy for crying. Some fathers will too. If you had a son and he tended to show emotion, especially by shedding tears, what would you say to him?

In this reading, David and his men first hear of Saul's death and the death of David's close friend, Jonathan. Nobody among David's men takes it well. Some might say that they should rejoice because now David can take his rightful place as king. But celebrating isn't part of their reaction. You'll learn a valuable lesson from their response.

As you read, note also how to tell the difference between persistence (good) and stubbornness (bad), how revenge can backfire, and how important it is to do justice to others.

Read 2 Samuel 1:1–4:12

When David and his men learned of Saul and Jonathan's deaths, "they mourned and wept and fasted all day" (2 Samuel 1:12). David and his men were visibly shaken over the tragic news. Their actions showed their genuine sorrow over the loss of their king, their friend Jonathan, and the other soldiers of Israel who had died that day. They were not ashamed to grieve. Today, some people consider expressing emotions to be a sign of weakness. Those who wish to appear strong try to hide their feelings. But expressing our grief can help us deal with our intense sorrow when a loved one dies.

¹David returned from his victory over the Amalekites and spent two days in Ziklag. ²On the third day a man arrived from Saul's army camp. He had torn his clothes and put dirt on his head to show that he was in mourning. He fell to the ground before David in deep respect. ³"Where have you come from?" David asked. "I escaped from the Israelite camp," the man replied. ⁴"What happened?" David demanded. "Tell me how the battle went." The man replied, "Our entire army fled from the battle. Many of the men are dead, and Saul and his son Jonathan are also dead." . . . ¹¹David and his men tore their clothes in sorrow when they heard the news. ¹²They mourned and wept and fasted all day for Saul and his son Jonathan, and for the LORD's army and the nation of Israel, because they had died by the sword that day.

2 SAMUEL 1:1-4, 11-12

Do you tend to keep your feelings inside? Because "sadness has a refining influence on us" (Ecclesiastes 7:3), find ways to express sorrow when you feel it. Tell God exactly how you feel—he understands. And share your feelings with a close friend.

¹⁶As the Ark of the LORD entered the City of David, Michal, the daughter of Saul, looked down from her window. When she saw King David leaping and dancing before the LORD, she was filled with contempt for him. . . . ²⁰When David returned home to bless his own family, Michal . . . said in disgust, "How distinguished the king of Israel looked today, shamelessly exposing himself to the servant girls like any vulgar person might do!" ²¹David retorted to Michal, "I was dancing before the LORD, who chose me above your father and all his family! He appointed me as the leader of Israel, the people of the LORD, so I celebrate before the LORD. ²²Yes, and I am willing to look even more foolish than this, even to be humiliated in my own eyes! But those servant girls you mentioned will indeed think I am distinguished!"

2 SAMUEL 6:16, 20-22

Being embarrassed by someone you love ranks as one of life's most inevitable experiences. No matter how carefully you guard against it, it's bound to happen. Has it happened to you lately?

This is the story of David's consolidation of power. He takes Jerusalem, defeats some of his enemies, and brings the Ark of the Covenant back to Jerusalem (it had been captured by the Philistines). Now it's time to celebrate, and David dances before the Lord. But Michal, David's wife, is too embarrassed by David to enjoy the festivities. How could he *do* such a thing?

Look for important lessons in this passage on waiting for the fulfillment of God's promises; how to fight; and why God sometimes says no to our requests.

Read 2 Samuel 5:1–7:29

Michal was so concerned about David's undignified actions that she did not rejoice in the Ark's return to the city (2 Samuel 6:16-20). Her contempt for David probably did not start with David's grand entrance into the city. She may have resented David's taking her from her former husband, Paltiel (see 2 Samuel 3:13-14). Whatever her reason, this contempt that Michal felt toward David escalated into a difficult confrontation.

Close friends and married couples know each other extremely well, including each other's faults, weaknesses, and annoying habits. Minor irritations can lead to anger, and bitterness can lead to hatred. Unchecked feelings of resentment will destroy any relationship. Deal with your negative emotions before they escalate into open warfare.

Michal focused on appearances while David emphasized the condition of his heart before God. David was willing to look foolish in order to worship God fully and honestly. Don't be afraid to express *your* feelings toward God, even when others are present.

You decided to take up a just cause. You knew it was right—that God was for it. But then you lost the fight, and you wonder what happened.

In the process of consolidating his power, David conquers the surrounding nations. His general, Joab, gives advice to David's men that can teach us a lot about the fights we take up for God.

Watching David in this section of Scripture will also teach us that God keeps his promises, and that we need to show kindness even when it isn't what other people are doing.

|||||||||||||||||||||||||||||||||||||||||||||||||||||| **Read 2 Samuel 8:1–10:19**

David and his men fought many battles as they established their control over Israel. As they prepared to attack the Ammonites, David's general, Joab, said, "Let us fight bravely" (2 Samuel 10:12). He was urging the men to do the best they could by using their minds to figure out the best techniques and using their resources strategically. But in the very same breath Joab also said, "May the Lord's will be done." Joab knew that God would determine the outcome of the battle.

We need to keep our actions and our faith in God in balance. Some seem to think that all believers need to do is to sit passively and wait for God to act. Others seem to think that everything depends on them, on their cleverness and effort. In reality, God expects us to use our minds and our muscles *while* we depend on him. We use our resources to obey God, while at the same time trusting him for the outcome.

⁸The Ammonite troops came out and drew up their battle lines at the entrance of the city gate, while the Arameans from Zobah and Rehob and the men from Tob and Maacah positioned themselves to fight in the open fields. ⁹When Joab saw that he would have to fight on both the front and the rear, he chose some of Israel's elite troops and placed them under his personal command to fight the Arameans in the fields. ¹⁰He left the rest of the army under the command of his brother Abishai, who was to attack the Ammonites. ¹¹"If the Arameans are too strong for me, then come over and help me," Joab told his brother. "And if the Ammonites are too strong for you, I will come and help you. ¹²Be courageous! Let us fight bravely for our people and the cities of our God. May the LORD's will be done."

2 SAMUEL 10:8-12

The next time you have a task to accomplish or a problem to solve, turn it over to God and then do your best. Trust God for the result and then accept what he brings.

²Late one afternoon, after his midday rest, David got out of bed and was walking on the roof of the palace. As he looked out over the city, he noticed a woman of unusual beauty taking a bath. ³He sent someone to find out who she was, and he was told, "She is Bathsheba, the daughter of Eliam and the wife of Uriah the Hittite." ⁴Then David sent messengers to get her; and when she came to the palace, he slept with her. . . . Then she returned home. ⁵Later, when Bathsheba discovered that she was pregnant, she sent David a message, saying, "I'm pregnant."

2 SAMUEL 11:2-5

Temptations seldom appear as ugly or dangerous as they really are. Think of it from a fish's perspective, or from that of a mouse approaching a trap. They bite the worm and pounce on the cheese that seem so good and harmless—until they have done their damage. People do the same.

This is the tragic story of David and Bathsheba. David sees her (the "bait"), makes a choice, and he's "hooked." The results are devastating to David, to Bathsheba, to Uriah, and to the nation. As you read this passage, ask yourself, *What could David have done to prevent this?*

This story also teaches the futility of trying to cover up a sin; the importance of correcting a friend; and the best way to respond when you get caught.

Read 2 Samuel 11:1–12:31

As David looked from the roof of the palace, he saw a beautiful woman bathing (2 Samuel 11:2-4). He didn't see a dangerous situation that could damage the rest of his life. As his heart filled with lust, he pushed aside the cautions that must have filled his head and asked about Bathsheba. David should have left the roof and fled the temptation; instead, he entertained it. As a result, David succumbed to temptation and committed adultery and murder.

To escape temptation, (1) ask God to help you stay away from people, places, and situations that may strongly tempt you. (2) Memorize and meditate on portions of Scripture that combat your specific weaknesses. At the root of most temptation is a real need or desire that God can fill, but we must trust in his timing. (3) Find another believer with whom you can openly share your struggles, and call this person for help when temptation strikes.

When tempted, move away from the temptation and toward a good place or safe activity. Fight the temptation; don't just stay there and look into the possibilities.

As you get older, do you notice how much you are becoming like your parents? You may think, *I'm just like my father or mother.* It's funny how we leave adolescence eager to be *unlike* our parents, and then the plan goes afoul. There's a part of Mom and Dad that we just can't escape.

David's kids are all grown up now, and his sons are bringing him a lot of grief. Unfortunately, by this time there's little he can do about it—indeed he does little. In this way, David sees his own sins coming back to haunt him. As you read this passage, think of the parenting implications David's actions have brought (disciplining, being a good role model, spending time together).

In this section of Scripture, you will also see the difference between love and lust, and the damage that can result from a rebellious attitude.

Read 2 Samuel 13:1–14:33

David faced sins in his own family similar to those that he had committed earlier. David's son, Amnon, raped his half sister Tamar. Amnon was then murdered by another of David's sons, Tamar's brother, Absalom (2 Samuel 13:1-29). David's sin was magnified in the lives of his children. David was angry with Amnon for raping Tamar, but he did not punish this wayward son (13:21-22). David probably hesitated because he didn't want to cross Amnon, who was his firstborn son (see 1 Chronicles 3:1), and next in line to be king. David was guilty of a similar sin himself in his adultery with Bathsheba. While unsurpassed as a king and military leader, David had problems as a husband and father.

¹David's son Absalom had a beautiful sister named Tamar. And Amnon, her half brother, fell desperately in love with her. . . . ⁶So Amnon lay down and pretended to be sick. And when the king came to see him, Amnon asked him, "Please let my sister Tamar come and cook my favorite dish as I watch. Then I can eat it from her own hands." . . . ¹¹But as she was feeding him, he grabbed her and demanded, "Come to bed with me, my darling sister." ¹²"No, my brother!" she cried. "Don't be foolish! Don't do this to me! Such wicked things aren't done in Israel. ¹³Where could I go in my shame? And you would be called one of the greatest fools in Israel. Please, just speak to the king about it, and he will let you marry me." ¹⁴But Amnon wouldn't listen to her, and since he was stronger than she was, he raped her.

2 SAMUEL 13:1, 6, 11-14

If you are a parent, you can't always control what your children will do. You can, however, live by God's standards and give them a good example to follow. What changes should you make in order to be a better mother or father?

¹Absalom bought a chariot and horses, and he hired fifty bodyguards to run ahead of him. ²He got up early every morning and went out to the gate of the city. When people brought a case to the king for judgment, Absalom would ask where in Israel they were from, and they would tell him their tribe. ³Then Absalom would say, "You've really got a strong case here! It's too bad the king doesn't have anyone to hear it. ⁴I wish I were the judge. Then everyone could bring their cases to me for judgment, and I would give them justice!" ⁵When people tried to bow before him, Absalom wouldn't let them. Instead, he took them by the hand and kissed them. ⁶Absalom did this with everyone who came to the king for judgment, and so he stole the hearts of all the people of Israel.

2 SAMUEL 15:1-6

Public opinion polls give solid proof that public opinion changes faster than a traffic light. They tell minute by minute what people are thinking—which is good, because people change their minds just as fast.

Absalom knows that aspect of human nature all too well. In this story of national rebellion against David, Absalom is the chief perpetrator, appealing directly to the crowds. His rebellion is popular, showing that the crowd will follow just about anybody. Learn from the fickle nature of the crowds.

Other lessons in this passage include evaluating leaders (making sure they're not schemers); ignoring unjustified criticism; avoiding flattery; thinking before acting; and using diplomacy and tact.

Read 2 Samuel 15:1–20:26

For a short time, most of Israel was supporting the rebel ruler, Absalom. Soon, however, the people wanted David back as their king (2 Samuel 19:8-10).

Crowds are often fickle, changing their minds with the wind. That's just one of the reasons we need to live by a higher moral code than the pleasure of the majority. One day the people will want this, the next day they will want that. What the crowd wants, and what people pressure us to do, will rarely conform to what God wants.

Although there is much pressure to conform to the world, rather than trying to be popular and acceptable to the crowd, guide your life by the moral principles given in God's Word. God never changes, and he knows and wants what is best for you.

"It's all right," Billy said forgivingly, and you couldn't help but smile. You had accused him of conspiring to keep you out of the clubhouse, but that wasn't what was truly going on. In fact, Billy had been decorating the clubhouse for your surprise birthday party. Now the truth was out, and so was your sheepish apology.

These are the later years of David's rule, a song of praise that David wrote, and some of David's last words. In this song, David brings up the subject of his own guilt. It's a telling speech. As you read, you will see that, to paraphrase, "forgiveness is cool."

You'll find other lessons, too, about bringing justice to others and placing our security in God instead of money.

Read 2 Samuel 21:1–24:25

"I am blameless before God; I have kept myself from sin" (2 Samuel 22:24). With these words, David was not denying that he had *ever* sinned. Psalm 51 shows his tremendous anguish over his sins against Uriah and Bathsheba. But David understood God's faithfulness and was writing this hymn from God's perspective. He knew that God had made him pure again—"whiter than snow," with a "clean heart" (Psalm 51:7, 10).

God will forgive our sins if we bring them to him in sorrow and repentance. Through the death and resurrection of Jesus Christ, we can be cleansed and made perfect in God's eyes. God replaces our sin with his purity—he sees us as forgiven and clean.

Stop right now and confess your sins to your loving heavenly Father. Accept his total forgiveness through Christ.

26To the faithful you show yourself faithful; to those with integrity you show integrity. 27To the pure you show yourself pure, but to the wicked you show yourself hostile. 28You rescue the humble, but your eyes watch the proud and humiliate them. 29O LORD, you are my lamp. The LORD lights up my darkness. 30In your strength I can crush an army; with my God I can scale any wall. 31God's way is perfect. All the LORD's promises prove true. He is a shield for all who look to him for protection. 32For who is God except the LORD? Who but our God is a solid rock? 33God is my strong fortress, and he makes my way perfect. 34He makes me as surefooted as a deer, enabling me to stand on mountain heights.

2 SAMUEL 22:26-34

⁵That night the LORD appeared to Solomon in a dream, and God said, "What do you want? Ask, and I will give it to you!" ⁶Solomon replied, "You showed faithful love to your servant my father, David, because he was honest and true and faithful to you. And you have continued your faithful love to him today by giving him a son to sit on his throne. ⁷Now, O LORD my God, you have made me king instead of my father, David, but I am like a little child who doesn't know his way around. ⁸And here I am in the midst of your own chosen people, a nation so great and numerous they cannot be counted! ⁹Give me an understanding heart so that I can govern your people well and know the difference between right and wrong. For who by himself is able to govern this great people of yours?" ¹⁰The LORD was pleased that Solomon had asked for wisdom.

1 KINGS 3:5-10

When was the last time someone asked you for advice and you didn't know what to say? It happens to everyone. Life throws some awful curve balls—problems that we've never seen before and have no idea how to confront.

Here we read where Solomon becomes king (after a conspiracy against him is quashed) and first gains his great wisdom. He already shows some wisdom, but he's wise enough to know that he doesn't know enough. Solomon's humility serves him well. As you read, carefully watch this ultimate advice-giver in action.

Other lessons in this passage include parenting (in retrospect); interfering when someone is about to do an injustice; putting God at the center (even of government); and getting organized.

Read 1 Kings 1:1–4:34

When given a chance to have anything in the world, Solomon asked for wisdom—"an understanding heart"—in order to lead well and to make right decisions (1 Kings 3:6-9). This, in itself, showed wisdom, and God honored Solomon's request. Solomon became the wisest man ever (3:12) and, at the moving of God's Spirit, recorded much of his God-given insight in the book of Proverbs.

God wants to work *through* us, not *for* us. Notice that Solomon asked for understanding to carry out his job; he did not ask God to do the job for him.

Ask God to give you the wisdom to know what to do and the courage to follow through on it. And remember, if you ask for wisdom, God has promised to give you all you need (see James 1:5).

"What church do you attend?" Usually when asked that question, a person will respond with "Community Congregational," "First Presbyterian," or another church name. When pressed for more information, the person might describe the building. The building where the church meets is also important, makes a public statement about the church, and provides a focal point for a particular body of believers.

In this passage, at long last, Solomon gets to build the Temple. What a grand structure! David wanted to do it but couldn't. More than most people, David understood the Temple's significance. That's why it mattered so much to him and why God wouldn't let him build it. See what you can learn from this massive, monumental project.

Note in Solomon's foremanship two more lessons: balancing work and family life, and dedicating ourselves to God's service.

Read 1 Kings 5:1–8:66

For four hundred and eighty years after Israel's escape from Egypt, God did not ask his people, the Jews, to build a Temple for him (1 Kings 8:15-21). Instead, he emphasized the importance of his presence among them and their need for spiritual leaders.

It is easy to think of a building as the focus of God's presence and power, but God chooses and uses *people* to do his work. He can use you more than he can use any building of wood and stone. Building or enlarging our place of worship may be necessary, but it should never take priority over developing spiritual leaders.

[14][Solomon] turned around to the entire community of Israel standing before him and gave this blessing: [15]"Praise the Lord, the God of Israel, who has kept the promise he made to my father, David. For he told my father, [16]'From the day I brought my people Israel out of Egypt, I have never chosen a city among any of the tribes of Israel as the place where a Temple should be built to honor my name. But I have chosen David to be king over my people Israel.'" [17]Then Solomon said, "My father, David, wanted to build this Temple to honor the name of the Lord, the God of Israel. [18]But the Lord told him, 'You wanted to build the Temple to honor my name. Your intention is good, [19]but you are not the one to do it. One of your own sons will build the Temple to honor me.' [20]And now the Lord has fulfilled the promise he made."

1 KINGS 8:14-20

Remember that God's church is a community of believers, not a building of stone, brick, and wood. Do you worry more about the carpet in the hallway than about the people walking on it? Do you find yourself overly concerned about wear and tear on the building, while neglecting the people using it? While it is good to maintain the church building (as a responsible church member and good steward of God's resources), remember that people are infinitely more important.

¹King Solomon loved many foreign women. Besides Pharaoh's daughter, he married women from Moab, Ammon, Edom, Sidon, and from among the Hittites. ²The LORD had clearly instructed the people of Israel, "You must not marry them, because they will turn your hearts to their gods." Yet Solomon insisted on loving them anyway. ³He had 700 wives of royal birth and 300 concubines. And in fact, they did turn his heart away from the LORD. ⁴In Solomon's old age, they turned his heart to worship other gods instead of being completely faithful to the LORD his God, as his father, David, had been. ⁵Solomon worshiped Ashtoreth, the goddess of the Sidonians, and Molech, the detestable god of the Ammonites. ⁶In this way, Solomon did what was evil in the LORD's sight; he refused to follow the LORD completely, as his father, David, had done.

1 KINGS 11:1-6

Dagwood is always making a sandwich or taking a nap. Blondie is always hoping he will do something more productive—like fixing the sink. We laugh at the comic strip because it mirrors life. And we know that two people coming to marriage from two different directions can lead to bumps and even collisions.

This passage tells of Solomon's greatness and his downfall. His greatness was asking God to be with him and the people and to bless them. Solomon's downfall involves a domestic problem—marriage doesn't work for him at all. As you read, determine to emulate Solomon's good decisions and to avoid the ones that led to disaster. You will also find cautions about indulging in luxuries and about flirting with false gods.

Read 1 Kings 9:1–11:43

Solomon had hundreds of wives. Most of these he married for political reasons, but eventually they exerted significant influence on Solomon and changed him. Unfortunately, most of Solomon's wives worshiped idols, and this put tremendous pressure on Solomon to do the same. Faced with such pressure, at first he *resisted* it, maintaining his own purity of faith while tolerating his wives' private preferences. Then Solomon *tolerated* a more widespread practice of idolatry throughout Israel. Finally, he involved himself in the idolatrous worship, *rationalizing* away the potential dangers to himself and to the kingdom. Solomon could handle great pressures in running the government, but he could not handle the pressure from his wives (1 Kings 11:4).

In marriage and in close friendships, it is difficult to resist pressure to compromise. Our love leads us to identify with the desires of those we care about. Because of this strong desire to please our loved ones, God tells his people not to marry those who do not share a commitment to him. Build your closest relationships with those who share your faith and values.

When was the last time you got some bad advice? Did you have any clue that the counsel had cracks in it? Or was it your own foolish fault for listening in the first place?

In this reading, Solomon's death brings about a national crisis. After Solomon's successor, Rehoboam, listens to the bad advice of poor counselors, he makes unwise and unpopular decrees. The northern tribes of Israel then revolt and set up their own kingdom under Jeroboam. Only the southern tribes of Judah and Benjamin remain loyal to Rehoboam. We can't entirely blame the northern rebels for their actions—Rehoboam helps them along, whether he realizes it or not. As you read this passage, look for the strong lesson about seeking wise counsel and rejecting bad advice.

Other lessons in this section of Scripture include being careful in what you accept as messages from God; how *not* to pick church leaders; the consequences of flagrant disregard for God's commands; and what happens to those who don't learn from the mistakes of their parents (Baasha).

Read 1 Kings 12:1–16:34

At a time when he really needed it, Rehoboam asked for advice. That was a great idea, but he didn't carefully evaluate what he was told, nor did he weigh the quality of the advisors (1 Kings 12:6-14). It's no wonder that Rehoboam rejected the greater wisdom of his elders in favor of that of his peers. It's often difficult for those who are younger to listen to those who are older. The young may think that the old don't understand them, the current times, or anything, well enough. Or perhaps they just lack the humility to submit to their elders even though they see the wisdom of their counsel.

When receiving advice, carefully evaluate it, asking if it is realistic, workable, and consistent with biblical principles. The next time you ask for advice, determine if the results of following it will make improvements and give a positive solution or direction. Seek counsel from those who are wiser and more experienced. Advice is helpful only if it is consistent with God's standards.

³Jeroboam and the whole assembly of Israel went to speak with Rehoboam. ⁴"Your father was a hard master," they said. "Lighten the harsh labor demands and heavy taxes that your father imposed on us. Then we will be your loyal subjects." ⁵Rehoboam replied, "Give me three days to think this over. Then come back for my answer." . . . ⁶King Rehoboam discussed the matter with the older men who had counseled his father, Solomon. "What is your advice?" he asked. "How should I answer these people?" ⁷The older counselors replied, "If you are willing to be a servant to these people today and give them a favorable answer, they will always be your loyal subjects." ⁸But Rehoboam rejected the advice of the older men and instead asked the opinion of the young men who had grown up with him and were now his advisers.

1 KINGS 12:3-8

³Elijah was afraid and fled for his life. He went to Beersheba, a town in Judah, and he left his servant there. ⁴Then he went on alone into the wilderness, traveling all day. He sat down under a solitary broom tree and prayed that he might die. "I have had enough, LORD," he said. "Take my life, for I am no better than my ancestors who have already died." ⁵Then he lay down and slept under the broom tree. But as he was sleeping, an angel touched him and told him, "Get up and eat!" ⁶He looked around and there beside his head was some bread baked on hot stones and a jar of water! So he ate and drank and lay down again. ⁷Then the angel of the LORD came again and touched him and said, "Get up and eat some more, or the journey ahead will be too much for you." ⁸So he got up and ate and drank.

1 KINGS 19:3-8

Sally is ready to quit her job. Her coworkers have shut her out, and she feels as if she gets no support from her boss. She has tried to endure the isolation and do her best, but after three years, the situation has not improved. She's thoroughly discouraged.

This is the first half of the story of Elijah's ministry. Elijah is one of Israel's most significant prophets, yet he fights great discouragement. In fact, it's more like depression or despair. "It's all over," he moans, and he really believes it. But God has a cure for Elijah's ills—check it out.

In this passage you will learn that God sends rescuers when they're needed, and that God's people can always get the resources to do what God commands them to do.

Read 1 Kings 17:1–19:21

Elijah fell into the depths of fatigue and discouragement immediately following two of his great spiritual triumphs: the defeat of the prophets of Baal and the answered prayer for rain. After experiencing God's astounding victory at Mount Carmel, Elijah ran for his life. Then, tired, lonely, and discouraged, he felt sorry for himself, believing that he was the only person left who was still true to God (1 Kings 19:10). To lead Elijah out of depression, God first allowed him to rest and to eat. Then God confronted Elijah with the need to return to his mission—to speak God's words in Israel. Elijah's battles were not over; there was still work for him to do (1 Kings 19:15-18).

Often discouragement sets in after great spiritual experiences, especially those requiring physical effort or involving great emotion. When you feel let down after a great spiritual experience, remember that God's purpose for your life is not yet over. When you are tempted to think that you are the only one remaining faithful to a task, don't wallow in self-pity—it will only dilute the good you are doing. Be assured that even if you don't know who they are, others are faithfully obeying God and fulfilling their duties as well. God is at work in the world as well as in your life.

Polite conversation is designed to insulate us from certain forms of the truth. How many cashiers, for example, total strangers to you, really need to know how you are doing that day? But most people confine polite conversation to contacts with the public. Only close friends get to hear—and tell—the truth.

There's precious little polite conversation here in Micaiah's prophesies against Ahab. This is truth straight from God to Ahab—no glossy public coating in sight. If Ahab really knew God, he would realize that he's hearing from a friend. Instead he takes offense, and the warnings have no effect. For us, this story means "CAUTION, Negative Examples Here."

Also, don't miss the point of the judgments in this passage: things can get rough when we refuse to listen to God, and they can get downright deadly when we keep it up.

Read 1 Kings 20:1–22:53

"I will go out and inspire all of Ahab's prophets to speak lies" (1 Kings 22:22). Does God allow angels to entice people to do evil? No. What Micaiah saw was either a picture of a real incident in heaven, or a parable of what was happening on earth—illustrating that the seductive influence of the false prophets would be part of God's judgment upon Ahab (22:23). Whether or not God sent an angel in disguise, he used the system of false prophets to snare Ahab in his sin. The lying spirit (22:22) symbolized the mind-set of these prophets who told the king only what he wanted to hear.

15When Micaiah arrived before the king, Ahab asked him, "Micaiah, should we go to war against Ramoth-gilead, or should we hold back?" Micaiah replied sarcastically, "Yes, go up and be victorious, for the LORD will give the king victory!" 16But the king replied sharply, "How many times must I demand that you speak only the truth to me when you speak for the LORD?" 17Then Micaiah told him, "In a vision I saw all Israel scattered on the mountains, like sheep without a shepherd. And the LORD said, 'Their master has been killed. Send them home in peace.'" 18"Didn't I tell you?" the king of Israel exclaimed to Jehoshaphat. "He never prophesies anything but trouble for me."

1 KINGS 22:15-18

Don't be like Ahab! Don't surround yourself with people who only tell you what you want to hear, or you may make it impossible to hear the truth from anyone. The very people you trust with your life may lead you right into a dead end. Instead, seek out people who will be honest with you. Then when they tell you the hard truth, accept it graciously.

⁹Naaman went with his horses and chariots and waited at the door of Elisha's house. ¹⁰But Elisha sent a messenger out to him with this message: "Go and wash yourself seven times in the Jordan River. Then your skin will be restored, and you will be healed of your leprosy." ¹¹But Naaman became angry and stalked away. "I thought he would certainly come out to meet me!" he said. "I expected him to wave his hand over the leprosy and call on the name of the LORD his God and heal me!" . . . ¹³But his officers tried to reason with him and said, "Sir, if the prophet had told you to do something very difficult, wouldn't you have done it? So you should certainly obey him when he says simply, 'Go and wash and be cured!'" ¹⁴So Naaman went down to the Jordan River and dipped himself seven times, . . . and he was healed!

2 KINGS 5:9-11, 13-14

Cures are seldom pleasant. Usually they involve taking pills, getting stuck by needles, having surgery, enduring nauseating side effects, or getting into embarrassing positions. It's no wonder our aversion to doctors and dentists can be as strong as our dependence on them.

In this reading, Naaman has great trouble with the cure offered to him, even though his disease is terminal, not to mention degrading. The problem is not needles or side effects—it's something else. As you read, learn a lesson about obeying God and finding his sure cures.

This section of Scripture is loaded with other lessons, such as talking about your faith; making fun of God's appointed messengers; listening to God's appointed messengers; showing concern for hurting people; blaming others; and sharing good news with others.

Read 2 Kings 1:1–8:15

Naaman, a great military hero, was used to getting respect and was outraged when Elisha treated him like an ordinary person (2 Kings 5:9-15). A proud man, he expected royal treatment. To wash in a great river would be one thing, but the Jordan was small and dirty. To wash there, Naaman thought, was beneath a man of his position. But Naaman had to humble himself and obey Elisha's commands in order to be healed.

Obedience to God begins with humility. We must believe that his way is better than our own. We may not always understand his ways, but by humbly obeying, we will receive his blessings.

When confronted with a choice of doing something God's way (that may seem unusual or could prove to be embarrassing) or your way (that may seem logical and would certainly be easier), remember that (1) God's ways are best; (2) God wants your obedience more than anything else; and (3) God can use anything to accomplish his purposes.

In 1908, Israel Zangwill, a British Jew, published *The Melting Pot*, a play about America that portrayed it as, well, a huge melting pot. He observed that people from all over the world go to America, rub shoulders with each other, and mix until their individual ways of life disappear. What ends up inside the vat bears no resemblance to what went in. It's a whole new concoction—like a cake mix.

People try to do that with religion, too, melting and stirring until the result is a personal belief system that looks nothing like any of the original ingredients. This reading is about several of the kings of Israel and Judah: Jehoram, Ahaziah, Jehu, Joram, and Ahab. They have a lot in common—most notably that they become experts on cooking up new religions in the name of tolerance. Are these really God's people? Learn from their bad examples.

The other lessons in this passage fall into two categories: when to seek peace and when to seek war.

Read 2 Kings 8:16–10:36

Israel was supposed to be intolerant of any religion that did not worship the true God. The religions of surrounding nations were evil and corrupt. They were designed to destroy life, not uphold it. Israel was God's special nation, chosen to be an example of what was right. Instead of obeying God, however, Israel's kings, priests, and elders first tolerated and then incorporated surrounding pagan beliefs. This led to their becoming apathetic and even hostile toward God's way (2 Kings 10:31).

²³Jehu went into the temple of Baal with Jehonadab son of Recab. Jehu said to the worshipers of Baal, "Make sure no one who worships the LORD is here—only those who worship Baal." ²⁴So they were all inside the temple to offer sacrifices and burnt offerings. Now Jehu had stationed eighty of his men outside the building and had warned them, "If you let anyone escape, you will pay for it with your own life." ²⁵As soon as Jehu had finished sacrificing the burnt offering, he commanded his guards and officers, "Go in and kill all of them. Don't let a single one escape!" So they killed them all with their swords, and the guards and officers dragged their bodies outside. Then Jehu's men . . . ²⁶dragged out the sacred pillar used in the worship of Baal and burned it. . . . ²⁸In this way, Jehu destroyed every trace of Baal worship from Israel.

2 KINGS 10:23-26, 28

Be completely intolerant of any sin—especially false religion. You should always be tolerant of *people* who hold differing views, but you should never tolerate or follow any belief or practice that is contrary to God's Word. It will lead you away from God and his standards for living.

⁴One day King Joash said to the priests, "Collect all the money brought as a sacred offering to the LORD's Temple, whether it is a regular assessment, a payment of vows, or a voluntary gift. ⁵Let the priests take some of that money to pay for whatever repairs are needed at the Temple." ⁶But by the twenty-third year of Joash's reign, the priests still had not repaired the Temple. ⁷So King Joash called for Jehoiada and the other priests and asked them, "Why haven't you repaired the Temple? Don't use any more money for your own needs. From now on, it must all be spent on Temple repairs." ⁸So the priests agreed not to accept any more money from the people, and they also agreed to let others take responsibility for repairing the Temple.

2 KINGS 12:4-8

It seems that every workplace depends on a humming core of borderline workaholics. These people have a true devotion to their work. Both master and slave to their jobs, they work because they *want* to. Who do you know like that?

You will find out more about the kings of Israel and Judah in this reading. The most notable is King Joash—an actual good king (there weren't many)—who sets out to finish repairing the Temple. His crew can't find the time to do their jobs, however, so Joash has to make some new assignments. Read this passage and learn about the importance of doing God's work.

See if you can find insights on going far enough when making changes.

Read 2 Kings 11:1–13:25

Much had to be done to repair the Temple, but many years had gone by without progress. The priests simply hadn't done any of the work. So King Joash took them off the task and gave the assignment to laypeople. As it turns out, these people proved to be exceedingly honest and dedicated—to the point of not having to account for the money given to them for the job. What a contrast between these workmen and the priests (2 Kings 12:8, 15)! As trained men of God, the priests should have been responsible and concerned, for the Temple was their life's work. But they did not have the necessary commitment.

God's work is best accomplished by people devoted to it. Don't let your lack of training or position stop you from making a solid contribution to God's kingdom. Give your energy wherever it can be used to carry out his work. What task does God have for you to do today?

If you have enough money, you can go places, buy things, hire lawyers, and protect yourself in ways that others can't. In our society, it seems as though money is power. In what ways have you seen this to be true? How has that been frustrating to you?

This reading continues the (mostly) sad story of the kings of Israel and Judah. Here the spotlight falls on Jeroboam II, who gets extremely rich. Success is his middle name. Yet in this passage, we see the pitfalls of money and power.

You will also notice these other cautions: the problem of overrating oneself; the difference it can make when leaders love and obey God; remaking God to suit our preferences; and discerning when imitation is *not* flattering.

Read 2 Kings 14:1–17:41

Jeroboam II had no devotion to God, yet under his warlike policies and skillful administration, Israel enjoyed more national power and material prosperity than at any time since the days of Solomon (2 Kings 14:28). God's prophets, Amos and Hosea, however, tell us what was really happening within the kingdom (see Hosea 13:4-8; Amos 6:11-14). Because Jeroboam's administration ignored the policies of justice and fairness, the rich became richer and the poor, poorer. The people became self-centered, relying more on their power, security, and possessions than on God. The poor were so oppressed that they found it difficult to believe God cared about their plight.

²³Jeroboam II, the son of Jehoash, began to rule over Israel in the fifteenth year of King Amaziah's reign in Judah. Jeroboam reigned in Samaria forty-one years. ²⁴He did what was evil in the LORD's sight. He refused to turn from the sins that Jeroboam son of Nebat had led Israel to commit. ²⁵Jeroboam II recovered the territories of Israel between Lebo-hamath and the Dead Sea, just as the LORD, the God of Israel, had promised through Jonah son of Amittai, the prophet from Gath-hepher. ²⁶For the LORD saw the bitter suffering of everyone in Israel, and that there was no one in Israel, slave or free, to help them. ²⁷And because the LORD had not said he would blot out the name of Israel completely, he used Jeroboam II, the son of Jehoash, to save them.

2 KINGS 14:23-27

Material prosperity is not always an indication of God's blessing; it can also be a result of self-centeredness. If you are experiencing prosperity, remember that God holds you accountable for how you attain success and how you use your wealth. Everything you have belongs to him. Use God's gifts with his interests in mind.

¹Manasseh was twelve years old when he became king, and he reigned in Jerusalem fifty-five years. His mother was Hephzibah. ²He did what was evil in the Lord's sight, following the detestable practices of the pagan nations that the Lord had driven from the land ahead of the Israelites. ³He rebuilt the pagan shrines his father, Hezekiah, had destroyed. He constructed altars for Baal and set up an Asherah pole, just as King Ahab of Israel had done. He also bowed before all the powers of the heavens and worshiped them. ⁴He built pagan altars in the Temple of the Lord, the place where the Lord had said, "My name will remain in Jerusalem forever." ⁵He built these altars for all the powers of the heavens in both courtyards of the Lord's Temple. ⁶Manasseh also sacrificed his own son in the fire.

2 KINGS 21:1-6

How do you know that the money in your wallet isn't counterfeit? You probably don't—that's the genius of counterfeits; they can pass for the real thing, fooling all but the most determined experts.

This section of Scripture focuses on kings of Judah, mostly Hezekiah and Manasseh. King Manasseh makes up his own religion and passes it off as legitimate. But this just means that Israel is going spiritually bankrupt. As you read, look for the differences between true and false religions.

In this passage, you will also find positive lessons from Hezekiah: standing up to bullies and people who try to intimidate you; an object lesson for the arrogant; and the difference one person can make.

Read 2 Kings 18:1–21:26

Manasseh was an evil king, and he angered God with his sin (2 Kings 21:6). Listed among his sins are occult practices, sorcery, divination, and consulting mediums and spiritists. These acts were strictly forbidden by God (see Leviticus 19:31; Deuteronomy 18:9-13) because they demonstrated a lack of faith in him, involved sinful actions, and opened the door to demonic influences.

Today, many books, television shows, and games emphasize fortune-telling, seances, and other occult practices. Some people seem almost obsessed with knowing and controlling the future. Instead of trusting God, they read their horoscopes or consult their personal psychic. Others actually seek power through seances, black magic, and mysterious satanic rituals.

Don't let the desire to know what will happen to you lead you toward the occult. And don't believe that superstition is harmless. Occult practices are counterfeits of God's power and are based on a system of beliefs totally opposed to him.

The lights go out and everybody sings the familiar song as the cake enters the room. Then the partygoers gather around the center of attention. "Make a wish!" somebody says, and during a brief pause the birthday girl stares at the candles and thinks, then takes a deep breath and blows. Soon the room is a paradise of cake and ice cream.

This reading concludes the focus on Judah's kings. It's like a sandwich, with Judah's celebration right in the middle. From facing up to their sins at the beginning to getting hauled off into captivity, it's quite exciting at both ends.

In this passage, you will also learn that grief isn't all bad—sometimes it's the best thing that can happen to you; how to start over; and the painful consequences of poor choices.

Read 2 Kings 22:1–25:30

When Josiah rediscovered the meaning and significance of the Passover celebration in the Book of the Covenant, he ordered everyone to observe the ceremonies exactly as they were prescribed (2 Kings 23:21-23). The Passover was to have been celebrated yearly in remembrance of the nation's deliverance from slavery in Egypt (see Exodus 12), but it had not been celebrated "since the time when the judges ruled in Israel, nor throughout all the years of the kings of Israel and Judah" (2 Kings 23:22).

One common misconception holds that God is against celebrations and parties, and that he wants to take all the fun out of life. In reality, God wants to give us life in its fullness (see John 10:10), and those who love him have the most to celebrate—especially when we remember all that he has done for us.

Make Christian holidays special. And look for other ways to celebrate God's goodness and blessings with your family and loved ones.

[21]King Josiah then issued this order to all the people: "You must celebrate the Passover to the LORD your God, as required in this Book of the Covenant." [22]There had not been a Passover celebration like that since the time when the judges ruled in Israel, nor throughout all the years of the kings of Israel and Judah. [23]This Passover was celebrated to the LORD in Jerusalem in the eighteenth year of King Josiah's reign. [24]Josiah also got rid of the mediums and psychics, the household gods, the idols, and every other kind of detestable practice, both in Jerusalem and throughout the land of Judah. He did this in obedience to the laws written in the scroll that Hilkiah the priest had found in the LORD's Temple. [25]Never before had there been a king like Josiah, who turned to the LORD with all his heart and soul and strength.

2 KINGS 23:21-25

⁹There was a man named Jabez who was more honorable than any of his brothers. His mother named him Jabez because his birth had been so painful. ¹⁰He was the one who prayed to the God of Israel, "Oh, that you would bless me and expand my territory! Please be with me in all that I do, and keep me from all trouble and pain!" And God granted him his request. . . . ⁵:¹The oldest son of Israel was Reuben. But since he dishonored his father by sleeping with one of his father's concubines, his birthright was given to the sons of his brother Joseph. For this reason, Reuben is not listed in the genealogical records as the firstborn son. ²The descendants of Judah became the most powerful tribe and provided a ruler for the nation, but the birthright belonged to Joseph.

1 CHRONICLES 4:9-10; 5:1-2

Everyone leaves behind at least one legacy at death—the memories that others have of him or her. Each person leaves a name and a face, plus some experiences that a few close friends will remember long afterward. What would you want your loved ones to memorialize about you? How would you like to be remembered?

In this dateless family tree of mostly unpronounceable names, very few people are remembered for anything more than their name. But here and there, a note surfaces about a particular person. Jabez, for example, left an impression on the author of Chronicles. To be recognized in this way in such a massive genealogy says something important—there's a lesson to learn here.

This list contains other lessons from history as well: some people make a mark for good; some leave a trail of wreckage; and all leave behind a reputation—even if it's a blank one.

Read 1 Chronicles 1:1–9:44

The Bible records many heroes in Israel's history. Yet Jabez is remembered for a prayer request rather than a heroic act (1 Chronicles 4:9-10). In his prayer, Jabez asked God to do four things: (1) bless him, (2) help him in his work ("expand my territory"), (3) be with him in all he did, and (4) protect him from evil and harm. Jabez acknowledged God as the true center of his work and the protector of his life.

When we pray for God's blessing, we should also pray that we will rightfully regard him as Lord over everything we do—our work, our family time, and our recreation.

Do you want God's blessing on your life? Do you want to be remembered as a "hero"? Obey God in your daily responsibilities. That is heroic living, and it's something worth being remembered for.

When you see a glass filled to its halfway mark, is it half empty or half full? In fairness, the answer probably has more to do with how thirsty you are. And whether you see the glass as half empty or half full, you're still only getting half a glass of water.

This reading tells us about the death of King Saul, the halfway man. Even in dying Saul makes a bad choice. Was Saul half empty or half full? You decide.

What matters here is that his devotion to God is half-hearted. As you read, note how Saul's lackluster devotion influences his actions and leadership as king—in the end leading to severe consequences for himself and his family.

Read 1 Chronicles 10:1–12:40

Saul made two mistakes in the way he lived—he actively did wrong, and he failed to do right (1 Chronicles 10:13-14). He actively did wrong by disobeying God's instructions (see 1 Samuel 13:1-14; 15:1-23). He passively failed to do right by neglecting to ask God for guidance as he ran the kingdom.

Our responsibility to obey God is much the same—both passive and active. It is not enough just to avoid what is wrong; we need to actively pursue what is right. How can we do this? We can avoid doing wrong by keeping God's commandments—worshiping God alone, telling the truth, being faithful to a husband or wife, being content with what we have, loving our enemies. We can actively pursue what is right by seeking God's guidance through prayer and his Word. In addition, we should take advantage of opportunities to serve God and others.

¹The Philistines attacked Israel, and the men of Israel fled before them. Many were slaughtered on the slopes of Mount Gilboa. . . . ⁸The next day, when the Philistines went out to strip the dead, they found the bodies of Saul and his sons on Mount Gilboa. ⁹So they stripped off Saul's armor and cut off his head. Then they proclaimed the good news of Saul's death before their idols and to the people throughout the land of Philistia. ¹⁰They placed his armor in the temple of their gods, and they fastened his head to the temple of Dagon. ¹¹But when everyone in Jabesh-gilead heard about everything the Philistines had done to Saul, ¹²all their mighty warriors brought the bodies of Saul and his sons back to Jabesh. Then they buried their bones beneath the great tree at Jabesh, and they fasted for seven days.

1 CHRONICLES 10:1, 8-12

²⁵David and the elders of Israel and the generals of the army went to the house of Obed-edom to bring the Ark of the LORD's Covenant up to Jerusalem with a great celebration. ²⁶And because God was clearly helping the Levites as they carried the Ark of the LORD's Covenant, they sacrificed seven bulls and seven rams. ²⁷David was dressed in a robe of fine linen, as were all the Levites who carried the Ark, and also the singers, and Kenaniah the choir leader. David was also wearing a priestly garment. ²⁸So all Israel brought up the Ark of the LORD's Covenant with shouts of joy, the blowing of rams' horns and trumpets, the crashing of cymbals, and loud playing on harps and lyres.

1 CHRONICLES 15:25-28

Marguerite can't understand Robert's enthusiasm for football; he cannot understand her passion for reading. That's the way it often is from person to person—each individual gets excited over different experiences and for different reasons. What gets you excited?

In this reading, bringing the Ark of the Covenant to Jerusalem is cause for great excitement and celebration, and David dances for joy! But not everyone gets excited about the Ark's debut in Jerusalem. In fact, one person is more preoccupied with despising David and his enthusiasm than in celebrating the Ark's arrival. As you read this passage, think about worship and consider how you might celebrate God's entrance into your life.

There are other things besides the debut of the Ark to get excited about in this reading. Note, for example, David's victories over the Philistines and his prayer of thanks to God for his goodness and mercy.

Read 1 Chronicles 13:1-17:27

David worshiped God with music and exuberant dancing (1 Chronicles 13:8; 15:29). Because of his enthusiasm, David's wife, Michal, was disgusted with him. Today, some people may think that those who are more expressive in their worship of God look foolish. At the same time, those who are reserved in their worship may appear uninspired or somber.

Whether we fall into one of these categories or strike a balance between the two, we should not be critical of how others worship God, for we do not know their hearts like God does. On the other hand, we should not be concerned with what others think of us as we worship. We should instead use whatever expressions seem appropriate in pouring out our heartfelt praise and worship to God.

Don't be afraid to worship God with whatever expressions seem appropriate. What do you need in your life—more serious reflection or more joyous celebration?

Think of the people who have helped you get where you are today—those who have helped you succeed or who have taught you the skills you use every day. Who are they? How did they help you?

This is the story of some of David's military exploits. He's at war with the surrounding nations, including the Moabites, the Arameans, the Ammonites, and the Philistines. He's very successful, indeed, and that calls for handing out some accolades to the people who have helped him get there. See what you can learn about giving credit and expressing gratitude to the One who gives every success.

In this passage, David also shows us ways we need to show restraint—not being overly suspicious of others and avoiding overconfidence in ourselves.

Read 1 Chronicles 18:1–22:1

When David received gifts from King Toi for successfully defeating King Hadadezer's army, he dedicated them to God, realizing that all of the gifts had come from God and were to be used for him (1 Chronicles 18:9-11). In a similar way, the list of battles in this chapter makes it clear that *God* had given David victory after victory (18:13).

It is easy to think that our successes and material blessings are the result of our abilities and hard work rather than gifts coming from a loving God (see James 1:17). Unbelieving people think that victory and success come from their own skills and a little luck. But David acknowledged God's role in his success and prosperity, and so should we.

¹David defeated and subdued the Philistines by conquering Gath and its surrounding towns. ²David also conquered the land of Moab, and the Moabites who were spared became David's subjects and paid him tribute money. ³David also destroyed the forces of Hadadezer, king of Zobah, as far as Hamath, when Hadadezer marched out to strengthen his control along the Euphrates River. ⁴David captured 1,000 chariots, 7,000 charioteers, and 20,000 foot soldiers. He crippled all the chariot horses except enough for 100 chariots. ⁵When Arameans from Damascus arrived to help King Hadadezer, David killed 22,000 of them. ⁶Then he placed several army garrisons in Damascus, the Aramean capital, and the Arameans became David's subjects and paid him tribute money. So the LORD made David victorious wherever he went.

1 CHRONICLES 18:1-6

What has God given you? Dedicate all your gifts and resources to him, and use them for his service. He will lead you in the method you should use. The first step is to be willing. Don't take credit for the work God does.

²⁰Other Levites, led by Ahijah, were in charge of the treasuries of the house of God and the treasuries of the gifts dedicated to the LORD. ²¹From the family of Libni in the clan of Gershon, Jehiel was the leader. ²²The sons of Jehiel, Zetham and his brother Joel, were in charge of the treasuries of the house of the LORD. . . . ²⁶Shelomoth and his relatives were in charge of the treasuries containing the gifts that King David, the family leaders, and the generals and captains and other officers of the army had dedicated to the LORD. ²⁷These men dedicated some of the plunder they had gained in battle to maintain the house of the LORD. ²⁸Shelomoth and his relatives also cared for the gifts dedicated to the LORD by Samuel the seer, Saul son of Kish, Abner son of Ner, and Joab son of Zeruiah. All the other dedicated gifts were in their care, too.

1 CHRONICLES 26:20-22, 26-28

Just about everyone is willing to share their money and time with others—with a church, a charity, or even a relative in need. Charitable organizations count on these donations. But most people have one kind of need to which they are sensitive and will give a little more, a little extra, the kind of need for which a person will *sacrifice* and not just give a token amount. What sort of need gets that kind of response from you?

In this reading, David arranges for the building of the Temple. Many of David's military officers show grand support of this effort by giving generously from their own pockets. They've worked hard for their money. They deserve it. They don't have to do this. But they're not thinking of their pocketbooks, because this isn't just any other fund-raising drive. As you read this passage, learn a lesson about giving.

This portion of Scripture also teaches about preparing the way for our children and appreciating the different roles in God's work.

Read 1 Chronicles 22:2–27:34

As David went about securing his place as king, his victories meant there were spoils of war to divide among his soldiers. War plunder rightfully belonged to the victorious army, but some of the Israelite military commanders expressed their dedication to God by generously donating a portion of their plunder to help pay for the repair of the Temple (1 Chronicles 26:27).

Some people give a token amount to church and other worthy causes—as though they are tipping God. Gifts like that come out of a feeling of obligation, and not out of love and devotion. Like these commanders, God's people today should think of what we *can* give, rather than only what we are obligated to give.

Is your giving a matter of rejoicing rather than duty? Consider all that God has given to you. Then give to his work as a response of joy and love for him.

Who knows you better than anybody else? In answer to that question, some people would name a parent, others a spouse or a friend. Perhaps you have managed to escape that kind of scrutiny, so *nobody* really knows you well—your motives, desires, thoughts, feelings, and dreams.

Whether you've opened your life up to someone or have kept it a secret from others, there is one person who knows you intimately—God. In this reading, David reminds his son Solomon of this and cautions him to be open and honest with the Lord.

Nobody knows us better than God, David reminds his son, so why try to hide? His advice to Solomon is also great advice to us.

Other lessons in David's speech include the connections between present obedience to God and the future; how to give; and humility.

Read 1 Chronicles 28:1–29:30

David pointed out to his son Solomon that "the Lord sees every heart" (1 Chronicles 28:9). In other words, nothing can be hidden from God. He sees and understands everything: our desires, thoughts, motives, feelings, and dreams. David had found this out the hard way when God sent Nathan to expose David's sins of adultery and murder (see 2 Samuel 12). Out of this experience, David told Solomon to be completely open with God and dedicated to him.

⁵From among my sons . . . [the Lord] chose Solomon to succeed me on the throne of Israel. . . . ⁸So now, with God as our witness, and in the sight of all Israel—the Lord's assembly—I give you this charge. Be careful to obey all the commands of the Lord your God, so that you may continue to possess this good land and leave it to your children as a permanent inheritance. ⁹And Solomon, my son, learn to know the God of your ancestors intimately. Worship and serve him with your whole heart and a willing mind. For the Lord sees every heart and knows every plan and thought. If you seek him, you will find him. But if you forsake him, he will reject you forever. ¹⁰So take this seriously. The Lord has chosen you to build a Temple as his sanctuary. Be strong, and do the work.

1 CHRONICLES 28:5, 8-10

God's total knowledge of us can cause us fear and dread because we cannot hide our sinful thoughts and actions from him—we are totally vulnerable. But his knowledge of us can also cause great comfort and joy because he loves us—the *real* us—and wants the very best for us.

Rejoice in the fact that God knows your deepest needs and longings, and that he desires a better life for you than you could ever imagine. Be honest with him—express your doubts and questions, confess your sinful thoughts and actions, pour out your feelings, and ask him for help.

¹Solomon decided to build a Temple to honor the name of the LORD, and also a royal palace for himself. ²He enlisted a force of 70,000 laborers, 80,000 men to quarry stone in the hill country, and 3,600 foremen. ³Solomon also sent this message to King Hiram at Tyre: "Send me cedar logs as you did for my father, David, when he was building his palace. ⁴I am about to build a Temple to honor the name of the LORD my God. It will be a place set apart to burn fragrant incense before him, to display the special sacrificial bread, and to sacrifice burnt offerings each morning and evening, on the Sabbaths, at new moon celebrations, and at the other appointed festivals of the LORD our God. He has commanded Israel to do these things forever. ⁵This must be a magnificent Temple because our God is greater than all other gods."

2 CHRONICLES 2:1-5

New Year's Day, Easter, Thanksgiving, and Christmas are just a few of the holidays marked on our calendars. Most of our holidays exist for a significant reason. The Fourth of July, for instance, is celebrated as the birthday of our nation.

The Israelites also celebrated holidays of great significance. To aid in their celebration, Solomon wants to establish a central place to observe these holidays. So he begins to carry out his responsibility of building the Temple. But before construction can begin, Solomon has to find craftsmen skilled enough to work on God's house. As you read, think of possible celebrations you could include in your schedule.

Also in this passage you will find the kind of wish God will grant; decorations suitable for a place of worship; and the importance of following instructions.

Read 2 Chronicles 1:1–5:1

A celebration is an occasion of joy, and remembering God's goodness to his people was certainly a reason to be joyful (2 Chronicles 2:4). God wanted Israel to celebrate certain historical events regularly because the people were so forgetful, so quick to turn to other gods, so quick to find more important actions to do than to worship him. The celebrations were designed to turn their attention and their hearts to the Lord.

Today, our church celebrations recall God's goodness. Because, like the people of Israel, we also have short memories, Christmas, Easter, and other special occasions help us remember what God has done for us. To some people, these holidays are just an excuse to have some fun. They should be much more than that—they should help us remember God's work in the world and in our lives.

Use Christian holidays and traditional church celebrations to remember God's goodness to you. And create your own celebrations that commemorate special days in your walk with the Savior.

Getting up in front of an audience strikes fear in the hearts of most people. "That's not my idea of a good time," they might say. It's a big responsibility to be in the spotlight—being observed by everybody, critiqued by some, and copied by others.

Solomon is one of the few who can stand in front of an audience and not be stricken with fear. As he dedicates the recently finished Temple, he stands in front of the people—on a platform—and blesses them.

This is the second part of Solomon's story. After seven years of construction, Solomon's work crews finally finish the Temple. Solomon dedicates the magnificent edifice to God and inaugurates it into service. He brings the Ark of the Covenant into the Holy of Holies and prays a prayer of dedication, and God appears to him. Then we read of Solomon's riches and wisdom and of his many building projects. Follow closely—the best part is the prayer.

There's a lot here: the importance of the Old Testament Temple; what to pray about; what it means to dedicate ourselves to God; consequences of turning away from God; and the power of example.

Read 2 Chronicles 5:2–9:31

As the people received Solomon's blessing, they stood (2 Chronicles 6:3). As Solomon prayed, he knelt (6:12-13). Solomon showed love and respect for God by kneeling before him as the people of Israel looked on. His action wasn't just for public display, though. It showed that he acknowledged God as the ultimate king and authority, and it encouraged the people to do the same.

¹²Solomon stood before the altar of the LORD in front of the entire community of Israel, and he lifted his hands in prayer. . . . ¹⁴He prayed, "O LORD, God of Israel, there is no God like you in all of heaven and earth. You keep your covenant and show unfailing love to all who walk before you in wholehearted devotion. ¹⁵You have kept your promise to your servant David, my father. You made that promise with your own mouth, and with your own hands you have fulfilled it today. ¹⁶And now, O LORD, God of Israel, carry out the additional promise you made to your servant David, my father. For you said to him, 'If your descendants guard their behavior and faithfully follow my Law as you have done, one of them will always sit on the throne of Israel.'"

2 CHRONICLES 6:12, 14-16

When you stand or kneel in church or at prayer, make these actions reflect more than mere changes in posture. Let them indicate your love for God.

4When the army of Judah arrived in the hill country of Ephraim, Abijah stood on Mount Zemaraim and shouted to Jeroboam and all Israel: "Listen to me! 5Don't you realize that the LORD, the God of Israel, made a lasting covenant with David, giving him and his descendants the throne of Israel forever? 6Yet Jeroboam son of Nebat, a mere servant of David's son Solomon, rebelled against his master. 7Then a whole gang of scoundrels joined him, defying Solomon's son Rehoboam when he was young and inexperienced and could not stand up to them. 8Do you really think you can stand against the kingdom of the LORD that is led by the descendants of David? You may have a vast army, and you have those gold calves that Jeroboam made as your gods. 9But you have chased away the priests of the LORD."

2 CHRONICLES 13:4-9

There's more to babysitting than preventing food fights and keeping the kids alive. That's why when parents need a babysitter, they want someone who will care for the children the way they themselves would.

Kings are similar to babysitters—they're both in charge of caring for people and keeping order. In this reading, the Jews of the northern tribes of Israel need to choose a king because they have decided not to put up with the current tyrant. Unfortunately, they aren't careful as to who they choose. As you read this story, note especially Abijah's advice to Jeroboam, and learn God's lesson there.

In this passage, you also will find these lessons: how to avoid bad advice; trappings of greed and power; confession and repentance; and a source of peace.

Read 2 Chronicles 10:1–14:1

In setting up his own religion, Jeroboam discarded the worship of God and made idols. He appointed priests to serve in his new religion, but he tossed out the standards that God had set for the priesthood of his people. Literally anyone could qualify to be a priest—all the person had to do was to present a prescribed offering, much like paying a fee.

Abijah criticized Jeroboam for this (2 Chronicles 13:9). He wanted Jeroboam to follow the instructions of the Lord (13:11), because a priest is a representative of God. Anyone can represent a worthless god; but to represent the Lord God Almighty, a person must live by *God's* standards.

Those appointed to positions of responsibility in your church should not be selected merely because they are influential or are highly educated. Instead they should demonstrate sound doctrine, dedication to God, and strong spiritual character (see 1 Timothy 3; Titus 1). It matters who leads you in worship, so don't choose just anybody.

Suppose you suddenly had two hours to do whatever you wanted. This was *your* time—no one else could call or interrupt you, no one could lay claim to your priorities, no one could tell you to get up and start washing the dishes. What would you most like to do with that time?

For some good tips, read the story of Asa, king of Judah. Asa is a good king. He loves God and does what is right. And this has a wonderful, positive effect on his nation—peace. As you read, note how Asa uses free time.

In this passage, Asa shows us other good examples— like the importance of removing sin and corrupt practices from our lives, as well as listening to and following through on godly counsel.

Read 2 Chronicles 14:2–16:14

This passage notes that the nation of Judah had been given rest from its enemies, meaning that they had peace with all their neighbors (2 Chronicles 14:7). King Asa wisely used this time to build his defenses, fortifying the cities with walls and battlements. Times of peace are not just for resting; they allow us to prepare for times of trouble. King Asa recognized that this period of peace afforded the right time to build his defenses—the moment of attack would be too late.

It is also difficult to withstand spiritual attack unless adequate defenses are prepared beforehand. Decisions about how to face temptation must be made with a cool head long before the heat of battle.

¹When Abijah died, he was buried in the City of David. Then his son Asa became the next king. There was peace in the land for ten years. ²Asa did what was pleasing and good in the sight of the LORD his God. ³He removed the foreign altars and the pagan shrines. He smashed the sacred pillars and cut down the Asherah poles. ⁴He commanded the people of Judah to seek the LORD, the God of their ancestors, and to obey his law and his commands. ⁵Asa also removed the pagan shrines, as well as the incense altars from every one of Judah's towns. So Asa's kingdom enjoyed a period of peace. ⁶During those peaceful years, he was able to build up the fortified towns throughout Judah. No one tried to make war against him at this time, for the LORD was giving him rest from his enemies.

2 CHRONICLES 14:1-6

Build your defenses *before* temptation strikes by scheduling times of rest, and using those times to recover from stress and to refresh your spirit. Remember to include prayer and Bible reading to boost your defenses.

¹³As all the men of Judah stood before the Lord with their little ones, wives, and children, ¹⁴the Spirit of the Lord came upon one of the men standing there. His name was Jahaziel son of Zechariah, son of Benaiah, son of Jeiel, son of Mattaniah, a Levite who was a descendant of Asaph. ¹⁵He said, "Listen, all you people of Judah and Jerusalem! Listen, King Jehoshaphat! This is what the Lord says: Do not be afraid! Don't be discouraged by this mighty army, for the battle is not yours, but God's. ¹⁶Tomorrow, march out against them. You will find them coming up through the ascent of Ziz at the end of the valley that opens into the wilderness of Jeruel. ¹⁷But you will not even need to fight. Take your positions; then stand still and watch the Lord's victory. He is with you, O people of Judah and Jerusalem."

2 CHRONICLES 20:13-17

The odds are often against us in life. Finances, for example, are a continual struggle for many. Work always seems to exact much too high a price for the little reward it returns.

In this reading, the odds are against Jehoshaphat and his army. They're no match for the combined forces that are moving against them. But Jehoshaphat loves God and follows him. Although Jehoshaphat doesn't have military might, he is on God's side. Jehoshaphat keeps his trust in God throughout his military exploits, despite his allies' lack of faith. As you read this passage, look for the secret of Jehoshaphat's success.

Other lessons in this section include leading others in Bible reading and prayer; how *not* to take advice; and how to exercise authority.

Read 2 Chronicles 17:1–21:3

As the enemy bore down on the army of Judah, God spoke through the prophet Jahaziel: "Do not be afraid! Don't be discouraged . . . for the battle is not yours, but God's" (2 Chronicles 20:15).

We may not physically fight an enemy army, but every day we battle temptation, pressure, and "mighty powers in this dark world" (Ephesians 6:12), who want us to fail or to stop doing good. Remember that we who are believers have God's Spirit in us. If we ask for God's help when we face struggles, God will fight for us. And God always wins.

How can you let God fight for you? (1) By realizing the battle is not yours, but God's; (2) by recognizing human limitations and allowing God's strength to work through your fears and weaknesses; (3) by making sure that you are pursuing God's interests and not just your own selfish desires; (4) by asking God for help in your daily battles; (5) by not forcing outcomes that are not yours to control; (6) by trusting that God is in control and not panicking; and (7) by doing your part and trusting God with the results (see 2 Samuel 10:12).

Some people believe that the reason people do bad things is because they don't have enough material goods. Give them what they need and they will be good people. This theory breaks down, though, when those who have everything do horrible things.

This passage tells the stories of Jehoram, Ahaziah, Athaliah, and Joash—a succession of kings and a queen. To call this family dysfunctional would be a gross understatement. All except Joash consistently did evil and even he had a lapse in his later years. Was their problem a lack of material prosperity? Did they go wrong because they just didn't have enough stuff? Far from it. Wealth doesn't do the trick. As you read, look for the lesson about prosperity.

You also will find these lessons: the trouble with marrying someone who hates God; testing the advice you receive; and a time for executions.

Read 2 Chronicles 21:4–24:27

Under Joash's rule, the Israelites repaired the Temple and the nation prospered. But right after the death of his uncle (the priest Jehoiada), the nation again descended into the worship of false gods. Everything was going well in Judah, so why did they turn away from God (2 Chronicles 24:18)?

Having money may bring us some comforts, but it doesn't feed our spiritual needs. Wealth doesn't make us better people or insulate us from sin. Whatever our status, we must make decisions about whom to serve and worship every day. Serving God is something we must consciously choose.

[17]After Jehoiada's death, the leaders of Judah came and bowed before King Joash and persuaded him to listen to their advice. [18]They decided to abandon the Temple of the LORD, the God of their ancestors, and they worshiped Asherah poles and idols instead! Because of this sin, divine anger fell on Judah and Jerusalem. [19]Yet the LORD sent prophets to bring them back to him. The prophets warned them, but still the people would not listen. [20]Then the Spirit of God came upon Zechariah son of Jehoiada the priest. He stood before the people and said, "This is what God says: Why do you disobey the LORD's commands and keep yourselves from prospering? You have abandoned the LORD, and now he has abandoned you!" [21]Then the leaders plotted to kill Zechariah, and King Joash ordered that they stone him to death.

2 CHRONICLES 24:17-21

Don't let good circumstances lure you into false security. If your bankroll is always tight, don't think that having more will enhance your love for God. Be content with what you have, remembering that God owns all. He alone deserves our ultimate allegiance (see Deuteronomy 6:10-12; 8:11-14).

¹⁶At that time King Ahaz of Judah asked the king of Assyria for help. ¹⁷The armies of Edom had again invaded Judah and taken captives. ¹⁸And the Philistines had raided towns located in the foothills of Judah and in the Negev of Judah. They had already captured and occupied Beth-shemesh, Aijalon, Gederoth, Soco with its villages, Timnah with its villages, and Gimzo with its villages. ¹⁹The LORD was humbling Judah because of King Ahaz of Judah, for he had encouraged his people to sin and had been utterly unfaithful to the LORD. ²⁰So when King Tiglath-pileser of Assyria arrived, he attacked Ahaz instead of helping him. ²¹Ahaz took valuable items from the LORD's Temple, the royal palace, and from the homes of his officials and gave them to the king of Assyria as tribute. But this did not help him.

2 CHRONICLES 28:16-21

Imagine this scenario and see if it has ever been your experience: Carla is trying to get the attention of her husband, Bob, who is across the room. "Bob, would you come here for a moment?" Carla waits. No response. "Bob?" Still no response. "*Bob?*" The plea is more insistent now. Still no response. Finally, "BOB!" "Huh?" he finally replies. He heard, but he didn't *hear.*

This parallels how God tries to get Ahaz's attention. This passage tells the story of Amaziah, Uzziah, Jotham, and Ahaz, all kings of Judah. Ahaz wins the award for Most Stubborn Rebel. In this passage, God uses hardship after hardship to shout to Ahaz, "Listen to me!" God has a message for Ahaz, but Ahaz is too distracted by his wild living to notice. Take a close look at Ahaz and learn from his mistakes.

You will also see that Amaziah has a problem with half-hearted faith but still makes some wise choices; Uzziah has great success, then spoils it; and Jotham becomes a model leader.

Read 2 Chronicles 25:1–28:27

As king of Judah, Ahaz had nothing but trouble. When his troubles hit, he was already in the midst of terrible sins; these problems were his wake-up call— his opportunity to hear God. How did he respond? He refused to listen and committed even more evil (2 Chronicles 28:22).

No one knows why bad things happen to people. From the beginning of time, people have tried to invoke universal explanations. The truth is, we can't know exactly why tragedies occur. We cannot know why they happen to us. But when they do happen, we must remember to ask how God might be attempting to get our attention to correct us.

When troubles hit, we need to respond to them as our teachers. Through hardship, God disciplines his children in love (see Hebrews 12:7). Rough times give us a chance to grow (see James 1:2-4). When you are facing difficulties and struggles, don't turn away from God—turn *to* him.

Mistakes are always a two-edged sword. On the one hand, they hurt; on the other hand, they pack a lesson. If we get the point, it's something we'll likely never forget—which, in its own cruel way, is a good thing. There's no teacher like experience.

Hezekiah, king of Judah, is a prime example of this. He's a good man, and he enjoys many successes. But that doesn't mean that Hezekiah is perfect, as he learns from his experience with some visitors from Babylon. Their visit is a test of Hezekiah's character. See how Hezekiah does on his test, and learn from his experience.

Hezekiah's life also tells us about restoring old Christian servants; making sacrifices; inviting others to follow Christ; getting rid of idols; and dealing with frightening situations.

Read 2 Chronicles 29:1–32:33

Envoys from Babylon came to visit the king of Judah, and he foolishly showed them his supply of gold, treasures, and weapons (see Isaiah 39:1-8). Hezekiah did not perceive Babylon as a threat. When the envoys came, Hezekiah had to decide whether to show off his treasures. He did, thinking that nothing bad would come of it. But the Babylonians would one day carry away all his treasures. His flirtation with pride led to a disaster for all Judah.

God presented the king with a choice to see what his heart was really like. God wanted to show Hezekiah his own shortcomings and the attitude of his heart (2 Chronicles 32:31).

27Hezekiah was very wealthy and highly honored. He built special treasury buildings for his silver, gold, precious stones, and spices, and for his shields and other valuable items. 28He also constructed many storehouses for his grain, new wine, and olive oil; and he made many stalls for his cattle and pens for his flocks of sheep and goats. 29He built many towns and acquired vast flocks and herds, for God had given him great wealth. 30He blocked up the upper spring of Gihon and brought the water down through a tunnel to the west side of the City of David. And so he succeeded in everything he did. 31However, when ambassadors arrived from Babylon to ask about the remarkable events that had taken place in the land, God withdrew from Hezekiah in order to test him and to see what was really in his heart.

2 CHRONICLES 32:27-31

Life brings many choices—each a test of character. Many of the circumstances and opportunities that you experience every day will test you, even if only in small ways. Consistently turn to God and do what pleases him.

¹Josiah was eight years old when he became king, and he reigned in Jerusalem thirty-one years. ²He did what was pleasing in the Lord's sight and followed the example of his ancestor David. He did not turn away from doing what was right. ³During the eighth year of his reign, while he was still young, Josiah began to seek the God of his ancestor David. Then in the twelfth year he began to purify Judah and Jerusalem, destroying all the pagan shrines, the Asherah poles, and the carved idols and cast images. ⁴He ordered that the altars of Baal be demolished and that the incense altars which stood above them be broken down. He also made sure that the Asherah poles, the carved idols, and the cast images were smashed and scattered over the graves of those who had sacrificed to them. . . . ⁵And so he purified Judah and Jerusalem.

2 CHRONICLES 34:1-5

What did you have on your mind at the age of eight? Perhaps it was a long time ago, but think back if you can. What were your favorite subjects in school? What were your favorite activities? What did you want to be when you grew up?

Josiah didn't really have an opportunity to dream about what he wanted to be when he grew up. When Josiah was eight years old he became the king of Judah. Imagine the immense responsibility he had at such a young age. But his age wasn't a negative factor for the job. In fact, it may have been an asset. This story will make you rethink the potential that is packed in kids who love God.

As you read this passage, you will find other lessons in the lives of Judah's kings: exercising your second chances (Manasseh); not missing a cue (Amon); godly sorrow (Josiah); and the cost of overestimating one's own goodness (Josiah).

Read 2 Chronicles 33:1–36:1

Josiah became king when he was eight years old. In Josiah's day, boys were considered to be men at age twelve. By sixteen, Josiah understood the responsibility of his office (2 Chronicles 34:3). Even at this young age, Josiah showed greater wisdom than many of the older kings who had come before him, because he decided to seek the Lord God and his wisdom.

Some people use age as an excuse for not serving the Lord: "I'm too young," or "I'm too old," or "I've only been a Christian for a short time—I don't know enough." It is clear from this passage that God can use people of any age to make a difference for him. They just need to be willing and open.

Don't let your age make you feel disqualified from serving God. Learn from Josiah's example—that God can use you at any age if you will listen to him and obey his Word.

The people of Judah have "one of those days" when they are taken captive to Babylon. But don't feel sorry for them—God has warned his people for years that there would be consequences for their stubborn disobedience. Now they've used up their supply of warnings, and the consequences are at hand. This is a sad story, but its lesson is helpful for us.

Also in this passage, you should be able to find lessons on God keeping his promises and God's people making big mistakes.

Read 2 Chronicles 36:2-23

The book of 2 Chronicles focuses on the rise and fall of the worship of God as symbolized by the Jerusalem Temple. David planned the Temple (1 Chronicles 22:5), Solomon built it (2 Chronicles 2:1), and King Nebuchadnezzar destroyed it (36:19).

The kings were gone, the Temple lay in ruins, and many of the people had been taken to Babylon as captives. The nation had been stripped to its very foundation. Fortunately, there still existed a greater foundation—God himself. Forty-eight years after the Temple's destruction, the year after Cyrus conquered Babylon, he announced his plans to rebuild God's Temple (36:22-23). The situation seemed hopeless, at first, but God was there, working out his plan for his people all along.

At times our lives can seem devastated, conquered, and empty. After difficult defeats and struggles, every support can seem to have been stripped away. That's when we should remember that God is still with us and that he is working out his perfect plan for us.

¹⁷The LORD brought the king of Babylon against them. The Babylonians killed Judah's young men, even chasing after them into the Temple. They had no pity on the people, killing both young men and young women, the old and the infirm. God handed all of them over to Nebuchadnezzar. ¹⁸The king took home to Babylon all the articles, large and small, used in the Temple of God, and the treasures from both the LORD's Temple and from the palace of the king and his officials. ¹⁹Then his army burned the Temple of God, tore down the walls of Jerusalem, burned all the palaces, and completely destroyed everything of value. ²⁰The few who survived were taken as exiles to Babylon, and they became servants to the king and his sons until the kingdom of Persia came to power.

2 CHRONICLES 36:17-20

When tough times come, when you have "one of those days," don't despair and give up. Instead, use those difficulties to push you closer to your loving heavenly Father. Trust in God and his promises to get you through the day, and remember that the bad times will one day pass.

¹Here is the list of the Jewish exiles of the provinces who returned from their captivity. King Nebuchadnezzar had deported them to Babylon, but now they returned to Jerusalem and the other towns in Judah where they originally lived. . . . ⁶⁴A total of 42,360 people returned to Judah, ⁶⁵in addition to 7,337 servants and 200 singers, both men and women. ⁶⁶They took with them 736 horses, 245 mules, ⁶⁷435 camels, and 6,720 donkeys. ⁶⁸When they arrived at the Temple of the LORD in Jerusalem, some of the family leaders made voluntary offerings toward the rebuilding of God's Temple on its original site, ⁶⁹and each leader gave as much as he could. The total of their gifts came to 61,000 gold coins, 6,250 pounds of silver, and 100 robes for the priests.

EZRA 2:1, 64-69

A joke has been made out of the phrase, "I hate when I do that." That sentiment pokes fun at a truth about ourselves. The truth is that sometimes we regret what we voluntarily do. What in your life makes you say, "I hate when I do that"?

Israel often hurt itself through poor choices and wrong actions. Despite their regrets, God always gave them another chance. In this reading, the first group of exiles returns to the land of Israel after having been in captivity for forty-eight years. They suddenly get the opportunity to return—and a second chance—as Cyrus offers them safe passage back to rebuild the Temple. The heads of families along with the priests and Levites lead the way. This is more than a trip—it's a commitment to change. As you read, look for signs of God's love and forgiveness, and learn the lesson of the second chance.

In this passage, you will find these other lessons: hope and new beginnings; the importance of teamwork; God's protection; and giving.

Read Ezra 1:1–2:70

After forty-eight years of captivity, God's arrogant people had been humbled. When the people's attitudes and desires changed, God ended their punishment and gave them another opportunity to go home and try again.

Major changes occur on the inside when God works on our attitudes, beliefs, and desires. These inner changes lead to faithful actions. Paul wrote, "For God is working in you, giving you the desire and the power to do what pleases him" (Philippians 2:13). Doing God's will begins with one's desires.

Are you willing to be humble, to be open to God's opportunities, and to move at his direction? Ask God to give you the desire to follow him more closely. He's giving you another chance to change your mind. Change your desires and attitude to *want* to follow God.

You turn the key, open the door, and enter the vacant house. "Ahh," you say with sincere pleasure, inhaling the stale and stuffy air, "Home at last!" You plop down on the couch and relax for the first time in two weeks. After an exhausting time away, it's good to be back home!

The Jews know what this feeling is like. They are glad to be home, glad to have returned from exile in Babylon to rebuild the Temple in Jerusalem. There will be a lot to do, with planning, clearing the area, getting materials, and starting the work. But before they begin, they have some important business to take care of—"first things first" you might say. As you read, learn a lesson from the Israelites' priorities.

As the Israelites unpack, note also their lessons on avoiding partnerships with unbelievers; when (and how) to resist opposition; when (and how) to speak up for what is right; and God's sovereignty over even the most powerful people on earth.

Read Ezra 3:1–6:22

Almost immediately after arriving in their homeland, the returning exiles built an altar (Ezra 3:1-3). The people began worshiping God through sacrifices even before the Temple foundations were laid. After many years in captivity, they had learned their lesson—God was their source of strength and success. Their parents and grandparents had been carried off by the Babylonians when they were relatively strong; this group was few, weak, and surrounded by enemies. They knew that they needed to rely on God's power.

¹In early autumn, when the Israelites had settled in their towns, all the people assembled in Jerusalem with a unified purpose. ²Then Jeshua son of Jehozadak joined his fellow priests and Zerubbabel son of Shealtiel with his family in rebuilding the altar of the God of Israel. They wanted to sacrifice burnt offerings on it, as instructed in the Law of Moses, the man of God. ³Even though the people were afraid of the local residents, they rebuilt the altar at its old site. Then they began to sacrifice burnt offerings on the altar to the LORD each morning and evening. ⁴They celebrated the Festival of Shelters as prescribed in the Law, sacrificing the number of burnt offerings specified for each day of the festival. ⁵They also offered the regular burnt offerings and the offerings required for the new moon celebrations.

EZRA 3:1-5

Regardless of our good health and prosperity, God is our source of strength and help. We need to depend on him and make worshiping him our top priority. Make time for worship, even when you are very busy and tired. Submit to the Lord and depend on him to work through you.

²¹By the Ahava Canal, I gave orders for all of us to fast and humble ourselves before our God. We prayed that he would give us a safe journey and protect us, our children, and our goods as we traveled. ²²For I was ashamed to ask the king for soldiers and horsemen to accompany us and protect us from enemies along the way. After all, we had told the king, "Our God's hand of protection is on all who worship him, but his fierce anger rages against those who abandon him." ²³So we fasted and earnestly prayed that our God would take care of us, and he heard our prayer.

EZRA 8:21-23

Family camping trips are supposed to be great fun, but too often a sense of dread accompanies them. It's all too easy to leave something crucial behind. One time it's the tent. Another time it's the food. Sound familiar?

The second group of exiles returns to Jerusalem from Babylonia, led by Ezra. But before they set out they have some important preparations to make, and Ezra makes sure they don't forget the most crucial ones. As you read, learn how to get prepared for any task God gives you.

In this passage you will find these other lessons: the qualities of an exemplary leader in action; acknowledging God's help and protection; and using your gifts and abilities for God's service.

Read Ezra 7:1–8:36

Ezra knew God's promises to protect his people, but he didn't take God for granted. He also knew that God's blessings come through prayer. So Ezra and the people humbled themselves by fasting and praying (Ezra 8:21-23). Fasting humbled the people because going without food was a reminder of their complete dependence on God. Fasting also gave them time to pray and think about God.

Too often, we pray glibly and superficially. We don't take time out from our busy schedules to commune with God seriously. Fasting is one way to free up the time to pray to God earnestly.

We need to take time to pray seriously. Not taking the time is an insult to God. When we approach him with our quick, unthoughtful prayers, we reduce him to a quick-service pharmacist with painkillers for every ailment. Serious prayer puts us in touch with God's will for our lives and can really change our hearts and minds.

Make time for prayer in which you *concentrate* on what you are saying and why you're saying it. That's the only way to be fully prepared for life. How much time do you spend in preparation?

"I didn't know." If a driver says that when stopped for speeding, the police officer *may* let the speeder off, but he or she doesn't have to, because ignorance of the law is no excuse. If a child says it to Mom, she'll probably give the child another chance, but she'll also expect compliance from then on. It works best to learn the rules *before* the trouble comes, instead of the hard way.

Here, the Israelites are back in their homeland. Not knowing God's laws, some of the returned exiles carelessly end up breaking them. This causes Ezra much grief and shame before God, who has just brought his people back from being held in captivity and given them a second chance.

As you read, notice Ezra's incredible humility before God, as well as the great sacrifice the Israelites make in order to repent for their sin.

Other lessons in this passage include avoiding certain kinds of partnerships and crying out for justice.

Read Ezra 9:1–10:44

Ezra pointed out a sin that the Israelites had been committing without really knowing it. They had intermarried with the pagan tribes around them, something God had forbidden (see Exodus 34:12-16; Deuteronomy 7:1-4). God knew that marrying into a family or clan meant accepting their gods. In order to reestablish the nation's relationship with God, Ezra pleaded for God's forgiveness (Ezra 9:5-15). Then the Israelites chose the painful course of repentance— ending their wrongful marriages.

¹While Ezra prayed and made this confession, weeping and lying face down on the ground in front of the Temple of God, a very large crowd of people from Israel—men, women, and children—gathered and wept bitterly with him. ²Then Shecaniah son of Jehiel, a descendant of Elam, said to Ezra, "We have been unfaithful to our God, for we have married these pagan women of the land. But in spite of this there is hope for Israel. ³Let us now make a covenant with our God to divorce our pagan wives and to send them away with their children. We will follow the advice given by you and by the others who respect the commands of our God. Let it be done according to the Law of God. ⁴Get up, for it is your duty to tell us how to proceed in setting things straight. We are behind you, so be strong and take action."

EZRA 10:1-4

In this reading, we should note the willingness we should have to sacrifice anything that causes sin in our lives. The Israelites sacrificed family relations in order to maintain a right relationship with God. What sacrifices, big or small, do you need to make in order to return to a right relationship with God and walk more closely with him?

True repentance does not end with words of confession—it must lead to corrected behavior and changed attitudes.

¹Early the following spring, in the month of Nisan, during the twentieth year of King Artaxerxes' reign, I was serving the king his wine. I had never before appeared sad in his presence. ²So the king asked me, "Why are you looking so sad? You don't look sick to me. You must be deeply troubled." Then I was terrified, ³but I replied, "Long live the king! How can I not be sad? For the city where my ancestors are buried is in ruins, and the gates have been destroyed by fire." ⁴The king asked, "Well, how can I help you?" With a prayer to the God of heaven, ⁵I replied, "If it please the king, and if you are pleased with me, your servant, send me to Judah to rebuild the city where my ancestors are buried." . . . ⁶After I told him how long I would be gone, the king agreed to my request.

NEHEMIAH 2:1-6

Brenda got a phone call today and found out that her sister is financially strapped, has lost her job, and wrecked her car. Bad news aplenty, with no easy solutions in sight. What should Brenda do? Get depressed? Get a loan? Get a stiff drink?

Though Nehemiah lives in Babylon, he's a Jew and he's concerned about his homeland. When he gets the reports of how the settlers are doing, it's all bad news. He's heard from home and everything's a wreck. But Nehemiah doesn't despair or distract himself—he takes action. In this passage, learn from Nehemiah's example about how to respond to bad news.

Nehemiah teaches us three other lessons: how to care for people; praying for success; and asking for help.

Read Nehemiah 1:1–2:10

Nehemiah was deeply grieved about the condition of Jerusalem, but he didn't just brood about it. After his initial grief, he prayed, pouring his heart out to God (Nehemiah 1:4-11) and looking for ways to improve the situation. Nehemiah put all his resources—his knowledge, experience, and organization—into figuring out what should be done.

That's how we should confront bad news, too, responding with trust in God, belief in his sovereignty, and then constructive action.

When tragic or difficult news comes to you, don't wallow in self-pity or merely run and try to hide. First pray. Then seek ways to move beyond your grief to specific action that will help those who need it, including yourself.

Commercial aircraft have four levels of backup in their navigational systems. If something goes wrong with the hydraulic lines that control the flaps, for example, a second set can take over. These planes also carry far more fuel than they need for every trip. This is just planning ahead. From planes to personal projects, such preparations mean the difference between risking failure and having great probability of success.

Nehemiah needs a workable plan to successfully accomplish the desire God has placed in his heart—to rebuild the walls of Jerusalem. Before Nehemiah can come up with a plan, however, he must do his homework. Nehemiah knows that he has his work cut out for him—the settlers' morale is low, and the neighboring kingdoms don't want the Jews to get ambitious. As you read this story, watch how Nehemiah designs his plan.

Nehemiah's project also has lessons about sharing dreams and about each believer doing his or her part in the body of Christ.

Read Nehemiah 2:11–3:32

Nehemiah arrived quietly in Jerusalem and spent several days carefully observing and assessing the damage to the walls. Nehemiah kept his mission a secret, surveying the walls by moonlight to prevent enemies from being alerted to his plans. Only after careful planning would he go public with his mission. A premature announcement could have caused rivalry among the Jews over the best way to begin. In this case, Nehemiah didn't need brainstorming sessions; he needed one plan that would bring quick action. Following this time of thoughtful consideration, he confidently presented his plan (Nehemiah 2:11-17).

^{13}After dark I went out through the Valley Gate, past the Jackal's Well, and over to the Dung Gate to inspect the broken walls and burned gates. ^{14}Then I went to the Fountain Gate and to the King's Pool, but my donkey couldn't get through the rubble. ^{15}So, though it was still dark, I went up the Kidron Valley instead, inspecting the wall before I turned back and entered again at the Valley Gate. ^{16}The city officials did not know I had been out there or what I was doing, for I had not yet said anything to anyone about my plans. I had not yet spoken to the Jewish leaders—the priests, the nobles, the officials, or anyone else in the administration. ^{17}But now I said to them, "You know very well what trouble we are in. Jerusalem lies in ruins, and its gates have been destroyed by fire. Let us rebuild the wall of Jerusalem and end this disgrace!"

NEHEMIAH 2:13-17

Nehemiah demonstrated an excellent approach to problem solving. First, he got all the accurate information he needed to assess the situation. Then he presented a realistic strategy.

Before jumping into a project, follow Nehemiah's example and plan ahead. Check your information to make sure your ideas will work, and be realistic. Then you will be able to present your plan with confidence.

¹²The Jews who lived near the enemy came and told us again and again, "They will come from all directions and attack us!" ¹³So I placed armed guards behind the lowest parts of the wall in the exposed areas. I stationed the people to stand guard by families, armed with swords, spears, and bows. ¹⁴Then as I looked over the situation, I called together the nobles and the rest of the people and said to them, "Don't be afraid of the enemy! Remember the LORD, who is great and glorious, and fight for your brothers, your sons, your daughters, your wives, and your homes!" ¹⁵When our enemies heard that we knew of their plans and that God had frustrated them, we all returned to our work on the wall. ¹⁶But from then on, only half my men worked while the other half stood guard with spears, shields, bows, and coats of mail.

NEHEMIAH 4:12-16

A lot of work relationships form around competition. People show off skills and knowledge in subtle ways, jockeying for position and advantage. Yet smart people realize that teamwork has to thrive also. If individual assignments get tangled in a scramble to prove who's better than whom, sooner or later everyone will be helping close up shop. Teamwork is vital.

Nehemiah realized that teamwork was crucial to completing the wall. Without it, the Israelites would not only fail to complete the project, but could lose their lives as well. As Nehemiah continues leading the rebuilding of Jerusalem's city walls, he experiences opposition just as he had expected. He also faces poverty and other issues. It's too much for one man to handle alone, so he organizes the workers together to support each other as a team. As you read about Nehemiah, consider carefully his emphasis on teamwork, delegation, and supervision.

Other lessons in this section include how to tackle large tasks; how to loan money; what to do when someone attacks your character; and the importance of courage for leaders.

Read Nehemiah 4:1–7:73

Not only were the workers threatened by enemy attack; they were vulnerable because they were spread out along the wall. To solve this problem, Nehemiah devised a plan of defense that would unite and protect his people—half the men worked while the other half stood guard (Nehemiah 4:16).

Like Nehemiah's workers, Christians need to work together and look out for each other. We may not have to repair a wall to protect ourselves from an enemy army, but we do war against Satan and his forces (see Ephesians 6:12). Our battles may come in the form of persecution from a coworker or relative, or from adverse circumstances—such as losing a job, getting a divorce, or being estranged from a child. Don't cut yourself off from other Christians; instead join together for mutual benefit. You need fellow believers as much as they need you.

Think back to your childhood or adolescence. What is one lesson you have learned from that time? Get out a photo album if it'll help. What guiding principle did you pick up from those earlier years?

The Israelites seem to have forgotten the lessons learned from their past, so they ask Ezra to read the Scriptures to them. As the Levites explain the meaning of the passage, the Israelites weep. Nehemiah reminds the people, however, that this is not a time for weeping but for rejoicing. Let this passage prompt you to reflect on the mighty acts God has done for you and the profound lessons he has taught you over the years.

Read Nehemiah 8:1–10:39

Many prayers and speeches in the Bible include a long summary of Israel's history. The summary of God's work in Nehemiah 9:7-38 reminded the people of their great heritage and God's wonderful promises.

Like the Israelites, we, too, should remember our history. Reviewing the past serves two purposes: (1) it helps us to avoid repeating the mistakes of our past and (2) it shows us the pattern of our spiritual growth. This process, therefore, can strengthen our faith as we remember how God has forgiven us for our sins, and how he has been working in us and through us to make us more like Christ.

Take time to reflect on your personal history, then thank God for what he has done in your life. Learn from your past so that you can live for Christ in the present and become the person God wants you to be in the future.

¹The people assembled again, and this time they fasted and dressed in burlap and sprinkled dust on their heads. ²Those of Israelite descent separated themselves from all foreigners as they confessed their own sins and the sins of their ancestors. ³They remained standing in place for three hours while the Book of the Law of the LORD their God was read aloud to them. Then for three more hours they confessed their sins and worshiped the LORD their God. . . . ¹⁰:²⁸Then the rest of the people— the priests, Levites, gatekeepers, singers, Temple servants, and all who had separated themselves from the pagan people of the land in order to obey the Law of God, . . . ²⁹solemnly promised to carefully follow all the commands, regulations, and decrees of the LORD our Lord.

NEHEMIAH 9:1-3; 10:28-29

¹⁵In those days I saw men of Judah treading out their winepresses on the Sabbath. They were also bringing in grain, loading it on donkeys, and bringing their wine, grapes, figs, and all sorts of produce to Jerusalem to sell on the Sabbath. So I rebuked them for selling their produce on that day. ¹⁶Some men from Tyre, who lived in Jerusalem, were bringing in fish and all kinds of merchandise. They were selling it on the Sabbath to the people of Judah—and in Jerusalem at that! ¹⁷So I confronted the nobles of Judah. "Why are you profaning the Sabbath in this evil way?" I asked. ¹⁸"Wasn't it just this sort of thing that your ancestors did that caused our God to bring all this trouble upon us and our city? Now you are bringing even more wrath upon Israel by permitting the Sabbath to be desecrated in this way!"

NEHEMIAH 13:15-18

The word *leadership* usually evokes thoughts of people with titles and positions. But every person takes up the challenge of leadership from time to time. Have you ever led a group of kids in an activity? a group of adults in singing? a family devotion time? an out-of-town friend through the city? a child through the steps of learning a skill?

Although Nehemiah is a leader by title and position, he is also a leader by example. Nehemiah leads the Israelites in rebuilding the city walls and establishes policies for residents of the city. But he also helps renew the covenant and keeps the Israelites on track with God. Clearly, that is what good leaders should do.

Other lessons in this reading include appropriate kinds of separation; keeping the Sabbath; and dealing with weaknesses.

Read Nehemiah 11:1–13:31

Nehemiah's life story provides many principles of effective leadership that are still valid today: (1) Have a clear purpose and keep evaluating it in light of God's will. (2) Be straightforward and honest. (3) Live above reproach. (4) Be a person of constant prayer, deriving power and wisdom from your contact with God.

We may think of leadership as glamorous, but it can often be lonely, thankless, and filled with pressures to compromise values and standards. Nehemiah was able to accomplish a huge task against incredible odds because he learned that there is no success without risk of failure, no reward without hard work, no opportunity without criticism, and no true leadership without trust in God. The book of Nehemiah is about rebuilding the wall of a great city, but it is also about spiritual renewal, rebuilding a people's dependence on God.

Whatever your leadership position or role, don't lose sight of doing what is most important—being a spiritual leader. Keep your focus on being God's person and doing what he wants.

In baseball, whether you hit the ball out of the park or down the left field line depends a lot on timing—exactly when the bat hits the ball. Internal combustion engines won't even run if the timing is off. And just ask a baker if it matters when he or she takes the bread out of the oven. Timing is everything.

Esther knows this to be true. As her life changes for the better, knowing when to speak and what to say becomes a significant factor in preserving her life and the lives of her people. She learns that God placed her in her important position, and at just the right time, she acts.

As you read this exciting story, learn the lesson of God's perfect timing—and the importance of our well-timed obedience.

These chapters also present two other lessons: watching out for impulsive decisions and fulfilling God's purposes in the task at hand.

Read Esther 1:1–2:23

Esther was a queen. We might imagine that this gave her every right to do as she pleased. In reality, she had virtually no rights and little access to the king. Under the circumstances, it was better for Esther not to reveal her Jewish identity immediately (Esther 2:10). She waited for a better time, a time when she could reveal the truth after the king had been prepared.

While boldness in stating our identity as God's people is our responsibility, at times a good strategy is to keep quiet until we have won the right to be heard. This is especially true when dealing with those in authority over us. We can always let them see the difference God makes in our lives, but we should make sure the timing is right before we speak.

Think of how your life displays your faith to your friends, neighbors, and coworkers. Next, consider when the right time would be to explain your faith to them. When God gives you the opportunity, carefully and lovingly share what you believe (see 1 Peter 3:15).

[16]Esther was taken to King Xerxes at the royal palace in early winter of the seventh year of his reign. [17]And the king loved Esther more than any of the other young women. He was so delighted with her that he set the royal crown on her head and declared her queen instead of Vashti. [18]To celebrate the occasion, he gave a great banquet in Esther's honor for all his nobles and officials, declaring a public holiday for the provinces and giving generous gifts to everyone. [19]Even after all the young women had been transferred to the second harem and Mordecai had become a palace official, [20]Esther continued to keep her family background and nationality a secret. She was still following Mordecai's directions, just as she did when she lived in his home.

ESTHER 2:16-20

[13]Mordecai sent this reply to Esther: . . . [14]"If you keep quiet at a time like this, deliverance and relief for the Jews will arise from some other place, but you and your relatives will die. Who knows if perhaps you were made queen for just such a time as this?" [15]Then Esther sent this reply to Mordecai: [16]"Go and gather together all the Jews of Susa and fast for me. Do not eat or drink for three days, night or day. My maids and I will do the same. And then, though it is against the law, I will go in to see the king. If I must die, I must die." . . . [5:1]On the third day of the fast, Esther put on her royal robes and entered the inner court of the palace, just across from the king's hall. The king was sitting on his royal throne, facing the entrance. [2]When he saw Queen Esther standing there in the inner court, he welcomed her and held out the gold scepter to her.

ESTHER 4:13-16; 5:1-2

What is the risk in telling your deepest secret to a friend, starting a new job, or reconciling with an estranged relative? No matter how shy or bold a person is by nature, he or she must from time to time decide whether to take risks. It's inevitable. Some people find risk taking terrifying. Others think it's exhilarating. For every person the feeling has a lot to do with how successful other risks were. What's the feeling you get when you think of taking risks?

For Esther, risk taking is more terrifying than exhilarating. But in this reading, it is necessary for her survival, even though it may cost Esther her life. Learn from Esther about balancing risky living with doing God's will.

This passage also has other lessons on reverence, arrogance, and courage.

Read Esther 3:1–5:2

Esther risked her life by coming before the king (Esther 4:11–5:2). Her courageous act gives us a model to follow when approaching a difficult or dangerous task. Like Esther, we should (1) *calculate the cost.* Esther realized her life was at stake. (2) *Set priorities.* Esther believed that the safety of the Jewish people was more important than her life. (3) *Prepare.* Esther gathered support, fasted, and prayed. (4) *Determine a course of action and move ahead boldly.* Esther didn't second-guess herself or allow her commitment to lessen.

Do you have to face a hostile audience, confront a friend on a delicate subject, make a crucial decision at work, or talk to your family about changes to be made? When you find yourself in a difficult situation that could cost you your job, a close relationship, your reputation, or even your future—follow Esther's example and take action with confidence. You don't have to be brash or brazen; just move ahead with what needs to be done, quietly confident in God's sovereign control of the outcome.

Plant an azalea bush and hope it doesn't die; pull a dandelion blossom and watch it grow back. That's part of the difference between garden plants and weeds—one requires your careful attention; the other defies it.

The same is true for what people plant in their hearts. As you read this passage, notice the difference between the plants Esther grows in her heart and the weeds Haman doesn't root out of his. Esther's courage and love stand out against the hatred and anger that spreads in Haman's wicked heart. He's not a little pot of dirt with a seed growing in him; he's a concrete slab with jagged, ugly, nameless weeds cracking the surface. These weeds will require more than a once-over with the garden shears.

This conclusion to Esther's story contains other lessons: trusting in God's sovereign control; seeing how sin catches up with us; rewards for obeying God; and using Christian holidays to remember God's acts of goodness.

Read Esther 5:3–10:3

Hatred and bitterness are like weeds with long roots that grow in the heart and corrupt all of life. Haman is a perfect example of a person who let weeds grow in his heart. Haman was so consumed with hatred toward Mordecai that he could not even enjoy the honor of being invited to Esther's party (Esther 5:9).

Hebrews 12:15 warns us to "Watch out that no poisonous root of bitterness grows up to trouble you, corrupting many." Ignoring bitterness, hiding it from others, or making superficial changes in behavior is not enough. If bitterness and unbelief aren't completely removed, they will grow back, making matters worse.

Don't let hatred and bitterness build up in your heart. Like Haman, you will find it corrupting you (Esther 6:13; 7:9-10). If the mere mention of someone's name provokes you to anger, confess to God your bitterness and sin.

[10]Haman gathered together his friends and Zeresh, his wife, [11]and boasted to them about his great wealth and his many children. He bragged about the honors the king had given him and how he had been promoted over all the other nobles and officials. [12]Then Haman added, . . . "Queen Esther invited only me and the king himself to the banquet she prepared for us. And she has invited me to dine with her and the king again tomorrow! . . . [13]But this is all worth nothing as long as I see Mordecai the Jew just sitting there at the palace gate." [14]So Haman's wife, Zeresh, and all his friends suggested, "Set up a sharpened pole that stands seventy-five feet tall, and in the morning ask the king to impale Mordecai on it. When this is done, you can go on your merry way to the banquet with the king." This pleased Haman, and he ordered the pole set up.

ESTHER 5:10-14

¹The members of the heavenly court came again to present themselves before the Lord, and the Accuser, Satan, came with them. ²"Where have you come from?" the Lord asked Satan. Satan answered the Lord, "I have been patrolling the earth, watching everything that's going on." ³Then the Lord asked Satan, "Have you noticed my servant Job? . . . He is blameless—a man of complete integrity. He fears God and stays away from evil. And he has maintained his integrity, even though you urged me to harm him without cause." ⁴Satan replied to the Lord, . . . "A man will give up everything he has to save his life. ⁵But reach out and take away his health, and he will surely curse you to your face!" ⁶"All right, do with him as you please," the Lord said to Satan. "But spare his life." ⁷So Satan left the Lord's presence, and he struck Job with terrible boils.

JOB 2:1-7

Most of us have had fair-weather friends. Their friendship is a mirage. As long as you're rich and carefree, they love you, they stand by your side, and they laugh at your jokes. But as soon as you lose your job or popularity, those fair-weather friends disappear faster than your paycheck. The blows inflicted by such impostors do a lot of damage because they hit you when you're the most vulnerable.

In this reading, Satan thinks that Job's faith in God is that of a fair-weather friend. As long as life is good and things are going Job's way, of course his faith in God is secure. But the loss of loved ones here and a little disease there will make Job's faith extinct—at least that's what Satan thinks.

Also note in this passage who the real enemy is, what believers can expect from him, and how he attacks.

Read Job 1:1–2:13

Satan attacked Job's motives, saying that he was blameless and upright only because he had no reason to turn against God (Job 1:9). Everything was going well for Job. Satan wanted to prove that Job was worshiping God not out of love, but because God had given him so much.

Satan accurately analyzed why many people trust God. They are fair-weather believers, following God only when everything is going well. Adversity destroys such superficial faith. But adversity strengthens real faith by causing believers to dig their roots deeper into God in order to withstand the storms.

How deep does your faith go? Put the roots of your faith down deep into God when life's skies are sunny. Then when the storms come, you will be able to stand strong.

In any personal struggle or tragedy, more advice will come your way than you need or want. Some of it is helpful, but much of it is hurtful.

In this reading, Job receives the latter kind of advice—hurtful. In this first round of discussion between Job and his friends, the friends begin by gently explaining their belief that Job must have sinned to bring so much pain on himself. Job doesn't think so. Read and see who's right.

There are a lot of good points in this passage: despairing in suffering (Job); "messages from God" that aren't (Eliphaz); how to benefit from pain (Eliphaz); being slow to give advice to people who are upset (Job); a lasting source of security (Job); the effects of long-term suffering on our emotional state (Job); insensitivity (Zophar); and hope in life after death (Job).

Read Job 3:1–14:22

Part of what Eliphaz said in Job 4:7-8 is true, and part is false. It is true that those who promote sin and trouble eventually will be punished; it is false that good and innocent people never suffer.

Because we live in a fallen world, those who love God and obey his commands are not necessarily immune to suffering. Although suffering is not a pleasant experience, we should try to have a joyful attitude when we go through it, knowing that it will be used by God to transform our character to be more like Christ (see James 1:2-4). In addition, we should look at suffering as a test of our faithfulness to Christ, and we should strive to rely on his grace to pull us through these difficult times.

¹Eliphaz the Temanite replied to Job: . . . ⁸"My experience shows that those who plant trouble and cultivate evil will harvest the same. ⁹A breath from God destroys them. They vanish in a blast of his anger. ¹⁰The lion roars and the wildcat snarls, but the teeth of strong lions will be broken. ¹¹The fierce lion will starve for lack of prey, and the cubs of the lioness will be scattered. ¹²This truth was given to me in secret, as though whispered in my ear. ¹³It came to me in a disturbing vision at night, when people are in a deep sleep. ¹⁴Fear gripped me, and my bones trembled. ¹⁵A spirit swept past my face, and my hair stood on end. ¹⁶The spirit stopped, but I couldn't see its shape. There was a form before my eyes. In the silence I heard a voice say, ¹⁷"Can a mortal be innocent before God? Can anyone be pure before the Creator?'"

JOB 4:1, 8-17

If you are struggling with a painful illness or sorrow, don't be quick to blame yourself for your suffering. Instead, rely on God and his goodness. Ask him to teach you and to lead you through it.

[1]Job spoke again: . . . [9]"God hates me and angrily tears me apart. He snaps his teeth at me and pierces me with his eyes. [10]People jeer and laugh at me. They slap my cheek in contempt. A mob gathers against me. [11]God has handed me over to sinners. He has tossed me into the hands of the wicked. [12]I was living quietly until he shattered me. He took me by the neck and broke me in pieces. Then he set me up as his target, [13]and now his archers surround me. His arrows pierce me without mercy. The ground is wet with my blood. [14]Again and again he smashes against me, charging at me like a warrior. [15]I wear burlap to show my grief. My pride lies in the dust. [16]My eyes are red with weeping; dark shadows circle my eyes. [17]Yet I have done no wrong, and my prayer is pure."

JOB 16:1, 9-17

What do you most want from your friends? Think especially of your times of need, when you're emotionally down, defeated, confused, or vulnerable. What would you want your friends to do at times like that?

In the second round of discussion between Job and his friends, Job indirectly lists the ways in which his friends could comfort him. Unfortunately, they don't take the hint and, instead, go at him even harder. Some friends they are! As you read this passage, learn how *not* to relate to your friends in need.

Other lessons here include finding real wisdom; being defensive (Bildad); and having confidence in God (Job).

Read Job 15:1–21:34

Job's friends were supposed to be comforting him in his grief. Instead they condemned him for causing his own suffering (Job 16:1–17:16). Job began his second reply to Eliphaz by calling him and his friends "miserable comforters" (16:2).

Job's words reveal several ways to become a better comforter to those in pain: (1) don't talk just for the sake of talking; (2) don't sermonize by giving pat answers; (3) don't accuse or criticize; (4) put yourself in the other person's place; and (5) offer help and encouragement.

The next time someone close to you is suffering, try Job's suggestions to comfort him or her, knowing that these suggestions were given by a person who needed great comfort. The best comforters are those who know something about personal suffering.

Imagine that you've been framed for a crime. You feel frantic because no one believes your story. You're embarrassed because your name has been muddied. Despite your frustration and gloom, you decide not to give up and determine to fight harder.

In trying to explain why Job is suffering, his friends have falsely accused him of sinning. Job has denied that this is true, but the friends don't believe that Job is innocent—there is too much circumstantial evidence against him. Job isn't ready to give in yet, so he digs in his heels and defends his innocence.

Is Job innocent? Judge for yourself and learn from his defense.

See these other lessons as well: being careful in applying God's commands and moral standards to others (Eliphaz); showing compassion rather than giving advice (Job); and attacking others (Bildad).

Read Job 22:1–31:40

In the middle of all the accusations, Job declared that he was not a sinner and that his conscience was clear (Job 27:6). How could he make this claim? Job was not claiming to be perfect, neither was he belittling his need for God's redemption. He was simply saying that he had lived a righteous life before God (1:1). As a result, his conscience *was* clear.

Outward circumstances are not always an accurate indicator of a person's relationship with God. Some people who are blessed with health, power, or wealth are not righteous (see Matthew 5:45). Conversely, some people who are sick, poor, or powerless *are* righteous in God's eyes. Job's friends were wrong to assume that his suffering was a result of sin.

20"I cry to you, O God, but you don't answer. I stand before you, but you don't even look. 21You have become cruel toward me. You use your power to persecute me. 22You throw me into the whirlwind and destroy me in the storm. 23And I know you are sending me to my death—the destination of all who live. 24Surely no one would turn against the needy when they cry for help in their trouble. 25Did I not weep for those in trouble? Was I not deeply grieved for the needy? 26So I looked for good, but evil came instead. I waited for the light, but darkness fell. 27My heart is troubled and restless. Days of suffering torment me. 28I walk in gloom, without sunlight. I stand in the public square and cry for help. 29Instead, I am considered a brother to jackals and a companion to owls. 30My skin has turned dark, and my bones burn with fever."

JOB 30:20-30

We must be careful not to make the same mistake that Job's friends made. We can't claim to have sinless lives, but we *can* claim forgiven lives. When we confess our sins to God he forgives us. Then we, too, can live with a clear conscience (see 1 John 1:9).

Be slow to judge others. And make it your goal to keep a clear conscience before God.

¹Elihu said: . . . ⁵"Look up into the sky, and see the clouds high above you. ⁶If you sin, how does that affect God? Even if you sin again and again, what effect will it have on him? ⁷If you are good, is this some great gift to him? What could you possibly give him? ⁸No, your sins affect only people like yourself, and your good deeds also affect only humans. ⁹People cry out when they are oppressed. They groan beneath the power of the mighty. ¹⁰Yet they don't ask, 'Where is God my Creator, the one who gives songs in the night? ¹¹Where is the one who makes us smarter than the animals and wiser than the birds of the sky?' ¹²And when they cry out, God does not answer because of their pride. ¹³But it is wrong to say God doesn't listen, to say the Almighty isn't concerned. ¹⁴You say you can't see him, but he will bring justice if you will only wait."

JOB 35:1, 5-14

A child will question the actions of the wisest, most loving parent. "Why must I brush my teeth?" "Why do I have to eat my vegetables?" Wise parents, whether they try to explain or not, insist that a child do what is best for them. They understand far more about the bigger picture than kids do.

Job has been asking *why* for a while now, and no one has been able to give him a satisfactory answer. But one person hasn't spoken up yet. That person is Elihu, the youngest "comforter" of the group. He has held his tongue until now because of his age, but he, too, is not satisfied with the answers given by Bildad, Eliphaz, and Zophar. Elihu rightly says that Job's friends have been wrong to accuse Job of sin, and that Job has been wrong to defend his goodness.

Look for other lessons in the way these men talk: the importance of speaking at the right time; applying truth; and giving advice to others.

Read Job 32:1–37:24

It's natural to want to know what's happening in our lives because being informed brings a sense of security.

Elihu claimed to have the answer for Job's biggest question, "Why doesn't God tell me what is happening?" Elihu told Job that God was trying to answer him, but he was not listening. Elihu misjudged both Job and God on this point. If God were to answer all our questions, we would not be adequately tested. What if God had said, "Job, Satan's going to test you and afflict you, but in the end you'll be healed and get everything back"? Job's greatest test was not the pain, but that he did not know *why* he was suffering.

Learn to trust in God who is good; not in the goodness of life.

Educators know that much of a person's ability to learn a particular skill depends on *readiness*—having developed the mental tools to learn. At the point of readiness, learning is easy, even effortless. Until then, the student simply isn't ready.

Job is not ready to understand the reasons for his suffering. Despite his well thought out arguments and reasonable appeals, he does not have the mental capacity to understand God's ways.

The attacks of Job's friends have only reinforced Job's belief that he never deserved to suffer in the first place. This belief has made him bitterly uncomfortable with his situation. He wants to know why God has treated him so badly without explaining his reasons or purpose. God finally speaks, saying (in effect), "Do I answer to you? You wouldn't understand even if I explained it to you. You need to trust me."

Other lessons are here for us relate to that idea—finding the answer in God and realizing that God's understanding is beyond our grasp.

Read Job 38:1–41:34

Out of a whirlwind, God spoke to Job (Job 38:1). He didn't answer any of Job's questions. Instead, God used Job's ignorance of the earth's natural order to reveal his ignorance of God's moral order. If Job did not understand the workings of God's physical creation, how could he possibly understand God's mind and character? There is no standard or criterion higher than God himself by which to judge. God is the standard. Our option is to submit to his authority and rest in his care.

¹Then the LORD answered Job from the whirlwind: ²"Who is this that questions my wisdom with such ignorant words? ³Brace yourself like a man, because I have some questions for you, and you must answer them. ⁴Where were you when I laid the foundations of the earth? Tell me, if you know so much. ⁵Who determined its dimensions and stretched out the surveying line? ⁶What supports its foundations, and who laid its cornerstone ⁷as the morning stars sang together and all the angels shouted for joy? ⁸Who kept the sea inside its boundaries as it burst from the womb, ⁹and as I clothed it with clouds and wrapped it in thick darkness? . . . ¹²Have you ever commanded the morning to appear and caused the dawn to rise in the east? . . . ¹⁹Where does light come from, and where does darkness go? ²⁰Can you take each to its home?"

JOB 38:1-9, 12, 19-20

¹Then Job replied to the LORD: ²"I know that you can do anything, and no one can stop you. ³You asked, 'Who is this that questions my wisdom with such ignorance?' It is I—and I was talking about things I knew nothing about, things far too wonderful for me. ⁴You said, 'Listen and I will speak! I have some questions for you, and you must answer them.' ⁵I had only heard about you before, but now I have seen you with my own eyes. ⁶I take back everything I said, and I sit in dust and ashes to show my repentance."

Job 42:1-6

There are times when surrender makes more sense than the bravest fight. Consider three examples: fighting a war when your side has been decimated, campaigning for a candidate after he or she has lost the race, and arguing with a spouse when he or she is right and you're wrong. No honor comes from resisting at times like these.

In this reading, Job admits defeat and surrenders to God. This is not the end of Job, however, because God has plans for Job's future.

This concludes the story of Job. God has proven his point and Job's reply is an admission of defeat. It's the good kind of surrender. Don't feel sorry for Job—get in line yourself.

Other lessons in this passage include not judging others or interpreting their circumstances as a judgment on them; praying for our enemies; and the rewards of following God in trust.

Read Job 42:1-17

Throughout the book, Job's friends had asked him to admit his sin and ask for forgiveness. Eventually Job did indeed repent. Ironically, Job's repentance was not the kind called for by his friends. He did not ask for forgiveness for committing secret sins, but for questioning God's sovereignty and justice. Job repented of his attitude and acknowledged God's great power and perfect justice (Job 42:1-6).

We sin when we angrily ask, "If God is in control, how could he let this happen?" Because we are locked into time and are unable to see beyond today, we cannot know the reasons for everything that happens. Job openly and honestly faced God and admitted that he was the one who had been foolish.

Are you using what you can't understand as an excuse for your lack of trust? Admit to God that you don't have enough faith to trust him. True faith begins in such humility. Will you trust God with your unanswered questions?

How well do you sleep when everything seems to be going wrong in your life? Do you lie awake all night worrying about the problems you'll face in the morning?

In this reading, David reveals his secret for sleeping through the night during an overwhelming crisis. David wrote Psalm 3 when he was on the run from his son, Absalom, who was bent on usurping his father's throne. Absalom orchestrated a slick revolt against David, and pretty soon David was running for his life. Wouldn't that make *you* sleepless? But David found a cure. As you read Psalm 3, watch how David praises the aspects of God's character that give every believer cause to sleep well.

The other psalms in this section have other lessons if you're willing to pursue them: good reasons to live God's way (Psalm 1); God's ultimate rule (Psalm 2); and God's protection and peace (Psalm 4).

Read Psalms 1:1–4:8

Sleep does not come easily during a crisis. Most people toss and turn with the anxiety, thinking about the problem. David may have had sleepless nights when Absalom rebelled and gathered an army to kill him. But he slept peacefully, even during the rebellion (Psalm 3:5). What made the difference? He knew that the Lord was watching over him.

It is easier to sleep well when we trust God to control our circumstances. The next time you lie awake at night worrying about circumstances you cannot change, pour out your concerns to him until he brings the sleep you need. Ask him to intervene. And thank him for being in control.

¹O Lord, I have so many enemies; so many are against me. ²So many are saying, "God will never rescue him!" ³But you, O Lord, are a shield around me; you are my glory, the one who holds my head high. ⁴I cried out to the Lord, and he answered me from his holy mountain. ⁵I lay down and slept, yet I woke up in safety, for the Lord was watching over me. ⁶I am not afraid of ten thousand enemies who surround me on every side. ⁷Arise, O Lord! Rescue me, my God! Slap all my enemies in the face! Shatter the teeth of the wicked! ⁸Victory comes from you, O Lord. May you bless your people.

PSALM 3:1-8

¹I come to you for protection, O Lord my God. Save me from my persecutors—rescue me! ²If you don't, they will maul me like a lion, tearing me to pieces with no one to rescue me. ³O Lord my God, if I have done wrong or am guilty of injustice, ⁴if I have betrayed a friend or plundered my enemy without cause, ⁵then let my enemies capture me. Let them trample me into the ground and drag my honor in the dust. ⁶Arise, O Lord, in anger! Stand up against the fury of my enemies! Wake up, my God, and bring justice! ⁷Gather the nations before you. Rule over them from on high. ⁸The Lord judges the nations. Declare me righteous, O Lord, for I am innocent, O Most High! ⁹End the evil of those who are wicked, and defend the righteous. For you look deep within the mind and heart, O righteous God.

PSALM 7:1-9

Being falsely accused or slandered is inevitable, especially if you are living your life for God. But how should you respond to such an injustice? Should you defend yourself and fight back? Or should you turn the other cheek?

David knew how to respond to injustice. Psalm 7 reveals his response and solution for dealing with unjust people. David knows that restoring justice is God's responsibility, so he submits a request rather than taking matters into his own hands. Learn from David how to respond when you're angry about an injustice.

Other psalms in this section tell us that God defends us against slander (Psalm 5); God rescues us when we're in trouble (Psalm 6); and God the Creator cares for us (Psalm 8).

Read Psalms 5:1–8:9

David wrote Psalm 7 in response to the personal attacks of those who claimed that he was trying to kill Saul and seize the throne (see 1 Samuel 24:9-11). Instead of taking matters into his own hands and striking back, David entrusted himself to God and cried out to him for justice. David did not have the authority to enact justice himself, so he did not try.

That should be our response. Whenever we are slandered, we should pray, not slander back; whenever we are insulted, we should pray, not give a retort. God says, "I will take revenge; I will pay them back" (Romans 12:19; see also Deuteronomy 32:35; Hebrews 10:30).

The next time someone attacks you, ask God to take over your case, bring justice, and protect your reputation. Only he can deal justly with the offender.

As much as we favor honesty, falsehood can be terribly convenient. If you want to impress someone, a *slight* exaggeration of your various strengths and accomplishments may do the trick. Or if you want to get in the good graces of a person who has influence or status, flattery comes in handy. When you do something wrong, you know how natural it is to cover it up. Telling the truth can take conscious effort.

The words of Psalm 12 verify this fact. They also reveal that lying was just as much a problem in David's time as it is today. But in all the deceit, there is hope—God is in control and will deal justly with those who make a lifestyle out of lying. What a great lesson to learn!

Other psalms in this reading contain encouraging news about how God responds to our cries for help (Psalm 9); his awareness of injustice (Psalm 10); and his sovereignty over wicked people (Psalm 11).

Read Psalms 9:1–12:8

It seems as though each day we are bombarded with news stories about violence and perversity. This may lead us to think that lying and other forms of deceit are relatively harmless and less sinful. Psalm 12 makes it perfectly clear, however, that God does not overlook lies, flattery, or boasting. He hates all kinds of deceit and commands us not to use them (see Exodus 20:16).

Deception comes from a desire to cover up what should not be hidden. In this, our tongue can be our greatest enemy. Though small, the tongue can do great damage (see James 3:5).

¹Help, O Lord, for the godly are fast disappearing! The faithful have vanished from the earth! ²Neighbors lie to each other, speaking with flattering lips and deceitful hearts. ³May the Lord cut off their flattering lips and silence their boastful tongues. ⁴They say, "We will lie to our hearts' content. Our lips are our own—who can stop us?" ⁵The Lord replies, "I have seen violence done to the helpless, and I have heard the groans of the poor. Now I will rise up to rescue them, as they have longed for me to do." ⁶The Lord's promises are pure, like silver refined in a furnace, purified seven times over. ⁷Therefore, Lord, we know you will protect the oppressed, preserving them forever from this lying generation, ⁸even though the wicked strut about, and evil is praised throughout the land.

PSALM 12:1-8

Watch how you use your tongue. When you are tempted to deceive someone, remember that God hates lies. Strive to make your speech entirely truthful all the time for God's glory.

¹Keep me safe, O God, for I have come to you for refuge. ²I said to the LORD, "You are my Master! Every good thing I have comes from you." ³The godly people in the land are my true heroes! I take pleasure in them! . . . ⁵LORD, you alone are my inheritance, my cup of blessing. You guard all that is mine. ⁶The land you have given me is a pleasant land. What a wonderful inheritance! ⁷I will bless the LORD who guides me; even at night my heart instructs me. ⁸I know the LORD is always with me. I will not be shaken, for he is right beside me. ⁹No wonder my heart is glad, and I rejoice. My body rests in safety. ¹⁰For you will not leave my soul among the dead or allow your holy one to rot in the grave. ¹¹You will show me the way of life, granting me the joy of your presence and the pleasures of living with you forever.

PSALM 16:1-3, 5-11

With what kind of people do you hang out? How would you describe your friends? Are they a good influence on you? Or do you do things when you're with them that make you feel uncomfortable?

Psalm 16 shows us the people with whom we should keep company—and it's not the popular or influential crowd. In this psalm we see that David seeks out a certain kind of person—the kind we should get to know.

In other psalms, we find help with several dilemmas: what to do when God doesn't answer prayers of distress (Psalm 13); how to respond when people deny that God exists (Psalm 14); and how to live a life that no one can fault (Psalm 15).

Read Psalms 13:1–16:11

Some people try to impress their friends by name-dropping. If they have met a famous person, for example, they may casually mention this fact to others to enhance their status. Others spend time with certain people to bolster their image. But truly noble people don't do that. They don't try to become famous or gain recognition; they strive to live as God desires.

Beware of temptations to seek someone's company solely to enhance your status. And remember that although hanging out with the wrong crowd can be fun at first, if you desire to please God, the fun you have will soon turn to spiritual conflict. Instead, like David, seek the company of those who can build you up spiritually—those who are committed to God and have the right perspective on life (Psalm 16:3).

One night you get a call from the Christmas pageant chairperson at church. The chairperson wants you to help out this year. You know that you don't have time, but you feel too guilty to say no. After hanging up, you feel guilty for taking on a responsibility for which you really don't have time.

Psalm 19 deals with guilt in a constructive way. Here, David sees his guilt and talks to God about it. As you read this passage, look for the right way to deal with guilt.

Other psalms in this reading teach about crying to God for justice (Psalm 17); asking God for help and strength against evil (Psalm 18); and trusting in God for strength when facing challenges (Psalm 20).

Read Psalms 17:1–20:9

Guilt plagues most people. We worry that we may have committed a sin without knowing it, done something good but with selfish intentions, failed to put our best efforts into an important task, or brushed off a significant responsibility. Guilt isn't always bad, however—it can alert us to changes we need to make in our behavior or beliefs. But at the same time, we should be careful not to let our guilt cripple us or make us afraid to act.

We should follow David's example by asking God to "cleanse" us of our "hidden faults" and keep us from deliberately doing wrong. For when we confess our sins, we can take comfort in the fact that our fellowship with God is restored and our conscience cleared (see 1 John 1:9). We no longer have a reason to feel guilty.

Take care of your *real* guilt before God by confessing your sins to him. Then thank God that he has forgiven you.

⁷The decrees of the LORD are trustworthy, making wise the simple. ⁸The commandments of the LORD are right, bringing joy to the heart. The commands of the LORD are clear, giving insight for living. ⁹Reverence for the LORD is pure, lasting forever. The laws of the LORD are true; each one is fair. ¹⁰They are more desirable than gold, even the finest gold. They are sweeter than honey, even honey dripping from the comb. ¹¹They are a warning to your servant, a great reward for those who obey them. ¹²How can I know all the sins lurking in my heart? Cleanse me from these hidden faults. ¹³Keep your servant from deliberate sins! Don't let them control me. Then I will be free of guilt and innocent of great sin. ¹⁴May the words of my mouth and the meditation of my heart be pleasing to you, O LORD, my rock and my redeemer.

PSALM 19:7-14

¹The Lord is my shepherd; I have all that I need. ²He lets me rest in green meadows; he leads me beside peaceful streams. ³He renews my strength. He guides me along right paths, bringing honor to his name. ⁴Even when I walk through the darkest valley, I will not be afraid, for you are close beside me. Your rod and your staff protect and comfort me. ⁵You prepare a feast for me in the presence of my enemies. You honor me by anointing my head with oil. My cup overflows with blessings. ⁶Surely your goodness and unfailing love will pursue me all the days of my life, and I will live in the house of the Lord forever.

PSALM 23:1-6

Ask children about their favorite pets and you're likely to get a short list: dogs, cats, hamsters, fish, gerbils, and rabbits.

The parallels between our relationship to God and that of a child to his or her pet hold many lessons for us. Psalm 23, while not about pets in particular, portrays our relationship with God as that of sheep to their shepherd. Although being compared to sheep isn't necessarily flattering, God's love for us becomes more concrete and real as we see how he cares for us.

The other psalms in this reading contain prayers about experiencing victory in battle (Psalm 21); finding joy in suffering (Psalm 22); and being a good owner (Psalm 24).

Read Psalms 21:1–24:10

In portraying the Lord as a shepherd (Psalm 23:1), David wrote from his own experience because he had spent his early years caring for sheep (see 1 Samuel 16:10-11). Sheep depend completely on their shepherd—good shepherds make sure that their sheep get plenty of green pasture as well as shelter from the elements and wild animals. When David wrote, "The Lord is my shepherd," he showed us that God, like a shepherd, cares and provides for us much the way that human shepherds care and provide for their sheep.

In the New Testament, Jesus is called the good shepherd (see John 10:11); the great Shepherd (see Hebrews 13:20); and the head Shepherd (see 1 Peter 5:4). What a great truth that God cares for us like this!

Whenever you doubt God's love and care for you, reread Psalm 23 and remember how God, your Shepherd, cares for you.

Waiting can feel like torture when you're afraid. David wrote Psalm 27 at a time when he was terribly afraid, but he didn't panic. Instead, he called upon the Lord and pleaded his case before him. Then he waited patiently for the Lord to rescue him. Any scared person knows that fear can cause people to make hasty, unwise decisions, and cause them to act before they're ready. Fear can make people impatient and reckless. As you read this psalm, learn from David's example about taking your fears to God.

The three other psalms in this reading also have something to say about times of fear: when you're afraid of losing your honor (Psalm 25); your reputation (Psalm 26); or even your life (Psalm 28).

Read Psalms 25:1–28:9

David's men wanted him to kill Saul. David knew that it was not his job—the fulfillment of God's promise would come about in God's own timing. So David placed his trust in God and waited for the Lord, despite his fear (Psalm 27:14). As it turns out, David had to wait fourteen years before being crowned king.

Waiting for God takes effort. It may seem as though God has refused to answer our prayers or doesn't feel the urgency of our situation. But God knows much more than we do. Lamentations 3:24-26 urges us to hope in and wait for the Lord because often God uses waiting to refresh, renew, and teach us.

David trusted God to do what was right. Trust in God's timing and make use of your times of waiting by discovering what God may be trying to teach you.

¹The Lord is my light and my salvation—so why should I be afraid? The Lord is my fortress, protecting me from danger, so why should I tremble? ²When evil people come to devour me, when my enemies and foes attack me, they will stumble and fall. ³Though a mighty army surrounds me, my heart will not be afraid. Even if I am attacked, I will remain confident. ⁴The one thing I ask of the Lord— the thing I seek most—is to live in the house of the Lord all the days of my life, delighting in the Lord's perfections and meditating in his Temple. ⁵For he will conceal me there when troubles come; he will hide me in his sanctuary. He will place me out of reach on a high rock. ⁶Then I will hold my head high above my enemies who surround me. At his sanctuary I will offer sacrifices with shouts of joy, singing and praising the Lord with music.

PSALM 27:1-6

¹O LORD, I have come to you for protection; don't let me be disgraced. Save me, for you do what is right. ²Turn your ear to listen to me; rescue me quickly. Be my rock of protection, a fortress where I will be safe. ³You are my rock and my fortress. For the honor of your name, lead me out of this danger. ⁴Pull me from the trap my enemies set for me, for I find protection in you alone. ⁵I entrust my spirit into your hand. Rescue me, LORD, for you are a faithful God. . . . ¹⁴But I am trusting you, O LORD, saying, "You are my God!" ¹⁵My future is in your hands. Rescue me from those who hunt me down relentlessly.

PSALM 31:1-5, 14-15

Thirty seconds of bungee jumping requires more trust than many people have in God over a lifetime. People entrust their lives to a total stranger and an unknown piece of equipment—all for a few seconds of excitement.

Unlike many people today, David knows where to place his trust—and it isn't in the hands of strangers. In Psalm 31, David unloads anguish over his circumstances—feeling alone, helpless, and threatened. His source of hope, however, is that he knows he's in good hands.

Trust is the theme of the psalms in this reading: trusting God to give us peace and strength through life's storms (Psalm 29); trusting ourselves to God (Psalm 30); and trusting God to free us from guilt (Psalm 32).

Read Psalms 29:1–32:11

David wrote many psalms about the attacks of his enemies and the utter ruin they made of his peace of mind. Psalm 31 is one of them. David was so plagued by opponents that he felt he was "dying from grief" (Psalm 31:10). Yet in the same prayer he added the words, "I entrust my spirit into your hand" (31:5), showing that he had complete trust in God.

Jesus used this phrase as he was dying on the cross—showing his absolute dependence on God the Father (see Luke 23:46). Stephen expressed a similar sentiment as he was being stoned to death (see Acts 7:59), confident that he was passing from God's earthly care to God's eternal care.

Having faith in God—really trusting him—risks nothing. That's why we can safely commit our possessions, our families, and our jobs to God.

If you were to make a wish list, what would you include? Would you write down what you truly have a great need for, or just what you crave? Life, after all, isn't fair, and few people have enough money for all that they want.

Psalm 34 deals with needs and the wonderful way that God provides for them. Do you need something? Follow David's advice—his observation from his own experience is a truth more durable than any earthly goods.

There are many other things to praise God for in this group of psalms as well, such as the protection he gives us from death (Psalm 33) and unjust enemies (Psalm 35), and for his great goodness (Psalm 36).

Read Psalms 33:1–36:12

David said that "those who trust in the LORD will lack no good thing" (Psalm 34:10). Can this be true? How can it be that God's people lack *nothing* good?

God knows what we truly need. Even though many Christians live in poverty and endure hardship, God gives them the spiritual nourishment they need in order to live for him. This is what David is saying here—if we have a relationship with God, we have all we need, despite our circumstances.

If you feel you don't have everything you need, ask yourself several questions: (1) Is this really a need? (2) Is this really good for me? (3) Is this the best time for me to have what I want? Even if you answer yes to all three questions, remember that God's thoughts are completely different from yours (see Isaiah 55:8). He may want you to learn that you need *him* more than you think.

¹I will praise the LORD at all times. I will constantly speak his praises. ²I will boast only in the LORD; let all who are helpless take heart. ³Come, let us tell of the LORD's greatness; let us exalt his name together. ⁴I prayed to the LORD, and he answered me. He freed me from all my fears. ⁵Those who look to him for help will be radiant with joy; no shadow of shame will darken their faces. ⁶In my desperation I prayed, and the LORD listened; he saved me from all my troubles. ⁷For the angel of the LORD is a guard; he surrounds and defends all who fear him. ⁸Taste and see that the LORD is good. Oh, the joys of those who take refuge in him! ⁹Fear the LORD, you his godly people, for those who fear him will have all they need. ¹⁰Even strong young lions sometimes go hungry, but those who trust in the LORD will lack no good thing.

PSALM 34:1-10

¹Don't worry about the wicked or envy those who do wrong. ²For like grass, they soon fade away. Like spring flowers, they soon wither. ³Trust in the LORD and do good. Then you will live safely in the land and prosper. ⁴Take delight in the LORD, and he will give you your heart's desires. ⁵Commit everything you do to the LORD. Trust him, and he will help you. ⁶He will make your innocence radiate like the dawn, and the justice of your cause will shine like the noonday sun. ⁷Be still in the presence of the LORD, and wait patiently for him to act. Don't worry about evil people who prosper or fret about their wicked schemes. ⁸Stop being angry! Turn from your rage! Do not lose your temper—it only leads to harm. ⁹For the wicked will be destroyed, but those who trust in the LORD will possess the land.

PSALM 37:1-9

Sometimes it seems as if wicked people enjoy the most fulfilling lives. They live in luxury, get what they want, and commit awful deeds to maintain their lifestyle. It's very difficult not to look at these people and feel envious. Have you envied people who have little or no concern for God?

Psalm 37 lists a whole host of cures for envy. Focus your attention on verses 3 through 6, the cures that head up the list. Also keep a look out for other cures in this psalm—they're delightful!

As you read these psalms, note also the outcome of confessing sin (Psalm 38); the benefits of waiting for God's timing (Psalm 40); and how to pray when you feel sick or abandoned (Psalm 41).

Read Psalms 37:1–41:13

Taking delight in the Lord is the cure for envy. David urged us to do this and to commit to him everything we have and do (Psalm 37:3-6). But how does a person "take delight in the LORD" (37:4)? To *delight* means to enjoy, so to take delight in God means to enjoy his presence, his company, and his will. Our goal should be to enjoy God, to want what God wants, to seek his presence, to enjoy his company.

Review any goals you have for your life. Do they match what God wants for you? Make it your goal to take delight in God today. Change your desires and goals to match his.

A human being can go without food for about thirty to forty days, but he or she can go only about three days without water. Extreme thirst will put you on a single-minded hunt for water. That makes *thirst* a good word for describing deep cravings, doesn't it?

In Psalm 42 we see a person thirsting for God, craving his presence, and still feeling alone or even abandoned by him. This person has longed for God's presence and found no ready source of relief. As you read this psalm, find, with the author, the answer to your own thirst.

Also, find hope in times of discouragement (Psalm 43); help when feeling weary and defeated (Psalm 44); and rejoicing in God's gift of marriage (Psalm 45).

Read Psalms 42:1–45:17

Do you ever feel alone in your faith? There come times in life when we thirst for God, weep for his help, or even endure ridicule for our faith while waiting for him to answer our prayers (Psalm 42:1-3). We want desperately to feel God's presence or to have some other tangible sign of his help and support. Times like these can lead to depression and discouragement for any Christian.

The writer of Psalm 42 discovered a remedy for these spiritually dry times. He remembered God's great blessings on his life. He realized that although God seemed silent, he was there and was worthy to be praised (42:4-5). He soaked in God's beautiful creation (42:6). He realized that he was never adrift from God's love (42:7-8). He faithfully expected God to act (42:11).

¹As the deer longs for streams of water, so I long for you, O God. ²I thirst for God, the living God. When can I go and stand before him? ³Day and night I have only tears for food, while my enemies continually taunt me, saying, "Where is this God of yours?" ⁴My heart is breaking as I remember how it used to be: I walked among the crowds of worshipers, leading a great procession to the house of God, singing for joy and giving thanks amid the sound of a great celebration! ⁵Why am I discouraged? Why is my heart so sad? I will put my hope in God! I will praise him again—my Savior and ⁶my God! Now I am deeply discouraged, but I will remember you—even from distant Mount Hermon, the source of the Jordan, from the land of Mount Mizar.

PSALM 42:1-6

¹God is our refuge and strength, always ready to help in times of trouble. ²So we will not fear when earthquakes come and the mountains crumble into the sea. ³Let the oceans roar and foam. Let the mountains tremble as the waters surge! . . . ⁸Come, see the glorious works of the LORD: See how he brings destruction upon the world. ⁹He causes wars to end throughout the earth. He breaks the bow and snaps the spear; he burns the shields with fire. ¹⁰"Be still, and know that I am God! I will be honored by every nation. I will be honored throughout the world." ¹¹The LORD of Heaven's Armies is here among us; the God of Israel is our fortress.

PSALM 46:1-3, 8-11

In metropolitan areas, you might find a sliver of quiet in the early morning hours; to get a taste of true silence, however, you have to go to more rural areas. Have you ever heard the difference? True silence contains no background noise at all. No one is driving by, shouting, or honking, and there is no hum and buzz of a thousand little noises in the distance. There are few places left on earth where you can truly experience silence.

Psalm 46 invites us to sample some silence. Read and consider it, even if you value the hustle and bustle of the big city. Silence allows us to meditate on God's goodness and the other lessons in this reading, such as his lordship over the whole world (Psalm 47) and his role as our guide and protector (Psalm 48).

Read Psalms 46:1–49:20

God is almighty and all-powerful. Psalm 46 says "God's voice thunders, and the earth melts" (46:6). God has far greater power than even the most powerful forces of nature (46:2-3) or of humankind (46:6, 9). How fitting, then, for us to show him some respect—to stand quietly before him, reverently honoring him and his power and majesty (46:10).

With life's busyness and burdens weighing us down, why should we take the time to stand still? What is the benefit of being silent before God? Spending time in silence is an opportunity to forget about all of the worldly distractions that keep us from entering into God's presence. It's an opportunity to focus on God's goodness, mercy, might, and power.

Take time each day to experience silence, and use it to ponder the awesome greatness of God. Be still and silent before God so that you can exalt him. Let silence give you the opportunity to worship.

Psalm 51 is the result of a tough—but right—decision. Here, David confesses his sins in order to restore his broken relationship with God. The other psalms in this reading also involve tough decisions about how we live and relate to God. The relationship we have with God can suffer ups and downs just as our human relationships can, and this involves confession and reconciliation.

Other lessons in this section of Scripture include being sincere (Psalm 50); having confidence that God will defeat all evil in his own time (Psalm 52); and admitting our need for God to save us from sin (Psalm 53).

Read Psalms 50:1–53:6

Has sin ever driven a wedge between you and God, making him seem distant? David's sins destroyed his ability to enjoy anything, even God's salvation (Psalm 51:3-17). David was confronted with his adultery with Bathsheba, could not deny it, and sought to repent. In his prayer he confessed his sin and cried, "Restore to me the joy of your salvation" (51:12).

God wants us to be obedient to his Word so that we can have a close relationship with him. But when we disobey God and try to cover up our sin rather than confess it, we hurt our relationship with him, driving the wedge between us and God even further. Confess any sin that stands between you and God. You may still have to face the consequences, as David did, but God will give back the joy of your relationship with him.

⁷Purify me from my sins, and I will be clean; wash me, and I will be whiter than snow. ⁸Oh, give me back my joy again; you have broken me—now let me rejoice. ⁹Don't keep looking at my sins. Remove the stain of my guilt. ¹⁰Create in me a clean heart, O God. Renew a loyal spirit within me. ¹¹Do not banish me from your presence, and don't take your Holy Spirit from me. ¹²Restore to me the joy of your salvation, and make me willing to obey you. ¹³Then I will teach your ways to rebels, and they will return to you. . . . ¹⁶You do not desire a sacrifice, or I would offer one. You do not want a burnt offering. ¹⁷The sacrifice you desire is a broken spirit. You will not reject a broken and repentant heart, O God.

PSALM 51:7-13, 16-17

[1] O God, have mercy on me, for people are hounding me. My foes attack me all day long. [2] I am constantly hounded by those who slander me, and many are boldly attacking me. [3] But when I am afraid, I will put my trust in you. [4] I praise God for what he has promised. I trust in God, so why should I be afraid? What can mere mortals do to me? [5] They are always twisting what I say; they spend their days plotting to harm me. [6] They come together to spy on me—watching my every step, eager to kill me. [7] Don't let them get away with their wickedness; in your anger, O God, bring them down. [8] You keep track of all my sorrows. You have collected all my tears in your bottle. You have recorded each one in your book. [9] My enemies will retreat when I call to you for help. This I know: God is on my side!

PSALM 56:1-9

Everyone is afraid of something:

gangs

disease

the future

a spouse

the government

failure

speaking in public

Have you ever been stopped at a traffic light and seen one of those bumper stickers that reads "NO FEAR"? But the fact that the driver isn't running the red light reveals the truth.

Psalm 56 deals with fear. Although the author, David, was a mighty warrior, he was not immune to this emotion—especially when his enemies were out to get him. Fortunately, David found a cure for his fear and recorded it in this psalm.

Other psalms in this reading contain invaluable truths about God as well as important lessons on prayer.

Read Psalms 54:1–56:13

What could be more frightening than being surrounded by an enemy who is pressing in from all sides (Psalm 56:1-6)? David faced exactly that situation many times. As a man who had great trust in God, this is what he learned about dealing with fear: (1) remember that God is with you; (2) trust God for protection; (3) praise God for fulfilling his promises; and (4) use the resources that God has given you.

Our fear often comes from our overestimating our attackers and underestimating our own resources in God and the church. Whenever you are faced with persecution, insecurity, or poor odds, take the fear-fighting steps that David took and overcome your fear.

Betrayal from a close friend or relative often results in a significant turning point in life. Devastated and angry, we wonder how we could have ever trusted that person in the first place. What is worse, though, is that this one experience may affect our future relationships. Will we ever trust anyone again?

Few people know what it is like to be betrayed better than David. In Psalm 59, David prays to God for protection from those who have turned against him. Yes, he has been betrayed. This is his prayer—it's also his solution. We can learn from his example.

The other psalms in this reading provide prayers for healing and examples for scarred and beaten pilgrims who are looking for a reason believe. They speak of enjoying God's faithful love and help in times of trouble (Psalm 57), and leaving ultimate justice in God's hands (Psalm 58).

Read Psalms 57:1–59:17

David was hunted by those whose love had turned to jealousy, and this was driving them to try to murder him (Psalm 59:1-4). Trusted friends, and even one of David's sons, had turned against him. Despite the fact that their love for David had eroded, God's love for him was constant. David knew that he could count on God to deliver him from his enemies.

When people betray and hurt you, remember that God still loves you and that he will never betray you. So rest in his enduring love, even if you feel that he is allowing bad things to happen to you. When the situation passes, you will be able to see that God was with you, sustaining you through the whole ordeal.

[1]Rescue me from my enemies, O God. Protect me from those who have come to destroy me. [2]Rescue me from these criminals; save me from these murderers. [3]They have set an ambush for me. Fierce enemies are out there waiting, LORD, though I have not sinned or offended them. [4]I have done nothing wrong, yet they prepare to attack me. Wake up! See what is happening and help me! [5]O LORD God of Heaven's Armies, the God of Israel, wake up and punish those hostile nations. Show no mercy to wicked traitors. [6]They come out at night, snarling like vicious dogs as they prowl the streets. [7]Listen to the filth that comes from their mouths; their words cut like swords. "After all, who can hear us?" they sneer. [8]But LORD, you laugh at them. You scoff at all the hostile nations. [9]You are my strength; I wait for you to rescue me.

PSALM 59:1-9

¹I wait quietly before God, for my victory comes from him. ²He alone is my rock and my salvation, my fortress where I will never be shaken. ³So many enemies against one man—all of them trying to kill me. To them I'm just a broken-down wall or a tottering fence. ⁴They plan to topple me from my high position. They delight in telling lies about me. They praise me to my face but curse me in their hearts. ⁵Let all that I am wait quietly before God, for my hope is in him. ⁶He alone is my rock and my salvation, my fortress where I will not be shaken. ⁷My victory and honor come from God alone. He is my refuge, a rock where no enemy can reach me. ⁸O my people, trust in him at all times. Pour out your heart to him, for God is our refuge.

PSALM 62:1-8

If you have ever harbored resentment toward a person who attacked your character, welcome to the club. We expect people to treat us with a certain amount of basic respect, and when they don't, it's quite natural to resent them.

Often attacked by his enemies, David had every excuse to resent others. Instead of doing that, however, he dealt with the situation in a more positive way. Read Psalm 62 and learn how to handle resentment.

Other themes in this section of Scripture include regaining control when chaos reigns (Psalm 60), and turning to God for security and help (Psalm 61).

Read Psalms 60:1–62:12

David was well acquainted with unjust personal attacks (Psalm 62:3-4), but he made a conscious effort not to harbor resentments or build up anger. Instead, he expressed his feelings to God and reaffirmed his faith. Through prayer, he released the tension of the emotional stress and handed it over to God. David was confident that the Lord would bring about justice, care for his life, and safeguard his reputation (62:2).

Choosing this attitude can change your entire outlook on life. You do not need to be held captive by resentment toward others when they hurt you. Instead, trust in God the Rock, and nothing will be able to shake you.

No one likes to listen to whining and complaining—no matter how legitimate the gripe. Negative talk is tiring and depressing. Where do you take your complaints? Do you torture your loved ones with a diatribe, yell at the mirror, scream at the television, write a letter, or just hold it in?

Psalm 64 talks about whining and griping and offers a solution. Read and learn that there *is* a legitimate place and time for complaints.

The other psalms in this reading encourage us to look to God for satisfaction (Psalm 63) and give thanks to God for all he provides (Psalm 65).

Read Psalms 63:1–65:13

Like many people today, David often complained about his circumstances and vented his feelings. *Unlike* most people, however, he took his complaints to God, as he did in Psalm 64:1-6.

Many people think it would be disrespectful to complain in prayer, supposing that God doesn't want to hear the complaints or that voicing negative thoughts directly to God is somehow unspiritual. David's model shows that in addition to our praise, confession, and requests, God wants to hear *everything*—even matters that we may not want to tell him. We cannot hide from God, so why should we try?

David expressed his complaints honestly to God, knowing that God would listen to him as a loving father listens to his children. The next time you feel like complaining, take it to God. He will listen to you.

¹O God, listen to my complaint. Protect my life from my enemies' threats. ²Hide me from the plots of this evil mob, from this gang of wrongdoers. ³They sharpen their tongues like swords and aim their bitter words like arrows. ⁴They shoot from ambush at the innocent, attacking suddenly and fearlessly. ⁵They encourage each other to do evil and plan how to set their traps in secret. "Who will ever notice?" they ask. ⁶As they plot their crimes, they say, "We have devised the perfect plan!" Yes, the human heart and mind are cunning. ⁷But God himself will shoot them with his arrows, suddenly striking them down. ⁸Their own tongues will ruin them, and all who see them will shake their heads in scorn. ⁹Then everyone will be afraid; they will proclaim the mighty acts of God and realize all the amazing things he does.

PSALM 64:1-9

⁸Let the whole world bless our God and loudly sing his praises. ⁹Our lives are in his hands, and he keeps our feet from stumbling. ¹⁰You have tested us, O God; you have purified us like silver. . . . ¹⁶Come and listen, all you who fear God, and I will tell you what he did for me. ¹⁷For I cried out to him for help, praising him as I spoke. ¹⁸If I had not confessed the sin in my heart, the LORD would not have listened. ¹⁹But God did listen! He paid attention to my prayer. ²⁰Praise God, who did not ignore my prayer or withdraw his unfailing love from me.

PSALM 66:8-10, 16-20

Do you remember when you were a kid and your mother would make you apologize when you didn't really feel like it? The real blow came when she insisted that you do it nicely. Even though you eventually said the words, in your heart true repentance was nowhere in sight.

Psalm 66 contains advice about saying you're sorry, even when you don't feel like it. In fact, this psalm shows us the good that can come from apologizing.

The psalms in this reading also show us different ways to pray: by example and by command. These life-changing prayers include a request for God's blessing (Psalm 67) and praise to God for his glory and power (Psalm 68).

Read Psalms 66:1–68:35

"If I had not confessed the sin in my heart, the Lord would not have listened" (Psalm 66:18). Confession of sin must be continual because we continually do wrong. But true confession requires us to listen to God and to want to stop sinning. David confessed his sin and prayed, "Keep your servant from deliberate sins" (see Psalm 19:13).

When we refuse to repent or when we harbor and cherish certain sins, we place a wall between us and God. We cannot remember every sin we have ever committed, but we can set our sights on doing right. True confession involves more than just saying words that describe the offense—it also involves taking a step toward change.

Tear down that wall between you and God. Be honest with him, admit your weakness, confess your sin, and share your feelings. Then he will listen to you!

The rumor mill is in full swing, and you're the target. People are making statements about you that would pierce the toughest skin. Although nothing they're saying about you is true, the more you try to stop the rumors, the more guilty you look.

Psalm 69 talks about the damage rumors can cause and offers hope for those whose lives are left in the wake of hurtful rumors. People don't like it when others appear better than they are. If people who notice your faith don't necessarily like it, they may hate you for it. They may go to extremes to get you in trouble or to embarrass you. This psalm offers a prayer for times like that.

Other themes in this reading include asking for God's help in emergencies (Psalm 70); celebrating God's constant help (Psalm 71); and leading and ruling others (Psalm 72).

Read Psalms 69:1–72:20

Many believers feel tempted to turn from God, give up on life, or even go into hiding when they encounter the kind of persecution that David endured. Rather than turning away from God at times like these, we should run to him. He will strengthen us for the trial and rescue us from our enemies.

When you are persecuted for your faith in God, continue to pray to him no matter how you feel or how difficult it may be. God promises to hear your prayer and rescue you. Remember that God is your most faithful friend. Don't turn away from him, especially in your time of need.

⁴Those who hate me without cause outnumber the hairs on my head. Many enemies try to destroy me with lies, demanding that I give back what I didn't steal. ⁵O God, you know how foolish I am; my sins cannot be hidden from you. ⁶Don't let those who trust in you be ashamed because of me, O Sovereign Lord of Heaven's Armies. Don't let me cause them to be humiliated, O God of Israel. ⁷For I endure insults for your sake; humiliation is written all over my face. ⁸Even my own brothers pretend they don't know me; they treat me like a stranger. . . . ¹²I am the favorite topic of town gossip, and all the drunks sing about me. ¹³But I keep praying to you, Lord, hoping this time you will show me favor. In your unfailing love, O God, answer my prayer with your sure salvation.

PSALM 69:4-8, 12-13

⁹We no longer see your miraculous signs. All the prophets are gone, and no one can tell us when it will end. . . . ¹²You, O God, are my king from ages past, bringing salvation to the earth. . . . ¹⁸See how these enemies insult you, LORD. A foolish nation has dishonored your name. ¹⁹Don't let these wild beasts destroy your turtledoves. Don't forget your suffering people forever. ²⁰Remember your covenant promises, for the land is full of darkness and violence! ²¹Don't let the downtrodden be humiliated again. Instead, let the poor and needy praise your name. ²²Arise, O God, and defend your cause. Remember how these fools insult you all day long. ²³Don't overlook what your enemies have said or their growing uproar.

PSALM 74:9, 12, 18-23

For many years it appeared as if Communists were succeeding in wiping out religion. When Soviet cosmonauts entered space, they boasted that they looked for God but found no trace of him. Ever since the days of Noah, skeptics have had such disbelief.

Psalm 74 is a plea for God to show himself to people who don't believe that he exists. If you have ever felt frustrated by God's silence in a day and age when people so brazenly say, "There is no God," you will find that this psalm has your answer.

The other themes in this reading include looking to future rewards (Psalm 73); getting help in times of need (Psalm 74); and relying on God to judge those who are wicked (Psalm 75).

Read Psalms 73:1–75:10

People who hate God have often thought that they could destroy God by wiping out his people. This attitude prevails today—many people try to eliminate religious holidays and traditions and erase God from subjects taught in our schools.

Christians should not become discouraged, because those attempts cannot succeed. We should strive to be more of an influence in our communities by truly caring for people the way Christ did and by living an exemplary life—with God's power and grace—before our neighbors.

What can you do to stand up for the truth? What changes should you make in your lifestyle to reflect Christ to your friends, coworkers, and neighbors?

How many photo albums do you have? Scrapbooks, curio boxes, and hope chests are valuable primarily because of the memories we attach to them. We all have special memories, and we cherish the things that help us remember.

Psalm 77 is about memories. The writer, Asaph, feels distraught, and he reaches into the past for comfort. What he finds there provides a valuable lesson.

The other themes in this section include asking God to punish evil-doers (Psalm 76); finding a source of courage (Psalm 77); and learning from history (Psalm 78).

Read Psalms 76:1–78:72

The story of the parting of the Red Sea (Psalm 77:16) was a memory that every Israelite would recall and cherish because it reminded them of God's power, protection, and love for them as a nation. Memories of God's miracles and faithfulness often sustained Israel through their difficulties (Psalm 77:11-12), reminding them that God was capable and trustworthy.

When encountering trials and tribulations, it is good to recall God's goodness and faithfulness. We can do this by reading favorite Bible verses, singing favorite songs, reviewing prayer journals, or discussing past blessings and miracles with a friend. Those remembrances can provide hope and strength for today.

Think of what you can do to help you remember how God has worked in your life. And if you are discouraged by your present circumstances, find a Christian friend to pray for you and to reminisce with you about God's blessings in the past.

⁷Has the LORD rejected me forever? Will he never again be kind to me? ⁸Is his unfailing love gone forever? Have his promises permanently failed? ⁹Has God forgotten to be gracious? Has he slammed the door on his compassion? ¹⁰And I said, "This is my fate; the Most High has turned his hand against me." ¹¹But then I recall all you have done, O LORD; I remember your wonderful deeds of long ago. ¹²They are constantly in my thoughts. I cannot stop thinking about your mighty works. ¹³O God, your ways are holy. Is there any god as mighty as you? ¹⁴You are the God of great wonders! You demonstrate your awesome power among the nations. ¹⁵By your strong arm, you redeemed your people, the descendants of Jacob and Joseph.

PSALM 77:7-15

⁵O LORD, how long will you be angry with us? Forever? How long will your jealousy burn like fire? ⁶Pour out your wrath on the nations that refuse to acknowledge you—on kingdoms that do not call upon your name. ⁷For they have devoured your people Israel, making the land a desolate wilderness. ⁸Do not hold us guilty for the sins of our ancestors! Let your compassion quickly meet our needs, for we are on the brink of despair. ⁹Help us, O God of our salvation! Help us for the glory of your name. Save us and forgive our sins for the honor of your name. ¹⁰Why should pagan nations be allowed to scoff, asking, "Where is their God?" Show us your vengeance against the nations, for they have spilled the blood of your servants. ¹¹Listen to the moaning of the prisoners. Demonstrate your great power by saving those condemned to die.

PSALM 79:5-11

Injustice. Unfairness. These are two ugly realities that everyone must face and deal with at some point in life. When will injustices in this world stop?

Psalm 79 is the prayer of a man with that question on his mind. It's the burning cry of a man who truly loves God, a man who really cares, a man who has been the victim. This psalm is a prayer for justice in Israel's time of distress, but it is still applicable to injustices committed today.

Other prayers in this passage include how to pray after experiencing defeat (Psalm 80) and celebrating God's goodness in view of our unfaithfulness (Psalm 81).

Read Psalms 79:1–81:16

Asaph (the author of Psalm 79) wanted to see the wrong that had been done made right. Like Asaph, we, too, want justice. However, the question remains: Can we expect to get it in this lifetime? We know for sure that, eventually, God will deal justly with everyone, but what about the present, the here and now?

We shouldn't expect to receive earthly justice in our lifetimes. This is not because God doesn't care, but because he often has a higher purpose in mind. So, we must endure injustice with patience and allow God to use it to strengthen us. In the meantime, we can bring our requests for justice to God. He won't ignore them.

Be ready to live in an unjust world—life *isn't* fair. And be prepared for criticism, jokes, and unkind remarks, because God does not always shield his people from the attacks of this world. Remember, however, that in the end the righteous will be vindicated. God will remember you!

Do you enjoy browsing in the library, going to see a friend, relaxing on the sofa, or walking through the woods? Sometimes the world becomes a pressure cooker, and we need to go to a place that refreshes us. Where is that place for you?

Psalm 84 talks of the place to go when we need refreshment.

Other psalms in this section of Scripture speak of ways to turn the tables and affect the world by defending the weak against unfair people (Psalm 82) and praying for people who hate or oppose God (Psalm 83).

Read Psalms 82:1–84:12

The writer of Psalm 84 had a deep desire to dwell in God's presence (84:1-4). In fact, he loved the Lord so much that he envied the sparrows because they could build nests near the altar (84:3). He recognized that those who seek God are richly rewarded (84:5-7). This was his cure for a meaningless and hectic existence.

We, like the psalmist, need to have a desire to know God intimately and a desire to dwell in his presence. Fortunately, we don't have to visit the Temple to commune with God. Today, because of the death and resurrection of Christ, we can meet God anywhere, at any time. If we belong to him, his Holy Spirit lives within us, and his presence is always with us. We need only to go to God in prayer to enjoy being in his presence (see Hebrews 4:16).

When the busyness of this world catches up with you, get away and spend time alone with God. It will be well worth your time to do so.

---

¹How lovely is your dwelling place, O LORD of Heaven's Armies. ²I long, yes, I faint with longing to enter the courts of the LORD. With my whole being, body and soul, I will shout joyfully to the living God. ³Even the sparrow finds a home, and the swallow builds her nest and raises her young at a place near your altar, O LORD of Heaven's Armies, my King and my God! ⁴What joy for those who can live in your house, always singing your praises. ⁵What joy for those whose strength comes from the LORD, who have set their minds on a pilgrimage to Jerusalem. ⁶When they walk through the Valley of Weeping, it will become a place of refreshing springs. The autumn rains will clothe it with blessings. ⁷They will continue to grow stronger, and each of them will appear before God in Jerusalem. ⁸O LORD God of Heaven's Armies, hear my prayer.

PSALM 84:1-8

¹I will sing of the LORD's unfailing love forever! Young and old will hear of your faithfulness. ²Your unfailing love will last forever. Your faithfulness is as enduring as the heavens. ³The LORD said, "I have made a covenant with David, my chosen servant. I have sworn this oath to him: ⁴'I will establish your descendants as kings forever; they will sit on your throne from now until eternity.'" ⁵All heaven will praise your great wonders, LORD; myriads of angels will praise you for your faithfulness. ⁶For who in all of heaven can compare with the LORD? What mightiest angel is anything like the LORD? ⁷The highest angelic powers stand in awe of God. He is far more awesome than all who surround his throne. ⁸O LORD God of Heaven's Armies! Where is there anyone as mighty as you, O LORD? You are entirely faithful.

PSALM 89:1-8

You can learn a lot about a person by the way he or she keeps or breaks promises. Each promise kept endears that person to you, proves the person's character to you, and builds trust between you. On the other hand, each promise broken disappoints you, makes you wonder about the person's character, and breaks down trust between you.

Psalm 89 celebrates some of the promises of the greatest promise keeper of all—God. The promises he keeps here have not only endeared him to the writer of this psalm but should also endear him to us.

Notice also the fulfilled promises in other psalms from this reading—promises of blessing, restoration, and answered prayer.

Read Psalms 85:1–89:52

God promised that he would preserve David's throne (Psalm 89:29). Even though Israel disobeyed God almost continually throughout its history, God promised to never fail his pledge to David (89:33). Through God's patient reminders and warnings, a small portion, or "remnant" of God's people always remained faithful to him. Centuries later, the Messiah arrived, the eternal King from David's line, just as God had promised.

We all have worries, some great, some small, and some just plain bothersome. Yet we can trust God to help us overcome our worries because he has taken care of our biggest worry—sin. God can be trusted to save us as he promised he would (see Hebrews 6:13-18).

God is completely reliable. Trust him in times of trouble. Relax in the security that God always keeps his promises.

It's easy to pass the time when it's spent in an enjoyable activity. No wonder many of us reach old age wondering, *Where has the time gone?* Time passes quickly. In fact, the longer you live the faster the time seems to go.

Psalm 90 is Moses' reflection on the passing of time. What he has to say is pure wisdom and should stir us not only to appreciate the time we have but to live godly lives as well.

In this section we are also reminded to look to God for protection from danger (Psalm 91) and to be thankful every day (Psalm 92).

Read Psalms 90:1–92:15

Moses was well qualified to write the lines, "Teach us to realize the brevity of life, so that we may grow in wisdom" (Psalm 90:12). He had experienced life from all sides—from a wealthy, powerful existence in Egypt to a frugal, nomadic life in Midian. He knew, perhaps better than most people, how to put life's short amount of time to good use.

Unless we train ourselves to value time as a priceless treasure, we will never realize how short life really is. Then when we are older, with little time left, we will regret the time we wasted.

To make the most of your time on earth, avoid those activities that benefit no one. Spend less time watching TV. Learn to manage your time better and set goals for yourself. Ask yourself these questions: What do I want to see happen in my life before I die? What small step could I take toward that purpose today? Seek God's opinion on your goals. Then, if he doesn't direct otherwise, set out to accomplish them by his power and grace.

¹Lord, through all the generations you have been our home! ²Before the mountains were born, before you gave birth to the earth and the world, from beginning to end, you are God. ³You turn people back to dust, saying, "Return to dust, you mortals!" ⁴For you, a thousand years are as a passing day, as brief as a few night hours. ⁵You sweep people away like dreams that disappear. They are like grass that springs up in the morning. ⁶In the morning it blooms and flourishes, but by evening it is dry and withered. ⁷We wither beneath your anger; we are overwhelmed by your fury. ⁸You spread out our sins before you—our secret sins—and you see them all. ⁹We live our lives beneath your wrath, ending our years with a groan. ¹⁰Seventy years are given to us! Some even live to eighty. But even the best years are filled with pain and trouble.

PSALM 90:1-10

⁸Think again, you fools! When will you finally catch on? ⁹Is he deaf—the one who made your ears? Is he blind—the one who formed your eyes? ¹⁰He punishes the nations—won't he also punish you? He knows everything—doesn't he also know what you are doing? ¹¹The LORD knows people's thoughts; he knows they are worthless! ¹²Joyful are those you discipline, LORD, those you teach with your instructions. ¹³You give them relief from troubled times until a pit is dug to capture the wicked. ¹⁴The LORD will not reject his people; he will not abandon his special possession. ¹⁵Judgment will again be founded on justice, and those with virtuous hearts will pursue it.

PSALM 94:8-15

If you've ever been around a cynical person, you know how maddening such company can be. A cynical outlook on life has two problems: (1) Negative attitudes are rarely necessary and rarely appreciated. (2) A cynical outlook makes every situation *look* bleak, even when it is not. What cures the cynic?

Psalm 94 has the answer. You'll notice a lot of contemporary problems here, such as crime and corruption. That's because some things, namely, human wickedness, never change. But the psalmist did not forget to look on the bright side.

The other two psalms in this reading contain similar lessons, but from different angles: learning from God's creation (Psalm 93) and worshiping God (Psalm 95).

Read Psalms 93:1–95:11

Today we have technology's mixed blessing of finding out about events more quickly and in greater detail than ever before. So much of it, however, is negative news. When negative news fills our minds, it's hard not to be cynical.

In the first half of Psalm 94, it seems as if the psalmist could think of nothing but bad news. He saw evil people prospering and oppressing others (94:3-7), corrupt governments (94:20), and the condemnation of the innocent (94:21), much like what we see in our world today. But he had come to realize and take comfort in the fact that God would not allow evil to continue forever. By the end of the psalm, he expressed trust in God and a commitment to take responsibility for his life and to obey God.

The next time you feel overwhelmed by negative news, do what this psalm writer did: tell God how you feel, declare confidence in his wisdom and timing, and reaffirm your commitment to follow him.

What do you strongly dislike? If you included all the categories that question could cover—foods, locations, television shows, ideas, organizations, people—you would have a nearly endless list. So could anybody; much of what we do from day to day involves a feeling of love or hate.

Psalm 97 provides *the* criterion for selecting things not only to dislike but to really hate. That's right, *hate*. What God's people should hate should not surprise you, however. In fact, hatred toward this, as you will learn, is good.

Other psalms in this section focus on more positive themes: how to praise God (Psalm 96) and celebrating God's victories over evil (Psalm 98).

Read Psalms 96:1–98:9

"You who love the LORD, hate evil!" (Psalm 97:10). This means that those who sincerely desire to please God should realign their desires with God's desires. Their affections will begin to change; that is, they will begin to love what God loves and hate what God hates. As they grow in their love for the Lord, they will grow in their hatred for evil.

If you do not despise the actions of people who take advantage of others, if you admire people who only look out for themselves, or if you envy those who get ahead through cruelty, your desires are not God's desires. Learn to love God's ways and to hate evil in every form—not just the obvious sins, but also the ones that are easy to consider acceptable or to overlook.

¹The LORD is king! Let the earth rejoice! Let the farthest coastlands be glad. ²Dark clouds surround him. Righteousness and justice are the foundation of his throne. ³Fire spreads ahead of him and burns up all his foes. ⁴His lightning flashes out across the world. The earth sees and trembles. ⁵The mountains melt like wax before the LORD, . . . ⁶The heavens proclaim his righteousness; every nation sees his glory. ⁷Those who worship idols are disgraced—all who brag about their worthless gods—for every god must bow to him. ⁸Jerusalem has heard and rejoiced, and all the towns of Judah are glad because of your justice, O LORD! ⁹For you, O LORD, are supreme over all the earth; you are exalted far above all gods. ¹⁰You who love the LORD, hate evil! He protects the lives of his godly people and rescues them from the power of the wicked.

PSALM 97:1-10

¹I will sing of your love and justice, LORD. I will praise you with songs. ²I will be careful to live a blameless life—when will you come to help me? I will lead a life of integrity in my own home. ³I will refuse to look at anything vile and vulgar. I hate all who deal crookedly; I will have nothing to do with them. ⁴I will reject perverse ideas and stay away from every evil. ⁵I will not tolerate people who slander their neighbors. I will not endure conceit and pride. ⁶I will search for faithful people to be my companions. Only those who are above reproach will be allowed to serve me. ⁷I will not allow deceivers to serve in my house, and liars will not stay in my presence. ⁸My daily task will be to ferret out the wicked and free the city of the LORD from their grip.

PSALM 101:1-8

It's a noble deed when kids stick up for siblings on the playground. That shouldn't surprise us, however, because family honor pulls family members together like nothing else does. But have you noticed how different it *usually* is between siblings? The politeness level quickly drops.

David knew all too well about how poorly family members treat each other. In Psalm 101, he wrote a prayer in which he asked God to help him act as he should at home. It's a prayer that every family member could benefit from reading.

Other prayers in this section concern trust in God's fairness and holiness (Psalm 99) and entering God's presence joyfully (Psalm 100).

Read Psalms 99:1–101:8

Living in close proximity to those with whom you have close relationships will always lead to conflict. Nowhere do we have more close relationships than at home. Thus, our homes can be difficult places in which to always be civil and kind. In most families, parents and children relax and remove their mask of good behavior, often treating each other with less respect and kindness than they show to friends, coworkers, or even strangers. David must have had this problem as he prayed to God for help (Psalm 101:2).

Like David, pray about your behavior and attitudes toward other family members. Pray that God will help you imitate Christ at home so that you will be able to genuinely love your family and show them kindness and respect.

Some people live on the dark side of the moon. Phone them and they give you an earful about how the world is mistreating them. They can't think of anything for which to be thankful, and reminding them of their blessings only seems to irritate them.

Psalm 103 provides a great example. It's a count-your-blessings psalm, a simple reminder to be thankful.

The other two psalms in this reading also give us reasons to be thankful. Psalm 102 teaches us how to receive God's comfort when we're in distress. Psalm 104 helps us appreciate God through his creation and the way he cares for it.

Read Psalms 102:1–104:35

David's praise in Psalm 103 focused on God's glorious deeds (103:3-19). People often complain when they are tired, needy, and frustrated. But David's list gives us plenty for which to praise God: God forgives our sins, heals our diseases, redeems us from death, crowns us with love and compassion, satisfies our desires, and intervenes for people who suffer injustice (103:1-22).

The best part is that we receive all these blessings without deserving any of them. And God never shows partiality—giving good things to his favorites and leaving out the others.

No matter how difficult your circumstances are today, count your blessings—past, present, and future. Keep them in mind when you feel as though you have nothing for which to praise God. If that doesn't work, remind yourself of what God has done for you by reading David's list.

²Let all that I am praise the LORD; may I never forget the good things he does for me. ³He forgives all my sins and heals all my diseases. ⁴He redeems me from death and crowns me with love and tender mercies. ⁵He fills my life with good things. My youth is renewed like the eagle's! ⁶The LORD gives righteousness and justice to all who are treated unfairly. . . .

⁸The LORD is compassionate and merciful, slow to get angry and filled with unfailing love. ⁹He will not constantly accuse us, nor remain angry forever. ¹⁰He does not punish us for all our sins; he does not deal harshly with us, as we deserve. ¹¹For his unfailing love toward those who fear him is as great as the height of the heavens above the earth. ¹²He has removed our sins as far from us as the east is from the west.

PSALM 103:2-6, 8-12

¹Give thanks to the LORD and proclaim his greatness. Let the whole world know what he has done. ²Sing to him; yes, sing his praises. Tell everyone about his wonderful deeds. ³Exult in his holy name; rejoice, you who worship the LORD. . . . ⁵Remember the wonders he has performed, his miracles, and the rulings he has given, ⁶you children of his servant Abraham, you descendants of Jacob, his chosen ones. ⁷He is the LORD our God. His justice is seen throughout the land. ⁸He always stands by his covenant—the commitment he made to a thousand generations. ⁹This is the covenant he made with Abraham and the oath he swore to Isaac. ¹⁰He confirmed it to Jacob as a decree, and to the people of Israel as a never-ending covenant: ¹¹"I will give you the land of Canaan as your special possession."

PSALM 105:1-3, 5-11

When I pray, it doesn't feel as if God is listening. When I read the Bible, it seems dull and lifeless. Have either of those concerns ever crossed your mind?

Consider the words of Psalm 105, which recall the many wonders God did for Israel—the miracles that helped them and the judgments on their enemies. David knows about spiritual dryness, and he knows that *remembering* can help a believer get through these times.

Also, if you make the mistake of not remembering God's goodness to you, Psalm 106 will teach you about learning from your mistakes.

Read Psalms 105:1–106:48

David knew that even God's people sometimes lose heart in their pursuit of God. Yet he also had discovered a remedy: remembering the way that God had helped his people in the past (Psalm 105:5).

God has always worked in the lives of his people, and he will continue to do so today. He is not far away but close by. That's why we should "search for the LORD . . . [and] continually seek him" (105:4).

Whenever you feel far from God, remember his specific deeds in your life, as David did. Persist in seeking God. If you can't remember them, start writing them down, and read the Bible's reminders of God's past works. Then pray through your needs and thank God for his help.

What has caused you to feel worried, anxious, or anguished lately? Don't feel awkward or uniquely rotten if you think of these easily; our adversary the devil sends a steady stream of troubles to distress us. He loves it when we worry about family members, money shortages, ill health, direction in life, conflicts with others, and consequences for mistakes.

Psalm 107 celebrates God's help for people in distress. Perhaps you can relate to some of the circumstances mentioned here.

Meanwhile, Psalm 108 urges us to rely on God's strength, and Psalm 109 teaches us how to pray for enemies and those who anger us.

Read Psalms 107:1–109:31

We don't know who wrote Psalm 107, but we can tell that the person was well acquainted with distress. The writer described four kinds of struggling people and how God helped them: people who were lost (107:4-9), prisoners who wanted to change (107:10-16), sick people (107:17-20), and storm-tossed sailors (107:23-30).

Everyone can identify with these kinds of people. At one time or another, we have all been lost, caught doing something wrong, sick, or afraid for our lives. But no matter how extreme the hardship, God never loses control of the situation and can help those who are in distress.

The next time you feel overwhelmed by worry, call on God to help you, and trust him to do what is right. You can bring him all your needs—he is able and willing to help.

¹Give thanks to the LORD, for he is good! His faithful love endures forever. ²Has the LORD redeemed you? Then speak out! Tell others he has redeemed you from your enemies. ³For he has gathered the exiles from many lands, from east and west, from north and south. . . . ³³He changes rivers into deserts, and springs of water into dry, thirsty land. ³⁴He turns the fruitful land into salty wastelands, because of the wickedness of those who live there. ³⁵But he also turns deserts into pools of water, the dry land into springs of water. ³⁶He brings the hungry to settle there and to build their cities. ³⁷They sow their fields, plant their vineyards, and harvest their bumper crops. . . . ⁴²The godly will see these things and be glad, while the wicked are struck silent.

PSALM 107:1-3, 33-37, 42

¹Praise the Lord! I will thank the Lord with all my heart as I meet with his godly people. ²How amazing are the deeds of the Lord! All who delight in him should ponder them. ³Everything he does reveals his glory and majesty. His righteousness never fails. ⁴He causes us to remember his wonderful works. How gracious and merciful is our Lord! ⁵He gives food to those who fear him; he always remembers his covenant. ⁶He has shown his great power to his people by giving them the lands of other nations. ⁷All he does is just and good, and all his commandments are trustworthy. ⁸They are forever true, to be obeyed faithfully and with integrity. ⁹He has paid a full ransom for his people. He has guaranteed his covenant with them forever. What a holy, awe-inspiring name he has!

PSALM 111:1-9

Schools test children to measure intelligence, but they give no tests for wisdom. Moral choices fall outside the line of what schools can track, so you can be a brain (and a fool) and your foolishness will never show up on your report card. More to the point, if you want to be wise, you'll have to do an independent study. No one will make you stay after school if you don't.

So are you wise or foolish? Psalm 111 will help you assess your wisdom. If you don't measure up, this psalm will also get you going in the right direction.

Other sources of wisdom in this reading focus on getting to know the Messiah (Psalm 110), and reviewing the benefits of being faithful to God (Psalm 112).

Read Psalms 110:1–112:10

The only way to become truly wise begins with having reverence for God (Psalm 111:10, see also Proverbs 1:7). Too often we forget this and think that our own observations, a healthy dose of common sense, and a good college education will do the trick. But true wisdom doesn't come from any of these human sources. If we do not acknowledge God as the only source of wisdom, our foundation for making wise decisions will not be solid, and we will often make foolish choices that will lead to big mistakes.

Get into the habit of reading and studying God's Word to become familiar with God's principles and his timeless truths. Once you're familiar with the principles, review them again and again. Open your mind to what God says. He wants to fill you with wisdom.

Everyone is, to an extent, indebted to someone else for teaching them a valuable lesson or skill. Some acknowledge that person's contribution, while others take all the credit themselves for their achievements and success.

Psalm 115 deals with giving credit where it's due. The author of this psalm makes absolutely sure that God is given the glory for the success he sees around him. There are no false claims to fame here. As you read, learn the lesson about glorifying your Lord.

Other psalms here also give the glory to God. Psalm 113 praises God for his care for the poor, weak, and needy. Psalm 114 celebrates God's help in our lives.

Read Psalms 113:1–115:18

The writer of Psalm 115 asked that God's name, not the nation's, be glorified (115:1). Note the lack of false humility—this writer could do nothing but call attention to God's greatness and sincerely praise him.

It's natural to want to take credit for something we've accomplished. Instead, we should ask God to glorify *his* name, not ours. No one can fault us for leaving a good impression as a by-product of doing our duty; the problem comes when we try to get praise from others and withhold praise that belongs to God.

Before you pray, consider who will get the credit if God answers your prayer. Ask God to glorify *his* name through your achievements and success, not yours. Then when you do succeed, remember to give credit and thanks to God for his love and faithfulness.

¹Not to us, O Lord, not to us, but to your name goes all the glory for your unfailing love and faithfulness. ²Why let the nations say, "Where is their God?" ³Our God is in the heavens, and he does as he wishes. ⁴Their idols are merely things of silver and gold, shaped by human hands. ⁵They have mouths but cannot speak, and eyes but cannot see. ⁶They have ears but cannot hear, and noses but cannot smell. ⁷They have hands but cannot feel, and feet but cannot walk, and throats but cannot make a sound. ⁸And those who make idols are just like them, as are all who trust in them. ⁹O Israel, trust the Lord! He is your helper and your shield. ¹⁰O priests, descendants of Aaron, trust the Lord! He is your helper and your shield. ¹¹All you who fear the Lord, trust the Lord! He is your helper and your shield.

PSALM 115:1-11

¹I love the LORD because he hears my voice and my prayer for mercy. ²Because he bends down to listen, I will pray as long as I have breath! ³Death wrapped its ropes around me; the terrors of the grave overtook me. I saw only trouble and sorrow. ⁴Then I called on the name of the LORD: "Please, LORD, save me!" ⁵How kind the LORD is! How good he is! So merciful, this God of ours! ⁶The LORD protects those of childlike faith; I was facing death, and he saved me. ⁷Let my soul be at rest again, for the LORD has been good to me. ⁸He has saved me from death, my eyes from tears, my feet from stumbling. ⁹And so I walk in the LORD's presence as I live here on earth!

PSALM 116:1-9

Everyone has a perspective on death. Some welcome its coming. Others fear death and try to prolong their time on earth as long as possible. But what should Christians think? Should we welcome it or fear it?

The author of Psalm 116 was near death and feared for his life. But he didn't just worry about it—he cried out to God, "Save me!" God did, and the psalm writer praised him. This psalm speaks a lot about what he has learned. Read it and you can learn, too.

This reading gives other reasons for praising God: his unlimited love for us (Psalm 117) and the security his eternal love provides for us when our circumstances keep changing (Psalm 118).

Read Psalms 116:1–118:29

God stays close to us even when we face death (Psalm 116:15). The death of a person matters to God; he does not take it lightly or count it cheaply. When someone we love nears death, we may become angry or feel abandoned. But God considers every believer precious, and he carefully chooses the time when they will be called into his presence.

Let this truth guide you when a loved one has a grave illness or a life-threatening injury; let it provide comfort when a loved one has died. God sees and cares for each and every life. No one takes death more seriously than God.

State lotteries have thrived in this country. Each week, millions of dollars are promised to a handful of winners. For a chance to be set for life financially, just buy a ticket.

Psalm 119, the longest chapter in the Bible, discusses something that has much more value than money: God's law. Almost every verse mentions the virtues of knowing, learning, loving, keeping, and telling others about God's law. In a word, God's law is *valuable!* And where does this leave the yardstick of all worldly value? Read on for some perspective.

Other lessons in this psalm include appreciating the value of God's Word; appreciating God's rules; and asking God for insight into his Word.

Read Psalm 119:1-176

In today's world, where advertisements continually entice us to buy things, thinking selfishly comes almost automatically. We can easily imagine that contentment and happiness lie just beyond the next income level. Making the lust for money even stronger is the fact that in our society money represents power, influence, and success.

Certainly, money can buy comforts and offer some security, but it offers nothing that will last or that can ultimately satisfy us. Besides, God determines what we have (see Proverbs 22:2). The Bible, God's Word, offers far more than money. In Scripture we find direction, guidance, and the meaning to life.

What means more to you? Knowing God or being rich? Make the psalm writer's prayer your own—that God will give you a love for his statutes and not for making money.

33Teach me your decrees, O Lord; I will keep them to the end. 34Give me understanding and I will obey your instructions; I will put them into practice with all my heart. 35Make me walk along the path of your commands, for that is where my happiness is found. 36Give me an eagerness for your laws rather than a love for money! 37Turn my eyes from worthless things, and give me life through your word. 38Reassure me of your promise, made to those who fear you. 39Help me abandon my shameful ways; for your regulations are good. 40I long to obey your commandments! Renew my life with your goodness. 41Lord, give me your unfailing love, the salvation that you promised me. 42Then I can answer those who taunt me, for I trust in your word. 43Do not snatch your word of truth from me, for your regulations are my only hope.

PSALM 119:33-43

¹I took my troubles to the LORD; I cried out to him, and he answered my prayer. ²Rescue me, O LORD, from liars and from all deceitful people. ³O deceptive tongue, what will God do to you? How will he increase your punishment? ⁴You will be pierced with sharp arrows and burned with glowing coals. ⁵How I suffer in far-off Meshech. It pains me to live in distant Kedar. ⁶I am tired of living among people who hate peace. ⁷I search for peace; but when I speak of peace, they want war!

PSALM 120:1-7

Psalm 120 was written by a man who had some thoughts on fighting. He had seen a lot of action and wanted a little peace. But chances are he didn't get any—at least not from his adversaries. As you read this psalm, learn the value of being a peacemaker.

The other psalms in this reading cover many different topics: knowing where your help comes from (Psalm 121); entering God's presence (Psalm 122); looking to God for mercy (Psalm 123); and celebrating God's protection when you are attacked by others (Psalm 124).

Read Psalms 120:1–124:8

The psalm writer wrote, "I search for peace; but . . . they want war" (Psalm 120:7). Many people feel that way and would rather fight for what they believe in than back down or compromise for the sake of peace. For those people, the glory of battle lies in winning. But when someone wins like that, somebody else loses.

In contrast, the glory of peacemaking lies in the fact that it can produce two winners. Peacemaking is God's way (see Matthew 5:9), so we, too, should strive to be peacemakers by carefully and prayerfully trying to resolve conflicts without force. But at the same time, we should keep in mind that peace at all costs is not peace. Therefore, we should not sacrifice God's principles to achieve a lesser peace.

The next time you are involved in a disagreement, look for things on which you both can agree. Work from there toward a solution that is mutually beneficial and pleasing to God. Be a peacemaker.

Does our society today think highly of children? It's hard to tell. Never have the laws against child abuse been tougher. Never have children had so many enjoyable opportunities geared just for them. But never have more abortions been performed, and never have so many children spent their early years in day care.

If ever we needed a "family psalm," it's now! And God has given it to us in Psalm 127. Among this psalm's pearls you will find a blanket statement about children, leaving little doubt as to what God thinks of them. As you read, consider whether this requires an adjustment of *your* attitude.

Other psalms in this reading give a plan for overcoming insecurity (Psalm 125); for celebrating God's great works on our behalf (Psalm 126); for letting God rule in the home (Psalm 128); and for looking to God when others oppose us (Psalm 129).

Read Psalms 125:1–129:8

God values children highly (Psalm 127:3-5). When God grants children to a couple, he grants them a blessing—bringing good to them, rewarding them. Therefore, we should value children and treat them as precious gifts.

Children are not annoying distractions, but an opportunity to shape the future. Too often we treat children like burdens rather than blessings.

If you have children, consider what you can do today to show them how much you love and care for them. If you don't have children of your own, consider how you can affirm and help the children at your church and in your neighborhood and extended family. Begin today to cultivate care and value for children.

¹Unless the LORD builds a house, the work of the builders is wasted. Unless the LORD protects a city, guarding it with sentries will do no good. ²It is useless for you to work so hard from early morning until late at night, anxiously working for food to eat; for God gives rest to his loved ones. ³Children are a gift from the LORD; they are a reward from him. ⁴Children born to a young man are like arrows in a warrior's hands. ⁵How joyful is the man whose quiver is full of them! He will not be put to shame when he confronts his accusers at the city gates.

PSALM 127:1-5

¹How wonderful and pleasant it is when brothers live together in harmony! ²For harmony is as precious as the anointing oil that was poured over Aaron's head, that ran down his beard and onto the border of his robe. ³Harmony is as refreshing as the dew from Mount Hermon that falls on the mountains of Zion. And there the LORD has pronounced his blessing, even life everlasting.

PSALM 133:1-3

We don't have to look far to find examples of unity and its benefits. Any choir, sports team, play, or family will work far better if there's unity among its members. What area of your life depends on unity?

When we have to work with others, sometimes it helps to be reminded of the value of unity. Psalm 133 is just such a reminder—check it out.

Other psalms in this reading will remind you of God's forgiveness (Psalm 130); of where to find contentment (Psalm 131); of the source of public honor (Psalm 132); and of finding joy in God's blessings (Psalm 134).

Read Psalms 130:1–134:3

David described unity as pleasant and precious (Psalm 133:1-3). Unfortunately, unity does not come without effort—in fact, it costs a great deal. We naturally disagree and divide ranks, usually over issues that matter, but just as often over unimportant ones, too. It takes work to overcome this nature. Yet unity is important enough to work at making this change for several reasons: (1) It makes God's people a positive example and helps draw others to him. (2) It helps us cooperate as God meant us to, giving us a foretaste of heaven. (3) It renews and revitalizes ministry because there is less tension to sap our energy.

Living in unity does not mean that God's people have to agree on everything. But we must agree on the issue that matters most—our ultimate purpose in life—loving God and one another.

DO YOU LOVE ME?

If you want to reassure someone of your love, whether a child, spouse, or friend, you have several methods available. You could give a gift, give a hug, spend some time with that person, or say, "I love you." Many people say those words so easily, but the proof—their actions—isn't always there.

Psalm 136 recites many ways in which God has shown his love to his people. Read this extensive list and praise your loving heavenly Father.

This reading also teaches how to praise God (Psalm 135) and how to pray during times of sadness (Psalm 137).

Read Psalms 135:1–137:9

Psalm 136 repeats the phrase "His faithful love endures forever" twenty-six times, once in every verse. This psalm may have been a responsive reading, with the congregation saying these words in unison after phrases spoken by a leader.

The repetition makes the importance of this message obvious: God loves us, and that love doesn't die, stop, wear out, fade, or lessen. It lives on, continues, keeps going, lasts. God has done more for us than we could ever deserve: He created us, gave us life to enjoy, and, through Christ, freed us from sin. But he didn't stop with the deeds; he went on to write it down—to say the words.

You never have to worry that God will run out of love for you. If you ever do, just reread Psalm 136.

¹Give thanks to the Lord, for he is good! His faithful love endures forever. ²Give thanks to the God of gods. His faithful love endures forever. ³Give thanks to the Lord of lords. His faithful love endures forever. ⁴Give thanks to him who alone does mighty miracles. His faithful love endures forever. ⁵Give thanks to him who made the heavens so skillfully. His faithful love endures forever. ⁶Give thanks to him who placed the earth among the waters. His faithful love endures forever. . . . ²³He remembered us in our weakness. His faithful love endures forever. ²⁴He saved us from our enemies. His faithful love endures forever. ²⁵He gives food to every living thing. His faithful love endures forever. ²⁶Give thanks to the God of heaven. His faithful love endures forever.

PSALM 136:1-6, 23-26

¹O LORD, you have examined my heart and know everything about me. ²You know when I sit down or stand up. You know my thoughts even when I'm far away. ³You see me when I travel and when I rest at home. You know everything I do. ⁴You know what I am going to say even before I say it, LORD. ⁵You go before me and follow me. You place your hand of blessing on my head. ⁶Such knowledge is too wonderful for me, too great for me to understand! ⁷I can never escape from your Spirit! I can never get away from your presence! ⁸If I go up to heaven, you are there; if I go down to the grave, you are there. ⁹If I ride the wings of the morning, if I dwell by the farthest oceans, ¹⁰even there your hand will guide me, and your strength will support me.

PSALM 139:1-10

A really close friend can help you identify and overcome weaknesses, identify and use your strengths, and make other important changes. The help you get from someone who knows you well—yet still accepts you—can make more difference than a hundred self-help books.

Psalm 139 is a celebration, from first verse to last, of a close friend—God. He knows us better than our closest confidant, even better than we know ourselves. As you read this psalm, celebrate with the writer God's great knowledge and love.

One psalm in this reading celebrates God's love in answering our prayers (Psalm 138), while the other one teaches how to survive slander and threats (Psalm 140).

Read Psalms 138:1–140:13

God knows everything about us, even down to the number of hairs on our heads (see Matthew 10:30). He knows what we do as well as what we are. He even knows what we think about (Psalm 139:1-5). Should we expect anything less from our Creator (139:13-14)?

Sometimes we don't let people get to know us because we are afraid they will discover something about us that they won't like. Or we try to pull back from them because we fear that they've already found something distasteful and will reject us. That cannot happen with God. He knows us completely, and still he accepts and loves us.

When you fear (or actually face) rejection from others—whether coworkers, neighbors, friends, or even family members—remember that God made you and has already accepted you, exactly as you are.

When was the last time someone criticized you? How did you respond? How do you *wish* you had responded? What leftover conflicts has it created? Most people find criticism difficult to take, even when it's given by someone who knows what he or she is talking about.

As he does in many of his psalms, in Psalm 141 David talks to God about his many enemies. As you read, you will see that David knows he can dismiss his enemies' accusations, taunts, and lies. There is one type of criticism, however, that he cannot discount.

David provides other lessons on prayer in this reading as well: how to pray whenever you are overwhelmed or desperate (Psalm 142); how to pray whenever you feel hopeless or depressed (Psalm 143); and how to pray when you are hemmed in or outnumbered by unbelievers (Psalm 144).

Read Psalms 141:1–144:15

David said that being corrected by a righteous person would be doing him a favor (Psalm 141:5). He knew that though no one really likes to hear criticism, everyone can benefit from the kind that makes good points, but only if the criticism is taken with humility. According to David we should take these three steps to accept well-given and well-placed criticism: (1) don't refuse it, (2) consider it a kindness, and (3) keep quiet (don't fight back).

The next time critics target you, put these suggestions into practice. They'll help you control how you react, making your response productive rather than destructive, no matter what the motives behind the critique.

¹O LORD, I am calling to you. Please hurry! Listen when I cry to you for help! ²Accept my prayer as incense offered to you, and my upraised hands as an evening offering. ³Take control of what I say, O LORD, and guard my lips. ⁴Don't let me drift toward evil or take part in acts of wickedness. Don't let me share in the delicacies of those who do wrong. ⁵Let the godly strike me! It will be a kindness! If they correct me, it is soothing medicine. Don't let me refuse it. But I pray constantly against the wicked and their deeds. ⁶When their leaders are thrown down from a cliff, the wicked will listen to my words and find them true. ⁷Like rocks brought up by a plow, the bones of the wicked will lie scattered without burial. ⁸I look to you for help, O Sovereign LORD. You are my refuge.

PSALM 141:1-8

¹I will exalt you, my God and King, and praise your name forever and ever. ²I will praise you every day; yes, I will praise you forever. ³Great is the LORD! He is most worthy of praise! No one can measure his greatness. ⁴Let each generation tell its children of your mighty acts; let them proclaim your power. ⁵I will meditate on your majestic, glorious splendor and your wonderful miracles. ⁶Your awe-inspiring deeds will be on every tongue; I will proclaim your greatness. ⁷Everyone will share the story of your wonderful goodness; they will sing with joy about your righteousness. . . . ¹⁷The LORD is righteous in everything he does; he is filled with kindness. ¹⁸The LORD is close to all who call on him, yes, to all who call on him in truth. ¹⁹He grants the desires of those who fear him; he hears their cries for help and rescues them.

PSALM 145:1-7, 17-19

What do you think when someone says, "Praise the Lord"? Does it strike you as strange, appropriate, logical, or weird? Does it make you uncomfortable? Or does it make you feel at ease?

David, the author of Psalm 145, didn't feel shy about expressing his love for God. In 2 Samuel 6:14, he danced for joy before the Lord, and here he says boldly, "Praise the Lord!" As you read, see what you can learn about praise.

Other psalms in this section give advice for people in need (Psalm 146); tell how to please God (Psalm 147); and list many reasons and ways to praise and worship God (Psalm 148-150).

Read Psalms 145:1–150:6

Sometimes life goes on with such an even rhythm that we may wonder why we should praise God. In Psalm 145, David gives us many good reasons: God is great (v. 3). God does mighty, wonderful deeds (vv. 4-6). God is righteous (v. 7). God is gracious, compassionate, patient, and loving (vv. 8-9). God rules over an everlasting kingdom (v. 13). God lifts us up when we are down (v. 14). God meets all our daily needs (vv. 15-16). God is righteous and loving in all he does (v. 17). God stays near to those who call on him (v. 18). God hears our cries and saves us (vv. 19-20).

If you are looking for a reason to praise God, start here. He is ready to listen.

You can spot the compulsive know-it-all by the way he or she dodges all possibility of admitting wrong. This person will use his or her knowledge to impress others, using words that people won't understand just to have the satisfaction of seeing them concede his or her superior knowledge. People like this are the ones that everyone tries to avoid at social gatherings.

This first chapter of Proverbs begins, appropriately, with a brief discourse on know-it-alls. The truth presented here is one that you've probably thought about before, but never really expressed in words.

Other lessons in this chapter highlight the difference between knowledge and wisdom; dangers in what you hear; and how to get God's advice.

Read Proverbs 1:1-33

Know-it-alls may have a great deal of knowledge, but they usually have little wisdom. Solomon called this kind of person a fool (Proverbs 1:7-9).

Much of what we know has no connection to how wise we are; for example, a brilliant surgeon can live a foolish life. Truly wise people know their knowledge is not complete and go to God for wisdom and more knowledge. All that we know has been granted to us by God as a gift for use in serving others and him. Therefore, we should use our knowledge with humility.

Don't act like a know-it-all, even if you have a lot of knowledge. Remember that all knowledge and wisdom come from God. Give him the glory!

⁴These proverbs will give insight to the simple, knowledge and discernment to the young. ⁵Let the wise listen to these proverbs and become even wiser. Let those with understanding receive guidance ⁶by exploring the meaning in these proverbs and parables, the words of the wise and their riddles. ⁷Fear of the Lord is the foundation of true knowledge, but fools despise wisdom and discipline. . . . ²⁰Wisdom shouts in the streets. She cries out in the public square. ²¹She calls to the crowds along the main street, to those gathered in front of the city gate: ²²"How long, you simpletons, will you insist on being simpleminded? How long will you mockers relish your mocking? How long will you fools hate knowledge? ²³Come and listen to my counsel. I'll share my heart with you and make you wise."

PROVERBS 1:4-7, 20-23

¹My child, listen to what I say, and treasure my commands. ²Tune your ears to wisdom, and concentrate on understanding. ³Cry out for insight, and ask for understanding. ⁴Search for them as you would for silver; seek them like hidden treasures. ⁵Then you will understand what it means to fear the LORD, and you will gain knowledge of God. ⁶For the LORD grants wisdom! From his mouth come knowledge and understanding. ⁷He grants a treasure of common sense to the honest. He is a shield to those who walk with integrity. ⁸He guards the paths of the just and protects those who are faithful to him. ⁹Then you will understand what is right, just, and fair, and you will find the right way to go. ¹⁰For wisdom will enter your heart, and knowledge will fill you with joy. ¹¹Wise choices will watch over you. Understanding will keep you safe.

PROVERBS 2:1-11

Modern technology presents new moral dilemmas almost daily: the abortion pill, pornography on the internet, movies and TV, life-support systems, and many others. When these technologies are created, they are often in widespread use before anyone even has the chance to ask, *Is this wrong?* The quest for broader insight (wisdom) will speak to these specific dilemmas, even when there are no Bible verses that speak directly to the problem at hand.

This chapter contains some advice about becoming wise. It takes more than an afternoon at a good seminar, and *much* more than an aptitude for common sense. Read Proverbs 2 to discover some of the sources of wisdom and to learn how long the process of getting it can take.

Other lessons to get out of this chapter include how and where to get wisdom and ways in which wisdom can save you.

Read Proverbs 2:1-22

Some people naturally have more insight than discretion; others have more knowledge than common sense. But no one is born wise. Growing wise doesn't happen quickly—it happens only through a consistent effort and only through God's Word. Wisdom comes through reading the Bible on a regular basis, accepting it, and putting its principles into practice.

Seek wisdom daily. Study and apply God's Word. Ask God to make your searches fruitful—you will be amazed at what you will learn and how your life will change.

Some people absolutely love leftovers for dinner. Other people just plain dislike them, preferring a freshly made meal every night.

Although leftovers from meals are good, other kinds of "leftovers" can cause problems. For instance, giving your spouse a little time at the end of a day rather than investing your free time with him or her is not a good idea. The same applies to our relationships with God. As you read this chapter, hear the challenge to give God your *best part,* not your leftovers.

This chapter also has lessons on how to live a long and prosperous life; how to make good choices; the benefits of wisdom; and how to treat one's neighbor.

Read Proverbs 3:1-35

God wants us to honor him with the "best part" of what we earn (Proverbs 3:9-10). The "best part" refers to the practice of giving to God the first and best portion of the harvest (see Deuteronomy 26:9-11).

For Christians today, this means writing the first check from their income to their local church or other Christian ministry. Unfortunately, many Christians give God what is left after they pay the bills and buy groceries. Then if they can afford to donate anything, they do so. But it is better to give God the *first* part of our income. This demonstrates that God, not possessions, has top place in our lives and that our resources belong to him—we are only managers of what he has given us. Giving to God first helps us conquer greed, helps us properly manage God's resources, demonstrates our faith in God to provide for our needs, and prepares us to receive his special blessings.

¹Never forget the things I have taught you. Store my commands in your heart. ²If you do this, you will live many years, and your life will be satisfying. ³Never let loyalty and kindness leave you! Tie them around your neck as a reminder. Write them deep within your heart. ⁴Then you will find favor with both God and people, and you will earn a good reputation. ⁵Trust in the LORD with all your heart; do not depend on your own understanding. ⁶Seek his will in all you do, and he will show you which path to take. ⁷Don't be impressed with your own wisdom. Instead, fear the LORD and turn away from evil. ⁸Then you will have healing for your body and strength for your bones. ⁹Honor the LORD with your wealth and with the best part of everything you produce. ¹⁰Then he will fill your barns with grain, and your vats will overflow with good wine.

PROVERBS 3:1-10

[10]Listen to me and do as I say, and you will have a long, good life. [11]I will teach you wisdom's ways and lead you in straight paths. [12]When you walk, you won't be held back; when you run, you won't stumble. [13]Take hold of my instructions; don't let them go. Guard them, for they are the key to life. [14]Don't do as the wicked do, and don't follow the path of evildoers. [15]Don't even think about it; don't go that way. Turn away and keep moving. [16]For evil people can't sleep until they've done their evil deed for the day. They can't rest until they've caused someone to stumble. [17]They eat the food of wickedness and drink the wine of violence! [18]The way of the righteous is like the first gleam of dawn, which shines ever brighter until the full light of day. [19]But the way of the wicked is like total darkness. They have no idea what they are stumbling over.

PROVERBS 4:10-19

The process of fending off temptation always involves a conversation with our feelings. *You really don't need this, you know. You just want it.* But desires tug at the heart. If there were no enjoyment to be had, where would the struggle be?

Proverbs 4 has some instructions about affection—those feelings of love and desire. It's about disciplining that part of the person that feels and desires the wrong pleasures (or the right ones at the wrong time). This is a difficult struggle—no one wants to go through life never doing what he or she enjoys. Read and learn.

Other areas of life covered in this chapter include lessons from parents; a goal that everyone should have; and the benefits of following wise advice and consequences of ignoring it.

Read Proverbs 4:1-27

Our affections can give us both pain and pleasure. On one hand, we can desire and enjoy good—such as wanting to help someone solve a problem or enjoying sexual pleasure in marriage. On the other hand, we can desire and enjoy what we shouldn't—such as being lazy or enjoying sex outside of marriage. Our affections define what we enjoy, but what we enjoy isn't always what we should do. Proverbs 4:23-27 tells us to guard these affections above all else, making sure we concentrate on those desires that will keep us on the right path.

Many people have the idea that God is against pleasure, but they are mistaken. He's only against letting pleasure rule our lives. Living in obedience to God begins with knowing the difference between our wants and our needs—and then making the right choice regardless of the pleasure involved.

In America, 95 percent of all adults eventually marry. In a country where arranged marriages hardly ever happen, these couples marry because they *want* to. No one forces them to get married; there are no penalties for staying single. But there is one problem for many of those couples who marry—individuals can still change their minds. Some will no longer want to stay with their spouse, or they might desire another companion.

Proverbs 5 gives advice on how to have a happy marriage, as well as good reasons why we should avoid infidelity. This chapter prohibits sex outside of marriage, but it encourages enjoyment of sexual pleasure within marriage. This reading also includes lessons on the consequences of adultery.

Read Proverbs 5:1-23

"Drink water from your own well" (Proverbs 5:15). In desert lands, water is incredibly precious, and a family's very survival depends on a well or cistern. In Old Testament times, it was considered a crime to steal water from someone else's well. In the sexual context of this passage, the message is clear: don't take what doesn't belong to you, especially someone else's husband or wife.

To a thirsty person in a hot, dry land, water satisfies like nothing else. If you're thirsty, you should go to your well and drink. God wants married couples to look only to each other for lifelong satisfaction and companionship. That is his provision. That is his desire. Enjoy.

¹My son, pay attention to my wisdom; listen carefully to my wise counsel. ²Then you will show discernment, and your lips will express what you've learned. ³For the lips of an immoral woman are as sweet as honey, and her mouth is smoother than oil. ⁴But in the end she is as bitter as poison, as dangerous as a double-edged sword. ⁵Her feet go down to death; her steps lead straight to the grave. ⁶For she cares nothing about the path to life. She staggers down a crooked trail and doesn't realize it. . . . ¹⁵Drink water from your own well—share your love only with your wife. ¹⁶Why spill the water of your springs in the streets, having sex with just anyone? ¹⁷You should reserve it for yourselves. Never share it with strangers. ¹⁸Let your wife be a fountain of blessing for you. Rejoice in the wife of your youth.

PROVERBS 5:1-6, 15-18

⁶Take a lesson from the ants, you lazybones. Learn from their ways and become wise! ⁷Though they have no prince or governor or ruler to make them work, ⁸they labor hard all summer, gathering food for the winter. ⁹But you, lazybones, how long will you sleep? When will you wake up? ¹⁰A little extra sleep, a little more slumber, a little folding of the hands to rest—¹¹then poverty will pounce on you like a bandit; scarcity will attack you like an armed robber. ¹²What are worthless and wicked people like? They are constant liars, ¹³signaling their deceit with a wink of the eye, a nudge of the foot, or the wiggle of fingers. ¹⁴Their perverted hearts plot evil, and they constantly stir up trouble. ¹⁵But they will be destroyed suddenly, broken in an instant beyond all hope of healing.

PROVERBS 6:6-15

If there were a television show called *Important Inventions That Everyone Takes for Granted*, the series would no doubt feature a profile of the snooze button. This workhorse feature of the alarm clock gives many people those few, crucial, extra minutes of rest. Its value far outweighs its price! For those who love to sleep, the snooze button lets them make the transition to wakefulness a little more slowly.

Proverbs 6 contains some advice on sleeping in and its close cousin, laziness. Don't sleep through this lesson.

Other proverbs in this chapter deal with the hazards of too much generosity and the consequences of scheming, displeasing God, and moral compromise.

Read Proverbs 6:1-35

Some days, a little extra sleep seems like a necessity—and to some people it actually is. But Proverbs warns us against sleeping in too much (Proverbs 6:10-11). Of course, God isn't saying that people should never rest. He commanded the Jews to observe the Sabbath, a weekly day of rest and restoration. But he also knows that human beings find it easier to sleep in than to get up and work.

Take responsibility for getting up and starting your day. Don't wait for someone else to do it for you. Get a good night's rest, but when the alarm goes off, be sure to get up and get to work.

One of the best ways to survive a walk through a minefield is to avoid it altogether. Don't go there, and you won't get blown up. But the idea behind a minefield is the element of surprise—you don't know where the mines are because they're hidden. Therefore, the most realistic defense against getting blown up is to have a healthy suspicion of where the mines might be laid. Heads up and don't be naive, we might say.

Proverbs 7 is a map to help you navigate your way through your own minefields—those areas of life in which you are susceptible to temptation. Self-defense comes in many forms, and this one should be a part of everyone's arsenal.

The other lessons in this chapter relate to sexual purity.

Read Proverbs 7:1-27

This chapter of Proverbs contains a dark description of a young woman seducing a young man into sexual compromise (Proverbs 7:6-23). The underlying principle applies to young women as well: Don't be naive. The person who has no purpose in life is simpleminded (7:7). Without aim or direction, an empty life is unstable and vulnerable to many temptations. Even though the young man in this passage doesn't know where he is going, the adulteress knows where she wants him. She preys on his naiveté: she dresses seductively (7:10); she boldly kisses him (7:13); she invites him over to her place (7:16-18); she cunningly answers his every objection (7:19-20); she persuades him with smooth talk (7:21). When she's done, he succumbs, as though he were a trapped animal (7:23).

⁶While I was at the window of my house, . . . ⁷I saw some naive young men, and one in particular who lacked common sense. ⁸He was crossing the street near the house of an immoral woman, strolling down the path by her house. . . . ¹⁰The woman approached him, seductively dressed and sly of heart. . . . ²²He followed her at once, like an ox going to the slaughter. He was like a stag caught in a trap, ²³awaiting the arrow that would pierce its heart. He was like a bird flying into a snare, little knowing it would cost him his life. ²⁴So listen to me, my sons, and pay attention to my words. ²⁵Don't let your hearts stray away toward her. Don't wander down her wayward path. ²⁶For she has been the ruin of many; many men have been her victims. ²⁷Her house is the road to the grave. Her bedroom is the den of death.

PROVERBS 7:6-8, 10, 22-27

The best way to avoid being entrapped by temptation is to have your eyes wide open about such schemes. Don't be naive—know your weaknesses, and run away.

¹Listen as Wisdom calls out! Hear as understanding raises her voice! ²On the hilltop along the road, she takes her stand at the crossroads. ³By the gates at the entrance to the town, on the road leading in, she cries aloud, ⁴"I call to you, to all of you! I raise my voice to all people. ⁵You simple people, use good judgment. You foolish people, show some understanding. ⁶Listen to me! For I have important things to tell you. Everything I say is right, ⁷for I speak the truth and detest every kind of deception. ⁸My advice is wholesome. There is nothing devious or crooked in it. ⁹My words are plain to anyone with understanding, clear to those with knowledge. ¹⁰Choose my instruction rather than silver, and knowledge rather than pure gold. ¹¹For wisdom is far more valuable than rubies. Nothing you desire can compare with it."

PROVERBS 8:1-11

Ice cream can sometimes be bought in a "swirl"—a mix of two flavors, usually chocolate and vanilla. It's for those who can't decide on one or the other, or who like both equally well, or who like the mix itself. But what is good in ice cream is bad in moral habits.

Proverbs 8 is a call to make right choices—to hate evil. There is no mixing of good and evil here.

Other proverbs in this chapter teach us why wisdom is more valuable than gold and even priceless.

Read Proverbs 8:1-36

"All who fear the LORD will hate evil. Therefore, I hate pride and arrogance, corruption and perverse speech" (Proverbs 8:13). Most of us have a mix of love and hate for evil. We know we should hate lying and hypocrisy, yet there are times when they come in handy. We know we should love sexual purity and honesty, yet there are times when our minds turn to impure thoughts, and deceit seems less painful than being honest.

Respect for God clears away the inconsistencies. Think about the place God deserves to have in your life, and fear the consequences of not giving him proper place. When you make the decision to love God wholeheartedly, love for sin will not be able to coexist in your life.

Columnists tell what's right and wrong with society. Theater critics explain who performed well and who faltered. Literary critics pronounce what's worth reading and what's not. Others, such as friends, neighbors, coworkers, and fellow drivers, give personal criticism in the many areas of life.

Proverbs 9 includes several principles regarding how to respond—or not respond—to criticism. As you read, be sure to notice the difference between being a wise person and a "mocker."

Other lessons here include how to tell the difference between wisdom and foolishness, and good reasons for avoiding prostitutes.

Read Proverbs 9:1-18

Are you a wise person or a "mocker"? You can tell by the way you respond to criticism (Proverbs 9:7-10). For instance, how do you normally respond to these situations? A relative rebukes you for something relatively insignificant that you did a while back; a coworker questions your judgment on a project; your spouse critiques your attire; your kids demand that you spend more time with them. Do you toss back a quick put-down or clever retort? Or do you listen to what is being said? A wise person learns from rebukes and criticism (9:8-9).

Instead of dismissing every critique of your behavior, try to see each from the critic's perspective. Search their words for ways you can improve yourself. Look for lessons in what they have to say and do not mock them. It bears repeating: How you respond to criticism tells a lot about you. A wise person accepts it and tries to learn from it. A fool throws it back. Don't be a fool.

¹Wisdom has built her house; she has carved its seven columns. ²She has prepared a great banquet, mixed the wines, and set the table. ³She has sent her servants to invite everyone to come. She calls out from the heights overlooking the city. ⁴"Come in with me," she urges the simple. To those who lack good judgment, she says, ⁵"Come, eat my food, and drink the wine I have mixed. ⁶Leave your simple ways behind, and begin to live; learn to use good judgment." ⁷Anyone who rebukes a mocker will get an insult in return. Anyone who corrects the wicked will get hurt. ⁸So don't bother correcting mockers; they will only hate you. But correct the wise, and they will love you. ⁹Instruct the wise, and they will be even wiser. Teach the righteous, and they will learn even more. ¹⁰Fear of the LORD is the foundation of wisdom.

PROVERBS 9:1-10

⁸The wise are glad to be instructed, but babbling fools fall flat on their faces. ⁹People with integrity walk safely, but those who follow crooked paths will slip and fall. ¹⁰People who wink at wrong cause trouble, but a bold reproof promotes peace. ¹¹The words of the godly are a life-giving fountain; the words of the wicked conceal violent intentions. ¹²Hatred stirs up quarrels, but love makes up for all offenses. ¹³Wise words come from the lips of people with understanding, but those lacking sense will be beaten with a rod. ¹⁴Wise people treasure knowledge, but the babbling of a fool invites disaster. ¹⁵The wealth of the rich is their fortress; the poverty of the poor is their destruction. ¹⁶The earnings of the godly enhance their lives, but evil people squander their money on sin.

PROVERBS 10:8-16

Are there certain people, who, even just the mention of their name can set you off in three seconds flat? Although you don't particularly care for the way you respond, you can't forget how badly that person treated you. Normally you're not a hateful person, but your feelings for so-and-so cross the line of hatred.

Proverbs 10 urges us to deal with this ugly emotion head-on. That's easy to say but not so easy to do. The principles in this reading, however, will help you out.

Other lessons in this chapter will teach you how to avoid sorrow; how to keep your foot out of your mouth; and how to avoid aggravating your employer.

Read Proverbs 10:1-32

Many people spend their whole lives hating certain people. They cannot let go of wrongs done to them, or forgive offenses from the distant past. Their statements about these people become laced with unkind words and slander. Harboring hatred destroys the person doing the hating and causes nothing but conflict with others (Proverbs 10:12). "Hiding hatred makes you a liar; slandering others makes you a fool" (10:18). In contrast, those who love bring forgiveness and healing because "love makes up for all offenses" (10:12). Love forgives and forgets.

Beware of hatred. If you try to conceal your hatred, you only lie about your true feelings. If you slander the other person, you become a fool. The only way out is to admit your hateful feelings to God, ask him to change your heart, and forgive the other person. Let God's love go beyond the other person's offense and help you to actually forgive the offender (10:12). Ask God to help you love instead of hate.

The power of words is amazing. Say a word and you can make a roomful of people laugh; say another and you can make them cry. An entire nation's morale can change with the words of its leaders. You could even completely destroy a person's reputation with a thoughtless word or two. It has been said that the pen is mightier than the sword—and for good reason.

Proverbs 11 contains some thoughts on the destructiveness of words and stands as a good reminder for us to watch what we say.

This chapter also has thoughts on wealth; abuse of power; leadership; and generosity.

Read Proverbs 11:1-31

Like power tools, words have the potential to do great good or enormous damage, depending on how we use them. We can either use words to damage a relationship or make it better (Proverbs 11:9, 11–13). Unfortunately, most people use words to destroy more often than to build up.

Each bit of gossip and each word of slander we speak not only hurts those around us, but it also wastes an opportunity to help. Every day brings many opportunities to use words negatively or positively. Sadly, it takes less effort to gossip than to praise; less skill to cut with sarcasm than to repair with thanks. So most people hear far more destructive comments than constructive ones.

Remember that every person with whom you interact today will be either better or worse off as a consequence of your words. Your words could make the difference. Think before you talk!

²Pride leads to disgrace, but with humility comes wisdom. ³Honesty guides good people; dishonesty destroys treacherous people. ⁴Riches won't help on the day of judgment, but right living can save you from death. ⁵The godly are directed by honesty; the wicked fall beneath their load of sin. ⁶The godliness of good people rescues them; the ambition of treacherous people traps them. ⁷When the wicked die, their hopes die with them, for they rely on their own feeble strength. ⁸The godly are rescued from trouble, and it falls on the wicked instead. ⁹With their words, the godless destroy their friends, but knowledge will rescue the righteous. ¹⁰The whole city celebrates when the godly succeed; they shout for joy when the wicked die. ¹¹Upright citizens are good for a city and make it prosper, but the talk of the wicked tears it apart.

PROVERBS 11:2-11

²The LORD approves of those who are good, but he condemns those who plan wickedness. ³Wickedness never brings stability, but the godly have deep roots. ⁴A worthy wife is a crown for her husband, but a disgraceful woman is like cancer in his bones. ⁵The plans of the godly are just; the advice of the wicked is treacherous. ⁶The words of the wicked are like a murderous ambush, but the words of the godly save lives. ⁷The wicked die and disappear, but the family of the godly stands firm. ⁸A sensible person wins admiration, but a warped mind is despised. ⁹Better to be an ordinary person with a servant than to be self-important but have no food. ¹⁰The godly care for their animals, but the wicked are always cruel. ¹¹A hard worker has plenty of food, but a person who chases fantasies has no sense.

PROVERBS 12:2-11

Cheating, cutting in line, fudging the numbers, covering up your mistakes, and working so many hours that you neglect your family responsibilities—these are the techniques people use to get ahead. This is the "American way." Is it yours?

When it comes to achieving success, there is a tremendous contrast between the techniques used by the wicked and those used by the righteous. There's also a big difference between whom the wicked and the righteous worship. In the end, only one will really be successful. As you read, look for the proverbs that teach how to attain real success.

You will also find these topics in Proverbs 12: a smart step that everyone can take; tips for responding to insults; how to use words; and laziness.

Read Proverbs 12:1-28

"Wickedness never brings stability, but the godly have deep roots" (Proverbs 12:3). This proverb refers to success. Everyone knows people who have cheated to pass a test or to get a larger tax refund. While they may get away with it and enjoy a good grade or a bigger refund, don't be tempted to view them as successful or desire to emulate them. Real success comes only to those who do what is right (12:3). Although the efforts of the righteous may not always be successful from the world's point of view, their efforts will have lasting worth. The apparent successes of the wicked will not last.

The choices that will set you on the path to real success—obedience to God and doing his will—have everlasting consequences. If you are not a success by God's standards, you have not achieved success at all.

Determine to be firmly rooted in living God's way. Don't sell your character to achieve worldly success.

What kind of advice do you get from your friends? Are you satisfied with it? Do you sometimes sense that some of your problems baffle your friends, leaving them unable to offer wise and insightful counsel? You may even wonder where you would turn if you ever needed counseling for a true problem.

Proverbs 13 contains many helpful words of advice about choosing friends and how to benefit from the people who walk the same path. You're right if you've been thinking you need some wise friends, friends who can guide you along the way. Here's how to get them.

There's much more here on several other subjects, including ways to benefit from your words; the benefits of being poor and the hazards of having wealth; a warning about pride; and the importance of disciplining children.

Read Proverbs 13:1-25

When seeking friends, most people look for those who make them feel good about themselves. But that's not the most important ingredient in friendship. In fact, people who make us feel good about ourselves may not be the best influence on us, and they may not have our best interests at heart.

Our friends help determine the direction that our lives take. If our friends are wise, we will be too. If they are fools, so will we be (Proverbs 13:20). Thus, we need to choose our friends very carefully. We should seek out friends who can advise us, set an example for us, and help us stay on the right track. Some of them should be older, and the best ones should be wiser.

¹³People who despise advice are asking for trouble; those who respect a command will succeed. ¹⁴The instruction of the wise is like a life-giving fountain; those who accept it avoid the snares of death. ¹⁵A person with good sense is respected; a treacherous person is headed for destruction. ¹⁶Wise people think before they act; fools don't—and even brag about their foolishness. ¹⁷An unreliable messenger stumbles into trouble, but a reliable messenger brings healing. ¹⁸If you ignore criticism, you will end in poverty and disgrace; if you accept correction, you will be honored. ¹⁹It is pleasant to see dreams come true, but fools refuse to turn from evil to attain them. ²⁰Walk with the wise and become wise; associate with fools and get in trouble. ²¹Trouble chases sinners, while blessings reward the righteous.

PROVERBS 13:13-21

Seek out wise people who have experienced life—and have succeeded. Seek out friends who are not afraid to tell you the truth, who will move you in God's direction.

9Fools make fun of guilt, but the godly acknowledge it and seek reconciliation. 10Each heart knows its own bitterness, and no one else can fully share its joy. 11The house of the wicked will be destroyed, but the tent of the godly will flourish. 12There is a path before each person that seems right, but it ends in death. 13Laughter can conceal a heavy heart, but when the laughter ends, the grief remains. 14Backsliders get what they deserve; good people receive their reward. 15Only simpletons believe everything they're told! The prudent carefully consider their steps. 16The wise are cautious and avoid danger; fools plunge ahead with reckless confidence. 17Short-tempered people do foolish things, and schemers are hated. 18Simpletons are clothed with foolishness, but the prudent are crowned with knowledge.

PROVERBS 14:9-18

"Hackers," or people who write destructive computer viruses, don't feel at fault when their viruses destroy people's data. *If I can hack my way into your computer,* many of them reason, *it's your own fault for not better protecting yourself.* What's wrong with that way of thinking?

Proverbs 14 contains the answer for those who can accept it. It's also the answer to Cain's infamous question, "Am I my brother's keeper?" (see Genesis 4:9).

Other proverbs in this chapter touch on many areas of relationships: advice for women; a way to avoid some unnecessary trouble; certain people to avoid; where to find help; reasons for controlling one's temper; and treatment of the poor.

Read Proverbs 14:1-35

People who love God care about what happens to others and try to do what will be helpful to them, not hurtful. They practice good will toward others (Proverbs 14:9, 21). They (1) think the best of others, (2) assume that others have good motives and intend to do what is right, (3) look out for others, and (4) make amends whenever they wrong someone.

In everything you do that affects others, ask yourself, *Does this show good will?* And in each interaction with another person, whether a phone call, gesture, E-mail, or face-to-face conversation, ask, *How can I help this person?*

A construction crew has been tearing up your route to work lately. It looks—as usual—as if they have chosen to do more than they can manage. Lanes and road shoulders are torn up, heavy equipment is scattered throughout the construction zone, and mud and debris are everywhere. As you pass through this mess, what do you see? Do you see a colossal inconvenience, or do you see a new era of smooth rides to work? Which would you rather do—curse the potholes or bless the highway department for filling them in?

Several verses in Proverbs 15 discuss attitudes—both cheerful and gloomy. They offer common sense on human emotions that you won't find in a modern-day psychology book.

You will find these other lessons in this reading: how to defuse erupting fights; what God loves; what your reading material says about you; the value of love; one way to protect your family; and one way to attract honor.

Read Proverbs 15:1-33

Our attitudes color every experience we have (Proverbs 15:4, 13, 15, 30). The way we interpret and respond to our experiences is entirely up to us. We can choose to respond cheerfully, or we can choose to respond grumpily. The secret to responding optimistically and having a good day is to have a cheerful heart (15:15). We can have this positive attitude despite wretched circumstances if we focus our attention on God—his character, his sovereignty, and his goodness to us.

⁴Gentle words are a tree of life; a deceitful tongue crushes the spirit. ⁵Only a fool despises a parent's discipline; whoever learns from correction is wise. ⁶There is treasure in the house of the godly, but the earnings of the wicked bring trouble. ⁷The lips of the wise give good advice; the heart of a fool has none to give. ⁸The LORD detests the sacrifice of the wicked, but he delights in the prayers of the upright. ⁹The LORD detests the way of the wicked, but he loves those who pursue godliness. ¹⁰Whoever abandons the right path will be severely disciplined; whoever hates correction will die. ¹¹Even Death and Destruction hold no secrets from the LORD. How much more does he know the human heart! ¹²Mockers hate to be corrected, so they stay away from the wise.

PROVERBS 15:4-12

As you face the struggles of daily living, look at your attitudes and examine what you choose to dwell on. If you have a bad attitude, shift your focus from your circumstances to God. It will make all the difference.

¹We can make our own plans, but the LORD gives the right answer. ²People may be pure in their own eyes, but the LORD examines their motives. ³Commit your actions to the LORD, and your plans will succeed. ⁴The LORD has made everything for his own purposes, even the wicked for a day of disaster. ⁵The LORD detests the proud; they will surely be punished. ⁶Unfailing love and faithfulness make atonement for sin. By fearing the LORD, people avoid evil. ⁷When people's lives please the LORD, even their enemies are at peace with them. ⁸Better to have little, with godliness, than to be rich and dishonest. ⁹We can make our plans, but the LORD determines our steps.

PROVERBS 16:1-9

Many people fear getting married. Marriage changes everything—for the rest of your life. No one should blame a bride or groom for being nervous. Uncertainty over the future is the most nerve-racking kind of all. How do they know this will work? So many marriages don't last. Will theirs?

Predicting the future has many hazards. A better approach would be to consider the advice in Proverbs 16 about committing your way (or future) to God.

In this chapter you will also learn about making plans; dealing with pride; being fair in business; using pleasant words; and strengthening the bond between friends.

Read Proverbs 16:1-33

Proverbs 16:3 says, "Commit your actions to the LORD, and your plans will succeed." What does this mean? To "commit your work to the Lord" means to dedicate everything you do to God's purposes through prayer—turning it over to him. It also means doing your best for God's glory and depending on him for the results.

What work should you commit to God? Any plan, task, or endeavor that you want to succeed: buying a car, starting school, initiating a new church program, getting engaged or married, going on vacation, changing jobs, entering retirement—these all qualify.

Think of a specific effort in which you are involved right now—how might you commit it to the Lord?

It's not surprising to see a winning team celebrate a victory. That's what victors are entitled to do. Some fans, however, dislike winning teams that take the celebration too far. They know that there's a place for respecting the loser, even if the gap between winner and loser is quite wide. They also hope that someday the roles will be reversed.

In an indirect way, Proverbs 17 talks about winners and losers. More to the point, it's about people who mock those less fortunate than they—the losers, you might say. As you read this chapter, be prepared to put away that "We're Number One!" chant.

Also in this chapter you will find one reason for suffering; one reward in getting old; one hazard in associating with a fool; one rule to being a best friend; one use for a positive attitude; and one more reason to hold your tongue.

Read Proverbs 17:1-28

Making fun of those less fortunate than others is an old tradition for humankind. The vulnerable can count on being ridiculed and exploited—especially the poor, but also children and senior citizens.

Those who take advantage of the vulnerable do so because it makes them feel stronger or more successful than the less fortunate. But mocking the poor mocks the God who made them (Proverbs 17:5), and we might reasonably extend that to the weak and downtrodden as well.

The next time you catch yourself putting others down, stop and think about who created them.

¹Better a dry crust eaten in peace than a house filled with feasting—and conflict. ²A wise servant will rule over the master's disgraceful son and will share the inheritance of the master's children. ³Fire tests the purity of silver and gold, but the LORD tests the heart. ⁴Wrongdoers eagerly listen to gossip; liars pay close attention to slander. ⁵Those who mock the poor insult their Maker; those who rejoice at the misfortune of others will be punished. ⁶Grandchildren are the crowning glory of the aged; parents are the pride of their children. ⁷Eloquent words are not fitting for a fool; even less are lies fitting for a ruler. ⁸A bribe is like a lucky charm; whoever gives one will prosper! ⁹Love prospers when a fault is forgiven, but dwelling on it separates close friends.

PROVERBS 17:1-9

[15]Intelligent people are always ready to learn. Their ears are open for knowledge. [16]Giving a gift can open doors; it gives access to important people! [17]The first to speak in court sounds right—until the cross-examination begins. [18]Casting lots can end arguments; it settles disputes between powerful opponents. [19]An offended friend is harder to win back than a fortified city. Arguments separate friends like a gate locked with bars. [20]Wise words satisfy like a good meal; the right words bring satisfaction. [21]The tongue can bring death or life; those who love to talk will reap the consequences. [22]The man who finds a wife finds a treasure, and he receives favor from the LORD. [23]The poor plead for mercy; the rich answer with insults. [24]There are "friends" who destroy each other, but a real friend sticks closer than a brother.

PROVERBS 18:15-24

When you were a little kid, best friends really meant *best friends*. You played together every day. You invited each other over all the time. You stuck up for each other when the neighborhood bully showed up. You shared secrets, passwords, and favorite things. It was all about one thing: loyalty.

Proverbs 18 covers friends—the loyal ones, the kind you can't do without. As you read, you will find a challenge to live up to the standard of an ideal friend. You will also find a warning to avoid those who pretend to be friends but aren't.

Other verses here deal with sharing your opinion; a popular myth about wealth; and getting both sides of the story.

Read Proverbs 18:1-24

Today, more than ever, friendlessness plagues many people. With all the advances in technology, people, for the most part, are no longer dependent upon one another. It's no wonder, then, why some people feel cut off and alienated from others, even those they consider "friends."

God, however, made us to be social beings, in need of close, meaningful relationships. Each one of us needs a friend who will listen, care, stick close, and offer help whenever we need it—in good times and bad. One such friend means more than dozens of superficial acquaintances (Proverbs 18:24).

If you're lonely and in need of a good friend, take the first step to developing great friendships: seek to become a true and loyal friend to someone else. Ask God to reveal this person to you. Then take on the challenge of being a true friend by caring, listening, helping, and affirming. Your friends need your friendship as much as you need theirs.

Some things have been disappearing from the office lately—small but expensive items. Talk turns to speculation on who could be doing it. Circumstantial evidence points to one person in particular, but no one is willing to believe that he could be guilty. He just isn't the kind of person who would do that—he's too honest.

Proverbs 19 addresses the subject of dishonesty. The consequences of dishonesty are not pleasant. As you read, you'll see what I mean . . . honest!

In addition, this chapter contains five don'ts and one do: don't be hasty; don't lie; don't be quarrelsome; don't be lazy; don't be stingy; but do listen to advice.

Read Proverbs 19:1-29

"A false witness will not go unpunished"—those words appear twice in this chapter (Proverbs 19:5, 9). Other verses make similar statements about the practical value of truth and the foolishness of deceiving others (19:1, 28).

Honesty is God's policy. Having a reputation for speaking the truth is better than lying and living well. Unfortunately, however, most people don't believe this, so in order to get ahead they cut moral corners when it comes to telling the truth.

Don't buy the world's line that lying is OK. Remember, being honest will keep you out of trouble with God, and it may also build your reputation. Be known as a person who tells the truth.

¹Better to be poor and honest than to be dishonest and a fool. ²Enthusiasm without knowledge is no good; haste makes mistakes. ³People ruin their lives by their own foolishness and then are angry at the Lord. ⁴Wealth makes many "friends"; poverty drives them all away. ⁵A false witness will not go unpunished, nor will a liar escape. ⁶Many seek favors from a ruler; everyone is the friend of a person who gives gifts! ⁷The relatives of the poor despise them; how much more will their friends avoid them! Though the poor plead with them, their friends are gone. ⁸To acquire wisdom is to love oneself; people who cherish understanding will prosper. ⁹A false witness will not go unpunished, and a liar will be destroyed. . . . ¹¹Sensible people control their temper; they earn respect by overlooking wrongs.

PROVERBS 19:1-9, 11

¹Wine produces mockers; alcohol leads to brawls. Those led astray by drink cannot be wise. ²The king's fury is like a lion's roar; to rouse his anger is to risk your life. ³Avoiding a fight is a mark of honor; only fools insist on quarreling. ⁴Those too lazy to plow in the right season will have no food at the harvest. ⁵Though good advice lies deep within the heart, a person with understanding will draw it out. ⁶Many will say they are loyal friends, but who can find one who is truly reliable? ⁷The godly walk with integrity; blessed are their children who follow them. ⁸When a king sits in judgment, he weighs all the evidence, distinguishing the bad from the good. ⁹Who can say, "I have cleansed my heart; I am pure and free from sin"? ¹⁰False weights and unequal measures—the LORD detests double standards of every kind.

PROVERBS 20:1-10

Everyone has wasted time. Perhaps you've watched a mindless television program when the lawn needed mowing. Maybe you've played games on your computer at work when you really needed to finish a report. Or perhaps you've put off doing a necessary but unpleasant task by immersing yourself in a magazine or newspaper. There are countless other ways to kill time. What is your favorite time-wasting activity?

Proverbs 20 says that there's a problem with wasting time, with putting off responsibilities in favor of puttering around. In some cases the consequences of wasting time can be serious. As you read, you will discover good reasons for being responsible.

Note also the other consequences here for getting drunk, sleeping in too much, and cursing one's parents. This chapter doesn't just dwell on consequences, though. It shows the many blessings for children of an honest parent; for those who have good sense; and for a leader who is fair, honest, and kind.

Read Proverbs 20:1-30

"Those too lazy to plow in the right season will have no food at the harvest" (Proverbs 20:4). You've probably heard similar warnings: "If you don't study, you'll fail the test," or "If you don't save, you won't have money when you need it." Although God will provide for our needs, he wants us to take responsibility for ourselves and use wisely what he has given us. Refusing to take responsibility for ourselves today can mean suffering the consequences of our irresponsibility tomorrow. And we cannot expect God to come to our rescue whenever we foolishly do not plan ahead.

What's on your must-do list? Let nothing hold you back from fulfilling your responsibilities and promises.

Do you know someone who seems to have an answer for every critic? In conversation you may have come to realize that this person can rationalize their every action. In fact, this person seems to have good reasons for all the wrong choices that he or she has ever made!

Yesterday's reading, Proverbs 20, urged us to be honest with others. This reading, Proverbs 21, urges us to bring the lesson home and be honest with ourselves. Call it a true/false test for motives.

Other topics in this chapter challenge us to be honest with ourselves in the areas of business, pleasure, pride, and savings.

Read Proverbs 21:1-31

"People may be right in their own eyes, but the LORD examines their heart" (Proverbs 21:2). It's amazing how readily we can justify whatever we set out to do. Every action seems right, so with a little thought, we can find an excuse for doing almost anything. The truth can often hurt, so we tend to deceive ourselves about why we're really doing what we're doing. But God always looks behind our excuses to our motives. We can't hide the truth from him; so we should be honest about why we're really doing something.

To cure this tendency to deceive ourselves and rationalize, we must examine our excuses carefully to make sure they aren't covering up sinful actions, poor choices, or wrong motives. A test to use to cut through an excuse is to ask, *Would God be pleased with my real reasons for doing this?* If the answer is no, then we shouldn't do it.

God wants you to be honest, to admit when you've done wrong, and to do what is right. He also wants you to do good deeds for the right reasons. If you do, you will find life!

¹The king's heart is like a stream of water directed by the LORD; he guides it wherever he pleases. ²People may be right in their own eyes, but the LORD examines their heart. ³The LORD is more pleased when we do what is right and just than when we offer him sacrifices. ⁴Haughty eyes, a proud heart, and evil actions are all sin. ⁵Good planning and hard work lead to prosperity, but hasty shortcuts lead to poverty. ⁶Wealth created by a lying tongue is a vanishing mist and a deadly trap. ⁷The violence of the wicked sweeps them away, because they refuse to do what is just. ⁸The guilty walk a crooked path; the innocent travel a straight road. ⁹It's better to live alone in the corner of an attic than with a quarrelsome wife in a lovely home.

PROVERBS 21:1-9

¹⁷Listen to the words of the wise; apply your heart to my instruction. ¹⁸For it is good to keep these sayings in your heart and always ready on your lips. ¹⁹I am teaching you today—yes, you—so you will trust in the LORD. ²⁰I have written thirty sayings for you, filled with advice and knowledge. ²¹In this way, you may know the truth and take an accurate report to those who sent you. ²²Don't rob the poor just because you can, or exploit the needy in court. ²³For the LORD is their defender. He will ruin anyone who ruins them. ²⁴Don't befriend angry people or associate with hot-tempered people, ²⁵or you will learn to be like them and endanger your soul. ²⁶Don't agree to guarantee another person's debt or put up security for someone else. ²⁷If you can't pay it, even your bed will be snatched from under you.

PROVERBS 22:17-27

With few exceptions, bullies use fear and intimidation only against people who are weaker than they are. They don't threaten those who are bigger and stronger because they don't want to lose. Their reign of terror depends on scaring people. That's why they'll hurt people just to make a point.

In Proverbs 22 you will find warnings for leaders who rule by fear and intimidation, just like bullies. Take heed.

You will also find thoughts on pursuing a good reputation; responding to dangers and hazards; rearing children; being rewarded for doing good; avoiding the sure road to poverty; and learning a skill.

Read Proverbs 22:1-29

God hates it when people use fear and intimidation to control others. Although he has given leaders the freedom to lead as they see fit, he doesn't stand back and ignore their abuse of power and influence. When abuse of power occurs, God will sometimes intervene directly and destroy the tyrant, but more often he uses other rulers or even the oppressed people to remove the tyrant from power (Proverbs 22:8, 22-23).

If you must live or work under an abusive leader, take these verses as a message of hope: God has not forgotten you and does not overlook your leader's abuses. If you lead or have any authority at all—either at church, work, or home—remember what happens to tyrants.

Leadership through kindness works better and lasts longer than leadership by force. Fear and intimidation are the human way, not God's way. Jesus never led by fear and intimidation and neither should we.

"You're not overweight!" friends tell Juan. "Diet any more and you're going to blow away!" Ruth tells Nancy. "I only drink at weddings and other celebrations," explains Jolene. "I don't have a drinking problem—I can quit any time I want," Mike insists. Eating and drinking—sources of pleasure and sources of grief.

Does the Bible talk about food and drink? You better believe it. Here in Proverbs 23 are some of the choicest morsels. Dig in.

Other verses in this chapter say more to modern living than the advice columns of most major newspapers. They address accepting bribes; the wrong reason to work hard; what to think of party animals; what to do with your parents when they are old; and the truth about alcohol.

Read Proverbs 23:1-35

Gluttony and drunkenness make poor friends. They not only make us overweight (and possibly alcoholic); they can also weaken our character and drain our pockets (Proverbs 23:19-21).

Not everyone struggles with overeating or alcoholism, but those who do certainly never planned on it. If you do have these struggles, there are some steps that you can take to overcome them: (1) realize you have a problem; (2) ask God to grant you the strength to resist the temptation; (3) seek professional help if necessary; and (4) avoid the source of your temptation.

Work at getting control of your appetites—God desires that you live a life of freedom!

¹While dining with a ruler, pay attention to what is put before you. ²If you are a big eater, put a knife to your throat; ³don't desire all the delicacies, for he might be trying to trick you. ⁴Don't wear yourself out trying to get rich. Be wise enough to know when to quit. ⁵In the blink of an eye wealth disappears, for it will sprout wings and fly away like an eagle. ⁶Don't eat with people who are stingy; don't desire their delicacies. ⁷They are always thinking about how much it costs. "Eat and drink," they say, but they don't mean it. ⁸You will throw up what little you've eaten, and your compliments will be wasted. . . . ¹⁷Don't envy sinners, but always continue to fear the LORD. ¹⁸You will be rewarded for this; your hope will not be disappointed.

PROVERBS 23:1-8, 17-18

⁷Wisdom is too lofty for fools. Among leaders at the city gate, they have nothing to say. ⁸A person who plans evil will get a reputation as a troublemaker. ⁹The schemes of a fool are sinful; everyone detests a mocker. ¹⁰If you fail under pressure, your strength is too small. ¹¹Rescue those who are unjustly sentenced to die; save them as they stagger to their death. ¹²Don't excuse yourself by saying, "Look, we didn't know." For God understands all hearts, and he sees you. He who guards your soul knows you knew. He will repay all people as their actions deserve. ¹³My child, eat honey, for it is good, and the honeycomb is sweet to the taste. ¹⁴In the same way, wisdom is sweet to your soul. If you find it, you will have a bright future, and your hopes will not be cut short.

PROVERBS 24:7-14

Many people are terrified of going to the dentist. The mere thought of the needle and the drill gives them the shivers. They long to overcome this fear, because they know what awaits them if they don't go to the dentist regularly—dentures.

Proverbs 24 talks about adversity and what our responses to it reveal about us. The wisdom here is a prescription for the fear of pain. If you suffer from this fear, don't forget to take your medicine regularly.

Other prescriptions in this chapter should be taken if you envy others; are struggling through tough times; associate with radicals; worry about the future; or struggle with laziness.

Read Proverbs 24:1-34

Adversity does us a favor—it gives us opportunity to see what we're made of (Proverbs 24:10). If we whine and whimper at every threat of illness, inconvenience, or irritation, we may have a character problem. People who love and obey God don't cave in easily because God sustains them (Proverbs 24:16; see also Nehemiah 9:21; Jeremiah 15:15-16).

How do you respond when you're not feeling well, when it rains, or when you have a bad day? Do you whine and complain? Don't grumble about your problems. Realize that the adversity you face today is training you to be strong for more difficult situations in the future.

One day a friend reveals a major problem. You're uncomfortable with this disclosure and your friend's ensuing tears. "Buck up!" you say. "Tough times never last, but tough people do! It's just so much water under the bridge! Cheer up! You'll feel better soon!"

Proverbs 25 contains a critique of the classic stoic approach to counseling, and the review is not good.

In this chapter you will also find these lessons: not exalting yourself; appropriate rebukes; how to ensure your plans will fail; and the value of self-control.

Read Proverbs 25:1-28

Proverbs 25:20 urges us to avoid being light and cheery around those who are grieving and sad. In fact, to say "Cheer up!" and discount the feelings of a hurting or distraught friend can have the opposite effect.

Whenever you encounter people who are sad or hurting, don't deny or minimize their pain, or belittle them for feeling the way they do. Instead, respect their feelings. Parents, do this for your children. Married person, do this for your spouse. Do this for your friends. Do this for anyone who confides in you. Listen with compassion and offer support. Give them a shoulder to lean on.

[11]Timely advice is lovely, like golden apples in a silver basket. [12]To one who listens, valid criticism is like a gold earring or other gold jewelry. . . . [17]Don't visit your neighbors too often, or you will wear out your welcome. [18]Telling lies about others is as harmful as hitting them with an ax, wounding them with a sword, or shooting them with a sharp arrow. [19]Putting confidence in an unreliable person in times of trouble is like chewing with a broken tooth or walking on a lame foot. [20]Singing cheerful songs to a person with a heavy heart is like taking someone's coat in cold weather or pouring vinegar in a wound. [21]If your enemies are hungry, give them food to eat. If they are thirsty, give them water to drink. [22]You will heap burning coals of shame on their heads, and the LORD will reward you.

PROVERBS 25:11-12, 17-22

¹⁰An employer who hires a fool or a bystander is like an archer who shoots at random. ¹¹As a dog returns to its vomit, so a fool repeats his foolishness. ¹²There is more hope for fools than for people who think they are wise. ¹³The lazy person claims, "There's a lion on the road! Yes, I'm sure there's a lion out there!" ¹⁴As a door swings back and forth on its hinges, so the lazy person turns over in bed. ¹⁵Lazy people take food in their hand but don't even lift it to their mouth. ¹⁶Lazy people consider themselves smarter than seven wise counselors. ¹⁷Interfering in someone else's argument is as foolish as yanking a dog's ears.

PROVERBS 26:10-17

Lazy people never seem to begin their responsibilities. Those they do start they never seem to finish. They let things wait until the last minute. They would rather listen to the radio or watch television than do their job. You know the type—maybe you've had to pick up the resulting slack.

Read through Proverbs 26 and look for verses on laziness. See what areas of your life could benefit from a hardworking perspective.

Two other major themes deserve attention: (1) fools (what they're like and what they deserve), and (2) gossip (its power and its harmfulness).

Read Proverbs 26:1-28

The person who doesn't want to work can find an excuse for avoiding every form of physical exertion (Proverbs 26:13-16). But laziness does more than just leave work undone. The less you do, the less you want to do—and the worse the cycle becomes. Unless you live and work entirely alone, others will have to do the work that you neglect.

If you struggle with the temptation to be lazy in any area of your life, apply these three steps: (1) Identify the responsibilities that you avoid and always do them first. (2) Identify the leisure pursuits that you overpursue and do them last. (3) Each time you feel the temptation to be lazy, take one small step toward doing what you need to do. Then take another.

If temptations to laziness plague you constantly, set simple, realistic goals for yourself. Figure out the steps needed to reach each goal and follow those steps one at a time. All along the way, ask God for strength and persistence.

"When are you going to fix the sink? Will you *please* fix the sink? I'm tired of waiting for you to fix the sink." That's a great conversation, isn't it?

Proverbs 27 takes aim at nagging. What alternatives are there to this persistent complaining? Words of love, for starters.

As you read about nagging, note the other lessons in this chapter on not boasting about tomorrow; not withholding a rebuke; and not making promises for others.

Read Proverbs 27:1-27

Nagging, a persistent attempt to make another person do something, has been called a mild form of domestic torture. Unfortunately, this steady stream of unwanted advice abuses the person our advice is meant to help. People also nag to make others do things, but that isn't right, either (Proverbs 27:15-16). Besides, constantly pushing someone will only make them less willing to sympathize with your agenda.

The next time you're tempted to nag, try to imagine *why* the person might not be acting on your advice or wishes. You may discover that those reasons may be as legitimate as your own. In addition, you may want to examine your motives: are you more concerned about yourself—getting your way—than about the other person? If you truly care about other people, try using a more effective way to communicate your concerns. For example, ask the person to do something in an open-ended way, leaving the person some options for accomplishing the task. You could even offer to help.

⁵An open rebuke is better than hidden love! ⁶Wounds from a sincere friend are better than many kisses from an enemy. ⁷A person who is full refuses honey, but even bitter food tastes sweet to the hungry. ⁸A person who strays from home is like a bird that strays from its nest. ⁹The heartfelt counsel of a friend is as sweet as perfume and incense. ¹⁰Never abandon a friend—either yours or your father's. When disaster strikes, you won't have to ask your brother for assistance. It's better to go to a neighbor than to a brother who lives far away. ¹¹Be wise, my child, and make my heart glad. Then I will be able to answer my critics. ¹²A prudent person foresees danger and takes precautions. The simpleton goes blindly on and suffers the consequences.

PROVERBS 27:5-12

⁶Better to be poor and honest than to be dishonest and rich. ⁷Young people who obey the law are wise; those with wild friends bring shame to their parents. ⁸Income from charging high interest rates will end up in the pocket of someone who is kind to the poor. ⁹God detests the prayers of a person who ignores the law. ¹⁰Those who lead good people along an evil path will fall into their own trap, but the honest will inherit good things. ¹¹Rich people may think they are wise, but a poor person with discernment can see right through them. ¹²When the godly succeed, everyone is glad. When the wicked take charge, people go into hiding. ¹³People who conceal their sins will not prosper, but if they confess and turn from them, they will receive mercy. ¹⁴Blessed are those who fear to do wrong, but the stubborn are headed for serious trouble.

PROVERBS 28:6-14

You can't tell whether your friend is serious or not at first, but then his face convinces you. He's just confessed a bitterness he's had against you and asked for your forgiveness. At first you're surprised, not because you didn't think he would have this problem, but because you never expected him to be so honest. Mostly you admire him for taking the risk of being vulnerable.

Since admitting that we're wrong comes at great expense, Proverbs 28 goes over some of the benefits to help us move in that direction. If you're not used to doing this, take it slow. But there's a lot to gain by confessing your mistakes. Swallow hard and give it a try.

Other thoughts in this chapter include keeping the law; avoiding quick riches; and working hard.

Read Proverbs 28:1-28

"People who conceal their sins will not prosper, but if they confess and turn from them, they will receive mercy" (Proverbs 28:13). Despite this wisdom, something in each of us strongly resists admitting our mistakes and sins. That may be why we admire people who openly and graciously do exactly that. These people have a strong self-image. They do not always have to be right to feel good about themselves.

It may be painful to admit our mistakes and sins, but this is the path we must take if we want to truly correct our behavior and to seek others' forgiveness.

Be willing to admit when you're wrong and to seek forgiveness from others. Being open and honest is the first step to experiencing peace and joy in your relationship with Christ and with others. To be successful in life—admit your mistakes.

"You're the best!" "You're so beautiful!" "I couldn't possibly do that as fast as you!" Do you notice anything suspicious here?

Proverbs 29 discusses flattery, as well as how to appropriately respond to other people's anger, how to vent your frustration, and how to get justice.

Read Proverbs 29:1-27

"To flatter friends is to lay a trap for their feet" (Proverbs 29:5). That states it clearly. Everyone wants to be liked, so we tend to encourage and excuse flattery. In fact, many people do not even consider flattery wrong, but use it as a handy tool for advancing themselves and their agendas. But each use of flattery, as the Scriptures say, sets a trap and endangers those who get caught in it.

Avoid using flattery to manipulate people. Instead, be sincere when you praise others for their achievements, appearance, or character. At the same time, don't believe everything you hear about yourself. Honestly evaluate your abilities, appearance, and personality. Know your strengths and weaknesses so you will know when others are flattering you. Learn to distinguish between truth and flattery, and learn to accept compliments graciously.

2When the godly are in authority, the people rejoice. But when the wicked are in power, they groan. 3The man who loves wisdom brings joy to his father, but if he hangs around with prostitutes, his wealth is wasted. 4A just king gives stability to his nation, but one who demands bribes destroys it. 5To flatter friends is to lay a trap for their feet. 6Evil people are trapped by sin, but the righteous escape, shouting for joy. 7The godly care about the rights of the poor; the wicked don't care at all. 8Mockers can get a whole town agitated, but the wise will calm anger. 9If a wise person takes a fool to court, there will be ranting and ridicule but no satisfaction. 10The bloodthirsty hate blameless people, but the upright seek to help them. 11Fools vent their anger, but the wise quietly hold it back.

PROVERBS 29:2-11

[5]Every word of God proves true. He is a shield to all who come to him for protection. [6]Do not add to his words, or he may rebuke you and expose you as a liar. [7]O God, I beg two favors from you; let me have them before I die. [8]First, help me never to tell a lie. Second, give me neither poverty nor riches! Give me just enough to satisfy my needs. [9]For if I grow rich, I may deny you and say, "Who is the LORD?" And if I am too poor, I may steal and thus insult God's holy name. [10]Never slander a worker to the employer, or the person will curse you, and you will pay for it. [11]Some people curse their father and do not thank their mother. [12]They are pure in their own eyes, but they are filthy and unwashed. [13]They look proudly around, casting disdainful glances. [14]They have teeth like swords and fangs like knives. They devour the poor from the earth.

PROVERBS 30:5-14

Winning the lottery or getting some other financial windfall plays itself out in the imaginations of almost everyone. We imagine how our lives would be different, better, easier. Sure, there might be higher taxes, strained relationships, and uncontrollable spending habits, but that would be better than poverty, right?

Proverbs 30 contains some profound thoughts about riches, as well as thoughts on God's character; false accusations; mockers; and pride.

Read Proverbs 30:1-33

Agur, the writer of these proverbs, prayed, "Give me neither poverty nor riches!" (Proverbs 30:8). Some people imagine that money can solve all their problems. Others believe that it will solve none of them. Both miss the point—it is the *love* of money that is at the root of evil (see 1 Timothy 6:10). Having too much money can give us the false impression that we don't need God. Like the apostle Paul, we should learn to live whether we have little or plenty (see Philippians 4:12), but our lives are likely to be more effective for God if, like Agur, we have "neither poverty nor riches."

Make Agur's prayer your prayer. Ask God to keep you from desiring material wealth, knowing that it isn't eternal and will one day be gone. At the same time, pray that God will strengthen your trust in him to provide for your needs.

Many women today have come to a difficult cross-roads. Some "career women" regret not devoting more time to their kids; some "stay-at-home moms" regret not having a career.

A wise woman will give serious thought to Proverbs 31. Contrary to popular belief, this passage does not describe an ideal too lofty to attain—no, the chief characteristic of the truly noble woman is *balance*. That's what happens when each of us takes our cues from God and God alone—it's the message of the entire book of Proverbs, isn't it?

Proverbs 31 doesn't discuss only female roles; other topics include drinking; leading; fulfilling responsibilities; and working.

Read Proverbs 31:1-31

Proverbs ends with a positive description of a godly woman—a woman of strong character, great wisdom, many skills, and compassion.

Some people have the mistaken idea that the ideal woman in the Bible is passive, submissive, and domestic. Not so! This woman takes her roles as a wife and mother quite proactively. She does not delegate her responsibilities to someone else. She manufactures, imports, manages, invests, farms, sews, buys, sells, and shares. Her strength and dignity do not come from amazing achievements, but from reverence for God. Her attractiveness comes from her strength of character. And that's the point.

Whoever you are, you can learn this lesson: A godly person is one who strives to be a person of character, integrity, devotion, and balance.

[10]Who can find a virtuous and capable wife? She is more precious than rubies. [11]Her husband can trust her, and she will greatly enrich his life. [12]She brings him good, not harm, all the days of her life. . . . [25]She is clothed with strength and dignity, and she laughs without fear of the future. [26]When she speaks, her words are wise, and she gives instructions with kindness. [27]She carefully watches everything in her household and suffers nothing from laziness. [28]Her children stand and bless her. Her husband praises her: [29]"There are many virtuous and capable women in the world, but you surpass them all!" [30]Charm is deceptive, and beauty does not last; but a woman who fears the LORD will be greatly praised. [31]Reward her for all she has done. Let her deeds publicly declare her praise.

PROVERBS 31:10-12, 25-31

¹These are the words of the Teacher, King David's son, who ruled in Jerusalem. ²"Everything is meaningless," says the Teacher, "completely meaningless!" ³What do people get for all their hard work under the sun? ⁴Generations come and generations go, but the earth never changes. ⁵The sun rises and the sun sets, then hurries around to rise again. ⁶The wind blows south, and then turns north. Around and around it goes, blowing in circles. ⁷Rivers run into the sea, but the sea is never full. Then the water returns again to the rivers and flows out again to the sea. ⁸Everything is wearisome beyond description. No matter how much we see, we are never satisfied. No matter how much we hear, we are not content. ⁹History merely repeats itself. It has all been done before. Nothing under the sun is truly new.

ECCLESIASTES 1:1-9

At one time or another, everyone thinks, *If only.* The thought usually ends with a dream of some fantastic ideal—a different job, a new house, a hot car, or more money. The fountain of happiness always lies just beyond our grasp. If only . . .

Solomon begins the book of Ecclesiastes by reflecting on his past and noting how he has changed. You can detect some "if only" thoughts in his observations. Like each of us, Solomon wanted to be happy—this is what he found.

Read Ecclesiastes 1:1–2:26

Would you be happier if you had more money, fame, or power? Solomon wasn't (Ecclesiastes 1:1-2, 12-15; 2:1-11). The world tells us to demand happiness, to do all we can to attain it, and to make personal satisfaction our chief goal. The world holds out many promises, all of which require dependence on some thing or experience that won't last. Solomon had attained everything the world thought he needed to guarantee happiness and fulfillment, but reflecting back on his life, he discovered that his wealth, power, position, wives, and accomplishments had not made him happy or brought meaning to his life.

In contrast to the world's view, the Bible says that true and lasting happiness comes from pleasing God. (Eventually Solomon found this to be true.) Real happiness can only be received through a right relationship with God.

Children who have reached the "Why?" stage remind us that they live in a smaller, simpler world than adults do. Often, the questions and truths that intrigue the young are beyond their comprehension.

Solomon lists several disappointments he has observed in the world and asks why they have to exist. Unable to grasp the answers, he has to come to a sort of compromise. Let him lead you to the "grown-up" who can explain.

This reading also comments further on three areas of life that touch us all: death, work, and friendship.

Ecclesiastes 3:1–5:20

In Ecclesiastes 3:16–4:12, Solomon reflects on six apparent contradictions in the world. First, wickedness rules where justice should (3:16). Second, people created in God's image die just as the animals do (3:18-21). Third, no one comforts oppressed people (4:1). Fourth, many people work because they envy what others have, not because they love their work (4:4). Fifth, people are lonely (4:7-12). Sixth, fame doesn't last (4:13-16).

Many questions in life cannot be answered to our satisfaction because we lack the ability to understand the answers, not because the answers don't exist. Although we cannot understand the answers today, one day we will. In the meantime, we should trust life's apparent contradictions to God and not lose faith in him when we don't understand something.

⁹What do people really get for all their hard work? ¹⁰I have seen the burden God has placed on us all. ¹¹Yet God has made everything beautiful for its own time. He has planted eternity in the human heart, but even so, people cannot see the whole scope of God's work from beginning to end. ¹²So I concluded there is nothing better than to be happy and enjoy ourselves as long as we can. ¹³And people should eat and drink and enjoy the fruits of their labor, for these are gifts from God. ¹⁴And I know that whatever God does is final. Nothing can be added to it or taken from it. God's purpose is that people should fear him. ¹⁵What is happening now has happened before, and what will happen in the future has happened before, because God makes the same things happen over and over again.

ECCLESIASTES 3:9-15

⁵Better to be criticized by a wise person than to be praised by a fool. ⁶A fool's laughter is quickly gone, like thorns crackling in a fire. This also is meaningless. ⁷Extortion turns wise people into fools, and bribes corrupt the heart. ⁸Finishing is better than starting. Patience is better than pride. ⁹Control your temper, for anger labels you a fool. ¹⁰Don't long for "the good old days." This is not wise. ¹¹Wisdom is even better when you have money. Both are a benefit as you go through life. ¹²Wisdom and money can get you almost anything, but only wisdom can save your life. ¹³Accept the way God does things, for who can straighten what he has made crooked? ¹⁴Enjoy prosperity while you can, but when hard times strike, realize that both come from God. Remember that nothing is certain in this life.

ECCLESIASTES 7:5-14

Sam is repulsed by his neighbor Doug, an outspoken Christian. Doug is always calling attention to his good deeds and overly stating his revulsion toward immorality and decadence. Most of the neighbors call him obnoxious. The kinder ones say he's just trying too hard.

This reading exposes some "negative" aspects of goodness and wisdom. Can you have too much of a good thing? Apparently so.

There is additional insight on meaningless activities; on work and earning money; and on fame, death, sorrow, and happiness. You will also find some sober advice on how to enjoy life, even when everything seems meaningless.

Read Ecclesiastes 6:1–8:17

"Don't be too good or too wise!" (Ecclesiastes 7:16). That's a warning against religious conceit—taking pride in your goodness or righteousness. How can a person be too righteous or too wise? Some people invent grand schemes for appearing righteous and accomplish nothing in the process. They sit atop poles, deny themselves food, give up pleasurable things, and pursue other drastic steps that do little more than ruin their health. "Why destroy yourself?" Solomon asks.

Don't lose sight of true goodness—honoring God—in favor of a nearly suicidal effort to make yourself artificially perfect. Do whatever God asks of you, and leave it at that.

Many years ago the phenomenon of a *midlife crisis* was given its name. Many people approaching the second half of their adult lives want to ensure that all they've ever worked for, lived for, and hoped for hasn't just been one big mistake.

The entire book of Ecclesiastes addresses the meaning of life, but this passage in particular punctuates his point. Solomon's summary makes it difficult to miss. Read on for help with that age-old set of questions that demand an answer somewhere around the halftime of your life.

In this passage you will also find specific lessons on death, wisdom, investing, and growing old.

Read Ecclesiastes 9:1–12:14

Solomon concludes this book by giving advice on how to live a full life. Solomon's final conclusion is that "everyone's duty" is to fear and obey God (Ecclesiastes 12:13). Solomon gave this advice because he knew that one day we will have to stand before God and be judged for how we have lived (12:14). We will not be able to use excuses to justify our failures and sins. So we need to learn how God wants us to live and then to do it. When we do this, we then complete our search for meaning.

Don't let the excitement of being young cause you to forget about your Creator. And don't spend your life trying to substitute your own rules for the ones God has given you—as if living your own way will somehow be easier, or as if God won't notice. Keep your values and priorities in line—keep God in first place in your life.

[1]Don't let the excitement of youth cause you to forget your Creator. Honor him in your youth before you grow old and say, "Life is not pleasant anymore." . . . [6]Yes, remember your Creator now while you are young, before the silver cord of life snaps and the golden bowl is broken. Don't wait until the water jar is smashed at the spring and the pulley is broken at the well. [7]For then the dust will return to the earth, and the spirit will return to God who gave it. . . . [12]But, my child, let me give you some further advice: Be careful, for writing books is endless, and much study wears you out. [13]That's the whole story. Here now is my final conclusion: Fear God and obey his commands, for this is everyone's duty. [14]God will judge us for everything we do, including every secret thing, whether good or bad.

ECCLESIASTES 12:1, 6-7, 12-14

⁸Come with me from Lebanon, my bride, come with me from Lebanon. Come down from Mount Amana, from the peaks of Senir and Hermon, where the lions have their dens and leopards live among the hills. ⁹You have captured my heart, my treasure, my bride. You hold it hostage with one glance of your eyes, with a single jewel of your necklace. ¹⁰Your love delights me, my treasure, my bride. Your love is better than wine, your perfume more fragrant than spices. ¹¹Your lips are as sweet as nectar, my bride. Honey and milk are under your tongue. Your clothes are scented like the cedars of Lebanon. ¹²You are my private garden, my treasure, my bride, a secluded spring, a hidden fountain.

SONG OF SONGS 4:8-12

The Song of Songs is a beautiful story of love between a husband and a wife. Also, in a day when marriages are falling apart all around us, this is an encouraging book to read. Marriage can last and still be passionate.

If you want to look for more specific treasures, dig for facets of this two-sided gem: what to say to your spouse and what to do for your spouse. If you are unmarried, look for ways to support your married friends and encourage them to make their marriages work. They need cheerleaders.

Read Song of Songs 1:1–8:14

As surely as time itself passes, the growth of familiarity in a marriage will cause the relationship to lose its initial sparkle. Glances and touches will no longer produce the same emotional responses. Conflicts and pressures will creep in, causing the man to lose his tenderness and the woman to lose her zeal for flirting. The world doesn't help, either; in fact, external stress often works against the marriage relationship. But spouses can learn to be shelters for each other, and they can learn to make marriage fun.

When intimacy and passion decline, remember that they can be renewed. Take time to remember those first thrills, the excitement of sex, your spouse's strengths, and the commitment you made in your wedding vows (Song of Songs 5:2-8). Be affectionate to each other every day and watch the excitement return to your relationship!

Although the latest style is supposedly always new, fashion and the fashion conscious have been around for a long time. The Judean women of Isaiah's time were no different than many women today—they were slaves to fashion. So much so that they angered God, who sent Isaiah to straighten them out.

The women of Judah aren't the only ones who need to set their priorities straight in this reading. Isaiah has a lot to say to the Judeans and to us about the importance we place (or don't place) on what God wants. As you read, notice the loving proposal God makes to his people; the good reasons to respect God; some bad mistakes to avoid; and how Isaiah became God's servant.

Read Isaiah 1:1–6:13

Isaiah's prophecies were not condemning the women for buying nice clothing, jewelry, and makeup. Rather he was condemning their prideful attitudes and self-centered concerns. Looking good is not wrong in and of itself. But when we become engrossed in our appearance while we neglect God's commands and others' needs, we've gone too far.

Strive for a balance between maintaining a well-groomed appearance and keeping your priorities and responsibilities straight. Remember that God is more concerned with your character than your looks (see 1 Samuel 16:7; Matthew 23:25-28). Use what you have to help others, not impress them.

[14]The Lord comes forward to pronounce judgment on the elders and rulers of his people: "You have ruined Israel, my vineyard. Your houses are filled with things stolen from the poor. [15]How dare you crush my people, grinding the faces of the poor into the dust?" demands the Lord, the Lord of Heaven's Armies. [16]The Lord says, "Beautiful Zion is haughty: craning her elegant neck, flirting with her eyes, walking with dainty steps, tinkling her ankle bracelets. [17]So the Lord will send scabs on her head; the Lord will make beautiful Zion bald." [18]On that day of judgment the Lord will strip away everything that makes her beautiful. . . . [25]The men of the city will be killed with the sword, and her warriors will die in battle. [26]The gates of Zion will weep and mourn. The city will be like a ravaged woman, huddled on the ground.

ISAIAH 3:14-18, 25-26

¹¹The Lord has given me a strong warning not to think like everyone else does. He said, ¹²"Don't call everything a conspiracy, like they do, and don't live in dread of what frightens them. ¹³Make the Lord of Heaven's Armies holy in your life. He is the one you should fear. He is the one who should make you tremble. ¹⁴He will keep you safe. But to Israel and Judah he will be a stone that makes people stumble, a rock that makes them fall. And for the people of Jerusalem he will be a trap and a snare. ¹⁵Many will stumble and fall, never to rise again. They will be snared and captured." ¹⁶Preserve the teaching of God; entrust his instructions to those who follow me. ¹⁷I will wait for the Lord, who has turned away from the descendants of Jacob. I will put my hope in him.

ISAIAH 8:11-17

Blame shifting kicks into high gear whenever someone has been caught. You can almost guarantee that the guilty person will try to blame somebody else (or some overpowering circumstance) for the offense.

Sadly, some believers do this, too, without even thinking about it. But this is nothing new for God's people. The Judeans, Isaiah predicted, would start pointing fingers as soon as the consequences of their sin came upon them. As you read, notice who gets blamed here.

This reading is an interesting mixture of hope and despair. Note the famous prophecies about Christ (Isaiah 7, 9, 11); the harsh words about conceit and favoring the strong (Isaiah 9–10); and the kind words for those who remain faithful to God (Isaiah 10, 12).

Read Isaiah 7:1–12:6

The people of Israel listened to false prophets instead of to Isaiah, and as a result they went "from one place to another, weary and hungry" (Isaiah 8:21). They blamed God for their troubles. After rejecting God's plan for them, the people tried to indict God for rejecting them!

Unfortunately, that's how we often behave. We blame God for problems that we have brought on ourselves instead of admitting that we deserve what has happened and making the appropriate changes.

How do you respond to the unpleasant results of your choices? Be honest with yourself and God—admit your sins, ask forgiveness, and, if necessary, make restitution.

The world stood up and took notice when the Apollo astronauts first landed on the moon. This was a truly great accomplishment because it had never been done before. But it also fed the belief that science would rescue us from all our ills.

A similar belief existed among the people living in Damascus. They made idols and placed their trust in them. Because they turned their backs on God, God gave them some bad news.

If you ever wondered whether God holds *groups* of people accountable, this reading should answer your question.

Read Isaiah 13:1–18:7

The people of Damascus looked to their idols and to their own strength for all the answers (Isaiah 17:8-11). They believed in gods they could see and control, not in an invisible God. God's message to them through Isaiah was that their cities would be completely destroyed (17:1-3). The people of Damascus had turned from the God who could save them and toward themselves, as represented by their man-made gods. They forgot God's place in the grand scheme of things.

Often we depend on technology (faster computers, more efficient energy sources, and more effective medical treatments) and our own knowledge to save us from our ills. But placing our trust in human technology rather than in God is wrong—it's idolatry. This is not to say that good technology doesn't have its place; it does, but not as an idol or god. We can appreciate progress, but we must never bow down to it.

¹This message came to me concerning Damascus: "Look, the city of Damascus will disappear! It will become a heap of ruins. ²The towns of Aroer will be deserted. Flocks will graze in the streets and lie down undisturbed, with no one to chase them away. ³The fortified towns of Israel will also be destroyed, and the royal power of Damascus will end. All that remains of Syria will share the fate of Israel's departed glory," declares the LORD of Heaven's Armies. ⁴"In that day Israel's glory will grow dim; its robust body will waste away. ⁵The whole land will look like a grainfield after the harvesters have gathered the grain. It will be desolate, like the fields in the valley of Rephaim after the harvest." . . . ⁷Then at last the people will look to their Creator and turn their eyes to the Holy One of Israel.

ISAIAH 17:1-5, 7

¹This message came to me concerning Jerusalem—the Valley of Vision: What is happening? Why is everyone running to the rooftops? ²The whole city is in a terrible uproar. What do I see in this reveling city? Bodies are lying everywhere, killed not in battle but by famine and disease. ³All your leaders have fled. They surrendered without resistance. The people tried to slip away, but they were captured, too. ⁴That's why I said, "Leave me alone to weep; do not try to comfort me. Let me cry for my people as I watch them being destroyed." ⁵Oh, what a day of crushing defeat! What a day of confusion and terror brought by the Lord, the Lord of Heaven's Armies, upon the Valley of Vision! The walls of Jerusalem have been broken, and cries of death echo from the mountainsides.

ISAIAH 22:1-5

Do you cry at movies? Some people do. Eyes and noses just drip, flow, and gush uncontrollably. People cry when overcome with great emotion—at the movies and in real life.

In this reading, Isaiah weeps because God's people are destroying themselves. He warns them repeatedly. But they just aren't listening. What's a prophet to do? What would you do?

This reading also contains the second half of the list of prophecies against Judah's neighbors (Egypt, Ethiopia, Babylon, Edom, Arabia, and Tyre). If you thought God was singling out Judah for punishment, think again.

Read Isaiah 19:1–23:18

Isaiah delivered God's messages to God's people, but that didn't mean that Isaiah was just a courier. As a fellow Judean, Isaiah cared deeply for his and God's people. Isaiah knew that because the Judeans did not heed God's warnings, they would experience his judgment. This saddened Isaiah and he wept for them (Isaiah 22:4).

Sometimes family and friends ignore our attempts to help, so they suffer the very grief we wanted to spare them. At these times we grieve because of our concern.

Have you pulled back from getting close to someone because of a fear of getting hurt? It can be tempting to insulate yourself from hurt by avoiding all close relationships. But God wants you, like Isaiah, to love others. To love someone carries with it the risk of getting hurt by that person's choices. But be willing to take that risk, and trust God for the outcome.

In George Orwell's classic novel *Animal Farm,* all the animals enjoy equal rights until it becomes apparent that some animals consider themselves "more equal" than others.

God doesn't judge superficially—he judges people by their character and not by their appearance. In this reading, Isaiah celebrates God's impartiality. God's only requirement is that we love and serve him.

Read Isaiah 24:1–27:13

Isaiah praised God for his greatness and described God's wonderful acts. Isaiah specifically praised God for making salvation available to all who would turn from their sin. God welcomes "all people of the world" (Isaiah 25:6). God's banquet has an international guest list. This means that men and women of every color, race, language, and custom who love God will dwell together in heaven. There will be no segregation there.

Be willing to share your life with people who differ from you. Don't discriminate against them just because they are a different sex or different color, have different customs or speak a different language. Remember, if they also trust in Christ, they are your brothers and sisters and will sit with you at God's banquet table. Include others—it's a very God-like action to take.

⁶In Jerusalem, the LORD of Heaven's Armies will spread a wonderful feast for all the people of the world. It will be a delicious banquet with clear, well-aged wine and choice meat. ⁷There he will remove the cloud of gloom, the shadow of death that hangs over the earth. ⁸He will swallow up death forever! The Sovereign LORD will wipe away all tears. He will remove forever all insults and mockery against his land and people. The LORD has spoken! ⁹In that day the people will proclaim, "This is our God! We trusted in him, and he saved us! This is the LORD, in whom we trusted. Let us rejoice in the salvation he brings!" ¹⁰For the LORD's hand of blessing will rest on Jerusalem. But Moab will be crushed. It will be like straw trampled down and left to rot.

ISAIAH 25:6-10

[23]Listen to me; listen, and pay close attention. [24]Does a farmer always plow and never sow? Is he forever cultivating the soil and never planting? [25]Does he not finally plant his seeds—black cumin, cumin, wheat, barley, and emmer wheat—each in its proper way, and each in its proper place? [26]The farmer knows just what to do, for God has given him understanding. [27]A heavy sledge is never used to thresh black cumin; rather, it is beaten with a light stick. A threshing wheel is never rolled on cumin; instead, it is beaten lightly with a flail. [28]Grain for bread is easily crushed, so he doesn't keep on pounding it. He threshes it under the wheels of a cart, but he doesn't pulverize it. [29]The LORD of Heaven's Armies is a wonderful teacher, and he gives the farmer great wisdom.

ISAIAH 28:23-29

Many descriptions of the 1980s and 1990s include a reference to male sensitivity—or lack of it. Because of women's liberation and concern over stereotypes, men have been encouraged to be more sensitive, to allow more feelings to show, and to have more concern for others in general. Some men squawked; others cheered.

This passage contains a lesson on sensitivity. As you read, you will see that power and sensitivity can live together.

Also in this reading, Isaiah pronounces a series of woes on those who resist being taught, who live double lives, and who go their own way instead of God's way.

Read Isaiah 28:1–31:9

The farmer uses special tools to plant and harvest tender herbs so he will not destroy them. He takes into account how fragile they are. In the same way God takes all our individual circumstances and weaknesses into account (Isaiah 28:23-29). He deals with each of us sensitively.

We should follow his example whenever we deal with others, because different people require different treatment. Sensitivity is required.

Be sensitive to the unique personalities and needs of those around you, being careful not to overpower the weak or to coddle the strong. Be aware of the special treatment that each person may need and the special circumstances in each one's life, then relate and lead accordingly.

Have you ever been hurt by a broken promise? Some people have been fortunate enough to escape the scars from broken promises, but others will forever feel the effects. They'll carry a memory, a regret, or a grudge.

The prophecies in this reading deal with promise-breakers and their victims. For the promise-breaking Assyrians, Isaiah brings a message of condemnation. For the Assyrians' victims, the Israelites, Isaiah brings a message of hope, comfort, and peace. For us, it's good to know God cares about promises—kept and broken. Read this passage for a message of hope.

Also in this reading you will find that God is out to take back what belongs to him.

Read Isaiah 32:1–35:10

The rulers of Assyria came under God's judgment because they broke their promises while demanding that others keep theirs (Isaiah 33:1). They observed a selfish double standard that protected them and exploited others.

Like the Assyrian rulers, we find it easy to expect a lot out of others while requiring less of ourselves. But God takes promises very seriously, and he wants us to be fair. Broken promises shatter trust and destroy relationships.

Determine to keep your promises. Negotiate in good faith. Demand the same faithfulness of yourself that you ask of everyone else.

¹What sorrow awaits you Assyrians, who have destroyed others but have never been destroyed yourselves. You betray others, but you have never been betrayed. When you are done destroying, you will be destroyed. When you are done betraying, you will be betrayed. ²But LORD, be merciful to us, for we have waited for you. Be our strong arm each day and our salvation in times of trouble. ³The enemy runs at the sound of your voice. When you stand up, the nations flee! ⁴Just as caterpillars and locusts strip the fields and vines, so the fallen army of Assyria will be stripped! ⁵Though the LORD is very great and lives in heaven, he will make Jerusalem his home of justice and righteousness. ⁶In that day he will be your sure foundation, providing a rich store of salvation, wisdom, and knowledge. The fear of the LORD will be your treasure.

ISAIAH 33:1-6

⁹Soon afterward King Sennacherib received word that King Tirhakah of Ethiopia was leading an army to fight against him. Before leaving to meet the attack, he sent messengers back to Hezekiah in Jerusalem with this message: ¹⁰"This message is for King Hezekiah of Judah. Don't let your God, in whom you trust, deceive you with promises that Jerusalem will not be captured by the king of Assyria. ¹¹You know perfectly well what the kings of Assyria have done wherever they have gone. They have completely destroyed everyone who stood in their way! Why should you be any different? ¹²Have the gods of other nations rescued them—such nations as Gozan, Haran, Rezeph, and the people of Eden who were in Telassar? My predecessors destroyed them all!

ISAIAH 37:9-12

How do you know if someone is lying to you? Often you can't tell—that's the trouble. You can't spot deceivers just by their appearance.

Hezekiah, a good king, has to deal with a smooth-talking deceiver here, the field commander of Assyria. According to the commander, Hezekiah has failed. "You're an incompetent leader and a disgrace to God," he basically says. Read this passage to see whether Hezekiah will believe the commander or God.

Even if you're not a leader, there are many lessons here on dealing with threats; praying; depending on God; coping with illness; and keeping a level head when your fortunes shift for the better.

Read Isaiah 36:1–39:8

The field commander from Assyria tried to talk Hezekiah out of resisting. He claimed that Hezekiah had insulted God by tearing down pagan altars and making the people worship only in Jerusalem (Isaiah 36:7). But Hezekiah knew better. His reform had sought to eliminate the worship of false gods, so that the people would worship only the true God, as they should. Either the Assyrian commander didn't know about the true God, or he wanted to trick the people into thinking they had angered a more powerful god than the Lord. But Hezekiah knew God and his Word well enough not to believe the lies. The field commander's plan failed.

Like Hezekiah, don't be naive. Study God's Word carefully and regularly. When you know what God says, you will not fall for lies.

Hectic work schedules, bad nutrition, poor health, small children, or just plain old age can make people weary. What makes you feel tired or weak?

In Isaiah 40:1–48:22 you will read about a tired people—Israel and Judah exiled in Babylon. They've been away from home for a long time. Isaiah brings them strong, energizing words.

The other sections in this passage all relate to Israel's release from captivity—a happy, joyous time. Here are words of encouragement and hope from this servant of the Lord.

Read Isaiah 40:1–48:22

Isaiah had words of encouragement for God's people: Their punishment wouldn't last forever, deliverance would come, and God would restore them. God didn't want them to despair, so he reassured them of his power (Isaiah 40:12-31).

Just as Israel and Judah's punishment overwhelmed them, so the pace of life overwhelms every person at times, even those who are strong (40:30). This may be because of our overzealous desire to do more than we should. Or it may be that we just don't trust in God and his power to help us move the mountain of work set before us. But God and his power should be our source of strength, especially when we feel overwhelmed.

Whenever you feel tired and weary, take time to rest—show your confidence in God's control over the events in your life. Let him renew your strength. Then wait for his timing before reentering the marathon called life, or you may not be able to finish the race at all. God will help you finish in good time.

[1]"Comfort, comfort my people," says your God. [2]"Speak tenderly to Jerusalem. Tell her that her sad days are gone and her sins are pardoned. Yes, the LORD has punished her twice over for all her sins." [3]Listen! It's the voice of someone shouting, "Clear the way through the wilderness for the LORD! Make a straight highway through the wasteland for our God! [4]Fill in the valleys, and level the mountains and hills. Straighten the curves, and smooth out the rough places. [5]Then the glory of the LORD will be revealed, and all people will see it together. The LORD has spoken!" . . . [31]Those who trust in the LORD will find new strength. They will soar high on wings like eagles. They will run and not grow weary. They will walk and not faint.

ISAIAH 40:1-5, 31

¹"Listen to me, all who hope for deliverance—all who seek the LORD! Consider the rock from which you were cut, the quarry from which you were mined. ²Yes, think about Abraham, your ancestor, and Sarah, who gave birth to your nation. Abraham was only one man when I called him. But when I blessed him, he became a great nation." ³The LORD will comfort Israel again and have pity on her ruins. Her desert will blossom like Eden, her barren wilderness like the garden of the LORD. Joy and gladness will be found there. Songs of thanksgiving will fill the air. ⁴"Listen to me, my people. Hear me, Israel, for my law will be proclaimed, and my justice will become a light to the nations. ⁵My mercy and justice are coming soon. My salvation is on the way. My strong arm will bring justice to the nations."

ISAIAH 51:1-5

If you are discouraged about your faith and are thinking about giving up on God, wait! Isaiah has something to say to you. And it's all good news! In this set of prophecies, Isaiah has many encouraging words for those who keep God's laws.

Other messages of good news in this passage concern Israel's homecoming from captivity and reasons not to fear other people.

Read Isaiah 49:1–52:12

Not everyone in Israel thumbed their nose at God. Some, a small minority, often called a "remnant" in the Bible, loved God and obeyed his laws. As often happens to minorities, they drew insults and slander from others for being different. In this case, they were abused for loving and obeying God. But Isaiah had prophecies for them, too (Isaiah 51:7). These prophecies gave them hope for when they faced others' reproach or insults because of their God-honoring lifestyle.

We need not fear when people insult us for our moral choices, because God is with us, and he will help us prevail.

If people make fun of you or dislike you because you go to church and stay faithful to your spouse, remember that they are not against you personally but against God. God will deal with them; you should concentrate on loving and obeying him. When you do, God will bless you for it!

Making big decisions usually takes a while. A person doesn't typically get married, buy a house, or have a child on a whim. On the other hand, some decisions *can't* wait. The opportunity is here today—it may be gone tomorrow.

This reading contains an offer from God to take advantage of *now*. So put it at the top of your list of things to do, and don't delay. This is one offer that definitely doesn't get any better and won't be around forever.

Other offers not to miss in this reading include Christ's payment for sin and a free reminder that God's ways are higher than ours.

Read Isaiah 52:13–55:13

Isaiah told his people to call on the Lord while he is near (Isaiah 55:6-7). He wanted them to respond to God while they still had the chance, and not delay.

God doesn't make occasional appearances and then leave us, but he also doesn't wait forever while we "think about" whether or not we'll respond to him. Deliberately putting off the decision to accept Christ as Savior tests God's patience.

Don't test God's patience or wait until you're "ready" to call on him. Turning to him later in life may be far more difficult than it is now. Or worse, you may die or Christ may return to judge the earth before you decide to follow him. Therefore, seek God now, while you can, before it is too late. Someday it will be.

[1]"Is anyone thirsty? Come and drink—even if you have no money! Come, take your choice of wine or milk—it's all free! [2]Why spend your money on food that does not give you strength? Why pay for food that does you no good? Listen to me, and you will eat what is good. You will enjoy the finest food. [3]Come to me with your ears wide open. Listen, and you will find life. I will make an everlasting covenant with you. I will give you all the unfailing love I promised to David. [4]See how I used him to display my power among the peoples. I made him a leader among the nations. [5]You also will command nations you do not know, and peoples unknown to you will come running to obey, because I, the LORD your God, the Holy One of Israel, have made you glorious." [6]Seek the LORD while you can find him. Call on him now while he is near.

ISAIAH 55:1-6

4"What good is fasting when you keep on fighting and quarreling? This kind of fasting will never get you anywhere with me. 5You humble yourselves by going through the motions of penance, bowing your heads like reeds bending in the wind. You dress in burlap and cover yourselves with ashes. Is this what you call fasting? Do you really think this will please the Lord? 6No, this is the kind of fasting I want: Free those who are wrongly imprisoned; lighten the burden of those who work for you. Let the oppressed go free, and remove the chains that bind people. 7Share your food with the hungry, and give shelter to the homeless. Give clothes to those who need them, and do not hide from relatives who need your help. 8Then your salvation will come like the dawn, . . . and the glory of the Lord will protect you from behind."

ISAIAH 58:4-8

It's easy to act like a religious person—to go to church, go along with what happens there, and go about your business. Many people go to church—anyone can do it, with or without sincerity.

The people of Israel were definitely religious. This portion of Isaiah's message supports that fact. But their piety doesn't please the Lord, and he lets them know it. He says, "What good is your religion if it doesn't affect the way you live?"

Two other messages come through loud and clear in this reading: God *loves* it when we love; God *hates* it when we sin.

Read Isaiah 56:1–59:21

To the people of Isaiah's day, worshiping God consisted entirely of religious ritual—going to the Temple every day, fasting, and listening to Scripture readings. They thought nothing of the fact that they oppressed the poor and denied help to the weak (Isaiah 58:1-12). In fact, they loved their worship practices, even as they refused to love hurting people.

Religious people who miss the point of a living, vital relationship with God forget that God cares about people, not performances. God does not want us merely to act pious—he wants our behavior to reflect our relationship with him. More important to God even than correct worship, liturgy, and doctrine is genuine compassion for people who are poor, helpless, homeless, or oppressed.

To God, true worship is simply this: doing deeds of love and kindness for others, especially those who need help or are defenseless. Set aside empty religious rituals and practice true worship. This is what really pleases God. Who needs a touch of God's love through you? Reach out to that person *today*.

Hardly anything happens to shoreline rocks each time a wave rolls in. The water is no match for the stone. Indeed, if you were to come back day after day to watch, you would see *no change:* waves pound, rocks win. Yet the waves are making an impact, and over a very long time, you would be able to see the cumulative effect. The rocks will wear down.

Like a relentless surf, Isaiah has spoken to his people time and time again. He has warned them about their need to change, and they, rocklike, have not responded—so far. Isaiah has no guarantee that they will *ever* respond in his lifetime. He certainly hasn't seen any change. So he faithfully gets on his knees. As you read this passage, learn from Isaiah's example.

Read Isaiah 60:1–66:24

When we warn or counsel others, sometimes they don't listen. Sometimes we can see their painful consequences, but they refuse to see the danger. After we've offered our warnings, our advice, and our pleas, we still have one potent option—prayer. That's why Jesus taught his followers to pray, "May your Kingdom come soon. May your will be done on earth, as it is in heaven" (Matthew 6:10).

You cannot control others who are about to make a foolish choice or when they're toying with a temptation that could bring painful consequences, but you can pray for them. Keep praying persistently for the people you love.

⁶O Jerusalem, I have posted watchmen on your walls; they will pray day and night, continually. Take no rest, all you who pray to the Lord. ⁷Give the Lord no rest until he completes his work, until he makes Jerusalem the pride of the earth. ⁸The Lord has sworn to Jerusalem by his own strength: "I will never again hand you over to your enemies. Never again will foreign warriors come and take away your grain and new wine. ⁹You raised the grain, and you will eat it, praising the Lord. Within the courtyards of the Temple, you yourselves will drink the wine you have pressed." ¹⁰Go out through the gates! Prepare the highway for my people to return! Smooth out the road; pull out the boulders; raise a flag for all the nations to see. ¹¹The Lord has sent this message to every land: "Tell the people of Israel, 'Look, your Savior is coming.'"

ISAIAH 62:6-11

⁴The Lord gave me this message: ⁵"I knew you before I formed you in your mother's womb. Before you were born I set you apart and appointed you as my prophet to the nations." ⁶"O Sovereign Lord," I said, "I can't speak for you! I'm too young!" ⁷The Lord replied, "Don't say, 'I'm too young,' for you must go wherever I send you and say whatever I tell you. ⁸And don't be afraid of the people, for I will be with you and will protect you. I, the Lord, have spoken!" ⁹Then the Lord reached out and touched my mouth and said, "Look, I have put my words in your mouth! ¹⁰Today I appoint you to stand up against nations and kingdoms. Some you must uproot and tear down, destroy and overthrow. Others you must build up and plant." ¹¹Then the Lord said to me, "Look, Jeremiah! What do you see?" And I replied, "I see a branch from an almond tree."

JEREMIAH 1:4-11

Youth is hampered in many ways: too little experience; not enough maturity; insufficient skills. If only we could have both the energy and the wisdom at the same time.

Welcome to the opening chapters of Jeremiah, the prophecies of a man who considers himself too young to serve God. True, Jeremiah is young. But you will see that when it comes to serving God, a person's age doesn't matter—it's the heart that counts.

Besides reading Jeremiah's call to service, in this passage you will learn that Judah has come under God's judgment because they have forsaken God and have been unfaithful to him.

Read Jeremiah 1:1–6:30

It's not unusual for people to struggle with new challenges because they feel too young or because they don't have enough ability, training, or experience. Jeremiah thought he was too young and inexperienced to be God's spokesman to the world. But God told him not to worry and to go ahead with his assignment (Jeremiah 1:6-8).

We must not allow our feelings of inadequacy to keep us from doing what God has called us to do. Instead, we should trust him to always be with us and to give us wisdom and guidance for the task.

When you find yourself avoiding something you know you should do, be careful not to use inadequacy as an excuse. Ask God for the courage to take on the job; then trust him wholeheartedly for the strength to complete it. Whether or not you succeed is God's concern. Leave your feelings of inadequacy with him so you can concentrate on doing his will. He will provide everything you need to do it.

Many people believe that lucky charms will protect or help them. Some people carry a rabbit's foot or wear a lucky hat, shirt, or tie. Many Christians have one of these charms, and many others have their own variations—a cross necklace, an angel pin, or maybe a way of praying that they think has special significance.

When it comes to lucky charms, the people of Judah were no different from people today. In this passage, Jeremiah exposes their misplaced dependence on one religious artifact. Unlike people's lucky charms today, however, Judah's charm wasn't small enough to wear or carry. In this passage you will find proof that objects don't bring luck to anyone.

Read Jeremiah 7:1–10:25

The people who lived in Jerusalem depended on the ultimate good-luck charm: the Temple. They thought that as long as the Temple stood in Jerusalem they would have God's favor and be protected from harm (Jeremiah 7:4, 10). Meanwhile, they lived sinful lives, oppressing aliens, widows, and orphans, and worshiping false gods (7:5-7). They had misplaced their faith—instead of trusting in God, they were trusting in the Temple.

True faith never involves superstitious belief in the power of an object. God wants us to respond personally to him and his will. Attending church, taking Communion, teaching Sunday school, singing in the choir, wearing a cross—these exercises grow out of our love for God; they don't gain us his favor or protection.

¹The LORD gave another message to Jeremiah. He said, ²"Go to the entrance of the LORD's Temple, and give this message to the people: 'O Judah, listen to this message from the LORD! Listen to it, all of you who worship here! ³This is what the LORD of Heaven's Armies, the God of Israel, says: "'Even now, if you quit your evil ways, I will let you stay in your own land. ⁴But don't be fooled by those who promise you safety simply because the LORD's Temple is here. They chant, "The LORD's Temple is here! The LORD's Temple is here!" ⁵But I will be merciful only if you stop your evil thoughts and deeds and start treating each other with justice; ⁶only if you stop exploiting foreigners, orphans, and widows; only if you stop your murdering; and only if you stop harming yourselves by worshiping idols.'"

JEREMIAH 7:1-6

¹⁸Then the LORD told me about the plots my enemies were making against me. ¹⁹I was like a lamb being led to the slaughter. I had no idea that they were planning to kill me! "Let's destroy this man and all his words," they said. "Let's cut him down, so his name will be forgotten forever." ²⁰O LORD of Heaven's Armies, you make righteous judgments, and you examine the deepest thoughts and secrets. Let me see your vengeance against them, for I have committed my cause to you. ²¹This is what the LORD says about the men of Anathoth who wanted me dead. They had said, "We will kill you if you do not stop prophesying in the LORD's name." ²²So this is what the LORD of Heaven's Armies says about them: "I will punish them! Their young men will die in battle, and their boys and girls will starve to death."

JEREMIAH 11:18-22

People like or dislike meteorologists depending on how accurately they predict the weather. But what is worse is that some people dislike meteorologists just for predicting bad weather, despite how accurate they may be. It's not their fault that it's raining—shouldn't we cut them some slack? At least they warned us about the bad weather, right?

Jeremiah gets about as much respect as a forecaster who predicts bad weather all the time. Even the folks he grew up with don't want him around. In fact, they want him *dead*. But unlike a meteorologist, Jeremiah can't leave this job or area because God has placed Jeremiah just where he wants him, so Jeremiah must continue to give the people the bad reports.

Read Jeremiah 11:1–15:21

People today sometimes oppose believers who share God's message for the same reasons that motivated the people of Anathoth to plot Jeremiah's death. Certainly it would be tempting to remain silent or to change the message in the face of such opposition. Instead, we must be faithful to our calling, faithful to our Lord.

If you speak to others about God, you don't need to be obnoxious, pushy, or abrasive. Like Jeremiah, speak respectfully, time what you say properly, and make sure that you're representing God and not your own biases. But also like Jeremiah, keep speaking, and pray that the plans of your opponents will fail (Jeremiah 11:20). Let God be your protection.

Cute, furry creatures talk, sing, and dance across the screen and entertain children. Mom and Dad know, however, that the entertainers are just puppets, controlled by puppeteers offstage and off camera. Have you ever wondered whether you are just a puppet in God's hand? He is, after all, *sovereign*. Doesn't that mean he controls your every move?

This passage answers that question directly. In one prophecy delivered by Jeremiah, he compares people to living clay in the hands of God.

Jeremiah's other prophecies tell of impending doom, but also how the people can avoid it. Jeremiah gets a rude reception anyway. (Aren't you glad you're not a prophet?)

Read Jeremiah 16:1–20:18

Because the people of Judah did not repent of their sins and return to the Lord, they were like a jar that didn't turn out as the potter had intended (Jeremiah 18:4-6). Defective jars are not useful. And even as a potter takes a defective jar and kneads it back into a lump of clay, so also was the Lord planning to destroy Judah and reshape it.

Choosing to live in sin makes our lives less moldable and more defective to God. He wants us to be useful to him—he wants to shape us into a beautiful creation. But he will only do so if we allow ourselves to be moldable.

The shape your life takes is a cooperative effort between you and God. Do not become hard and unreceptive to his molding, but be soft and receptive to his hand on you. As you yield to God, he will shape you into a valuable vessel. Submit to him, the divine, loving Potter.

¹The LORD gave another message to Jeremiah. He said, ²"Go down to the potter's shop, and I will speak to you there." ³So I did as he told me and found the potter working at his wheel. ⁴But the jar he was making did not turn out as he had hoped, so he crushed it into a lump of clay again and started over. ⁵Then the LORD gave me this message: ⁶"O Israel, can I not do to you as this potter has done to his clay? As the clay is in the potter's hand, so are you in my hand. ⁷If I announce that a certain nation or kingdom is to be uprooted, torn down, and destroyed, ⁸but then that nation renounces its evil ways, I will not destroy it as I had planned. ⁹And if I announce that I will plant and build up a certain nation or kingdom, ¹⁰but then that nation turns to evil and refuses to obey me, I will not bless it as I said I would."

JEREMIAH 18:1-10

⁹My heart is broken because of the false prophets, and my bones tremble. I stagger like a drunkard, like someone overcome by wine, because of the holy words the Lord has spoken against them. ¹⁰For the land is full of adultery, and it lies under a curse. The land itself is in mourning—its wilderness pastures are dried up. For they all do evil and abuse what power they have. . . . ¹⁵Therefore, this is what the Lord of Heaven's Armies says concerning the prophets: "I will feed them with bitterness and give them poison to drink. For it is because of Jerusalem's prophets that wickedness has filled this land." ¹⁶This is what the Lord of Heaven's Armies says to his people: "Do not listen to these prophets when they prophesy to you, filling you with futile hopes. They are making up everything they say. They do not speak for the Lord!"

JEREMIAH 23:9-10, 15-16

Some people just don't want to hear bad news. They don't watch the news on television because it gets them too depressed. The news stations keep broadcasting the negative stories, insisting that they are exactly what keep viewers tuned in. News directors say that if they air only good news, the viewers lose interest and switch to stations that feature murders, fires, and political scandals. So the question remains: Do we want to hear bad news or don't we?

From Jeremiah's experience, he'd probably tell you that people don't want to hear bad news at all. As he shares God's newsflashes with the people in this passage, they denounce him and God for the bad news. But the really bad news isn't coming from God or Jeremiah.

Read Jeremiah 21:1–24:10

You can ignore some criticism. "Where'd you get that awful tie?" for example. But sometimes the issue hits close to home and won't let you escape so easily: "You shouldn't use bad language or read those dirty magazines." It's the inescapable criticism that gave Jeremiah's listeners fits. When people deliver bad news that carries the weight of Scripture, we simply don't have the option to turn our backs on their words.

Have you ever rejected a message or made fun of it because it would require you to change your ways? Before dismissing someone who says something negative about you, consider what he or she has to say. The message this person brings may contain some invaluable truth that will help to change your life for the better.

When you're away at college, at boot camp, or almost anywhere else, there's nothing quite like a letter from home. You know that the familiar handwriting means the message inside is just for you

Jeremiah's friends, neighbors, and other fellow citizens were a long way from home. Conquered by invaders, they lived in exile in Babylon. In this set of prophecies, Jeremiah deals with lonely, grief-stricken people. They want only to go back home to Jerusalem. Jeremiah knows, however, that they will be in Babylon for a long time, so he sends them a letter to help them get on with their lives. Look for a lesson about making the most of a bad situation.

Read Jeremiah 25:1–29:32

We should not let our lives grind to a halt during troubled times. In an unpleasant or distressing situation, we must accept what we cannot change, adjust whatever we can, and get on with our responsibilities. Some circumstances are unavoidable. Perhaps they aren't going to change anytime soon, or there is no end in sight. God places us in these circumstances for good reasons, either to discipline us or to teach us a lesson.

When you enter times of trouble or sudden change, or when you realize that your difficult circumstances aren't going to change, pray often. Don't give in to fear or give up in discouragement; instead, do what you can to fulfill your responsibilities.

⁴This is what the LORD of Heaven's Armies, the God of Israel, says to all the captives he has exiled to Babylon from Jerusalem: ⁵"Build homes, and plan to stay. Plant gardens, and eat the food they produce. ⁶Marry and have children. Then find spouses for them so that you may have many grandchildren. Multiply! Do not dwindle away! ⁷And work for the peace and prosperity of the city where I sent you into exile. Pray to the LORD for it, for its welfare will determine your welfare." . . . ¹¹"For I know the plans I have for you," says the LORD. "They are plans for good and not for disaster, to give you a future and a hope. ¹²In those days when you pray, I will listen. ¹³If you look for me wholeheartedly, you will find me. ¹⁴I will be found by you," says the LORD. "I will end your captivity and restore your fortunes."

JEREMIAH 29:4-7, 11-14

¹⁰"Listen to this message from the Lord, you nations of the world; proclaim it in distant coastlands: The Lord, who scattered his people, will gather them and watch over them as a shepherd does his flock. ¹¹For the Lord has redeemed Israel from those too strong for them. ¹²They will come home and sing songs of joy on the heights of Jerusalem. They will be radiant because of the Lord's good gifts—the abundant crops of grain, new wine, and olive oil, and the healthy flocks and herds. Their life will be like a watered garden, and all their sorrows will be gone. ¹³The young women will dance for joy, and the men—old and young—will join in the celebration. I will turn their mourning into joy. I will comfort them and exchange their sorrow for rejoicing. ¹⁴The priests will enjoy abundance, and my people will feast on my good gifts."

JEREMIAH 31:10-14

When friends fight, as they sometimes do, it's as if they've blown a circuit. To reset the breaker, so to speak, they apologize and make amends. The same is true in our relationship with God—only we do all the breaking.

This reading is about God resetting the breaker with the people of Judah. Though they will be spending some time in Babylon as a punishment for their sins, God reassures them that this won't last forever. As proof of this promise, Jeremiah buys a field back home in Judah.

Read Jeremiah 30:1–33:26

People who don't know God typically make one of two false assumptions about him. First, some suppose that God loves them so much that he doesn't care about their sinful behavior. These people also don't believe in hell or that God would punish anybody. Second, others assume God is an angry tyrant. People caught in this falsehood imagine that God cannot possibly love them because they are too sinful. They don't believe in heaven (at least for them) or that God could accept anybody (as bad as they).

Jeremiah's prophecies in this reading address this second assumption. Though God doesn't like it when we sin, he loves us enough to reach out and draw us to him (Jeremiah 31:3). He is eager for us to repent of our sins and turn to him for salvation. He doesn't hold grudges or fume over our every past offense. Rather he forgives us and forgets each sin when we repent.

Every family has a special link to the past. Some remember their ethnic roots and can tell you about their proud heritage. Others have favorite stories of the struggles that their grandparents or great-grandparents endured. Still others remember the heroic acts, faith, wisdom, or accomplishments of an ancestor who made a mark and left a story (if not a photo), making the relatives who live today somehow special.

This passage contains Jeremiah's last-minute prophecies and what happened to him and to the nation around the time he was giving them. It's Judah's last hour—Jerusalem is under siege by the Babylonians (as Jeremiah predicted) and is about to fall. In case anyone doesn't understand *why,* Jeremiah provides a vivid illustration through the Recabite family and their cherished past.

Read Jeremiah 34:1–38:28

As Christians, we have a long and glorious family tradition of seeking God and living for him. Although we should not emulate our spiritual ancestors merely out of tradition, we can and should learn from their example. We should seek God with all our hearts and obey his Word in every aspect of life, even if it means dying for Jesus Christ.

Take some time to reflect on your personal spiritual heritage. Thank God for godly parents, grandparents, and other relatives who have kept your family on the right path. If you have no such memories or heritage, determine that it will begin with you and your family. Make spiritual memories that your children and grandchildren will reflect upon to gain strength and inspiration.

¹²Then the LORD gave this message to Jeremiah: ¹³"This is what the LORD of Heaven's Armies, the God of Israel, says: Go and say to the people in Judah and Jerusalem, 'Come and learn a lesson about how to obey me. ¹⁴The Recabites do not drink wine to this day because their ancestor Jehonadab told them not to. But I have spoken to you again and again, and you refuse to obey me. ¹⁵Time after time I sent you prophets, who told you, "Turn from your wicked ways, and start doing things right. Stop worshiping other gods so that you might live in peace here in the land I have given to you and your ancestors." But you would not listen to me or obey me. ¹⁶The descendants of Jehonadab son of Recab have obeyed their ancestor completely, but you have refused to listen to me.'"

JEREMIAH 35:12-16

¹Then all the guerrilla leaders, including Johanan son of Kareah and Jezaniah son of Hoshaiah, and all the people, from the least to the greatest, approached ²Jeremiah the prophet. They said, "Please pray to the Lord your God for us. As you can see, we are only a tiny remnant compared to what we were before. ³Pray that the Lord your God will show us what to do and where to go." ⁴"All right," Jeremiah replied. "I will pray to the Lord your God, as you have asked, and I will tell you everything he says. I will hide nothing from you." ⁵Then they said to Jeremiah, "May the Lord your God be a faithful witness against us if we refuse to obey whatever he tells us to do! ⁶Whether we like it or not, we will obey the Lord our God to whom we are sending you with our plea. For if we obey him, everything will turn out well for us."

JEREMIAH 42:1-6

Running errands, going on vacation, working on projects—all of these activities require planning. Planning makes things easier to accomplish. But sometimes even plans aren't enough to achieve success.

Enter the forward-thinking Johanan, who has some plans. Like any good Israelite, he wants God to bless his plans and asks Jeremiah to pray for him. But something rotten shows itself as soon as God reveals the truth about Johanan's true motives. As you read, look for the lesson about truly seeking and doing God's will.

Read Jeremiah 39:1–45:5

Johanan and his tiny band came to Jeremiah and asked him to pray for God's approval of their plan (Jeremiah 42:1–43:3). But they didn't really care what God wanted; they wanted approval of their wicked plans.

This is a common problem—seeking God's approval of our desires rather than asking him to shape our desires. We should not make plans unless we are willing to have God shape and change them, and it is not good to place conditions on our willingness to accept God's answer. Whenever we seek God's blessing, we should say, "*Your* will be done" (Matthew 6:10, emphasis added).

What plans are you making these days? How do they match up with what God wants? Talk to God; yield your goals and your plans to him and he'll bless your decisions.

Vaccinations have given the world a prevention for several deadly diseases, most notably, polio, smallpox, whooping cough, mumps, and diphtheria. Also, common antibiotics have all but eliminated the threat from bacterial diseases such as bubonic plague and strep throat. Death has fewer weapons in its arsenal, it appears, so scientists are going after the rest of them, including the biggest ones: cancer and AIDS. Though cures for these have proven much more difficult to discover, hope runs high. Medical scientists have succeeded before; surely they'll do it again. After all, medical science can do anything, right?

Not all diseases focus their attack on the body—some target the soul. Pride, for instance, is one of these diseases, and the final section of Jeremiah's prophecies concerns Babylon, a country infected with pride. Will we ever understand how much damage this sin can cause? Or will we always see it as a natural right? As you read this section, check your life for pride.

Read Jeremiah 46:1–52:34

Pride, or arrogance, was Babylon's characteristic sin (Jeremiah 50:32). At best, pride is an oversight—a failure to recognize our total dependence on God for everything (life, health, and every skill). At worst, pride is spitting in the face of the one who created us.

We depend on God for our very lives. Only a humble acknowledgment of this makes any sense at all. That is why God resists the proud (see James 4:6). Because of sin, we naturally want to hold on to our pride, but there are steps we can take to overcome it by God's power and grace.

25The Lord has opened his armory and brought out weapons to vent his fury. The terror that falls upon the Babylonians will be the work of the Sovereign Lord of Heaven's Armies. 26Yes, come against her from distant lands. Break open her granaries. Crush her walls and houses into heaps of rubble. Destroy her completely, and leave nothing! 27Destroy even her young bulls—it will be terrible for them, too! Slaughter them all! For Babylon's day of reckoning has come. 28Listen to the people who have escaped from Babylon, as they tell in Jerusalem how the Lord our God has taken vengeance against those who destroyed his Temple. 29"Send out a call for archers to come to Babylon. Surround the city so none can escape. Do to her as she has done to others, for she has defied the Lord, the Holy One of Israel.

JEREMIAH 50:25-29

⁸The LORD was determined to destroy the walls of beautiful Jerusalem. He made careful plans for their destruction, then did what he had planned. Therefore, the ramparts and walls have fallen down before him. ⁹Jerusalem's gates have sunk into the ground. He has smashed their locks and bars. Her kings and princes have been exiled to distant lands; her law has ceased to exist. Her prophets receive no more visions from the LORD. ¹⁰The leaders of beautiful Jerusalem sit on the ground in silence. They are clothed in burlap and throw dust on their heads. The young women of Jerusalem hang their heads in shame. ¹¹I have cried until the tears no longer come; my heart is broken. My spirit is poured out in agony as I see the desperate plight of my people. Little children and tiny babies are fainting and dying in the streets.

LAMENTATIONS 2:8-11

People go to a particular church for many different reasons. For some it's the architecture of the building. For some, it's the pastor's sermons. For others, it's Sunday School and church programs. In theory, everyone goes to worship God.

It seems as though the people of Jerusalem also went to church—in their case the Temple—for reasons other than to worship God. In Lamentations, Jeremiah reveals why God has "rejected his own altar" (Lamentations 2:7). It has everything to do with the people's worship practices, and what Jeremiah compares their worship to is startling. As you read, take an honest appraisal of your motives for attending church.

Read Lamentations 1:1–5:22

When we go to church and worship God, we should examine our motives for doing so. If we're there for any reason other than worshiping him, then we need to reorder our priorities for attending church. In addition, we can practice three steps to help us focus our attention on praising and worshiping God. First, we can meditate on God as we participate in the service each Sunday. Second, we can try to ignore the distractions that occur during the service. Third, we can let the service create in us a sense of wonder at God's greatness and great deeds.

When you attend church, enjoy the fellowship and company of other believers, but also go to worship God with a sincere heart. The sincerity of our worship matters more to God than where or how we worship.

Suppose you have a friend, relative, or neighbor who has made a lot of foolish mistakes in the past. He or she has paid a heavy price for these mistakes, but for some reason the lesson just hasn't sunk in yet. Now this person is on the verge of making another big mistake. Should you warn him or her?

Ezekiel is in this kind of position. Despite repeated warnings of punishment from several prophets, the Jews refused to listen and kept on sinning. As a result, God let the Babylonians destroy Israel and take the Jews into captivity. Apparently the Israelites didn't learn their lesson, however, and they continued to sin in Babylon. So God appointed Ezekiel to bring his message to the Jews there. God also told Ezekiel if he didn't give the Jews his message, he, too, would pay for their sins.

As you read this section of Ezekiel, note the prophet's faithfulness in carrying out his responsibilities. Also look for the many symbols of God in Ezekiel's call to prophesy. Let these symbols lead you in worship.

Read Ezekiel 1:1–3:27

Ezekiel was bitter and angry at God's people (Ezekiel 3:14-15), and understandably so. Ezekiel had no guarantee that they would listen to him either (3:11). Still, Ezekiel delivered the messages God gave him and sacrificed his own comforts to communicate God's warnings.

You may feel like Ezekiel when Christian brothers or sisters scorn God's Word. But don't be discouraged. If Christian friends have strayed from God, speak up, even if they aren't listening, and even if it seems unlikely that they will take your advice.

6"Son of man, . . . 7You must give them my messages whether they listen or not. But they won't listen, for they are completely rebellious! 8Son of man, listen to what I say to you. Do not join them in their rebellion. Open your mouth, and eat what I give you." 9Then I looked and saw a hand reaching out to me. It held a scroll, 10which he unrolled. And I saw that both sides were covered with funeral songs, words of sorrow, and pronouncements of doom. 3:1The voice said to me, "Son of man, eat what I am giving you—eat this scroll! Then go and give its message to the people of Israel." 2So I opened my mouth, and he fed me the scroll. 3"Fill your stomach with this," he said. And when I ate it, it tasted as sweet as honey in my mouth. 4Then he said, "Son of man, go to the people of Israel and give them my messages."

EZEKIEL 2:6–3:4

³"Proclaim this message from the Sovereign LORD against the mountains of Israel. This is what the Sovereign LORD says to the mountains and hills and to the ravines and valleys: I am about to bring war upon you, and I will smash your pagan shrines. ⁴All your altars will be demolished, and your places of worship will be destroyed. I will kill your people in front of your idols. ⁵I will lay your corpses in front of your idols and scatter your bones around your altars. ⁶Wherever you live there will be desolation, and I will destroy your pagan shrines. Your altars will be demolished, your idols will be smashed, your places of worship will be torn down, and all the religious objects you have made will be destroyed. . . . ¹⁴Then they will know that I am the LORD."

EZEKIEL 6:3-6, 14

When discussing with people about what makes America great, you may eventually come to the topic of religious freedom. In America, whatever people want to believe, they can believe. Whatever god they want, they can have. It is a nation of options.

The Jews had many gods, but they weren't supposed to. The Lord was their God, and they were not to worship anything or anyone else. That's why many of Ezekiel's prophecies in this reading foretell terrible punishments to come.

From the sidelines, also watch the prophet because he is a good example to us all. He goes to great lengths to get God's message across. (Whatever God asks, he does!) And see what happens when a man is exposed to God's glory.

Read Ezekiel 4:1–11:25

The people to whom Ezekiel had prophesied had abandoned God in many ways. They had worshiped man-made idols. They had disobeyed God's laws. They had ignored the words of several prophets. Even in exile they still had stubborn hearts. Many of the tragic events that Ezekiel foretold and spoke about had one aim: to impress upon God's people (and, incidentally, the rest of the world) that the Lord is the only true and living God.

It is easy to forget that the Lord alone is God, the supreme authority and the only source of eternal life. Sometimes God uses the difficulties of life to remind people of his authority. When trials happen, we should not ask, "Oh, how could God let this happen?" Rather, we should ask, "Have we forgotten the Lord? Have we replaced God with something else? Have we brought this on ourselves?" Have no other god but the Lord.

People who speak for someone else have a responsibility to represent their clients or constituents accurately and adamantly.

It's no wonder that God was upset with a group of false prophets. These people claimed to represent God, but the messages they gave to the Jews didn't even come close to representing God's views. So God sent his appointed representative, Ezekiel, to speak out against them. What God had to say wasn't comforting news for those who misrepresented him. Check it out.

Also, note the change that lies ahead for God's people as reported by the true prophet, Ezekiel, because of their choices. It can really make you stop and think.

Read Ezekiel 12:1–17:24

Anyone can say, "I speak for God." But who can actually represent him? The desire to draw attention to ourselves, to be liked, and to be seen as an authority can entrap us. This same desire entrapped the false prophets in a quest to gain admirers rather than God's approval.

Be careful how you represent God's viewpoint to others. Make sure your message does indeed come from God's Word and not just from your own opinions or biases. And don't look to approval from others as proof that you are right. Many people will willingly believe a falsehood if it suits them. Watch carefully what you believe, and be careful in how you represent it to others.

4"O people of Israel, these prophets of yours are like jackals digging in the ruins. 5They have done nothing to repair the breaks in the walls around the nation. They have not helped it to stand firm in battle on the day of the LORD. 6Instead, they have told lies and made false predictions. They say, 'This message is from the LORD,' even though the LORD never sent them. And yet they expect him to fulfill their prophecies! 7Can your visions be anything but false if you claim, 'This message is from the LORD,' when I have not even spoken to you? 8Therefore, this is what the Sovereign LORD says: Because what you say is false and your visions are a lie, I will stand against you, says the Sovereign LORD. 9I will raise my fist against all the prophets who see false visions and make lying predictions."

EZEKIEL 13:4-9

³⁶The Lord said to me, . . . "You must accuse Oholah and Oholibah of all their detestable sins. ³⁷They have committed both adultery and murder —adultery by worshiping idols and murder by burning as sacrifices the children they bore to me. . . . ³⁸They have defiled my Temple and violated my Sabbath day! ³⁹On the very day that they sacrificed their children to their idols, they boldly came into my Temple to worship! They came in and defiled my house. . . . ⁴⁶Now this is what the Sovereign Lord says: Bring an army against them and hand them over to be terrorized and plundered. ⁴⁷For their enemies will stone them and kill them with swords. They will butcher their sons and daughters and burn their homes. . . . ⁴⁸I will put an end to lewdness and idolatry in the land, and my judgment will be a warning to others not to follow their wicked example."

EZEKIEL 23:36-39, 46-48

Some of the Jewish children of Ezekiel's time were physically abused by their parents. They did not even have a chance to grow up. In this reading, Ezekiel confronts the Jews about one of their most heinous practices—child sacrifice. What may be even more shocking than this, however, is what the Jews did after sacrificing their children.

Also in this reading, you can see God's people trying to deflect their responsibility for their sin. They say it's unfair, that they're not guilty, that they don't deserve it. But Ezekiel won't accept these excuses.

Read Ezekiel 18:1–24:27

Today children aren't often killed in religious rituals, but they are sometimes sacrificed in other ways. Some are abused by adults who take out their anger on them or, worse, derive sexual pleasure from them. Some children are neglected by parents who are too busy to spend time with them. Other parents selfishly indulge their appetites and don't provide for their children's needs. All of these atrocities are modern-day examples of child sacrifice. Children have no power to stop those who treat them with contempt. We should not abuse or neglect children in any way. Rather, we should treat them as the precious gifts from God that they are.

Bob is proud. He has built his business from the ground up. He has worked long hours, pushed through lean times, hired many employees, and let a few go. Now he's selling what he so skillfully built, and the proceeds will set him up for an early retirement. He has what you might call "bragging rights."

In this set of prophecies, we learn a negative lesson on pride as demonstrated by Egypt. They've got a jewel in the Nile, and they know it. But along with this source of pride comes a caution.

You will find other cautions here—especially judgments against Ammon, Moab, Edom, Philistia, Tyre, and Egypt (all nations that bordered Israel). These show that *everybody* has to answer to God, even those who don't acknowledge him.

Read Ezekiel 25:1–32:32

The Egyptian people took great pride in the Nile River. This unstoppable source of fresh water cut through the desert and turned barren land into fertile soil, making life in Egypt possible. It was a reliable source of all the food they could ever need. All they had to do was work the land year after year, and it would yield abundant amounts of grain and vegetables. Rather than thanking God for this great provision, however, the Egyptians proudly boasted, "The Nile River is mine; I made it" (Ezekiel 29:9).

God's provisions come to us in many forms: a home, a job, a church, a business, a family, a reputation. Each gives us opportunity to say, "Thank you, Lord." Each also tempts us to boast, especially if we have invested a great deal of time and energy in the good we enjoy.

⁶"All the people of Egypt will know that I am the Lord, for to Israel you were just a staff made of reeds. ⁷When Israel leaned on you, you splintered and broke and stabbed her in the armpit. When she put her weight on you, you gave way, and her back was thrown out of joint. ⁸Therefore, this is what the Sovereign Lord says: I will bring an army against you, O Egypt, and destroy both people and animals. ⁹The land of Egypt will become a desolate wasteland, and the Egyptians will know that I am the Lord. Because you said, 'The Nile River is mine; I made it,' ¹⁰I am now the enemy of both you and your river. I will make the land of Egypt a totally desolate wasteland, from Migdol to Aswan, as far south as the border of Ethiopia. ¹¹For forty years not a soul will pass that way, neither people nor animals. It will be completely uninhabited."

EZEKIEL 29:6-11

²"Son of man, give your people this message: 'When I bring an army against a country, the people of that land choose one of their own to be a watchman. ³When the watchman sees the enemy coming, he sounds the alarm to warn the people. ⁴Then if those who hear the alarm refuse to take action, it is their own fault if they die. ⁵They heard the alarm but ignored it, so the responsibility is theirs. If they had listened to the warning, they could have saved their lives. ⁶But if the watchman sees the enemy coming and doesn't sound the alarm to warn the people, he is responsible for their captivity. They will die in their sins, but I will hold the watchman responsible for their deaths.' ⁷Now, son of man, I am making you a watchman for the people of Israel. Therefore, listen to what I say and warn them for me."

EZEKIEL 33:1-7

Suppose you really blow it. You feel quite certain that God could never forgive you or use you or care whether you get up the next morning. Where do you go from here?

This portion of Ezekiel has the answer. As you read, notice the Jews' change in attitude toward God. Once they were hardened—now they're repentant. The tone of Ezekiel's prophecies changes to match. The people begin to listen, and God responds. Here is the turning point: God's enemies will be wiped out and good times will return. Restoration and new life lie ahead.

Read Ezekiel 33:1–39:29

Thirty-two chapters of Ezekiel record how Judah, and many of the surrounding nations, would be punished for their sins. At first none of the people listened to these divine rebukes. Finally God's people admitted their guilt and set aside their stubborn rebellion. But then they felt overwhelmed by their sorrow: "Our sins are heavy upon us; we are wasting away!" (Ezekiel 33:10). God responded by saying that he would not punish those who repented (33:10-12).

God doesn't enjoy punishing people, nor does he abandon us when we stray from him. In every warning he calls us back. He prefers that we turn from our sins, seek his forgiveness, and begin to follow him again. No matter how far we've gone astray, we can always come back to God, because he *wants* us back.

When you sin, don't resign yourself to a pitiless fate of isolation from God. Simply confess your sins and acknowledge his right to guide you. Don't let past disobedience ever keep you from returning to God.

Surely no holiday generates more anticipation than Christmas—the waiting, the countdown of days till that bright morning when the ripping of wrapping paper becomes welcome chaos. Countless children have counted the days. Countless more have slept poorly—or not at all—the night before. The anticipation is just too much.

That's the point of this prophetic passage: anticipation. Ezekiel's vision contains such hope for the future that it can get you a little worked up. Don't speed-read through this and miss the splendor.

Read Ezekiel 40:1–48:35

King Nebuchadnezzar's invading armies had completely destroyed the Temple. But one day that terrible event would only be a distant memory. In one of Ezekiel's visions, he saw a new Temple of great beauty and splendor, where worship flourished. Ezekiel wrote down a very detailed description of that Temple and the worship that would take place there among God's people (Ezekiel 40:1–46:24). To a group of exiles in Babylon, with the memory of their devastated homeland still fresh in their minds, this vision came as a great encouragement. Ezekiel's vision meant that God had not abandoned his people, and that one day the Lord and his great blessings would once again become the focal point of Israel's life.

Don't let the details of this blueprint obscure the point of Ezekiel's vision. Eventually God's people will enjoy eternal life with him, and it will be indescribably wonderful. Our present troubles will end before long, and the life that awaits us will make all our service and obedience to God worthwhile.

⁵The Spirit took me up and brought me into the inner courtyard, and the glory of the Lord filled the Temple. ⁶And I heard someone speaking to me from within the Temple, while the man who had been measuring stood beside me. ⁷The Lord said to me, "Son of man, this is the place of my throne and the place where I will rest my feet. I will live here forever among the people of Israel. They and their kings will not defile my holy name any longer by their adulterous worship of other gods or by honoring the relics of their kings who have died. ⁸They put their idol altars right next to mine with only a wall between them and me. They defiled my holy name by such detestable sin, so I consumed them in my anger. ⁹Now let them stop worshiping other gods and honoring the relics of their kings, and I will live among them forever."

EZEKIEL 43:5-9

¹⁴Nebuchadnezzar said to them, . . . ¹⁵"I will give you one more chance to bow down and worship the statue I have made when you hear the sound of the musical instruments. But if you refuse, you will be thrown immediately into the blazing furnace. And then what god will be able to rescue you from my power?" ¹⁶Shadrach, Meshach, and Abednego replied, "O Nebuchadnezzar, we do not need to defend ourselves before you. ¹⁷If we are thrown into the blazing furnace, the God whom we serve is able to save us. He will rescue us from your power, Your Majesty. ¹⁸But even if he doesn't, we want to make it clear to you, Your Majesty, that we will never serve your gods or worship the gold statue you have set up."

DANIEL 3:14-18

Sometimes having a job means having to make some big ethical choices. For instance, your employer may ask you to do something that is wrong and then tell you that it's not optional. You have to decide whether you're going to go through with it.

This situation is similar to the one in which Shadrach, Meshach, and Abednego find themselves. They each have an important job in the Babylonian government, and they, too, have a big decision to make. But the consequence they face for upsetting their boss is serious—a decision to do what is right here means death. As you read, determine whether their actions are foolish or courageous.

Read Daniel 1:1–3:30

Shadrach, Meshach, and Abednego had been ordered to bow down and worship a statue, but they refused. To worship the image would violate God's command in Exodus 20:3, "You must not have any other god but me." When threatened with execution, they still refused. Then they were given one more chance (Daniel 3:15). At that point they could have used any number of excuses for bowing to the image to save their lives ("It's just one time"; "We had no choice"; "It's just a Babylonian custom"; "It isn't so bad"; "We're not hurting anybody"; "We can always say we did it against our will"). But instead of making excuses, Shadrach, Meshach, and Abednego simply obeyed God. The outcome of their courageous decision lay with God, so that is where they left it.

Don't make excuses for wrong choices. Like these young men, have the courage to do what's right. Know that God is pleased with your obedience, and trust him to work out the best for the situation.

Revenge is a natural response. Anyone can do it, and everyone does. Tell others about a time when you responded that way, and they will be able to sympathize with you. It's understandable and logical. It's even intuitive. For many, it's a way of life. For a few, it's not even an option.

Daniel was one of the few, the humble, the forgiving. In this reading, he learns of the tragic future awaiting King Nebuchadnezzar, a man who has offended Daniel beyond the limits of reason. As you read, notice especially Daniel's attitude toward the king. Daniel sets an example to follow.

Read Daniel 4:1–6:28

Daniel served King Nebuchadnezzar of Babylon—a mixed blessing. Nebuchadnezzar had destroyed Daniel's home, killed many of Daniel's people, and leveled the Temple of Daniel's God. Daniel, the servant of God, was forced to serve an enemy king. Yet as soon as Daniel understood Nebuchadnezzar's dream— foretelling a horrible future for this rogue—he was "aghast" and wondered how to break the news. He even told the king he wished that the dream's foreshadowed judgments would happen to the king's enemies and not to Nebuchadnezzar (Daniel 4:19)! How could Daniel so deeply grieve the fate of an enemy? He had forgiven the king.

You do not have to like or endorse hurtful actions. Perhaps you will even need to put a stop to them. But you *can* forgive the offender. God may even use you in an extraordinary way in that person's life, much as he used Daniel in Nebuchadnezzar's. The next time someone hurts or mistreats you, ask God to help you forgive him or her, and lay aside any plans you may have to get even.

24"This is what the dream means, Your Majesty, and what the Most High has declared will happen to my lord the king. 25You will be driven from human society, and you will live in the fields with the wild animals. You will eat grass like a cow, and you will be drenched with the dew of heaven. Seven periods of time will pass while you live this way, until you learn that the Most High rules over the kingdoms of the world and gives them to anyone he chooses. 26But . . . you will receive your kingdom back again when you have learned that heaven rules. 27King Nebuchadnezzar, please accept my advice. Stop sinning and do what is right. Break from your wicked past and be merciful to the poor. Perhaps then you will continue to prosper." 28But all these things did happen to King Nebuchadnezzar.

DANIEL 4:24-28

⁴"O Lord, you are a great and awesome God! You always fulfill your covenant and keep your promises of unfailing love to those who love you and obey your commands. ⁵But we have sinned and done wrong. We have rebelled against you and scorned your commands and regulations. ⁶We have refused to listen to your servants the prophets, who spoke on your authority to our kings and princes and ancestors and to all the people of the land. ⁷Lord, you are in the right; but as you see, our faces are covered with shame. This is true of all of us, including the people of Judah and Jerusalem and all Israel, scattered near and far, wherever you have driven us because of our disloyalty to you. ⁸O Lord, we and our kings, princes, and ancestors are covered with shame because we have sinned against you."

DANIEL 9:4-8

The word *confession* holds very different meanings for different people. Some think of it as an out-of-date religious custom. Others have good memories of relieving a guilty conscience in the privacy of a confessional. Still others think of the humiliation of secret sins being publicly revealed in a courtroom. What connotations does the word *confession* hold for you?

Confession has an important place in this set of prophecies. All of Daniel 7:1–12:13 concerns the future, and a lot of it does not bode well for God's people. As Daniel learns the bad news, he prays . . . and confesses.

Read Daniel 7:1–12:13

Daniel loved God and wanted to do God's will, yet the prayer he recorded in Daniel 9 included his confession of sin (Daniel 9:3-19). We have no record of any of Daniel's mistakes or sins. The book of Daniel always portrays him as an exceptional man of God. But even Daniel had offended God (see Romans 3:23-24), and he shared in the guilt of his people's rebellion. So in Daniel's prayers he took responsibility for the sins that he and his people had committed. He didn't gloss over them, excuse them, minimize them, or deny them. He admitted his guilt and placed it in God's merciful hands.

That's the pattern of confession that every believer should follow. Whenever we pray, we should openly admit our sins. We should not deny the faults we have and the sins we commit.

Like Daniel, be honest with God. Confess your sins to him and feel clean, relieved, prepared to serve him—forgiven.

You can tell how devoted fans are to a team by the way they act when the team isn't winning. You can also tell how devoted a dating couple is by how they act when they're separated by distance. And you can tell how devoted a spouse is by how he or she acts when the partner develops a severe disability.

In this reading, Hosea pays a huge price to maintain his relationship with God. Some people may think this is too high a price to pay, but not Hosea. He is devoted to God, and he obeys God regardless of the cost. As you read Hosea's story, consider whether you would be willing to go that far for God.

Read Hosea 1:1–3:5

God often required extraordinary obedience from his prophets. For Hosea that meant marrying a woman who would be unfaithful to him (Hosea 1:2-3). But God had good reasons for commanding Hosea to do this. Through this marriage, God would illustrate the way Israel had been unfaithful to him despite the fact that he remained faithful to them.

Sometimes God's commands make no sense to us at all, and the obligation to obey them seems really unattractive. But those who devote themselves to God, like Hosea, obey his teachings and commands without hesitation.

Always obey God, even if you don't understand his purposes. He has given us his commands for our own good, and he will reward us with more than we deserve for obeying him. What has God told you to do that you have put off? Obey him in response to his love for you.

²When the Lord first began speaking to Israel through Hosea, he said to him, "Go and marry a prostitute, so that some of her children will be conceived in prostitution. This will illustrate how Israel has acted like a prostitute by turning against the Lord and worshiping other gods." ³So Hosea married Gomer, the daughter of Diblaim, and she became pregnant and gave Hosea a son. ⁴And the Lord said, "Name the child Jezreel, for I am about to punish King Jehu's dynasty to avenge the murders he committed at Jezreel. In fact, I will bring an end to Israel's independence. ⁵I will break its military power in the Jezreel Valley."

HOSEA 1:2-5

¹Hear the word of the LORD, O people of Israel! The LORD has brought charges against you, saying: "There is no faithfulness, no kindness, no knowledge of God in your land. ²You make vows and break them; you kill and steal and commit adultery. There is violence everywhere—one murder after another. ³That is why your land is in mourning, and everyone is wasting away. Even the wild animals, the birds of the sky, and the fish of the sea are disappearing. ⁴Don't point your finger at someone else and try to pass the blame! My complaint, you priests, is with you. ⁵So you will stumble in broad daylight, and your false prophets will fall with you in the night. And I will destroy Israel, your mother. ⁶My people are being destroyed because they don't know me."

HOSEA 4:1-6

Steve Johnson is captain of the USS *Maxum,* a small but capable boat that can hold up to twelve passengers and crew. As captain, Steve has many responsibilities, but foremost is the safety of those on board. It's his job to make sure the boat is safe to operate and that everyone on board always gets to shore safely, no matter what. The people on board are his responsibility—that's what it means to be captain.

The leaders of Israel also have a responsibility for others. But they have been irresponsible—they've neglected their duty to teach and guide the people in God's ways. When Hosea confronts them about this, they try to shift the blame to someone else. Like bad ship captains, they have sunk the ship and stolen all the lifeboats. As you read this section of Scripture, look for the lessons on leadership.

Read Hosea 4:1–5:15

The priests had dropped their responsibility to correctly lead. Instead of instructing the nation in religion and morality, they had led the way toward idolatry and immorality. Yet they didn't want to face the consequences. When their sins came under scrutiny, they tried to divert attention from themselves to the people. They tried to justify their own irresponsible actions by pointing to the sins of others. But the sins of others didn't exonerate them.

All of us share a mandate to lead others—by setting an example if not by holding a position or responsibility (see 1 Timothy 4:12). The fact that some people won't follow doesn't excuse us from leading the way.

Take responsibility for the people who follow you. Teach them, guide them, and lead them in God's way.

When sitting in church, married people can often think of a thousand ways that their spouse should put the sermon they're hearing to good use. *More patience, less judging—yes, that's what he (or she) needs. If only my spouse would listen.*

In this reading, Hosea is talking directly to the Israelites. They have a tendency of finding fault with others far away. They need to take a good look in the mirror before pointing fingers.

That's not all Israel needs to do, however. There are more good lessons in this passage for them to hear, if they're willing: lessons such as how a person reaps what he or she sows; the cost of serving false gods; and prosperity not being an indicator of God's approval.

Read Hosea 6:1–10:15

God said, "Even though I gave them all my laws, they act as if those laws don't apply to them." (Hosea 8:12). The Israelites needed to look at how the laws applied to them, not to others. Anyone can listen to a sermon and think of other people who need to hear it. Everyone, at least occasionally, reads the Bible, comes upon a great truth, and thinks, *If only so and so would do what this passage teaches!* When we do that, we miss the point. God has given the message to *us,* and that's where the response must begin. Maybe the person we have in mind does need to change, but even then the best way to change him or her involves setting a good example ourselves.

Whenever you encounter a rule to live by, apply it to yourself first. Then pray for others who you think could also benefit from it.

¹"Sound the alarm! The enemy descends like an eagle on the people of the Lord, for they have broken my covenant and revolted against my law. ²Now Israel pleads with me, 'Help us, for you are our God!' ³But it is too late. The people of Israel have rejected what is good, and now their enemies will chase after them. ⁴The people have appointed kings without my consent, and princes without my knowledge. By making idols for themselves from their silver and gold, they have brought about their own destruction. ⁵O Samaria, I reject this calf—this idol you have made. My fury burns against you. How long will you be incapable of innocence? ⁶This calf you worship, O Israel, was crafted by your own hands! It is not God! Therefore, it must be smashed to bits. ⁷They have planted the wind and will harvest the whirlwind."

HOSEA 8:1-7

¹The people of Israel feed on the wind; they chase after the east wind all day long. They pile up lies and violence; they are making an alliance with Assyria while sending olive oil to buy support from Egypt. ²Now the LORD is bringing charges against Judah. He is about to punish Jacob for all his deceitful ways, and pay him back for all he has done. ³Even in the womb, Jacob struggled with his brother; when he became a man, he even fought with God. ⁴Yes, he wrestled with the angel and won. He wept and pleaded for a blessing from him. There at Bethel he met God face to face, and God spoke to him—⁵the LORD God of Heaven's Armies, the LORD is his name! ⁶So now, come back to your God. Act with love and justice, and always depend on him. ⁷But no, the people are like crafty merchants selling from dishonest scales.

HOSEA 12:1-7

The issue of reducing crime presents many dilemmas. Some believe that spending more money on social programs will help reduce the number of people who turn to crime as an alternative lifestyle. Others believe building more prisons and increasing the length of prison sentences will deter people from committing crimes. Each view has good and bad points. But neither is balanced. One involves love or caring without justice—the other uses justice without love or caring.

Hosea brings a simple message to God's people in this passage regarding the love-and-justice tug-of-war. As you read, look for God's desire that his people concern themselves with both love and justice.

Read Hosea 11:1–14:9

Hosea's people neither looked out for others nor transacted business honestly or fairly. God's prescription for their sins involved making a simple, two-sided adjustment: living by love and living by justice (Hosea 12:6).

Love and justice lie at the very foundation of God's character. If we are to live rightly at all, we must begin there. Some people love others so much that they excuse all wrongdoing. Others insist so vigorously on being just that they ignore the effects of their actions on people. But love without justice, because it aims at a low standard, leaves people in their sins. Justice without love, because it aims at an impossibly high standard, drives people away from God. We need to live by both principles, in imitation of God's character.

Consider your relationships at work, in the community, at church, and in your home. How should you act in order to be more loving? What should you change to be more just?

If you could convey one message to the next generation, what would it be? What piece of invaluable advice would you pass on to them? Would it be financial, political, spiritual, or something else?

In this passage, the prophet Joel urges parents to pass on to their children the stories he is about to tell them—to open up the details of their past, to tell what has happened to them, to reveal the hidden details that kids would never know. They're not pleasant stories, but they contain a valuable lesson: Obey God or endure the consequences.

Read Joel 1:1–2:27

God urged the parents of Judah to tell their children all about the terrible events that Joel was about to describe. God wanted them to pass along the important lessons they learned through these horrible events (Joel 1:3).

Is there any point in telling others about the downturns you've had because of bad choices? After all, some people think they have nothing to offer. They think that their mistakes have canceled out all successes, leaving them nothing to share. But they are wrong. God can use people's wounds to heal others. The apostle Paul, for example, wrote, "These things happened to them as examples for us. They were written down to warn us" (1 Corinthians 10:11).

Give younger people your own testimony of God's truth—disobeying God can bring pain and consequences—and you do them a world of good. Telling these stories can help others avoid your mistakes and duplicate your successes. God can use your wounds to heal others. God's rebukes and lessons to you can help teach others, especially if the lessons were painful or difficult to learn.

¹The Lord gave this message to Joel son of Pethuel. ²Hear this, you leaders of the people. Listen, all who live in the land. In all your history, has anything like this happened before? ³Tell your children about it in the years to come, and let your children tell their children. Pass the story down from generation to generation. . . . ⁶A vast army of locusts has invaded my land, a terrible army too numerous to count. Its teeth are like lions' teeth, its fangs like those of a lioness. ⁷It has destroyed my grapevines and ruined my fig trees, stripping their bark and destroying it, leaving the branches white and bare. ⁸Weep like a bride dressed in black, mourning the death of her husband. ⁹For there is no grain or wine to offer at the Temple of the Lord. So the priests are in mourning. The ministers of the Lord are weeping.

JOEL 1:1-3, 6-9

¹²"Let the nations be called to arms. Let them march to the valley of Jehoshaphat. There I, the LORD, will sit to pronounce judgment on them all. ¹³Swing the sickle, for the harvest is ripe. Come, tread the grapes, for the winepress is full. The storage vats are overflowing with the wickedness of these people." ¹⁴Thousands upon thousands are waiting in the valley of decision. There the day of the LORD will soon arrive. ¹⁵The sun and moon will grow dark, and the stars will no longer shine. ¹⁶The LORD's voice will roar from Zion and thunder from Jerusalem, and the heavens and the earth will shake. But the LORD will be a refuge for his people, a strong fortress for the people of Israel. ¹⁷"Then you will know that I, the LORD your God, live in Zion, my holy mountain. Jerusalem will be holy forever, and foreign armies will never conquer her again."

JOEL 3:12-17

He stands on the street corner every day, trumpeting a message of warning and doom. "The world is going to end soon," he says. "You'd better repent now while there's still time."

In this reading, Joel sounds like a doomsaying street preacher. But not all of his news is bad. For those who love the Lord, Joel's message is filled with hope. The Lord will be gentle with his people. For his enemies, however . . . it's not too late to repent!

Read Joel 2:28–3:21

Joel's messages included many references to the "Day of the Lord," a final day of judgment that still lay in the future. On that final judgment day, every person who has ever lived—dead, living, and yet to be born—will face God (Joel 3:2, 12, 14).

Today many people don't believe in a final day of judgment. Some even mock the idea, pointing to the many doomsayers who have come and gone with their warnings unfulfilled. But we don't disbelieve in medical science because some doctors are quacks. Likewise, we shouldn't disbelieve the Bible's prophecies because of false prophets in the present day.

God has told us that we will be held accountable for our actions, and we will. We need to acknowledge and prepare for that time.

To be prepared for the Judgment Day, live according to God's Word, and tell others of his love for them. Let the coming Day of the Lord motivate you to action.

If you follow football, you know that the game has seen a lot of changes over the past decade. Of all the changes though, the worst one has to be the new attitudes of many who play. These players often act cocky, intimidating, and unsportsmanlike.

In this set of prophecies, Amos takes aim at cockiness and unfettered bravado. Arrogant warriors, beware. God is not impressed.

Amos's other prophecies in this reading contain clues that God doesn't always respect what we do. Note, for example, what God can do with a mere shepherd and fig grower. Second, mark God's words toward some upper-class types who exploit the poor while giving extra tithes and sacrifices. It's kind of sobering.

Read Amos 1:1–2:16

Television and movies bombard us with heroes (and heroines) who defy death and all foes with a huge arsenal of skill, tools, intelligence, luck, and bravado. Because of their incredible fortune, they appear to fear nothing. Many people try to model their lives after these fake images, even though their heroes don't exist in real life. They try to be like these cellophane gods: tough, indestructible, and fearless. But God is not impressed with skill or bravado. He says that even the best, most skilled, and toughest people will be terrified when his judgment comes (Amos 2:16). And it *will* come.

Don't be swayed by the self-assured rhetoric of those who think they can make it through life without God. Don't let them lead you to conceit—don't trust in your own brain power, skill, or bravado. God fears no one, and one day all people will fear him.

¹⁰"It was I who rescued you from Egypt and led you through the desert for forty years, so you could possess the land of the Amorites. ¹¹I chose some of your sons to be prophets and others to be Nazirites. Can you deny this, my people of Israel?" asks the LORD. ¹²"But you caused the Nazirites to sin by making them drink wine, and you commanded the prophets, 'Shut up!' ¹³So I will make you groan like a wagon loaded down with sheaves of grain. ¹⁴Your fastest runners will not get away. The strongest among you will become weak. Even mighty warriors will be unable to save themselves. ¹⁵The archers will not stand their ground. The swiftest runners won't be fast enough to escape. Even those riding horses won't be able to save themselves. ¹⁶On that day the most courageous of your fighting men will drop their weapons and run for their lives."

AMOS 2:10-16

⁶Come back to the LORD and live! . . . ¹⁴Do what is good and run from evil so that you may live! Then the LORD God of Heaven's Armies will be your helper, just as you have claimed. ¹⁵Hate evil and love what is good; turn your courts into true halls of justice. Perhaps even yet the LORD God of Heaven's Armies will have mercy on the remnant of his people. ¹⁶Therefore, this is what the LORD, the LORD God of Heaven's Armies, says: "There will be crying in all the public squares and mourning in every street. Call for the farmers to weep with you, and summon professional mourners to wail. ¹⁷There will be wailing in every vineyard, for I will destroy them all," says the LORD.

AMOS 5:6, 14-17

How many times have you heard this scenario: Someone who is falsely accused can't afford a good lawyer and ends up being convicted. Or someone who is guilty but has money hires a good lawyer and goes free. For the poor, justice never seems to be affordable.

In this reading, you will find Amos accusing God's people of denying justice to the poor. "Stop cheating the poor and start helping them," Amos says.

You will also see that this isn't the only sin on Israel's record. The rap sheet God has on them is a mile long.

Read Amos 3:1–6:14

Amos prophesied against the people of Israel for neglecting and abusing powerless people (Amos 5:12). They favored the rich, took bribes, and exploited the poor.

Today we have our own excuses for not helping the poor or speaking out against those who exploit them ("They don't deserve help"; "I don't know any poor people"; "I've got to look out for myself"; "Any money I give will just be wasted or stolen"; "No one will listen to me—I'm not important"; "The little bit I could give wouldn't make any difference"). We still have a responsibility, however, to care for the poor just as much as the people of Israel did. To neglect them is sin.

What programs to help the needy does your church sponsor? With what poverty-fighting community groups could you work? In what mercy ministry can you serve? As an individual, you may think that you can't accomplish much, but with the love of God in your heart you can. And when you join with others who care, the difference you can make will be even more apparent.

It's funny how we appreciate some things only after they're gone. The kids grow up and move away, and suddenly the house is much too quiet. Or the job we once called boring now looks like the best one we ever had. Whether we took it for granted or not, something good has come and gone, and how we miss it now!

As Amos continues prophesying against Israel and Judah, his words reveal one precious commodity that they are about to lose: God's Word. Up to this point they haven't seen its value. They've taken it for granted and left it unused. It will soon be gone, and someday they will miss it—the day when they need it most.

That's why Amos sees visions of judgment, from which no one can escape. Fortunately for those who listen, the visions also include promise of restoration (a constant theme from our God, who disciplines those he loves). As you read this passage, consider how much you really value God's Word.

Read Amos 7:1–9:15

The people to whom Amos preached wanted nothing to do with God's Word. Though they had the law of Moses, they ignored it. When God graciously sent prophets like Amos to warn the Israelites to pay attention to his Word, they ignored that, too. They didn't want to hear what God had to say. It is no wonder, then, that the day would come when all this apathy toward Scripture would come back to haunt them. They would crave the opportunity to hear his Word and not be able to find it anywhere—taken for granted and taken away (Amos 8:11-13).

Amos's message speaks to us as well. We disregard the Bible to our own peril. If we set it aside, the day may come when we will need it and it will be gone. How we treat the Bible each day makes a huge difference.

9"In that day," says the Sovereign Lord, "I will make the sun go down at noon and darken the earth while it is still day. 10I will turn your celebrations into times of mourning and your singing into weeping. You will wear funeral clothes and shave your heads to show your sorrow—as if your only son had died. How very bitter that day will be!" 11"The time is surely coming," says the Sovereign Lord, "when I will send a famine on the land—not a famine of bread or water but of hearing the words of the Lord. 12People will stagger from sea to sea and wander from border to border searching for the word of the Lord, but they will not find it. 13Beautiful girls and strong young men will grow faint in that day, thirsting for the Lord's word."

AMOS 8:9-13

¹This is the vision that the Sovereign Lᴏʀᴅ revealed to Obadiah concerning the land of Edom. We have heard a message from the Lᴏʀᴅ that an ambassador was sent to the nations to say, "Get ready, everyone! Let's assemble our armies and attack Edom!" ²The Lᴏʀᴅ says to Edom, "I will cut you down to size among the nations; you will be greatly despised. ³You have been deceived by your own pride because you live in a rock fortress and make your home high in the mountains. 'Who can ever reach us way up here?' you ask boastfully. ⁴But even if you soar as high as eagles and build your nest among the stars, I will bring you crashing down," says the Lᴏʀᴅ. . . . ⁷"All your allies will turn against you. They will help to chase you from your land. They will promise you peace while plotting to deceive and destroy you."

OBADIAH 1:1-4, 7

Everyone gets a sense of security from something or someone. For young children, security may be found in a blanket or the arms of a parent. For adults it may be in a career, a big salary, or a relationship with a spouse.

Obadiah's little book is about securities—false securities to be exact. Edom, one of Israel's neighbors, has developed a false sense of security in the safety of their homeland (the cliffs, crags, and caves of Petra in modern-day Jordan). Their sense of security may have even led them to commit hateful acts against Israel. As you read, you will see that despite Edom's strategic location, they are not invulnerable. God will make sure of that.

Read Obadiah 1:1-21

The Edomites felt secure and were proud of their self-sufficiency. They lived in homes protected by high, inaccessible cliffs. Looking around, they analyzed their situation and thought, "*Who can ever reach us way up here?*" (Obadiah 1:3). God didn't appreciate their pride, however, and he wasn't happy with the way they were treating Israel (their relatives through Esau). Therefore, God sent Obadiah to the Edomites with a message of impending doom: The security they found in the cliffs would be their downfall, literally, as their friends and allies would turn against them and take their land.

Placing one's security in something other than God, such as a job, a family, a retirement plan, a relationship, or intellect is foolish—they can disappear in a moment. Only God is strong, sure, lasting, and trustworthy. Only he can supply true security.

Don't be like the Edomites. Don't rely only on yourself and your position. Recognize your vulnerability, ask God for help, and find your security in him.

People have strong feelings about cities. Some feel loyal to a particular city because that's their hometown, they have fond memories of a recent visit, or their favorite sports team resides there. Others absolutely detest certain cities because of a sports team rivalry, a bad experience during a recent visit, or a misunderstanding of the people who live there.

Jonah, one of God's prophets, has strong feelings toward a certain Assyrian city called Nineveh, and for good reason. The Assyrians were Israel's bitter enemies, and Ninevah stood as the symbol of evil. So when Jonah gets a call from God to go to Ninevah to warn them about God's judgment, he takes off running—in the opposite direction. But his travel plans end up taking a detour. In this passage, find a lesson about obeying God, no matter what.

Read Jonah 1:1–2:10

Every change for the better begins by giving up the attempt to flee and surrendering to God's will. We sometimes pull the same stunts as Jonah. Like him, we cannot get away with them forever. Sooner or later God will call us back.

From what responsibilities have you tried to run away? Has God been urging you to reconcile with an enemy, to reach out to someone obnoxious and uncaring, or to help a person who has wronged you in the past? In what ways have you tried to run from God? Stop running, and surrender to the Lord. Go his direction; do his appointed task.

¹The LORD gave this message to Jonah son of Amittai: ²"Get up and go to the great city of Nineveh. Announce my judgment against it because I have seen how wicked its people are." ³But Jonah got up and went in the opposite direction to get away from the LORD. He went down to the port of Joppa, where he found a ship leaving for Tarshish. He bought a ticket and went on board, hoping to escape from the LORD by sailing to Tarshish. ⁴But the LORD hurled a powerful wind over the sea, causing a violent storm that threatened to break the ship apart. . . . ¹⁵Then the sailors picked Jonah up and threw him into the raging sea, and the storm stopped at once! ¹⁶The sailors were awestruck by the LORD's great power, and they offered him a sacrifice and vowed to serve him.

JONAH 1:1-4, 15-16

⁵Jonah went out to the east side of the city and made a shelter to sit under as he waited to see what would happen to the city. ⁶And the LORD God arranged for a leafy plant to grow there, and soon it spread its broad leaves over Jonah's head, shading him from the sun. . . . ⁷But God also arranged for a worm! The next morning at dawn the worm ate through the stem of the plant so that it withered away. . . . ⁸God arranged for a scorching east wind to blow on Jonah. The sun beat down on his head until he grew faint and wished to die. "Death is certainly better than living like this!" he exclaimed. ⁹Then God said to Jonah, "Is it right for you to be angry because the plant died? ¹⁰You feel sorry about the plant, . . . ¹¹but Nineveh has more than 120,000 people living in spiritual darkness. . . . Shouldn't I feel sorry for such a great city?"

JONAH 4:5-11

If you want an example of anger, look no further than Jonah. He finally gets around to doing what God wants him to do, preaching to the people of Ninevah. Jonah would rather *not* be doing this, however; so when it goes well, he'd just as soon call it a loss. God would rather teach him a lesson about his anger.

In this reading, you will see an amazing picture of God's mercy. You will also find the lessons that it's never too late for repentance and that sometimes believers have bad reasons for being angry.

Read Jonah 3:1–4:11

Sometimes we wish only that terrible suffering or judgment would come upon evil people. Even David expressed those very wishes in many of the psalms that he wrote (see Psalms 3, 7, 28, 35, 54, 55, 58, 109, 140, 141, 143). But God is more merciful than we can imagine, and he feels compassion for the sinners that we want him to punish. Because of his great mercy, God devises plans to bring sinners to himself. David realized this. And although David hated wicked people, he also prayed for God's glory and that all people would come to know the Lord.

What is your attitude toward those who are especially wicked? Do you want them destroyed? Or do you wish that they could experience God's mercy and forgiveness? Pray for people who need to know God. Hate their evil deeds, but do what you can to persuade them to follow Christ. In addition, keep in mind that in many ways you, too, were once like the wicked and that God has been more merciful to you than you may ever realize.

When was the last time you lay awake at night eagerly awaiting the next day? Perhaps it was an upcoming fishing trip that you and Dad had been planning for weeks. Or maybe it was Christmas Eve, and you just couldn't get your mind off the presents, lights, excitement, cookies, and music.

Micah's prophecies comment on the thoughts for the next day that kept Israelites up at night. But their anticipation involves trips and activities far different from fishing and holiday decorating—theirs were plans for fraud, threats, and violence. That's why Micah's prophecies include visions of judgment for both Israel and Judah and messages directed to the kings who could have stopped it.

Read Micah 1:1–2:13

Today, many people fall prey to the ambitions of the powerful. Some lose their houses, jobs, life savings, and even their lives. Some of these wrongs are protected by the law. But just because the law allows us to do something doesn't mean that we should do it. Taking away people's possessions "by fraud and violence" invites God's judgment.

Never use position or power to take what you want by force. Instead, be content with what God has blessed you with, and rely on him to provide for your needs and fulfill your heart's desire.

[1]What sorrow awaits you who lie awake at night, thinking up evil plans. You rise at dawn and hurry to carry them out, simply because you have the power to do so. [2]When you want a piece of land, you find a way to seize it. When you want someone's house, you take it by fraud and violence. You cheat a man of his property, stealing his family's inheritance. [3]But this is what the LORD says: "I will reward your evil with evil; you won't be able to pull your neck out of the noose. You will no longer walk around proudly, for it will be a terrible time." [4]In that day your enemies will make fun of you by singing this song of despair about you: "We are finished, completely ruined! God has confiscated our land, taking it from us. He has given our fields to those who betrayed us."

MICAH 2:1-4

¹"Listen, you leaders of Israel! You are supposed to know right from wrong, ²but you are the very ones who hate good and love evil. You skin my people alive and tear the flesh from their bones. ³Yes, you eat my people's flesh, strip off their skin, and break their bones. You chop them up like meat for the cooking pot. ⁴Then you beg the LORD for help in times of trouble! Do you really expect him to answer? After all the evil you have done, he won't even look at you!" ⁵This is what the LORD says: "You false prophets are leading my people astray! You promise peace for those who give you food, but you declare war on those who refuse to feed you. ⁶Now the night will close around you, cutting off all your visions. Darkness will cover you, putting an end to your predictions. The sun will set for you prophets, and your day will come to an end."

MICAH 3:1-6

Many people regard teaching as an underpaid profession. "Teach because you love it," they say. "Don't do it for the money. The hours are long and the hassles are plenty." The same could be said for related professions, such as preaching and social work.

Ironically, this set of prophecies contains a harsh message for some preachers and teachers who have found a way around their profession's classic compensation problem. But their cure is worse than the disease, and God says it's *not* all right.

Micah's words also contain one promise that is still to be fulfilled, and another that already has been, and is still being, celebrated.

Read Micah 3:1–5:15

Some of Micah's sternest words condemned religious leaders who accepted bribes or who ministered only if they were compensated well for their work (Micah 3:11). The priests and prophets of Israel had come to love money more than their jobs—a serious problem of inverted values.

When Christians preach or teach for personal rewards, the point of their ministry evaporates. "Ministering" means "serving."

Whenever you serve or minister to others, do it cheerfully and willingly—for Christ—even if no one pays or rewards you for it. And encourage other Christian workers to do the same by never using your giving to impose your preferences on them.

The only thing worse than giving the sales pitch for a defective piece of merchandise is falling for it. Has that ever happened to you? At first you say no, but the insistent salesperson keeps at you until you cave in. Suddenly you feel like part of the problem. "Never again," you vow.

In this reading of Micah's prophecies you will see that the people of Israel tried to sell God on a bad idea. They thought that he could be bought or bribed into changing his mind about their sins. But a holy God won't exchange sacrifices for permission to sin. "No deal," God says.

Read Micah 6:1–7:20

Israel had forgotten how kind God had been to them. As a result, they were ungrateful and unresponsive to him and became cheaters, liars, and blackmailers. When Micah explained that they would suffer God's judgment for their sins, they tried to make a deal with God. "What's your price?" they asked him. "What do you want us to give you to leave us alone? Do you want more sacrifices?" Basically, the people wanted to continue sinning, appeasing God with some sort of penance or payment. But Micah told the Israelites that God wasn't interested in their offer and that he wanted them "to do what is right, to love mercy, and to walk humbly with . . . God" (Micah 6:8).

God cannot be bought, and we should not attempt to purchase the right to sin with confessions, penances, or sacrifices. We cannot "balance out" our bad deeds with good ones. Pleasing God means giving up all our sins, even the ones we love dearly, and living by God's standards of righteousness, as we depend on his help and presence at every step.

When you give to God, do it out of love and obedience, not out of a desire to buy him off.

[1]Listen to what the LORD is saying: "Stand up and state your case against me. Let the mountains and hills be called to witness your complaints. [2]And now, O mountains, listen to the LORD's complaint! He has a case against his people. He will bring charges against Israel. [3]O my people, what have I done to you? What have I done to make you tired of me? Answer me! [4]For I brought you out of Egypt and redeemed you from slavery. I sent Moses, Aaron, and Miriam to help you. [5]Don't you remember, my people, how King Balak of Moab tried to have you cursed and how Balaam son of Beor blessed you instead? And remember your journey from Acacia Grove to Gilgal, when I, the LORD, did everything I could to teach you about my faithfulness."

MICAH 6:1-5

¹¹You, Nineveh, will also stagger like a drunkard. You will hide for fear of the attacking enemy. ¹²All your fortresses will fall. They will be devoured like the ripe figs that fall into the mouths of those who shake the trees. ¹³Your troops will be as weak and helpless as women. The gates of your land will be opened wide to the enemy and set on fire and burned.... ¹⁵The fire will devour you; the sword will cut you down. The enemy will consume you like locusts, devouring everything they see. There will be no escape, even if you multiply like swarming locusts.... ¹⁹There is no healing for your wound; your injury is fatal. All who hear of your destruction will clap their hands for joy. Where can anyone be found who has not suffered from your continual cruelty?

NAHUM 3:11-13, 15, 19

Smooth talkers. Eve fell prey to one in the garden. Consumers fall prey to one when they enter a showroom and are enticed into making an unnecessary purchase. It seems that sooner or later everybody falls prey to one—a smooth talker who comes along and persuades us to do something foolish. It's hard not to admire these tempters, because they're so successful at what they do. They often dress, talk, and look like real winners.

Smooth talkers—or charmers—are the topic of Nahum. In his book by the same name, Nahum is prophesying against the people of Nineveh for their deceptive practices. He tells them that their wicked deeds have been seen by God and will cost them dearly. As you read, learn the lesson that doom is certain for those who oppose God.

Read Nahum 1:1–3:19

Nothing deceives quite like charm. Politicians know this. That's why they pour it on around election time. Unfortunately, they're not the only ones who know how to use charm to get what they want. Con artists use it to swindle people out of their life savings, other properties, and even their virginity or sexual purity. Charm bewitches us today just as much as it did in Nahum's day.

To escape the influence of evil charm, we need to be wise and have a healthy suspicion of people—and offers—who seem too good to be true.

Look closely at any company, salesperson, movement, or even ministry before you trust them. Make sure that people and institutions deal truthfully with you. And never forget to ask God for discernment when dealing with individuals or organizations with whom you're unfamiliar. Seek the counsel of wise and experienced Christians. God knows people's true motives, and you can trust his advice.

To enjoy some good things we must wait. For instance, farmers must wait until the crop is ripe before harvesting it. Expectant parents must wait the full nine months for their child to develop before they can enjoy a relationship with him or her. And employees must wait for the coffeemaker to finish brewing before they can enjoy that first cup at the office.

Justice is no different. In this reading, Habakkuk struggles with waiting for God to deal justly with the wicked. But through his struggle he learns two important lessons: patience and trust. He also encounters God and is blessed by his presence. By the end of this book, Habakkuk's outlook on life is remarkably different, and he no longer asks God if the time for justice has come yet.

Read Habakkuk 1:1–3:19

Habakkuk was disturbed that evil and injustice seemed to have the upper hand among his people (Habakkuk 1:3). Habakkuk questioned God about the situation and pleaded with him to do something. God promised that he would. God assured him that all would be put right. "Wait patiently," he said (2:3).

Like Habakkuk, we often feel angry and discouraged by what we see going on in the world. But we need to remember that God hates sin even more than we do. Certainly God will punish those who deserve it. If we preoccupy ourselves with the evil we see, however, and keep staring at headlines that mention rape and murder and watch the news programs that expose the latest scam, then we will continue to be frustrated and angry. But if we refuse to dwell on the evil in this world and trust God to deal justly with the wicked, then we will be able to wait for him to bring about justice.

⁵The Lord replied, "Look . . . and be amazed! For I am doing something . . . you wouldn't believe even if someone told you about it. ⁶I am raising up the Babylonians, a cruel and violent people. They will march across the world and conquer other lands. ⁷They are notorious for their cruelty and do whatever they like. ⁸Their horses are swifter than cheetahs and fiercer than wolves at dusk. Their charioteers charge from far away. Like eagles, they swoop down to devour their prey. ⁹On they come, all bent on violence. Their hordes advance like a desert wind, sweeping captives ahead of them like sand. ¹⁰They scoff at kings and princes and scorn all their fortresses. They simply pile ramps of earth against their walls and capture them! ¹¹They sweep past like the wind and are gone. But they are deeply guilty, for their own strength is their god."

HABAKKUK 1:5-11

⁷Stand in silence in the presence of the Sovereign LORD, for the awesome day of the LORD's judgment is near. The LORD has prepared his people for a great slaughter and has chosen their executioners. ⁸"On that day of judgment," says the LORD, "I will punish the leaders and princes of Judah and all those following pagan customs. ⁹Yes, I will punish those who participate in pagan worship ceremonies, and those who fill their masters' houses with violence and deceit. . . . ¹²I will search with lanterns in Jerusalem's darkest corners to punish those who sit complacent in their sins. They think the LORD will do nothing to them, either good or bad. ¹³So their property will be plundered, their homes will be ransacked. They will build new homes but never live in them. They will plant vineyards but never drink wine from them."

ZEPHANIAH 1:7-9, 12-13

In Zephaniah's time some of the people of Judah were financially secure. However, Zephaniah had a message from the Lord for them on investing. Apparently, some of them had received a bad investment tip and were at risk of losing it all. As you read this passage, learn the lesson that some things cannot be bought at any price.

Read Zephaniah 1:1–3:20

Israel had silver and gold, but no holiness. God said that their riches would not help them when it came time to account for their sins (Zephaniah 1:18).

In this life, we often rely on money for a sense of security and power. When we are poor, we feel weak. When we are rich, we feel strong. But wealth doesn't make us right with God. Nor can it buy our salvation or influence God's will. At the final judgment our riches will be worthless.

If you're already rich, ask God to help you maintain a humble attitude, use what you have for his glory, and live righteously. If you're middle class or poor, rather than working to accumulate wealth, work at cultivating holiness. It's the one thing you *can* take with you when you die.

Jake has a long list of unfinished projects. There's a hole in the stairwell wall still waiting for a patch, a bare window in the bedroom still awaiting curtains, and a tight pair of pants still waiting for his diet to get underway. But these things will have to wait. He's got more important things to do than patch walls, put up curtains, and improve his eating habits. These unfinished projects will have to wait.

That's what the people of Judah are saying about the Temple, which is badly in need of repair. It is their highest priority, but they've got their minds on their own home improvements. In this reading, Haggai prophesies to them about reprioritizing the items on their to-do list.

Read Haggai 1:1–2:23

The focal point of Judah's relationship with God, the Temple, lay in ruins. Instead of rebuilding it, the people had put their energies into beautifying their own homes. But the harder the people worked for themselves, the less they had. The harvests kept getting smaller. Their income never quite covered their expenses. Because of a coming drought, they would not even be able to meet their most basic needs. All of this resulted from one cause—neglecting their spiritual priorities (Haggai 1:2-6, 9-11).

If you never have enough, it may be because of a misplaced value. Guard your spiritual priorities. As you parcel out your time, money, and energy, don't forget the importance of activities and pursuits that matter to God. He will provide for you if you put him first.

³The Lord sent this message through the prophet Haggai: ⁴"Why are you living in luxurious houses while my house lies in ruins? ⁵This is what the Lord of Heaven's Armies says: Look at what's happening to you! ⁶You have planted much but harvest little. You eat but are not satisfied. You drink but are still thirsty. You put on clothes but cannot keep warm. Your wages disappear as though you were putting them in pockets filled with holes! ⁷This is what the Lord of Heaven's Armies says: Look at what's happening to you! ⁸Now go up into the hills, bring down timber, and rebuild my house. Then I will take pleasure in it and be honored, says the Lord. ⁹You hoped for rich harvests, but they were poor. And when you brought your harvest home, I blew it away. Why? Because my house lies in ruins, says the Lord."

HAGGAI 1:3-9

¹Then the angel showed me Jeshua the high priest standing before the angel of the LORD. The Accuser, Satan, was there at the angel's right hand, making accusations against Jeshua. ²And the LORD said to Satan, "I, the LORD, reject your accusations, Satan. Yes, the LORD, who has chosen Jerusalem, rebukes you. This man is like a burning stick that has been snatched from the fire." ³Jeshua's clothing was filthy as he stood there before the angel. ⁴So the angel said to the others standing there, "Take off his filthy clothes." And turning to Jeshua he said, "See, I have taken away your sins, and now I am giving you these fine new clothes." ⁵Then I said, "They should also place a clean turban on his head." So they put a clean priestly turban on his head and dressed him in new clothes while the angel of the LORD stood by.

ZECHARIAH 3:1-5

Everyone who has ever done laundry knows how stubborn some dirt can be. You treat it, soak it, scrub it, and rewash it, but nothing you do takes out the stain.

Dirt comes in more forms than just the physical. We say that we have dirt in our past and try to avoid airing our "dirty laundry." Like stained clothes, dirt in lives is hard to get out. That's why, for this set of prophecies, God shows Zechariah a vision of Jeshua, the high priest, in dirty clothes. As you read, pay close attention to this vivid illustration of God's work of mercy in our lives.

Read Zechariah 1:1–8:23

In Zechariah's vision, Satan made many accusations against Jeshua (Israel) (Zechariah 3:2-4). Jeshua could not deny them, either, because they were true. But God rejected the accusations and declared mercy on Jeshua. By having Jeshua's filthy clothes removed and replaced by fine new ones, God graphically portrayed how people receive his mercy. There is nothing they can do to earn it. God grants mercy and forgiveness out of his tremendous love for his people. He removes the filthy clothes (sins) and then provides new, clean, rich garments (his righteousness and holiness). (See also 2 Corinthians 5:21, Ephesians 4:24, and Revelation 19:8.)

Whenever you feel dirty and unworthy, go to God for cleansing. He can remove the stain of your sin and guilt and replace it with a clean conscience and pure heart.

What would you do if you went to work and your boss announced to you, "Clean out your desk. This is your last day." Would you be ready? Would your family be ready? Would you know what to do?

"Be prepared" is the theme of this passage. This portion of Zechariah contains many prophecies about the Messiah, some of which were fulfilled when Jesus Christ came and paid the penalty for sin. But God's people still await the fulfillment of the remaining prophecies—when Jesus comes back to take them to heaven with him. As you read, hear Zechariah's strong message: "Be ready."

Read Zechariah 9:1–14:21

Zechariah predicted the Triumphal Entry of Jesus riding into Jerusalem (see Matthew 21:1-11) more than five hundred years before it happened (Zechariah 9:9). Other portions of Zechariah's prophesies about Christ, such as the coming day of the Lord (14:1-9), have not yet been fulfilled. Jesus told his disciples that he would return (see Matthew 25:31). Meanwhile, he wants his followers to "watch" for his coming (a command often paired with prophecies about his return, as here in Zechariah 14:1).

We often make two mistakes with regard to the return of Christ: (1) we ignore it, or (2) we presume to know the date. We don't know when Christ will return, so we shouldn't pretend that we do. But we do know that he will come back, and God wants us to be ready at all times.

¹Watch, for the day of the Lord is coming when your possessions will be plundered right in front of you! ²I will gather all the nations to fight against Jerusalem. The city will be taken, the houses looted, and the women raped. Half the population will be taken into captivity, and the rest will be left among the ruins of the city. ³Then the Lord will go out to fight against those nations, as he has fought in times past. ⁴On that day his feet will stand on the Mount of Olives, east of Jerusalem. And the Mount of Olives will split apart, making a wide valley running from east to west. Half the mountain will move toward the north and half toward the south. ⁵You will flee through this valley, for it will reach across to Azal. . . . Then the Lord my God will come, and all his holy ones with him.

ZECHARIAH 14:1-5

If Christ were to come back today, would you be ready? If not, you can get ready by living according to God's Word consistently. Spread the Good News of Jesus Christ, live a morally pure life, and spend time with God on a regular basis. Be prepared by living each day in anticipation of his return.

¹"Look! I am sending my messenger, and he will prepare the way before me. Then the LORD you are seeking will suddenly come to his Temple. The messenger of the covenant, whom you look for so eagerly, is surely coming," says the LORD of Heaven's Armies. ²"But who will be able to endure it when he comes? Who will be able to stand and face him when he appears? For he will be like a blazing fire that refines metal, or like a strong soap that bleaches clothes. ³He will sit like a refiner of silver, burning away the dross. He will purify the Levites, refining them like gold and silver, so that they may once again offer acceptable sacrifices to the LORD. . . . ⁶"I am the LORD, and I do not change. That is why you descendants of Jacob are not already destroyed. ⁷Return to me, and I will return to you," says the LORD of Heaven's Armies.

MALACHI 3:1-3, 6-7

Imagine that all the money you have ever given to the Lord in tithes has been kept in a trust fund earning 10 percent a year. Before long, you will get it all back. Would you be rich? Or would you be no better off?

Malachi's audience have that sort of question to think about. They've been skimping on their tithes for some time now, and it's affecting their bottom line.

Read Malachi 1:1–4:6

Malachi urged the people to stop holding back their tithes, to stop keeping from God what he deserved (Malachi 3:8-12). The tithing system had begun during the time of Moses (see Leviticus 27:30-34; Deuteronomy 14:22). It was set up by God to provide an income for the Levites who ministered in the tabernacle and later the Temple of the Lord (see Numbers 18:20-21). During Malachi's day, the people did not give. They had forgotten that everything they had was from God; as a result, they stopped tithing. Because of this, the Levites were forced to earn a living and neglect their God-given responsibilities to care for the Temple and the service of worship.

We, too, can fall into this trap when we forget that God is our real provider—everything we have comes from him. When we stop giving God a portion of what he has given us, we essentially steal from him.

Be faithful in giving back a percentage of your income to God because there is still a practical reason for tithing: Your pastor and other church staff depend on it. In addition, you won't be disappointed with the interest rates God pays on your faithfulness to him.

Most people long to be smarter. To increase their IQ, some try the latest "brain foods," while others take up brain-stimulating hobbies. Intelligence is a priceless commodity. The smarter people are, the more money they can make, the more respect they will receive, and the more influence they will have.

Although it's good to be smart, intelligence isn't everything. In fact, three men in this reading have something more important—wisdom. Wisdom may seem to be more difficult to gain than intelligence, but these men show how easy it is to start down the road in that direction. As you read, follow the example of these men.

Read Matthew 1:1–4:25

Three astrologers from the east traveled a great distance to a foreign land to find Jesus. They said they wanted to worship him, but that was only half true. As soon as they found Jesus, they also honored him as king by giving gifts. Then they left (Matthew 2:1-12). Though their encounter with Jesus probably lasted only a day, the wisdom they displayed in worshiping him has been recorded for eternity.

Today, many people demonstrate foolishness in their attitudes and actions toward Jesus. Some treat him as a quaint and harmless idealist, too human to be worshiped. Others expect him to accommodate them. Some even treat Jesus with contempt and irreverence. Yet those who are wise recognize Jesus for who he is and feel a personal responsibility to bow down to and serve him.

¹Jesus was born in Bethlehem in Judea, during the reign of King Herod. About that time some wise men from eastern lands arrived in Jerusalem, asking, ²"Where is the newborn king of the Jews? We saw his star as it rose, and we have come to worship him." ³King Herod was deeply disturbed when he heard this, as was everyone in Jerusalem. ⁴He called a meeting of the leading priests and teachers of religious law and asked, "Where is the Messiah supposed to be born?" ⁵"In Bethlehem in Judea," they said, "for this is what the prophet wrote: ⁶'And you, O Bethlehem in the land of Judah, are not least among the ruling cities of Judah, for a ruler will come from you who will be the shepherd for my people Israel.'" ⁷Then Herod called for a private meeting with the wise men, and he learned from them the time when the star first appeared.

MATTHEW 2:1-7

Honor Jesus in your attitude and actions. Give your life to him because he gave his for you, and don't forget to give him the praise and worship he deserves. In doing this, you will be truly wise.

¹One day as he saw the crowds gathering, Jesus went up on the mountainside and sat down. His disciples gathered around him, ²and he began to teach them. ³"God blesses those who are poor and realize their need for him, for the Kingdom of Heaven is theirs. ⁴God blesses those who mourn, for they will be comforted. ⁵God blesses those who are humble, for they will inherit the whole earth. ⁶God blesses those who hunger and thirst for justice, for they will be satisfied. ⁷God blesses those who are merciful, for they will be shown mercy. ⁸God blesses those whose hearts are pure, for they will see God. ⁹God blesses those who work for peace, for they will be called the children of God. ¹⁰God blesses those who are persecuted for doing right, for the Kingdom of Heaven is theirs."

MATTHEW 5:1-10

Have you ever had a teacher who expected a lot out of you? What about a parent or relative who assumed that you would act responsibly and morally? People who believe in you usually expect a lot of you—your conduct and your work. Although it may be frustrating to have someone hold you to such high standards—not to mention trying to live up to them—it can be very beneficial.

Similar to this teacher, parent, or relative, Jesus wanted, and expected, the best for his followers, and he set high standards for them to live by. This passage, known as the Sermon on the Mount, spells out some of those standards. Jesus set them up to help you.

Read Matthew 5:1-48

Jesus' standards required a new way of holiness that neither the crowds nor the religious authorities could grasp. They couldn't understand because his standards turned their way and their world's way of thinking upside down. Consider some of Jesus' teachings: true happiness involves humility, mourning, longing, purity, and persecution (Matthew 5:3-11); anger can place you in danger of judgment (5:22); do not even *look* at others lustfully (5:28); never take revenge (5:39); and love your enemies (5:44). Jesus' listeners that day also didn't realize that to live by his standards required God's power, faith in Christ, and change brought by the Holy Spirit.

Although Jesus' standards are steep, they are his formula for happiness and success. Christians should strive to live up to them only with the help of the Holy Spirit. When we get discouraged by trying to live up to such high standards, we should remember that living by them will bring rewards—though not the kind most people seek, and not necessarily in this life (5:12).

'We're not worried," we say nervously, "just quite concerned."

Life is full of concerns—fleeting, chronic, financial, relational, mild, or severe. These worries can drive us crazy just thinking about them. They can also cause us to question our faith in God. Does God care about our concerns? Is he doing anything to help us out?

In this passage, Jesus points out the lessons in trust that we can learn from nature, assuring us of the futility of worry and of the certainty of God's care. As you read, strengthen your dependence on God's gracious care, and watch your worries melt away.

Read Matthew 6:1-34

Jesus knew that his disciples naturally worried about having enough of life's necessities, so he reassured them that God would provide for their needs. He pointed out that God provides for the animal kingdom, so he also would provide for them—they mattered much more than the animals (Matthew 6:25-34).

Worrying about our needs accomplishes nothing and ignores the fact that God works to meet those needs. Jesus didn't tell his disciples to be lazy or not to work, just to trust God and not to worry.

Do what you can about the concerns you have, but also realize that God, who loves and cares for you, has made provision for them as well. He will not let your needs overwhelm you. Whenever worries plague you, follow these three steps: (1) tell God about your concerns, asking him to provide for your needs; (2) do what you humanly can to work on your concerns; and (3) trust in God's goodness—remember that he cares for you more than even you care for yourself, and he will provide all you need at the right time.

24"No one can serve two masters. For you will hate one and love the other; you will be devoted to one and despise the other. You cannot serve both God and money. 25That is why I tell you not to worry about everyday life—whether you have enough food and drink, or enough clothes to wear. Isn't life more than food, and your body more than clothing? 26Look at the birds. They don't plant or harvest or store food in barns, for your heavenly Father feeds them. And aren't you far more valuable to him than they are? 27Can all your worries add a single moment to your life? 28And why worry about your clothing? Look at the lilies of the field and how they grow. They don't work or make their clothing, 29yet Solomon in all his glory was not dressed as beautifully as they are."

MATTHEW 6:24-29

¹"Do not judge others, and you will not be judged. ²For you will be treated as you treat others. The standard you use in judging is the standard by which you will be judged. ³And why worry about a speck in your friend's eye when you have a log in your own? ⁴How can you think of saying to your friend, 'Let me help you get rid of that speck in your eye,' when you can't see past the log in your own eye? ⁵Hypocrite! First get rid of the log in your own eye; then you will see well enough to deal with the speck in your friend's eye. ⁶Don't waste what is holy on people who are unholy. Don't throw your pearls to pigs! They will trample the pearls, then turn and attack you. ⁷Keep on asking, and you will receive what you ask for. Keep on seeking, and you will find. Keep on knocking, and the door will be opened to you."

MATTHEW 7:1-7

I pay attention to details; *she's* way too picky. *I* am a person of conviction; *he* is just plain stubborn. In these and a host of other ways, we justify our own behavior while condemning the same actions in others.

In this reading, Jesus' sermon continues with a rebuke for those who spend more time pointing out others moral shortcomings than correcting their own. Using the vivid imagery of boards and specks in the eye, Jesus explains how to fix the problem.

Other solutions can also be found in this passage. As you read, look for lessons on asking and faith building, as well as directions to heaven.

Read Matthew 7:1-29

Jesus told his disciples to be careful how they criticized others (Matthew 7:1-2). He said that to criticize and judge is like trying to extract a splinter from someone else's eye when you've got a piece of lumber in your own (7:3-6). If you want to help your friend get the splinter out, fine, but first get the board out of yours.

We tend to judge others much more harshly than we judge ourselves. Therefore, we need to be careful how severely we speak to others when we spot their defects.

If you find fault with someone else, first stop and ask whether or not you have the same problem. Don't deny or cover up your own faults. Don't be self-righteous in condemning others. Be as sensitive in dealing with others' faults as you would wish them to be with you.

rom the early grades in school, we worry that certain iendships might cause us embarrassment. "What will eople think if I'm seen with *them?*" we fret. Often e'll do just about anything to associate with people /ho might elevate our public image and avoid those /ho drag it down.

esus didn't worry about his social status. In fact, he isks social disgrace in this reading by going to Mathew's house for dinner. But in doing so, Jesus helps nother, regardless of his status. In this reading, we lso learn that when it comes to a person's receptivity o spiritual matters, appearances can be deceiving. As ou read, consider how you can focus on others and ot just yourself.

Read Matthew 8:1–10:42

ome of the Pharisees tried hard to find fault with esus. Often their attacks involved some sort of interiew over fine points of doctrine, but they also went fter his actions. On this occasion, they noticed what ooked like a perfect opportunity to trap Jesus in a olitical blunder—associating with criminals (Mathew 9:11-12). Jesus shocked them, first of all, by not aring about his image and second, by faulting *them* or doing so.

n the public eye, everyone notices whose company ve keep. But this shouldn't matter, provided that we re influencing others for good and aren't being influnced by them for evil.

f you are overly concerned with whom you're seen, ray for the courage to follow Jesus' example by loving and helping the social outcasts. Your reputation nay suffer on earth, but it won't suffer in heaven.

¹Jesus climbed into a boat and went back across the lake to his own town. ²Some people brought to him a paralyzed man on a mat. Seeing their faith, Jesus said to the paralyzed man, "Be encouraged, my child! Your sins are forgiven." ³But some of the teachers of religious law said to themselves, "That's blasphemy! Does he think he's God?" ⁴Jesus knew what they were thinking, so he asked them, "Why do you have such evil thoughts in your hearts? ⁵Is it easier to say 'Your sins are forgiven,' or 'Stand up and walk'? ⁶So I will prove to you that the Son of Man has the authority on earth to forgive sins." Then Jesus turned to the paralyzed man and said, "Stand up, pick up your mat, and go home!" ⁷And the man jumped up and went home! ⁸Fear swept through the crowd . . . and they praised God for sending a man with such great authority.

MATTHEW 9:1-8

²John the Baptist, who was in prison, heard about all the things the Messiah was doing. So he sent his disciples to ask Jesus, ³"Are you the Messiah we've been expecting, or should we keep looking for someone else?" ⁴Jesus told them, "Go back to John and tell him what you have heard and seen—⁵the blind see, the lame walk, the lepers are cured, the deaf hear, the dead are raised to life, and the Good News is being preached to the poor." . . . ⁷As John's disciples were leaving, Jesus began talking about him to the crowds. "What kind of man did you go into the wilderness to see? Was he a weak reed, swayed by every breath of wind? ⁸Or were you expecting to see a man dressed in expensive clothes? . . . ⁹Were you looking for a prophet? Yes, and he is more than a prophet."

MATTHEW 11:2-5, 7-9

Some people can second-guess themselves into a state of paralysis. "I don't know if I'm doing the right thing," they may say. Here's another favorite: "I just want to do what is right." They may pray for "peace" and do what gives them that peaceful feeling: "I know what I'm doing sounds crazy, but I just really have a sense of peace about it." If peace escapes them, they may look to others for reassurance that they are on the right track.

Although John the Baptist was not a double-minded man, this passage reports how he began to second-guess his original conclusions about Jesus. As you read, notice especially Jesus' reaction to John's doubts—it will teach you a bit about dealing with your own uncertainties.

Read Matthew 11:1–13:52

John's God-given mission had been to prepare people for the Messiah's coming. Now that he was in prison, his ministry wasn't going very well. Had he been wrong about Jesus? John wanted to be sure, so he sent some of his followers to talk with Jesus. Jesus told John's disciples to report to John what they saw and heard—the blind see, the deaf hear, the dead are raised to life. Jesus gave John the reassurance he sought (Matthew 11:2-6).

John did not come to his conclusion about who Jesus was based on his impressions or feelings. Instead, he went to the source, Jesus, to get the facts on which he would base his decision. We should take the same approach when dealing with our uncertainties.

When in doubt, check with the source of truth. Rather than relying on a feeling or conviction, search God's Word for reassurance that Jesus is the Messiah, the Son of God. If you study what Jesus said and did, your faith will be renewed and strengthened.

Look is one of the first words that many children learn to read. The command form of look—as in, "Look out!" is really important. Often in life we need to use or to heed this word.

Although it is usually good to *look out,* doing so can cause problems in the area of faith. In this passage, Jesus' most impulsive disciple literally steps out in faith. Unfortunately, he looks *out* and gets into deep trouble. As you read, note the importance of keeping your eyes on Christ and not on your circumstances.

Also in this passage you will see the action heating up as Herod kills John, Jesus feeds a huge crowd of people with a single entree, and more and more people are healed.

Read Matthew 13:53–15:39

When the disciples saw Jesus walking on the water, they could hardly believe their eyes. Peter asked Jesus to summon him to walk on the water (Matthew 14:28). That was quite a step of faith for Peter to take. When Jesus invited him to walk, Peter stepped out of the boat and began to walk on the water's surface. But as soon as he looked away from Jesus and looked around at the windswept waves and murky depths, he started to sink.

As Peter's example proves, a person's faith doesn't stay constant. It increases or decreases depending on where that person chooses to focus his or her attention. Those who focus on their problems are likely to find their faith decreasing. But those who focus their attention on Jesus are likely to find their faith increasing.

²²Jesus insisted that his disciples get back into the boat and cross to the other side of the lake, while he sent the people home. ²³After sending them home, he went up into the hills by himself to pray. . . . ²⁴Meanwhile, the disciples were in trouble far away from land, for a strong wind had risen, and they were fighting heavy waves. ²⁵About three o'clock in the morning Jesus came toward them, walking on the water. ²⁶When the disciples saw him walking on the water, they were terrified. In their fear, they cried out, "It's a ghost!" ²⁷But Jesus spoke to them at once. "Don't be afraid," he said. "Take courage. I am here!" ²⁸Then Peter called to him, "Lord, if it's really you, tell me to come to you, walking on the water." ²⁹"Yes, come," Jesus said. So Peter went over the side of the boat and walked on the water toward Jesus.

MATTHEW 14:22-29

Maintain and increase your faith by keeping your attention focused on Jesus. Remind yourself of his presence, power, care, and willingness to help, and keep your eyes off your inadequacies and circumstances.

⁵After they crossed to the other side of the lake, the disciples discovered they had forgotten to bring any bread. ⁶"Watch out!" Jesus warned them. "Beware of the yeast of the Pharisees and Sadducees." ⁷At this they began to argue with each other because they hadn't brought any bread. ⁸Jesus knew what they were saying, so he said, "You have so little faith! Why are you arguing . . . about having no bread? ⁹Don't . . . you remember the 5,000 I fed with five loaves, and the baskets of leftovers you picked up? ¹⁰Or the 4,000 I fed with seven loaves, and the large baskets of leftovers you picked up? ¹¹Why can't you understand that I'm not talking about bread?" . . . ¹²Then at last they understood that he wasn't speaking about the yeast in bread, but about the deceptive teaching of the Pharisees and Sadducees.

MATTHEW 16:5-12

Many people set standards of behavior for God as a condition for their faith. "If God would just solve this one problem for me, I'd have no trouble believing." Usually it involves some kind of miraculous appearance or deed.

Many people have set such conditions for God, but few have tried harder than the Pharisees and Sadducees. We see how they make their demands for a miracle quite plain to Jesus. But Jesus, just as plainly declines and leaves them in the dust of their doubt.

Believers and nonbelievers become harder to label in this passage. As the disciples pledge their belief in Jesus, they can't cope with his predictions of his death, and they even squabble over who will be the greatest in his kingdom. As you read, ask yourself, "What kind of proof would convince me of Christ's divinity?"

Read Matthew 16:1–18:35

Miracles never convince skeptical people. They have already committed themselves to disbelief. One more miracle would only compel them to explain it away. Today, many people demand proof of God's existence or power, but their demands mask the real issue—that they have already chosen not to believe in God. Until we believe that God *can* do miracles, we won't even entertain the possibility that something we saw *was* a miracle.

If you doubt Christ because you haven't "seen a miracle," ask whether a bona fide miracle would really convince you or just entrench your skepticism. Jesus said, "Blessed are those who believe without seeing me" (John 20:29). Seeing God's work in your life begins when you simply step forward in faith and believe in Jesus as God's Son and as the only way of salvation.

Anger, fatigue, frustration, insults, setbacks—some people will endure all this and more for the promise of an eventual reward. Without some future payoff, however, you would be hard-pressed to find one person who would be willing to endure a great deal of difficulty.

Reward is one of Peter's concerns in this reading. After Jesus makes a startling revelation about wealthy people and salvation, Peter begins to worry about his chances of being saved. In addition, he begins to wonder if leaving everything behind to follow Jesus is worth it. But Jesus knew that the cost of being one of his followers was great, and he didn't expect those who followed him to leave everything for nothing. He did, however, expect them to trust him and learn the truth about who is doing the saving and why. As you read, check your level of commitment to the Lord.

Read Matthew 19:1–20:34

God's rewards don't appeal to those, like the rich young man, who desire instant gratification. If God gave out immediate and material rewards for obedience, some people would obey him for the wrong reasons. And God doesn't want people to obey him just for the potential rewards. He prefers that people obey him out of love and gratitude. That's why the rewards he offers for obedience and service to him appeal to those who long for something more than material prosperity, who long for such things as truth, justice, mercy, and peace.

Don't look for the immediate rewards of money, comfort, and status when serving God. Instead, be willing to wait for the greater reward of spending eternity in his presence. But most of all, serve God out of gratitude for what he has done for you and out of love for who he is, not for the rewards that he will give you.

[16]Someone came to Jesus with this question: "Teacher, what good deed must I do to have eternal life?" [17]"Why ask me about what is good?" Jesus replied. "There is only One who is good. But to answer your question—if you want to receive eternal life, keep the commandments." [18]"Which ones?" the man asked. And Jesus replied: "'You must not murder. You must not commit adultery. You must not steal. You must not testify falsely. [19]Honor your father and mother. Love your neighbor as yourself.'" [20]"I've obeyed all these commandments," the young man replied. "What else must I do?" [21]Jesus told him, "If you want to be perfect, go and sell all your possessions and give the money to the poor, and you will have treasure in heaven. Then come, follow me."

MATTHEW 19:16-21

25"What sorrow awaits you teachers of religious law and you Pharisees. Hypocrites! For you are so careful to clean the outside of the cup and the dish, but inside you are filthy—full of greed and self-indulgence! 26You blind Pharisee! First wash the inside of the cup and the dish, and then the outside will become clean, too. 27What sorrow awaits you teachers of religious law and you Pharisees. Hypocrites! For you are like whitewashed tombs—beautiful on the outside but filled on the inside with dead people's bones and all sorts of impurity. 28Outwardly you look like righteous people, but inwardly your hearts are filled with hypocrisy and lawlessness. 29What sorrow awaits you teachers of religious law and you Pharisees. Hypocrites! For you . . . 30say, 'If we had lived in the days of our ancestors, we would never have joined them in killing the prophets.'"

MATTHEW 23:25-30

Have you ever met someone who looked like they stepped out of a glamour magazine, yet whose attitude and character were as ugly as sin? It's amazing how a person's outward appearance can be so different from his or her character.

Today's reading includes strong words for people who are so concerned with how they appear to others that they neglect to take care of their character. Jesus directs his words at some of the Pharisees and Sadducees, but we can tell they are for anyone who focuses on life's minor issues instead of being concerned about what really matters to God. As you read, determine to focus on what's on the inside, instead of merely working on your outward appearance.

The passage also includes Jesus' entry into Jerusalem (which begins the final week of his life); more parables about the kingdom of God; and more vivid criticism of the scribes and Pharisees.

Read Matthew 21:1–23:39

Jesus condemned some of the Pharisees and religious leaders for hiding their corruption and greed behind a veneer of good behavior (Matthew 23:25-28). They kept a long list of rules by which they defined obedience to the Law. But they also harbored attitudes and behaviors that dishonored the God who had given them the Law, including greed, conceit, injustice toward others, pretense, and pride. That's the heart of hypocrisy—pretending to be what you're not.

Appearing to be a Christian isn't the same as being one. What's inside your heart? Are you hiding behind a mask? Are you pretending to be a Christian? Are you covering up sins? Work on your inner attitudes and motivations and not on your image. Don't be like the Pharisees. Don't be a hypocrite.

What a shame," people say. "She had so much poten-
al, but she has really wasted her talent." We hear it
id of athletes, young scholars, artists, and other tal-
nted people.

sus has more than head shaking for those who do
othing with their God-given talents. Here he uses
story about investing to convince his listeners that
hen God gives us an asset, he expects us to invest
. As you read, consider how you are investing the
esources that God has entrusted to your care.

n addition to this story, Jesus' teaching here includes
redictions about the future and warnings about
iod's judgment.

Read Matthew 24:1–25:46

n the parable of the loaned money, Jesus gave his
isciples a picture of our own service to God. The
naster entrusted three of his servants with money
o invest; in a similar way, God entrusts us with skills,
noney, time, and other resources. The master gave
ach servant only as much money as he felt the ser-
ant could handle; God gives us only what we can
andle. The master rewarded those who invested his
noney; God rewards us when we employ his gifts in
is service. And the master punished the servant who
id his money instead of investing it; God takes away
vhat we refuse to use.

iod has given each person many talents and other
esources to use for his service. What has God given
ou to glorify him? Invest those gifts by serving
im and the people he loves. He will ensure a good
eturn.

[14]"The Kingdom of Heaven can be illustrated by the story of a man going on a long trip. He called together his servants and entrusted his money to them while he was gone. [15]He gave five bags of silver to one, two bags of silver to another, and one bag of silver to the last—dividing it in proportion to their abilities. He then left on his trip. [16]The servant who received the five bags of silver began to invest the money and earned five more. [17]The servant with two bags of silver also went to work and earned two more. [18]But the servant who received the one bag of silver dug a hole in the ground and hid the master's money. [19]After a long time their master returned from his trip and called them to give an account of how they had used his money."

MATTHEW 25:14-19

[16]The eleven disciples left for Galilee, going to the mountain where Jesus had told them to go. [17]When they saw him, they worshiped him—but some of them doubted! [18]Jesus came and told his disciples, "I have been given all authority in heaven and on earth. [19]Therefore, go and make disciples of all the nations, baptizing them in the name of the Father and the Son and the Holy Spirit. [20]Teach these new disciples to obey all the commands I have given you. And be sure of this: I am with you always, even to the end of the age."

MATTHEW 28:16-20

The last words of many famous people have been recorded and pondered. Final statements from the lips of the dying become a rich source for everything from term paper quotations to attention grabbers in sermons.

This last passage of Matthew contains Jesus' famous last words. But unlike the somber, reflective words of a dying man, Christ's words have a triumphant ring to them. That's because he has overcome death and has faithfully completed the task given to him by his Father. As Jesus prepares to return to his Father, he gives his disciples their final mission. As you read, listen carefully to Jesus' commission to his disciples (and you)—to reach the world for him.

Read Matthew 26:1–28:20

Just before leaving the earth, Jesus gave his disciples some final instructions: "Go and make disciples" (Matthew 28:19).

Although Jesus gave this command to the disciples present at his ascension into heaven, it still applies to all believers today. Every disciple needs to make other disciples, to tell others about Jesus and his invitation to receive him as Savior and Lord. Some imagine that the job of sharing the good news about Christ falls mainly to full-time evangelists, but that's not what Jesus said on that mountain. Any method of communicating the gospel, any means of helping people feel or recognize their need for Christ, any help to others taking steps of faith makes disciples. Jesus didn't limit the spreading of the Good News to formal presentations in front of crowds. All believers can communicate the news about Christ, and we all have gifts that we can use to tell his story in a significant way.

When making a new acquaintance, you probably greet the person warmly, perhaps even with a friendly handshake, especially if the emotional connections or mutual friendships are right. But what if you learned that the person had AIDS? Would you feel shocked and fearful? Would you involuntarily put your hand back into your pocket?

The disease of leprosy received that kind of negative reaction in Jesus' day. As with AIDS today, leprosy was seen as a death sentence, wreaking horrible physical devastation on the infected person. Lepers were unclean outcasts—no one came near them.

Despite the social and physical consequences, Jesus, filled with compassion, reached out and touched a leper (Mark 1:41). The empathy and love demonstrated by our Lord challenges us to reach today's outcasts.

Read Mark 1:1–3:35

Understand this in context. People greatly feared lepers. Many kinds of leprosy had no cure—once a leper, always a leper. And the disease's side effects meant disfigurement and paralysis. In addition, the law in Leviticus 13 and 14 said that people with leprosy were unclean and were barred from all religious and social activities. Lepers had no status; they lived as total outcasts. Some people even threw rocks at lepers to keep them away.

Certainly you know people who wear the stigma of a disease (such as AIDS), a disability (such as cerebral palsy), or some other condition. The natural response of revulsion or disgust will only prevent you from reaching out to those people in any meaningful way. God's love compels his people to be friendly, accepting, and kind (and to help them, if possible). Reach out and touch an "untouchable."

³⁵Before daybreak the next morning, Jesus got up and went out to an isolated place to pray. ³⁶Later Simon and the others went out to find him. ³⁷When they found him, they said, "Everyone is looking for you." ³⁸But Jesus replied, "We must go on to other towns as well, and I will preach to them, too. That is why I came." ³⁹So he traveled throughout the region of Galilee, preaching in the synagogues and casting out demons. ⁴⁰A man with leprosy came and knelt in front of Jesus, begging to be healed. "If you are willing, you can heal me and make me clean," he said. ⁴¹Moved with compassion, Jesus reached out and touched him. "I am willing," he said. "Be healed!" ⁴²Instantly the leprosy disappeared, and the man was healed. ⁴³Then Jesus sent him on his way with a stern warning: ⁴⁴"Don't tell anyone about this."

MARK 1:35-44

[1]Jesus began teaching by the lakeshore. A very large crowd soon gathered around him, so he got into a boat. Then he sat in the boat while all the people remained on the shore. [2]He taught them by telling many stories in the form of parables. . . . [3]"A farmer went out to plant some seed. [4]As he scattered it across his field, some of the seed fell on a footpath, and the birds came and ate it. [5]Other seed fell on shallow soil with underlying rock. The seed sprouted quickly because the soil was shallow. [6]But the plant soon wilted under the hot sun, and since it didn't have deep roots, it died. [7]Other seed fell among thorns that grew up and choked out the tender plants so they produced no grain. [8]Still other seeds fell on fertile soil, and they sprouted, grew, and produced a crop that was thirty, sixty, and even a hundred times as much as had been planted!"

MARK 4:1-8

If you've ever tried to garden, you know that each plant, each vegetable or flower, is a unique living thing. Each grows differently. And one growing season can differ greatly from the next. But you're always hoping for the best *every* season.

Jesus knew that parables from the land would find receptivity from an audience who understood gardening and farming. We, too, can learn how faith can grow and thrive, or shrivel and die. We can see that there is more than one possible response to God (soil), more than one way that the seeds of faith can fare. As you read, consider what kind of soil you are. That is how receptive are you to God's seeds?

Read Mark 4:1–7:23

As the parable illustrates, not everyone who hears the Word of God receives it. Some forget what they hear almost immediately. Others receive it with joy but fall away when persecution comes. Some receive the Word but then let the attractions and wealth of this world crowd out God's Word from their lives. A few, however, receive God's Word and take it to heart, producing a good crop of righteousness.

When you hear or read God's Word, do you harden your heart and refuse to believe what you've just heard or read? Or are you easily distracted by the cares of this world from paying attention to God's message? If you struggle with one of these attitudes, here are some steps you can take to receive God's Word with joy: (1) Whenever you read the Bible or hear a sermon, do not close your heart to the message. (2) Watch out for the world's distractions that try to turn you off to God's Word. (3) Realize that although parts of God's message will bring joy, other parts may bring sorrow, especially when you examine your life in light of his Word.

When you join a club or organization, you do so because you know something of its philosophy, goals, and activities. When decisions are made and events planned that seem contrary to your knowledge of the club's purpose, you wonder what is going on. You may even speak up and question the club's integrity.

Peter thought he had signed up with the Triumphant King Club, but here he receives a rude awakening. Jesus sets Peter straight, gives him the proper picture, and puts him back on the path of service. As you read, consider what really is involved in becoming a follower of the King.

In this passage Jesus also heals the sick and blind, feeds the hungry, teaches the disciples, corrects the misapprehensions of others, and predicts his death for the first time.

Read Mark 7:24–8:38

When Jesus talked about the rejection, suffering, and death that he would soon face, Peter took him aside and told him to stop. In modern words Peter was saying, "Quit that negative talk!" Jesus' response left no doubt where Peter had steered wrong: "You are seeing things merely from a human point of view, not from God's" (Mark 8:33).

Perspective makes all the difference. Peter misjudged Jesus' statement because of his poor perspective. We need to look on our circumstances from God's point of view. This requires that we become familiar with God's priorities and values and see the big picture. This only comes by reading and studying the Scriptures.

The next time God's ways seem silly or out of line with "enlightened thinking," stop and ask God to help you see it all from his angle.

³¹Jesus began to tell them that the Son of Man must suffer many terrible things and be rejected by the elders, the leading priests, and the teachers of religious law. He would be killed, but three days later he would rise from the dead. ³²As he talked about this openly with his disciples, Peter took him aside and began to reprimand him for saying such things. ³³Jesus turned around and looked at his disciples, then reprimanded Peter. "Get away from me, Satan!" he said. "You are seeing things merely from a human point of view, not from God's." ³⁴Then, calling the crowd to join his disciples, he said, "If any of you wants to be my follower, you must turn from your selfish ways, take up your cross, and follow me. ³⁵If you try to hang on to your life, you will lose it. But if you give up your life for my sake and for the sake of the Good News, you will save it."

MARK 8:31-35

24 Jesus said again, "Dear children, it is very hard to enter the Kingdom of God. 25 In fact, it is easier for a camel to go through the eye of a needle than for a rich person to enter the Kingdom of God!" 26 The disciples were astounded. "Then who in the world can be saved?" they asked. 27 Jesus looked at them intently and said, "Humanly speaking, it is impossible. But not with God. Everything is possible with God." 28 Then Peter began to speak up. "We've given up everything to follow you," he said. 29 "Yes," Jesus replied, "and I assure you that everyone who has given up house or brothers or sisters or mother or father or children or property, for my sake and for the Good News, 30 will receive now in return a hundred times as many houses, brothers, sisters, mothers, children, and property—along with persecution."

MARK 10:24-30

Everyone lives with physical barriers—the doors, walls, and fences that keep valuables in and intruders out. These barriers have counterparts in the moral and spiritual arena—beliefs, attitudes, and actions that define and limit a person's choices. Think, for example, of the fences put up by prejudice, the doors shut by negative self-worth, and the walls built with pride or rebellion.

The young man in today's passage wasn't even aware of the barrier that he had put around his heart. Jesus knocked on the barrier, but the young man was unwilling even to make an opening, much less tear it down. This caused a problem. From the text we can see that all of the young man's good intentions and law-abiding behavior didn't count as much with Jesus as did removing that barrier around his heart.

Read Mark 9:1–10:52

When Jesus told the rich young man to sell all he had, the man walked away sadly (Mark 10:17-23). Jesus' challenge revealed the truth about the young man's law-abiding record: he loved his money more than God, thus breaking the first commandment (Exodus 20:3). And as Jesus pointed out, until he let go of this false god, he could not have eternal life (Mark 10:17, 23).

Boasting about goodness always presents a barrier to following Jesus—a false god who is *really* being served. Love of money blocked this man from following Christ; for others it may be career, relationships, security, power, or simply self-centeredness.

The next time you find yourself feeling pride in your own efforts, reevaluate your priorities. Confess your "idol worship" and give Christ first place in your life.

There are few things more frustrating than excuses. A slow driver in the left lane, perhaps. Another would be a church that doesn't care for people. You probably have a few pet peeves that would qualify as frustrating, too.

Jesus was also frustrated by people and things that didn't fulfill their purpose or potential. This passage records two accounts of his frustration. But Jesus doesn't just get bothered by these incidents—he does something about them. Today's passage exposes the misconception that Jesus was merely a soft-spoken, mild-mannered teacher. He reacted forcefully toward hypocritical religious leaders, profiteering Temple merchants, and an unproductive fig tree. His words and actions were strong, and the number of his enemies was growing.

Read Mark 11:1–12:44

In the hustle and bustle of cosmopolitan Jerusalem, true worship had given way to petty merchandising. People who came to participate in the festivals had to exchange their Roman coins for the Temple money. Some of the money changers were exploiting this for their own selfish gain. What should have been *fruitful* service became selfish pursuit.

People of God who don't produce godly behavior are as useless as a fig tree that produces no fruit. Genuine fruitfulness requires genuine faith.

As you watch your powerful Lord in action, compare your life with those he castigated for their unfruitfulness and self-centeredness. What can you do to deepen your relationship with God, pushing down your roots and drawing his nourishment?

¹²As they were leaving Bethany, Jesus was hungry. ¹³He noticed a fig tree in full leaf a little way off, so he went over to see if he could find any figs. But there were only leaves because it was too early in the season for fruit. ¹⁴Then Jesus said to the tree, "May no one ever eat your fruit again!" And the disciples heard him say it. . . .

²⁰The next morning as they passed by the fig tree . . . the disciples noticed it had withered from the roots up. ²¹Peter remembered what Jesus had said to the tree . . . and exclaimed, "Look, Rabbi! The fig tree you cursed has withered and died!" ²²Then Jesus said to the disciples, "Have faith in God. ²³I tell you the truth, you can say to this mountain, 'May you be lifted up and thrown into the sea,' and it will happen. But you must really believe it will happen and have no doubt in your heart."

MARK 11:12-14, 20-23

26"Everyone will see the Son of Man coming on the clouds with great power and glory. 27And he will send out his angels to gather his chosen ones from all over the world—from the farthest ends of the earth and heaven. 28Now learn a lesson from the fig tree. When its branches bud and its leaves begin to sprout, you know that summer is near. 29In the same way, when you see all these things taking place, you can know that his return is very near, right at the door. 30I tell you the truth, this generation will not pass from the scene before all these things take place. 31Heaven and earth will disappear, but my words will never disappear. 32However, no one knows the day or hour when these things will happen, not even the angels in heaven or the Son himself. Only the Father knows. 33And since you don't know when that time will come, be on guard! Stay alert!"

MARK 13:26-33

How do you think the world will end? Will a nuclear holocaust obliterate our home planet? Will an asteroid the size of Alaska collide with the earth, causing another ice age? Or will we deplete the ozone layer so much that the world's climates will be radically changed and no longer able to support life?

In this reading, Jesus reveals something about how the world will really end. It's a horrifying finish, but Jesus assures his followers that God is in control. He also encourages his followers who will live through this time to hold fast to their faith in him. Doing so will bring a great reward at the end of time. As you read, gain confidence in your heavenly Father who knows and controls the future.

Read Mark 13:1-37

The events of the end times are still to come in world history. We know that when these events happen Christ's return will follow soon (Mark 13:26-37). Unfortunately, before his return, some Christians may be deceived by false prophets who say they have received messages from God or false messiahs who claim to be God (13:5-6).

So how can we avoid being deceived? And how will we know when Christ has returned? We can look for his appearance in the clouds—one of the sure signs of his second coming (13:26; see Revelation 1:7). All people everywhere will be able to see him then.

When Jesus returns, *you will know.* In the meantime, be on your guard against false prophets and false messiahs. Don't believe what they say, because only God the Father knows when Christ will return (Mark 13:32). At the same time, be ready because he will come suddenly and unexpectedly, like a "thief in the night" (see Matthew 24:42-44; 1 Thessalonians 5:2).

Whether you have ever been to a funeral or not, you are probably familiar with what a grave site looks like. That's because you have probably passed by countless cemeteries and may have even ventured to walk through a few. So imagine how dismayed you would be if you passed by a grave a couple of days after the funeral, and found that the grave was open and the body was gone.

On the third day after Jesus' crucifixion, three women go to Jesus' tomb to embalm his body with spices. When they get there, they find an empty tomb. But then an angel tells them that Jesus is alive! As you read, rejoice with these women that Jesus has risen!

Read Mark 14:1–16:20

The fact that Jesus rose from the dead is important for several reasons. First, he paid the penalty for our sin that we could never pay ourselves. His resurrection was the final act in redeeming fallen humankind from a sinful nature. Second, coming back to life proved that he is the one and only God, the author of life. No leader of any other world religion has ever come back from the grave. Third, his resurrection was a fulfillment of Old Testament prophecies about the Messiah. Jesus' resurrection was a fulfillment of God's plan for redemption. Fourth, Christ's resurrection not only fulfilled prophecies but also kept the promise he made to rise again. He proved to his followers that he is trustworthy. Fifth, his resurrection is an assurance that all believers in Christ will one day be resurrected, too.

¹Saturday evening, when the Sabbath ended, Mary Magdalene, Mary the mother of James, and Salome went out and purchased burial spices so they could anoint Jesus' body. ²Very early on Sunday morning, just at sunrise, they went to the tomb. ³On the way they were asking each other, "Who will roll away the stone for us from the entrance to the tomb?" ⁴But as they arrived, they looked up and saw that the stone, which was very large, had already been rolled aside. ⁵When they entered the tomb, they saw a young man clothed in a white robe sitting on the right side. The women were shocked, ⁶but the angel said, "Don't be alarmed. You are looking for Jesus of Nazareth, who was crucified. He isn't here! He is risen from the dead! Look, this is where they laid his body. ⁷Now go and tell his disciples."

MARK 16:1-7

Jesus' resurrection is a miracle in and of itself that makes him worthy of our praise. Thank and worship him for his personal sacrifice to redeem you. At the same time, thank and worship the Father for raising his Son from the grave and for designing and implementing a wonderful plan for saving humanity.

25At that time there was a man in Jerusalem named Simeon. He was righteous and devout and was eagerly waiting for the Messiah to come and rescue Israel. The Holy Spirit was upon him 26and had revealed to him that he would not die until he had seen the Lord's Messiah. 27That day the Spirit led him to the Temple. So when Mary and Joseph came to present the baby Jesus to the Lord as the law required, 28Simeon was there. He took the child in his arms and praised God, saying, 29"Sovereign Lord, now let your servant die in peace, as you have promised. 30I have seen your salvation, 31which you have prepared for all people. 32He is a light to reveal God to the nations, and he is the glory of your people Israel!" 33Jesus' parents were amazed at what was being said about him.

LUKE 2:25-33

The older that people get today, the more they prefer to keep their age a secret. That's because our society values youth over age, and the potential contributions of the elderly are often ignored or dismissed as outdated and useless. That wasn't the case in Jesus' time. Age wasn't something to be embarrassed about and wasn't kept a secret. Luke's Gospel even salutes the value of the elderly by recording an incident in which two older people play an important role in Jesus' young life.

As you read this section, look for contrasts with modern views of age and youth and determine to be a person used by God, regardless of your age.

Read Luke 1:1–4:13

In Simeon and Anna's culture, elders were respected, and age wasn't a strike against their usefulness. But if Simeon and Anna had lived today, their lives and testimonies probably would not have meant as much.

Despite what our society believes, the elderly still have much to contribute. As Christians, we should value them not only as human beings but also as people from whom we can learn a great deal. If you're young, invite older people to share their wisdom and experience with you. Listen carefully when they speak. Offer them your friendship, and help them find ways to continue to serve God. If you are elderly, don't believe our society's views about you. Continue serving God, however he enables you. In God's view, you are never too old to be useful.

Sooner or later almost every person has at least one negative opinion about his or her boss. Some bosses definitely earn this reputation, while others come by it innocently through the instructions they give their employees. In this latter instance, it comes down to this: The boss has told you to do something, and you don't like it. What can you do?

You may have never thought of Jesus as a bosslike figure, but he was a leader while he was here on earth. This reading contains examples of his earthly leadership. Here he takes charge and gives orders, and gets flak for it—just as we might expect. As you read, watch Jesus lead, and learn from his example.

Read Luke 4:14–6:49

Many people think of Jesus as a nice man, even a great man, who taught great truths. But the problem is that these same people stop short of viewing Jesus as an authority figure. They don't think he has any right to influence even the most minuscule area of their lives. They don't understand that Jesus isn't just a nice teacher, a gentle giant, or a profound guru. He's the Creator and absolute ruler of the universe (see Colossians 1:16-20). He has all authority (see Matthew 28:18). He has the right to tell us how to live, and he has power over all forces in the universe—natural, physical, and spiritual.

Whenever you read Jesus' teachings, see them as your mandate for living. Read them as if they were directed right at you. Jesus didn't come just to inspire us, but to lay claim to us. Can you call him Lord, Master, King?

³¹Jesus went to Capernaum, a town in Galilee, and taught there in the synagogue every Sabbath day. ³²There, too, the people were amazed at his teaching, for he spoke with authority. ³³Once when he was in the synagogue, a man possessed by a demon—an evil spirit—began shouting at Jesus, ³⁴"Go away! Why are you interfering with us, Jesus of Nazareth? Have you come to destroy us? I know who you are—the Holy One sent from God!" ³⁵Jesus cut him short. "Be quiet! Come out of the man," he ordered. At that, the demon threw the man to the floor as the crowd watched; then it came out of him without hurting him further. ³⁶Amazed, the people exclaimed, "What authority and power this man's words possess! Even evil spirits obey him, and they flee at his command!" ³⁷The news about Jesus spread through every village.

LUKE 4:31-37

¹⁸One day Jesus left the crowds to pray alone. Only his disciples were with him, and he asked them, "Who do people say I am?" ¹⁹"Well," they replied, "some say John the Baptist, some say Elijah, and others say you are one of the other ancient prophets risen from the dead." ²⁰Then he asked them, "But who do you say I am?" Peter replied, "You are the Messiah sent from God!" ²¹Jesus warned his disciples not to tell anyone who he was. . . . ²³Then he said to the crowd, "If any of you wants to be my follower, you must turn from your selfish ways, take up your cross daily, and follow me. ²⁴If you try to hang on to your life, you will lose it. But if you give up your life for my sake, you will save it. ²⁵And what do you benefit if you gain the whole world but are yourself lost or destroyed?"

LUKE 9:18-21, 23-25

The start of a new year is a common occasion for making resolutions—from becoming more fit, to serving in the community, to sticking to spiritual disciplines. Our commitment is high; we can't be swayed by man or beast—and then the second week of the year rolls along, and we begin to wonder, *Is it really worth it?*

In this reading, Jesus speaks to those of us whose resolve has begun to dissolve. He demands commitment and speaks clearly about what it will take to follow him. But he does not ask us to do anything he would not do himself, and demonstrates his own commitment to people by reaching out to the lowest in society, calming John the Baptist's fears, and feeding thousands of people. As you read, consider what you can do to be more like Christ.

Read Luke 7:1–9:50

To follow Jesus, sooner or later we must submit our wants and desires to his desires for us. We must stop serving ourselves and start serving him. If that means selling something, we sell it. If it means stopping a certain behavior, we stop it. If it means doing something we don't want to do, we do it. It means the end of what we want and the beginning of what Jesus wants. That is why Jesus says, "If you try to keep your life for yourself, you will lose it"—because only by giving it up to Jesus can you gain eternal life.

Is it worth it? If you have any doubt, Jesus makes a good case for doing so: "What do you benefit if you gain the whole world but are yourself lost or destroyed?" (Luke 9:25). Sure, there's a price to be paid for following Jesus, but those who pay it also receive an eternal benefit.

A huge task confronts you, and you spring into action. You form committees. You buy supplies. You organize a phone-a-thon. Wait! Have you forgotten to pray?

When it came to accomplishing any task, prayer was at the top of Jesus' list. In addition to setting this example, Jesus also taught how to divide the labor—long before the days of personnel assessment profiles, project-management software, and planning calendars.

As you read this passage, understand the priority of prayer and place it at the top of your to-do list.

Read Luke 9:51–10:42

Jesus sent out seventy-two of his disciples in pairs to spread the good news about him. Despite this good start, his mission was still understaffed. The first step he took in solving this problem was to instruct his followers to "Pray to the Lord who is in charge of the harvest; ask him to send more workers into his fields" (Luke 10:2). They had a huge task, and getting it done meant asking God to send more people.

Likewise, we have a huge task today in furthering the spread of the gospel. No one person, however, can save the world single-handedly. You can't be a missionary to Rwanda, live at home and minister to your family, and tell your coworkers about Christ all at once. But you can list the people and causes that matter to you and pray that God will send people to each one. You can also ask him to help you take advantage of the opportunities to share the gospel that come your way.

If you have friends and relatives who don't know Christ, pray for them. Ask God to send believers into their lives who will address their concerns, objections, and needs—people who will lead them to the Savior.

[1]The Lord now chose seventy-two other disciples and sent them ahead in pairs to all the towns and places he planned to visit. [2]These were his instructions to them: "The harvest is great, but the workers are few. So pray to the Lord who is in charge of the harvest; ask him to send more workers into his fields. [3]Now go, and remember that I am sending you out as lambs among wolves. [4]Don't take any money with you, nor a traveler's bag, nor an extra pair of sandals. And don't stop to greet anyone on the road. [5]"Whenever you enter someone's home, first say, 'May God's peace be on this house.' [6]If those who live there are peaceful, the blessing will stand; if they are not, the blessing will return to you."

LUKE 10:1-6

43"What sorrow awaits you Pharisees! For you love to sit in the seats of honor in the synagogues and receive respectful greetings as you walk in the marketplaces. 44Yes, what sorrow awaits you! For you are like hidden graves in a field. People walk over them without knowing the corruption they are stepping on." 45"Teacher," said an expert in religious law, "you have insulted us, too, in what you just said." 46"Yes," said Jesus, "what sorrow also awaits you experts in religious law! For you crush people with unbearable religious demands, and you never lift a finger to ease the burden. 47What sorrow awaits you! For you build monuments for the prophets your own ancestors killed long ago. . . . 48They killed the prophets, and you join in their crime by building the monuments!"

LUKE 11:43-48

But what would people think? For many of us, this question springs to our mind and even our lips more than we would like to admit. Even as we think about making a moral choice, we ponder how popular or unpopular it would be.

Those who are concerned more with the popularity than the morality of their decisions need to think twice. This reading is full of warnings that Jesus aimed primarily at Pharisees and other "experts in religious law." But they could easily apply to any person today who, like these people, is more concerned with appearances than with justice and righteousness. As you read, consider how important being popular is to you.

Jesus' lessons are to the point in other areas as well, including prayer and unbelief.

Read Luke 11:1-54

Jesus criticized some of the Pharisees and experts in the Law harshly because they loved praise and attention (Luke 11:43). They went wrong by protecting their outward appearances while ignoring their attitudes and God's revealed desires.

Public recognition of our "religiosity" does not make us devout. We must guard against taking public admiration or honor from religious folks as proof of our own religious piety. God seeks sincere and unselfish devotion to him; this requires humility. Striving to be in the spotlight works against that. Seek God's praise and attention, not that of people.

What topics generate heated debate in your family? Politics, for example, is completely off-limits for some family gatherings because of the potential for misunderstandings and hurt feelings. There are many issues upon which families can disagree.

In this reading, Jesus speaks about more than mere dinnertime discussions. A person's relationship with God can—indeed, should—affect every earthly relationship. Sometimes the effect is negative, and Jesus wants his followers to be prepared. As you read, think of how your Christian faith has impacted your relationships.

Read Luke 12:1-59

Jesus came to bring strife and division, not peace. Wait—isn't Jesus supposed to be a peacemaker? Did he not say to turn the other cheek when others insult or injure us? Didn't he allow thugs to nail him to the cross? Why this talk of fighting? Why this bad news?

Jesus isn't asking us to pick fights, to be obnoxious with our views, or to brag about being enlightened until people can't stand to hear it anymore. He's merely warning us that not everyone will want to follow him. Some will accept him while others will reject him. Unlike choosing a favorite color, recognizing God's absolute authority, our sin, and Jesus' claim on our lives radically changes us. Because these changes affect many areas of great consequence, they will often ripple through the close relationships in a family.

[49]"I have come to set the world on fire, and I wish it were already burning! [50]I have a terrible baptism of suffering ahead of me, and I am under a heavy burden until it is accomplished. [51]Do you think I have come to bring peace to the earth? No, I have come to divide people against each other! [52]From now on families will be split apart, three in favor of me, and two against—or two in favor and three against. [53]Father will be divided against son and son against father; mother against daughter and daughter against mother; and mother-in-law against daughter-in-law and daughter-in-law against mother-in-law."

LUKE 12:49-53

Be patient with those who are slow to respond to God's gift of salvation or the changes he brings about in your life. Have faith that those loved ones who reject Christ may one day accept him. In the meantime endure their rejection, realizing that Christ understands what you are going through.

²²Jesus went through the towns and villages, teaching as he went, always pressing on toward Jerusalem. ²³Someone asked him, "Lord, will only a few be saved?" He replied, ²⁴"Work hard to enter the narrow door to God's Kingdom, for many will try to enter but will fail. ²⁵When the master of the house has locked the door, it will be too late. You will stand outside knocking and pleading, 'Lord, open the door for us!' But he will reply, 'I don't know you or where you come from.' ²⁶Then you will say, 'But we ate and drank with you, and you taught in our streets.' ²⁷And he will reply, 'I tell you, I don't know you or where you come from. Get away from me, all you who do evil.' ²⁸There will be weeping and gnashing of teeth, for you will see Abraham, Isaac, Jacob, and all the prophets in the Kingdom of God, but you will be thrown out."

LUKE 13:22-28

Have you ever joked about who will and will not get into heaven? Many comedians have placed famous people at the pearly gates, giving some excuse as to why they should be let in. These jokes are so popular (and often so funny) that they are heard from the pulpit as well.

Jesus, on the other hand, paints a less-than-humorous picture about entering heaven. In this passage, he shows us the meaning of being saved and describes God's criteria for his followers—living a life that imitates Christ. As you read, match your life with his criteria.

Also look for lessons on facing criticism for the right choice; being frustrated with concern over a city; seeking honor; and the cost of following Christ.

Read Luke 13:1–14:35

Many people will express great surprise when God judges the world. Some who escaped the notice of journalists and awards committees will receive great honor then; others who had great influence and authority here will have nothing to offer God (Luke 13:22-30). God doesn't care about a person's earthly popularity, status, achievements, reputation, wealth, heritage, influence, or power; he cares about a person's commitment to Christ. Many people whom God considers great get absolutely no worldly recognition.

Do not waste time trying to impress the world. Seek praise and honor instead from God alone. His approval counts for eternity.

If you ever have had the unfortunate experience of having two bosses at work, you know that opposing supervisory forces can make the workday a continual struggle of conflicting priorities and miscommunication. Yet when it comes to values, that's the way many people live. They try to go in two directions at the same time.

God and riches can be like two bosses, each demanding your allegiance. Perhaps no other spiritual struggle is as intense as this one. It is a struggle between two needs—God and money—and where to place your faith. Some place it in money. Some place it in God. Still others try to divide their faith between the two. In this reading, Jesus lets people know that this is not possible. You must choose to serve one or the other. As you read, ask God to reveal your values, to show you where your allegiance is.

Also, look for the down-to-earth lessons found in the stories of coins; an unforgiving fellow who gets his just desserts; and a son who learns from his father what true love is.

Read Luke 15:1–16:31

Money tests us at every turn. The way we earn it, the way we spend it, and the way we give it away all reveal who or what rules our heart (Luke 16:10-12). If we serve money, we will live for it and try to get it at all costs. But if we serve God, we will be honest in how we earn money, shrewd in how we spend it, and generous in how we give it. Most notably, we will be dependable with others' money.

⁹"Use your worldly resources to benefit others and make friends. Then, when your earthly possessions are gone, they will welcome you to an eternal home. ¹⁰If you are faithful in little things, you will be faithful in large ones. But if you are dishonest in little things, you won't be honest with greater responsibilities. ¹¹And if you are untrustworthy about worldly wealth, who will trust you with the true riches of heaven? ¹²And if you are not faithful with other people's things, why should you be trusted with things of your own? ¹³No one can serve two masters. For you will hate one and love the other; you will be devoted to one and despise the other. You cannot serve both God and money."

LUKE 16:9-13

Do riches have control over you? God wants your love and loyalty. He will not share what is rightfully his with anything or anyone. Do not fool yourself—you can't serve both God and money (16:13). Sooner or later you have to choose one over the other. Which will you choose?

¹⁵One day some parents brought their little children to Jesus so he could touch and bless them. But when the disciples saw this, they scolded the parents for bothering him. ¹⁶Then Jesus called for the children and said to the disciples, "Let the children come to me. Don't stop them! For the Kingdom of God belongs to those who are like these children. ¹⁷I tell you the truth, anyone who doesn't receive the Kingdom of God like a child will never enter it."

LUKE 18:15-17

Think back to when you were a young child, perhaps five years old. Didn't it mean the world to you when an adult would take the time to listen to you? How did you feel when an adult knelt down to your level and communicated that you were important?

In a brief but important scene in this reading, Jesus takes the time to do this with a group of children. He expresses his love for them and rebukes the grown-ups who try to prohibit them from coming to him. Through this incident he also teaches the disciples and all of his followers a key truth about the kingdom of God. As you read, learn with the disciples how much little children matter to God.

Read Luke 17:1–19:27

What does it mean to have the faith of a child? It means trusting in someone or something without giving it a second thought. A daughter, for example, will jump into her father's arms, knowing that he won't drop her. A son won't ponder the risks involved in going to a strange place if he knows Mom and Dad will be there, too. He will simply go. If only we would be like that with God.

Some of what God asks his people to do has no explanation or obvious benefit, but if we have the faith of a child, that should not matter. We should know that Daddy is strong enough to catch us, and we can assume that he won't take us to a bad place.

What has God asked you to do? Where has he told you to go? Take the risk of trusting God the way a child trusts his or her parents—completely and without hesitation.

Whether watching a television show, video, or movie, or reading a book, everyone likes happy endings, where the main characters triumph over tragedy and overwhelming odds. We like to see the hero or heroine get justice or some other reward. Ultimately, we like to see evil soundly defeated and, at times, completely eliminated. We want the events to happen this way because in real life there are few happy endings. Good hardly ever seems to triumph and never seems to win out.

The bad news is that things are not going to get better—yet. In this reading, Jesus warns his followers that in the end times they will be persecuted, arrested, and killed because of him. But he also reassures them that those who remain faithful to him during the difficult times will definitely experience a happy ending. If your present struggles seem overwhelming, take hope as you read this passage—God's story has a truly happy ending.

Read Luke 19:28–21:38

Jesus knew that the time would come when people would oppose both him and his disciples, even to the point of torturing and killing them. Some of his followers would even find relatives and former friends among their new enemies. Jesus told his disciples to expect this, but he also told them not to worry because God's Holy Spirit would tell them what to say and how to respond whenever they came under attack (Luke 21:14-19).

Following Christ has always entailed the risk of rejection from others. Jesus reassures us that whenever that happens, he stands right there with us, with his Holy Spirit guiding and helping us. Remember this the next time you need courage or hope, and then stand firm for Christ.

12"There will be a time of great persecution. You will be dragged into synagogues and prisons, and you will stand trial before kings and governors because you are my followers. 13But this will be your opportunity to tell them about me. 14So don't worry in advance about how to answer the charges against you, 15for I will give you the right words and such wisdom that none of your opponents will be able to reply or refute you! 16Even those closest to you—your parents, brothers, relatives, and friends—will betray you. They will even kill some of you. 17And everyone will hate you because you are my followers. 18But not a hair of your head will perish! 19By standing firm, you will win your souls."

LUKE 21:12-19

²³The disciples . . . ²⁴began to argue among themselves about who would be the greatest among them. ²⁵Jesus told them, "In this world the kings and great men lord it over their people, yet they are called 'friends of the people.' ²⁶But among you it will be different. Those who are the greatest among you should take the lowest rank, and the leader should be like a servant. ²⁷Who is more important, the one who sits at the table or the one who serves? The one who sits at the table, of course. But not here! For I am among you as one who serves. ²⁸You have stayed with me in my time of trial. ²⁹And just as my Father has granted me a Kingdom, I now grant you the right ³⁰to eat and drink at my table in my Kingdom. And you will sit on thrones, judging the twelve tribes of Israel."

LUKE 22:23-30

Some people have trouble remaining serious at somber occasions. The weight of the moment more than escapes them—its gravity causes their minds to wander. They are oblivious to their surroundings and the importance of the event.

The disciples fall prey to a form of this as Jesus shares some difficult news. Rather than listening to what he has to say, they begin to argue about who will be the greatest in God's kingdom. Jesus' response to their arguing is amazing. He could have rebuked them for their pettiness. Instead, he tells them how to be great and then sets the example. As you read, consider how *you* may be getting in the way of God's purpose for your life. Are you focused on yourself or on doing his will?

Read Luke 22:1-71

At Jesus' last supper with his disciples before his death, the disciples got into a lively discussion about who would be greatest in his upcoming kingdom. Why did they jockey for position at a time like this (Luke 22:24)? Did they simply not want to believe the bad news, or didn't they care? Capitalizing on their self-centeredness, Jesus explained that to be great they must serve others (22:25-27).

It's easy to criticize the disciples for their self-centeredness, but that's the way we are, too. Sometimes we have great concern for our own ascent to greatness, wealth, and prestige. But Christ commands us to do as he did by serving others.

About what desires for career advancement, better reputation, or public achievement do you dream? Rather than just serving your ambitions, look for opportunities to serve others.

You hurry for the train, bounding along the platform. You rush through the closing doors and eagerly settle into a seat. When the conductor calls out the stops and final destination of the train, you realize in a panic that you're on the wrong one!

In a way, this is the experience of the disciples. As Jesus reaches his final destination—the cross—his disciples begin to wonder what is going on. They thought that they had signed up with a triumphant army, but they see their leader, Jesus, dying with criminals. Did they get on the wrong train? What are your expectations in your walk with Christ?

Read Luke 23:1-56

Sometimes we expect to be rewarded too soon for following Christ. We expect congratulations (or at least grudging admiration) from coworkers and friends for our choice to do what is right. Most of all, we expect God to oversee everything with our own interests first in his mind. We can get a rude awakening when our expectations get ambushed by the exact opposite—trouble, tragedy, conflict, or disappointment. As Jesus' death on the cross shows, sometimes God's plan for us doesn't bring instant victory, justice, or reward. Suffering may precede or follow right choices.

Don't let your expectations get in the way of enjoying God's good plan for you now. He cares—you can be sure of that. Setbacks, unfairness, sufferings, and other trials enter the picture as part of it all. Exactly why, you may not know. But you can be sure that it isn't a surprise to God and that the timetable—though it may seem long—makes perfect sense to him.

[32] Two others, both criminals, were led out to be executed with him. [33] When they came to a place called The Skull, they nailed him to the cross. And the criminals were also crucified—one on his right and one on his left. [34] Jesus said, "Father, forgive them, for they don't know what they are doing." And the soldiers gambled for his clothes by throwing dice. [35] The crowd watched and the leaders scoffed. "He saved others," they said, "let him save himself if he is really God's Messiah, the Chosen One." [36] The soldiers mocked him, too, by offering him a drink of sour wine. [37] They called out to him, "If you are the King of the Jews, save yourself!" [38] A sign was fastened to the cross above him with these words: "This is the King of the Jews."

LUKE 23:32-38

¹³Two of Jesus' followers were walking to the village of Emmaus. . . . ¹⁴As they walked along they were talking about everything that had happened. ¹⁵As they talked and discussed these things, Jesus himself suddenly came and began walking with them. ¹⁶But God kept them from recognizing him. ¹⁷He asked them, "What are you discussing so intently as you walk along?" They stopped short, sadness written across their faces. ¹⁸Then one of them, Cleopas, replied, "You must be the only person in Jerusalem who hasn't heard about all the things that have happened there the last few days." ¹⁹"What things?" Jesus asked. "The things that happened to Jesus, the man from Nazareth," they said. "He was a prophet who did powerful miracles, and he was a mighty teacher in the eyes of God and all the people."

LUKE 24:13-19

When was the last time you scoured the house looking for the pen that was behind your ear? Have you ever needed to ask someone for your own phone number because you couldn't remember it? Or have you ever driven to work when you were supposed to be headed to the grocery store? Lapses of attention and memory afflict everyone from time to time.

The two disciples on the road to Emmaus have one of these lapses in memory. Their lapse, however, is more serious than forgetting where they placed a pen. Fortunately, the recently risen Jesus comes along, explains where they went wrong, and sets them straight. It may seem incredible that this couple could forget Christ, but consider the times that you have "forgotten" the Savior.

Read Luke 24:1-53

The two disciples on the road to Emmaus were depressed and hopeless. Despite others' testimony that Jesus was alive, these two still didn't believe or even grasp this fact. But when the risen Jesus met them on the road to Emmaus, he called them "foolish people" (Luke 24:25) because they found it difficult to believe the Scriptures. They had already forgotten what Jesus had told them several times before.

Sometimes our inability to enjoy the presence of Christ stems from our own disbelief of the Scriptures. We worry about life's problems despite God's promises to provide for our needs. Or we read the Bible, attend church, and even serve as Christian workers, only to wonder if God is at work in the world.

Don't easily forget this truth you have learned: Jesus has defeated sin and death, and he is alive today! He is with you through the Holy Spirit. Enjoy his presence.

It is a valiant way to serve God. It does not bring any earthly reward, and the costs of serving are tremendous, emotionally and sometimes physically. This is the ministry of a soapbox preacher—one who stands in the middle of a college campus, for example, and proclaims the Word of God to sneering, mocking students. He is a modern-day John the Baptist—a lone voice crying in the wilderness.

At times, John the Baptist was probably treated like a soapbox preacher. But that did not dissuade him from completing his mission—to call the Jews to repentance, baptize Jesus, and introduce Jesus as the Messiah. As you read, learn from the courage and conviction of John the Baptist, and determine to introduce people to the Savior.

Read John 1:1–2:11

God sent John the Baptist to identify Jesus as God's living light (John 1:8). Today, all Christians, like John the Baptist, serve to bring God's light to the world. We are not the source of God's light—we merely reflect it. Jesus Christ is the true Light. He helps us see our way to God and shows us how to walk along that path. But Christ also has chosen to shine his light through his followers to an unbelieving world. As we reflect God's moral excellence, our lives and words help guide others.

If you belong to Christ, your lifestyle, habits, words, and actions should reflect God's goodness to the people around you. Take time today to examine your life carefully. Ask God to point out any area that does not reflect his goodness. Then ask for his grace and strength, to make the needed changes in your life and to brightly reflect his light.

⁶God sent a man, John the Baptist, ⁷to tell about the light so that everyone might believe because of his testimony. ⁸John himself was not the light; he was simply a witness to tell about the light. ⁹The one who is the true light, who gives light to everyone, was coming into the world. ¹⁰He came into the very world he created, but the world didn't recognize him. ¹¹He came to his own people, and even they rejected him. ¹²But to all who believed him and accepted him, he gave the right to become children of God. ¹³They are reborn—not with a physical birth resulting from human passion or plan, but a birth that comes from God. ¹⁴So the Word became human and made his home among us. He was full of unfailing love and faithfulness. And we have seen his glory, the glory of the Father's one and only Son.

JOHN 1:6-14

¹²"If you don't believe me when I tell you about earthly things, how can you possibly believe if I tell you about heavenly things? ¹³No one has ever gone to heaven and returned. But the Son of Man has come down from heaven. ¹⁴And as Moses lifted up the bronze snake on a pole in the wilderness, so the Son of Man must be lifted up, ¹⁵so that everyone who believes in him will have eternal life. ¹⁶For God loved the world so much that he gave his one and only Son, so that everyone who believes in him will not perish but have eternal life. ¹⁷God sent his Son into the world not to judge the world, but to save the world through him. ¹⁸There is no judgment against anyone who believes in him. But anyone who does not believe in him has already been judged for not believing in God's one and only Son."

JOHN 3:12-18

True love has inspired countless books, poems, movie scripts, and songs. Young men and women have spent endless hours dreaming about it. Wars have been fought over it, and people have ended their lives because of losing it. How can this emotion demand so much attention and cause so much misfortune?

Unfortunately, the popular perception of true love is wrong. It is *not* romantic feelings between a man and a woman. Jesus knows the answer, and in this reading, he explains true love to the truth-seeking Pharisee, Nicodemus. Earlier, Jesus revealed his love for his Father when he cleared the Temple. As you read, look for true love in action and think of how you should display your love for God.

Read John 2:12–3:36

The entire message of the Bible comes to a focus in John 3:16: "For God loved the world so much that he gave his one and only Son, so that everyone who believes in him will not perish but have eternal life." Did you feel the weight of every word? There is no greater love than the birth, death, and resurrection of Jesus Christ.

As seen in Jesus' sacrifice, there is a big difference between his *true* love and what we call "love." While we reserve our love for special cases and special occasions, Jesus gives his love freely to all. While we love up to a point, Jesus loves to the point of self-sacrifice. While we restrict love to those who've earned it, Jesus loves those who can never deserve it.

Where are you looking for love? Please know that God loves you unconditionally. In fact, he loves you so much that he sent his Son, Jesus, to die for you so you might be forgiven and spend eternity with him. Give your life to the one who truly loves you. Let him teach you true love so that you can truly love others.

"Hi, how are ya?"

"Oh, fine. How are you?"

"Fine. Nice weather we're having."

"Sure is. See ya."

If you went for months with conversations no deeper than that, you would begin to think that no one cared about you.

In this reading, Jesus has a conversation with a woman that goes way beyond small talk. When Jesus says, "Hi," it's not mere chitchat—he really wants to talk. Watch how Jesus approaches this conversation, and take some cues.

Jesus wants to help in a unique way—that's the theme you'll keep seeing in this reading. Watch for several examples of this in his conversations.

Read John 4:1-45

In Jesus' day, prejudice was strong against women and Samaritans. In addition, this woman had a reputation for living in sin in the nearby village of Sychar. No respectable Jewish man would talk to such a woman. Then came the surprise of this woman's life: Jesus engaged her in a meaningful, no-nonsense conversation.

Not all our conversations have to be a carbon copy of this one, but all should look past race, social position, or past sins, as this one did. All should bring others a glimpse of our heavenly Father's love and offer of forgiveness, as this one did. Note that such conversations don't have to happen in a church—this one didn't.

Be prepared to share God's love through your words and everyday conversations. That is where the Good News about Christ begins.

---

[6]Jesus, tired from the long walk, sat wearily beside the well about noontime. [7]Soon a Samaritan woman came to draw water, and Jesus said to her, "Please give me a drink." [8]He was alone at the time because his disciples had gone into the village to buy some food. [9]The woman was surprised, for Jews refuse to have anything to do with Samaritans. She said to Jesus, "You are a Jew, and I am a Samaritan woman. Why are you asking me for a drink?" [10]Jesus replied, "If you only knew the gift God has for you and who you are speaking to, you would ask me, and I would give you living water." [11]"But sir, you don't have a rope or a bucket," she said, "and this well is very deep. Where would you get this living water?"

JOHN 4:6-11

⁵³Jesus said again, "I tell you the truth, unless you eat the flesh of the Son of Man and drink his blood, you cannot have eternal life within you. ⁵⁴But anyone who eats my flesh and drinks my blood has eternal life, and I will raise that person at the last day. ⁵⁵For my flesh is true food, and my blood is true drink. ⁵⁶Anyone who eats my flesh and drinks my blood remains in me, and I in him. ⁵⁷I live because of the living Father who sent me; in the same way, anyone who feeds on me will live because of me. ⁵⁸I am the true bread that came down from heaven. Anyone who eats this bread will not die as your ancestors did (even though they ate the manna) but will live forever." ⁵⁹He said these things while he was teaching in the synagogue in Capernaum.

JOHN 6:53-59

"Can't be."

"No way."

"Get outta here."

"I'll believe it when I see it."

These are some of the responses used to dismiss claims that stretch the limits of probability. When hard-to-believe statements are made, critics zoom in and strafe the landscape with dismissals, improbabilities, and proofs against. Meanwhile, a small minority might believe. Sometimes the critics are right; sometimes they are not.

In this portion of Scripture, you will see Jesus make the kinds of statements that divide the audience—not down the middle, but sharply to one side. Most disbelieve. A few hold on. This is too wild to be true. Or is it?

As you read, imagine yourself in that audience—on which side do you stand?

Read John 4:46–6:71

Jesus' words caused many of his followers to desert him because they just couldn't accept what he said (John 6:66). Many people respond to Jesus that way. They hear the Word of God, learn a little of Jesus' teachings and actions, and decide to turn away from him. If you ask why, you will hear as many reasons as people you ask. But the bottom line is that they leave because he asks too much—the cost is too high.

What Jesus asks is sometimes difficult. But if we turn away from him, where will we go? As Peter said, "Lord, to whom would we go? You alone have the words that give eternal life" (6:68). If you feel that Jesus asks too much, ask him to change your heart. Then have the courage to keep on following in faith, as Peter did.

More than ever before, every problem demands an explanation. We want to know why the traffic is so slow today, why taxes are going up, why the job doesn't pay better. In an earlier day of fewer options, we didn't ask as many questions. But these days that's not good enough. We want to know why? who? how?

Jesus confronts that attitude in this passage. A man who has been suffering from blindness prompts the disciples to ask Jesus why. Jesus' answer sparks a controversy. Jesus knows what he's talking about, partly because he's the Son of God, and partly because he knows what it's like to suffer.

Read John 7:1–10:42

Many people of Jesus' day believed that calamity or suffering resulted from sin. So when his disciples came upon a blind man, they put the question directly to Jesus: Who's to blame for this man's blindness? Is it his or his parents' fault? Jesus answered that no one was to blame—God allowed it in order to teach them about faith and to glorify God through the man's healing (John 9:2-3).

Jesus' lesson teaches us that we must not make assumptions about why people suffer. Sometimes we may be able to identify cause-and-effect relationships between certain choices we make and their outcomes. But we can't blame specific hurts on specific sins. God does not work the way we do. In every kind of suffering, Jesus asks that we look not for scapegoats but for ways to help those who suffer and to learn from their suffering.

¹As Jesus was walking along, he saw a man who had been blind from birth. ²"Rabbi," his disciples asked him, "why was this man born blind? Was it because of his own sins or his parents' sins?" ³"It was not because of his sins or his parents' sins," Jesus answered. "This happened so the power of God could be seen in him. ⁴We must quickly carry out the tasks assigned us by the one who sent us. The night is coming, and then no one can work. ⁵But while I am here in the world, I am the light of the world." ⁶Then he spit on the ground, made mud with the saliva, and spread the mud over the blind man's eyes. ⁷He told him, "Go wash yourself in the pool of Siloam" (Siloam means "sent"). So the man went and washed and came back seeing!

JOHN 9:1-7

When you suffer from a disease, tragedy, or disability, try not to ask, "Why did this happen to me?" or, "What did I do wrong?" Instead, ask God to give you strength for the trial and a greater reliance on him.

[37]Despite all the miraculous signs Jesus had done, most of the people still did not believe in him. [38]This is exactly what Isaiah the prophet had predicted: "Lord, who has believed our message? To whom has the Lord revealed his powerful arm?" [39]But the people couldn't believe, for as Isaiah also said, [40]"The Lord has blinded their eyes and hardened their hearts— so that their eyes cannot see, and their hearts cannot understand, and they cannot turn to me and have me heal them." [41]Isaiah was referring to Jesus when he said this, because he saw the future and spoke of the Messiah's glory. [42]Many people did believe in him, however, including some of the Jewish leaders. But they wouldn't admit it for fear that the Pharisees would expel them from the synagogue. [43]For they loved human praise more than the praise of God.

JOHN 12:37-43

Suppose something miraculous happens to you. News of this miracle spreads quickly throughout your community, county, and state. People from miles around come to see you and the result of this incredible event. Soon, investigative reporters show up and start asking you pointed questions. The next day their stories appear under headlines containing words like *hoax* and *fraud*. There never seems to be a shortage of skeptics.

Even Jesus had to deal with skeptics. Despite the fact that he had performed many miracles, some people would not believe he was the Messiah. But, as John writes, Isaiah predicted that people would not believe. This is hard to imagine since Jesus performs one of his most amazing miracles in this reading—raising Lazarus from the dead. Some people never believe, even when the facts are undeniable.

Do you really believe that Jesus is the Messiah? How will you respond when friends, neighbors, and coworkers are skeptical about your experience with God?

Read John 11:1–12:50

Skepticism toward Jesus' identity and claims has always been the rule, not the exception. Most people will not believe our witness about Christ. Granted, that doesn't mean we shouldn't speak. Jesus didn't stop preaching and healing the day people first said, "So what?" He stayed faithful to the task his Father had given him, regardless of how people responded. Likewise, we need to commit to do God's work faithfully, no matter how people react.

Don't be discouraged if your witness for Christ doesn't turn as many to him as you would like. You can control only your own actions, not others' responses. Be a faithful worker and continue to reach out to others for Jesus.

On a cold, rainy night when you can't get to sleep, what thoughts arise? Do you think of people from your past who had a positive influence on your life? Do you remember the stories your mother or father read to you on nights like this? Or do you fantasize about your first kiss or marrying the person of your dreams?

All these thoughts have one thing in common: love. Appropriately, this reading has a lot to do with love, especially Jesus' love for his disciples. Here Jesus demonstrates his love for them before giving them the ultimate command by which they should live. Look for Jesus' dramatic demonstration of love, and compare your love with his.

Read John 13:1–14:31

Jesus commanded his disciples, "Just as I have loved you, you should love each other" (John 13:34). You know what happened next—Jesus died for their sins. This was the ultimate demonstration of love. As Christ's followers reflected that love, others would surely notice (13:35).

What separates Christians from the rest of the world is love. If you belong to Christ, love others as he loved you. Help people when it's not convenient. Give of your resources even when it hurts. Devote your energy to others' welfare rather than your own, and absorb hurts from others without complaining or fighting back. This kind of love does not come naturally. That is why only God's people, with the help of the Holy Spirit, can love unconditionally. This kind of love makes others sit up and notice.

[21]Jesus was deeply troubled, and he exclaimed, "I tell you the truth, one of you will betray me!" [22]The disciples looked at each other, wondering whom he could mean. [23]The disciple Jesus loved was sitting next to Jesus at the table. [24]Simon Peter motioned to him to ask, "Who's he talking about?" [25]So that disciple leaned over to Jesus and asked, "Lord, who is it?" [26]Jesus responded, "It is the one to whom I give the bread I dip in the bowl." And when he had dipped it, he gave it to Judas, son of Simon Iscariot. [27]When Judas had eaten the bread, Satan entered into him. Then Jesus told him, "Hurry and do what you're going to do." [28]None of the others at the table knew what Jesus meant. [29]Since Judas was their treasurer, some thought Jesus was telling him to go and pay for the food or to give some money to the poor.

JOHN 13:21-29

⁶"I have revealed you to the ones you gave me from this world. They were always yours. You gave them to me, and they have kept your word. ⁷Now they know that everything I have is a gift from you, ⁸for I have passed on to them the message you gave me. They accepted it and know that I came from you, and they believe you sent me. ⁹My prayer is not for the world, but for those you have given me, because they belong to you. ¹⁰All who are mine belong to you, and you have given them to me, so they bring me glory. ¹¹Now I am departing from the world; they are staying in this world, but I am coming to you. Holy Father, you have given me your name; now protect them by the power of your name so that they will be united just as we are."

JOHN 17:6-11

Some newspaper headlines can depress even entrenched optimists: crime and taxes on the rise, school test scores on the slide. But we shouldn't be surprised when we see these headlines. Bad news has been grabbing people's attention for a long time.

Even Jesus shared bad news occasionally. This passage records him talking about the hatred, grief, separation, pain, and injustice that lay ahead for his followers. But behind every dreary headline, he assures us, is a promise and a hope, realized in part now and in full later. Our reunion with Jesus is coming. The last headline is *really* good news.

Read John 15:1–17:26

In his final prayer for the disciples, Jesus told his Father that he would send them into the world as he had been sent into the world. He asked not that the disciples be isolated from hatred and persecution but that they be protected from falling prey to the devil. He asked that God would strengthen them and teach them through the opposition they would experience. Their presence in the world would be vital, and by God's grace and power, they would thrive there (John 17:13-18).

A glance around at our painful world may make you wish for an escape. But Jesus sends you, if you follow him, into that painful world the same way that God the Father sent him. He has not left you alone. The Holy Spirit lives inside you, protecting, guiding, and teaching you. His Spirit will work through you to tell others of Jesus, ease others' pain, and further God's work.

Jesus has sent you into the world. Carry on Christ's message today, trusting God for his protection of your soul even though your body and spirit may suffer.

Imagine that you are the only fan in a sold-out stadium cheering for the visiting team. Couple this with the fact that the sporting event you are attending is the championship game. Even though the stadium security forces are nearby, you know that if you raise your voice to celebrate your team's score, you will be in danger. At times like this, secrecy has its advantages.

Unfortunately, secrecy can also be a trap. Peter learns this lesson the hard way as he tries but fails to hide his faith in Jesus. In this reading, Peter is not the only one to learn this lesson. Joseph of Arimathea and Nicodemus also realize that it is better to acknowledge Jesus for who he is than to deny knowing him at all. For them, however, this realization comes a little too late.

The bottom line is that secrecy has disadvantages, too, especially when it comes to faith. Secret faith is no faith at all. As you read, determine to be open and honest about your faith in Christ.

Read John 18:1–19:42

We take a risk whenever we let others know that we follow Christ. We risk backlash—some may think less of us, some may question our judgment, some may even threaten our job or safety. Yet the time always comes when someone says, "Aren't you one of his?" Or we recognize that we must say or do something that many others will see and recognize as an act of faith in Christ.

[28]Jesus knew that his mission was now finished, and to fulfill Scripture he said, "I am thirsty." [29]A jar of sour wine was sitting there, so they soaked a sponge in it, put it on a hyssop branch, and held it up to his lips. [30]When Jesus had tasted it, he said, "It is finished!" Then he bowed his head and released his spirit. [31]It was the day of preparation, and the Jewish leaders didn't want the bodies hanging there the next day, which was the Sabbath (and a very special Sabbath, because it was the Passover). So they asked Pilate to hasten their deaths by ordering that their legs be broken. Then their bodies could be taken down. [32]So the soldiers came and broke the legs of the two men crucified with Jesus. [33]But when they came to Jesus, they saw that he was already dead, so they didn't break his legs.

JOHN 19:28-33

Exposing your faith may have some disadvantages. But doing so also may help you take an important step. If you're not willing to be bold for Christ, it begs the question, *Do you really believe?*

¹⁵After breakfast Jesus asked Simon Peter, "Simon son of John, do you love me more than these?" "Yes, Lord," Peter replied, "you know I love you." "Then feed my lambs," Jesus told him. ¹⁶Jesus repeated the question: "Simon son of John, do you love me?" "Yes, Lord," Peter said, "you know I love you." "Then take care of my sheep," Jesus said. ¹⁷A third time he asked him, "Simon son of John, do you love me?" Peter was hurt that Jesus asked the question a third time. He said, "Lord, you know everything. You know that I love you." Jesus said, "Then feed my sheep."

JOHN 21:15-17

Airplane banners occasionally announce love and sometimes propose marriage. Highway billboards have been known to do the same. These are shockingly public ways to get a normally private message to the object of one's affection.

Jesus' last recorded encounter with Peter brings about one of these public declarations of love. Unlike the voluntary action of flying a banner or renting a billboard, Peter has to be coaxed into admitting his love for Jesus. As you read this passage, notice the love God has declared for you in the resurrection of his Son, Jesus.

Read John 20:1–21:25

After Jesus rose from the dead, and shortly before he ascended into heaven, he asked Peter if he loved him (John 21:15-17). First Jesus asked if Peter's love (using the Greek word for love that means freely given, self-sacrificial love) excelled that of the other disciples. Peter said yes, using a different word for love, the one that signifies brotherly love. Then Jesus asked again, leaving out a comparison with the others. Again Peter said yes, and again he used brotherly love. Then Jesus asked Peter for a third time, this time referring to brotherly love, saying, in effect: "Are you even my friend?" Peter answered, "Lord, you know everything. You know I love you" (21:17).

Peter felt hurt at Jesus' persistence, but Jesus knew that it's all too easy to say glibly, "Sure, I love you." To face the question three times, each time pressed a little harder, forced Peter to face his true feelings and motives. A third declaration of his devotion would leave no doubt.

How would you respond if Jesus asked, "Do you truly love me? Do you *really* love me? Are you even my friend?" Be sure you can sincerely say to Jesus, "I love you. I am your friend."

Our very way of life depends on electricity. If you don't think so, see what happens when you turn off the power in your home. You can't use your lights when it gets dark, or your TV, stereo, or computer. If you have an electric oven or if your house has electric heat, forget about cooking or staying warm. You may also want to go out and buy some ice to keep your food cold.

The church without the Holy Spirit is like a house without electrical power. That is why Jesus sends his power source—the Holy Spirit—to the church soon after his ascension. When the Spirit comes, the church is radically transformed—Peter preaches his first sermon, converting thousands; a lame beggar is healed; and Peter and John boldly face Jesus' killers. The promise Jesus gave his disciples is coming true—they have received *real* power.

Read Acts 1:1–4:37

Jesus said that shortly after he ascended to heaven, the Holy Spirit would come and give his disciples power to take his message to the whole world (Acts 1:8). That's exactly what happened. First the disciples received the Holy Spirit (2:3-4). Then the Spirit gave them power that enabled them to speak in other languages and to perform miracles (2:4-12, 43; 3:6-8; 4:13). As a result, they took the message of Christ to the rest of the world (8:4).

Often, Christians try to use their own power and authority to persuade others to follow Christ. But sharing God's message should not involve slick debate or manipulation. Instead, we should share what God has done for us through the power of the Holy Spirit. Then we should depend on the Spirit for the results. The Holy Spirit works in people, helping them see that the incredible Jesus really did come to die for them, paying the penalty for their sins.

¹On the day of Pentecost all the believers were meeting together in one place. ²Suddenly, there was a sound from heaven like the roaring of a mighty windstorm, and it filled the house where they were sitting. ³Then, what looked like flames or tongues of fire appeared and settled on each of them. ⁴And everyone present was filled with the Holy Spirit and began speaking in other languages, as the Holy Spirit gave them this ability. ⁵At that time there were devout Jews from every nation living in Jerusalem. ⁶When they heard the loud noise, everyone came running, and they were bewildered to hear their own languages being spoken by the believers. ⁷They were completely amazed. "How can this be?" they exclaimed. "These people are all from Galilee, ⁸and yet we hear them speaking in our own native languages!"

ACTS 2:1-8

27They brought the apostles before the high council, where the high priest confronted them. 28"Didn't we tell you never again to teach in this man's name?" he demanded. "Instead, you have filled all Jerusalem with your teaching about him, and you want to make us responsible for his death!" 29But Peter and the apostles replied, "We must obey God rather than any human authority. 30The God of our ancestors raised Jesus from the dead after you killed him by hanging him on a cross. 31Then God put him in the place of honor at his right hand as Prince and Savior. He did this so the people of Israel would repent of their sins and be forgiven. 32We are witnesses of these things and so is the Holy Spirit, who is given by God to those who obey him." 33When they heard this, the high council was furious and decided to kill them.

ACTS 5:27-33

Public speaking is usually listed among people's greatest fears. Yet every day, thousands of people speak in public, because they recognize that the importance of what they have to say exceeds the fear they feel.

Take Stephen, for example. His speech is brilliant. And Philip speaks well, too. So do Peter and John. We're not told if they enjoy the experiences, but we have lots of evidence that they have every reason to fear. For example, Peter and John are told by the Jewish Council never to speak of Jesus again. If they do, they will be in danger. But they ignore this threat and continue to preach. Because of Peter and John's courage and determination, the council members decide to silence them—permanently. Unlike Peter and John, Stephen never receives a warning for speaking about Jesus. Instead, his enemies stone him to death for telling the truth.

Read Acts 5:1–7:60

Many of Jesus' followers were imprisoned or killed for speaking the truth about his resurrection. It was not long before the first of his followers, Stephen, was martyred. James, the brother of Jesus, was also killed because of his faith in Christ. The apostle John was exiled to an island, and tradition says Peter was crucified upside down.

The fate of Stephen and the apostles does not sound appealing. However, we should remember that they gladly died for the sake of Christ because they knew without a doubt that he was—and still is—the Messiah. This knowledge led them to speak out even under threat of death. No one could silence them.

Don't let anyone silence you, either. Speak out boldly for Jesus. Share your faith with others. If you endure persecution for your testimony, keep in mind the attitude of the apostles (Acts 5:41), and try to follow their example.

Pulling off a surprise party takes the street smarts of a big-city detective and the logistical skill of an army general. Weeks of planning can crumble at any minute, but if done right, the moment of sweet surprise finally comes.

For the early church, the surprises keep coming. This reading contains some unique ones, including Philip's encounter with an Ethiopian official, Peter's vision, and Paul's conversion. Not all of the surprises are good, however—in particular, the church's persecution. But through it all, these first believers learn how powerful God is and how big their mission field has grown.

As you read, be alert for God's surprises, in the text but also in your life and church.

Read Acts 8:1–12:25

The introduction of Gentiles (non-Jews) into the church was a struggle. Up until this point, all the believers were Jews. When Peter brought the news that a Gentile named Cornelius had become a believer in Christ, the believers in Jerusalem were shocked and didn't know how to respond. But Peter said that God had overcome his objections and led him to Cornelius. In fact, God had given Cornelius the Holy Spirit—proof of salvation. After Peter's colleagues heard the whole story, they praised God and accepted this new development as great news (Acts 11:2-18).

[4]Peter told them exactly what had happened. [5]"I was in the town of Joppa," he said, "and while I was praying, I went into a trance and saw a vision. Something like a large sheet was let down by its four corners from the sky. And it came right down to me. [6]When I looked inside the sheet, I saw all sorts of small animals, wild animals, reptiles, and birds. [7]And I heard a voice say, 'Get up, Peter; kill and eat them.' [8]'No, Lord,' I replied. 'I have never eaten anything that our Jewish laws have declared impure or unclean.' [9]But the voice from heaven spoke again: 'Do not call something unclean if God has made it clean.'"

Acts 11:4-9

As this incident shows, conflict with other Christians may arise over important issues. When this happens, we should guard ourselves against the bias of our initial reaction. We need to listen and speak respectfully, not jump to conclusions.

Before judging the behavior of fellow believers, let them tell their side of the story. The Holy Spirit may have something important to teach you through them.

[23]"This letter is from the apostles and elders, your brothers in Jerusalem. It is written to the Gentile believers in Antioch, Syria, and Cilicia. Greetings! [24]We understand that some men from here have troubled you and upset you with their teaching, but we did not send them! [25]So we decided, having come to complete agreement, to send you official representatives, along with our beloved Barnabas and Paul, [26]who have risked their lives for the name of our Lord Jesus Christ. [27]We are sending Judas and Silas to confirm what we have decided concerning your question. [28]For it seemed good to the Holy Spirit and to us to lay no greater burden on you than these few requirements: [29]You must abstain from eating food offered to idols, from consuming blood or the meat of strangled animals, and from sexual immorality."

ACTS 15:23-29

Laws for the state of Illinois take up thirteen feet of shelf space. Add another twenty-three feet of shelving for federal laws and several more shelves containing court decisions, and you still are not done. You have city, county, and township rules to consider. If you go to school, work for a corporation, or attend church, you have even more rules to follow. It's a wonder a person doesn't need permission to take a breath.

The earliest Christians are Jewish, and they still live under the many religious rules that make up their culture. With the addition of numerous Gentile believers to the church, things get complicated. Should the Gentile Christians also follow all these rules? The solution comes straight from the truth about salvation itself.

Read Acts 13:1–15:35

Paul, Peter, James, and other leaders, under the guidance of the Holy Spirit, realized that Christ saves a person by faith alone and not by observing the law (Acts 15:1-29). This conclusion, though, did not mean that the Gentile believers did not have to keep any laws. Rather, they did not have to keep the laws of Moses, including the notable rite of circumcision, in order to be saved.

We often like to add conditions to the simple mandate to believe in Christ, but we must not. The more a Christian looks like us, the better we sometimes feel about their faith. But by *looks like us* do we mean "looks like Christ," or just "looks like me"? Resist the temptation to make other Christians act just like you. The commands of Christ are all the religious rules they need, and all that most can bear.

A wise person carefully checks out certain people, places, and things before utilizing them. A new babysitter, a public bathroom, and a new car should definitely be checked out before being used. Some people, however, just skip this step and assume that all is OK. They like to live dangerously.

Checking things out is also a good practice for people sitting in the pews. Take the Bereans for example. They do not take everything Paul says as gospel truth. They compare what he says about Jesus with the Old Testament texts and are blessed by it.

Unfortunately, not all of Paul's audiences are as studious as the Bereans. Each one presents a different challenge—jealousy, skepticism, and apathy. As you read, learn from the way Paul handles these challenges.

Read Acts 15:36–18:22

The people in Berea had more than a surface interest in the news about Christ when they heard it. They listened carefully to Paul's message, considered its merit, got out their copies of the Scriptures, and checked it all out for themselves (Acts 17:11). Always open but never careless, they verified each teaching diligently before embracing it wholeheartedly.

A preacher or teacher who gives God's true message will never contradict or explain away anything that is found in God's Word. That is why we need to think about what we hear, to evaluate sermons and teachings. If we do this and the message is true, we will benefit all the more by understanding it better and seeing more clearly how to apply it. If we do this and the message is false, we will spot the error and not follow a mistake.

¹Paul and Silas then traveled through the towns of Amphipolis and Apollonia and came to Thessalonica, where there was a Jewish synagogue. ²As was Paul's custom, he went to the synagogue service, and for three Sabbaths in a row he used the Scriptures to reason with the people. . . . ⁵But some of the Jews were jealous, so they gathered some troublemakers from the marketplace to form a mob and start a riot. . . . ¹⁰That very night the believers sent Paul and Silas to Berea. When they arrived there, they went to the Jewish synagogue. ¹¹And the people of Berea were more open-minded than those in Thessalonica, and they listened eagerly to Paul's message. They searched the Scriptures day after day to see if Paul and Silas were teaching the truth.

ACTS 17:1-2, 5, 10-11

¹³A group of Jews was traveling from town to town casting out evil spirits. They tried to use the name of the Lord Jesus in their incantation, saying, "I command you in the name of Jesus, whom Paul preaches, to come out!" ¹⁴Seven sons of Sceva, a leading priest, were doing this. ¹⁵But one time when they tried it, the evil spirit replied, "I know Jesus, and I know Paul, but who are you?" ¹⁶Then the man with the evil spirit leaped on them, overpowered them, and attacked them with such violence that they fled from the house, naked and battered. ¹⁷The story of what happened spread quickly all through Ephesus, to Jews and Greeks alike. A solemn fear descended on the city, and the name of the Lord Jesus was greatly honored. . . . ²⁰So the message about the Lord spread widely and had a powerful effect.

ACTS 19:13-17, 20

"What are your personal goals?" a corporate interviewer asked the young man hoping for his first job. "Oh," came the reply, "I'd like to dabble in sales."

"What are your long-range interests?" an interviewer asked a young woman seeking admission to medical school. "Hmm," she said, "I'd love to dabble in neurosurgery."

Dabblers are casual hobbyists, not the people stockholders want running corporate operations and not the doctors most people choose. Spiritual dabblers are hobbyists, too, and if you think a casual neurosurgeon is dangerous, note what can happen because of these folks. Some ideas are too important to dabble with, and some are too dangerous—especially those tied to the occult.

Also look for the tale of poor Eutychus. He should have left at intermission, or called for one.

Read Acts 18:23–21:14

The city of Ephesus was a center for black magic and other occult practices. Some professionals made a living inventing and promoting magical formulas for wealth, happiness, and success in marriage. Most Ephesians followed superstitions and practiced sorcery. But those who believed in Christ renounced these sins and burned their occult implements in a public bonfire (Acts 19:18-19).

God clearly forbids sorcery and occult practices (see Deuteronomy 18:9-14). You cannot follow Christ and dabble in the occult, black magic, or sorcery. God's power is greater than Satan's (see 1 John 4:4; Revelation 20:10). Once you begin to engage in these evils superficially, however, you invite Satan to draw you in even further.

If you tend to dabble in the occult, learn a lesson from the Ephesians, and get rid of anything that could keep you trapped in such practices.

What's worse than running out of gas on a busy freeway during rush hour? Being told that such problems are wonderful opportunities for character growth.

Paul has flat tires at nearly every turn. Yet each time, his delay or detour becomes an opportunity to preach, witness, and spread the Good News about Christ. Paul must have considered his itinerary to be completely in God's hands, for he doesn't complain about hunger, cold, shipwreck, snakebite, imprisonment, or the injustice of his own court case. He adjusts marvelously to change, as his last recorded speech makes clear. In an exemplary way, Paul sees each pothole as just part of the trip, which makes his life an adventure in faith.

Read Acts 21:15–28:31

Paul was arrested by a Roman commander because he was the center of attention in a riot. But the reason for his arrest is not as important as how he handled this humiliation, setback, and injustice. As military officers and prominent city leaders met with King Agrippa to hear Paul's case, Paul prepared his thoughts for another speech about Jesus. He saw his troubled situation not as a cause for lodging a formal complaint with the government, but as another opportunity to present the Good News about Christ that mattered so much to him (Acts 25:23–26:32).

²⁴Festus shouted, "Paul, you are insane. Too much study has made you crazy!" ²⁵But Paul replied, "I am not insane, Most Excellent Festus. What I am saying is the sober truth. ²⁶And King Agrippa knows about these things. I speak boldly, for I am sure these events are all familiar to him, for they were not done in a corner! ²⁷King Agrippa, do you believe the prophets? I know you do—" ²⁸Agrippa interrupted him. "Do you think you can persuade me to become a Christian so quickly?" ²⁹Paul replied, "Whether quickly or not, I pray to God that both you and everyone here in this audience might become the same as I am, except for these chains."

Acts 26:24-29

Every offense and injustice you suffer will test you. It will force you—as it forced Paul—to choose what to "preach" about. Will you see your humiliation only as a problem, barrier, or roadblock to your happiness? Or will you see it as an opportunity, given to you by God, to demonstrate his power and love in your life? Rather than complain at every hint of brokenness in this world, why not try to fix it? Look for ways to turn your painful experiences into an opportunity to serve God and share him with others.

⁵Through Christ, God has given us the privilege and authority as apostles to tell Gentiles everywhere what God has done for them, so that they will believe and obey him, bringing glory to his name. ⁶And you are included among those Gentiles who have been called to belong to Jesus Christ. ⁷I am writing to all of you in Rome who are loved by God and are called to be his own holy people. May God our Father and the Lord Jesus Christ give you grace and peace. ⁸Let me say first that I thank my God through Jesus Christ for all of you, because your faith in him is being talked about all over the world. ⁹God knows how often I pray for you. Day and night I bring you and your needs in prayer to God, whom I serve with all my heart by spreading the Good News about his Son.

ROMANS 1:5-9

Whether or not you are a sports fan, you are undoubtedly familiar with braggadocio, or empty boasting. Many in our society—in particular athletes and their rabid fans—have made this an art form. "We're Number 1" signs and childish antics pop up everywhere. Even those who can back up their words are often full of hot air.

For those who think they are the greatest, Paul has some sobering news: You are not as great as you may think. Paul reminds us that we are all great at one thing: sinning. But that is not all that Paul has to say. The good news of Paul's letter to the Romans is that God has a great message of hope and forgiveness. Now that is something to really brag about!

Read Romans 1:1–3:20

Paul knew how thoroughly kind God had been to him. He called himself and everyone else in need of Christ's forgiveness "terrible people" (Romans 2:1). That's why he had no trouble obeying God's call to travel all over the Roman Empire preaching and spreading the good news about Christ. It only made sense to him that he would share the message of God's forgiveness with others after all God had done for him (1:5).

Being a Christian is a privilege. God has taken away more of our sin than we can realize, more sin than we deserve to have forgiven. The more we appreciate the depth of this, the more we'll understand Paul's gratitude here.

If you have received Christ's forgiveness, you have an important story to tell. You don't have to be a clone of Paul, just motivated by the same gratitude, driven by the same love, committed to the same end: God's greater glory. In what way can you share the news about God's goodness today?

If you want to view the smallest leaves in the hardwood kingdom, look at a silk tree. Next to a maple or oak leaf, the silk tree leaflet is tiny. But despite its small leaves, the silk tree is one of the hardiest species in the world. It is a short but significant plant.

Some sins, like silk leaves, are small. But just as silk leaves are still leaves, so small sins are still sins. Paul reminds us that small acts of lying, lusting, and coveting all produce the same result as murder, adultery, and stealing—separation from God. Paul also explains how people can draw close to God and acquire joy. As you read, compare your life with Paul's inspired words and determine to root out every sin.

In addition, in this section Paul shows how two men made significant changes in the world—one for the worse, the other for the better.

Read Romans 3:21–5:21

The Bible says that every person's sin has separated them from God (Romans 3:23). Most people consider some sins to be bigger than others because they have such serious consequences. For example, murder is thought to be worse than hatred, and adultery worse than lust. In one sense they are, because they hurt others. But the fact that a person commits "smaller" sins does not mean that he or she is somehow less damned. Sin is incompatible with God, who is holy and without sin. All sin, therefore, leads to death, regardless of how great or small it may seem.

Don't minimize "little" sins or overrate "big" ones. Understand and fear the effects of all sins, and ask God to help you live blamelessly before him.

[21]But now God has shown us a way to be made right with him without keeping the requirements of the law, as was promised in the writings of Moses and the prophets long ago. [22]We are made right with God by placing our faith in Jesus Christ. And this is true for everyone who believes, no matter who we are. [23]For everyone has sinned; we all fall short of God's glorious standard. [24]Yet God, with undeserved kindness, declares that we are righteous. He did this through Christ Jesus when he freed us from the penalty for our sins. [25]For God presented Jesus as the sacrifice for sin. People are made right with God when they believe that Jesus sacrificed his life, shedding his blood.

ROMANS 3:21-25

28And we know that God causes everything to work together for the good of those who love God and are called according to his purpose for them. 29For God knew his people in advance, and he chose them to become like his Son, so that his Son would be the firstborn among many brothers and sisters. 30And having chosen them, he called them to come to him. And having called them, he gave them right standing with himself. And having given them right standing, he gave them his glory. 31What shall we say about such wonderful things as these? If God is for us, who can ever be against us? 32Since he did not spare even his own Son but gave him up for us all, won't he also give us everything else? 33Who dares accuse us whom God has chosen for his own? No one—for God himself has given us right standing with himself.

ROMANS 8:28-33

Rock climbers are a unique group of people. Some of them are extremely adventurous and like to climb without the aid of a rope. Others are a little more cautious and climb with the security a rope provides. This added confidence helps them scale the most difficult surfaces, even those that jut out and require them to hang over empty space.

In many ways, going through tough times is like climbing a sheer rock face. Trying to get through these times without God is like climbing without a rope. In this reading, Paul makes Christians aware of the "rope" that God extends to all his followers. That rope is God's promise to never let anything separate us from his love. As you read, take hope in God's rope.

Read Romans 6:1-8:39

Like Paul, we face hardships in many areas of life. We may be unemployed or working under strenuous conditions. Some may be punished for doing right. Others may be going through a debilitating illness or even facing death. These experiences, or the idea of having to face them, often cause us to fear that God has abandoned us or no longer loves us. But the truth is that *nothing* can separate us from Christ's love. The fact that he died for us proves it, and this promise reminds us.

When you experience doubt about God's constant love for you, remember Paul's experience. Then reread and meditate on Romans 8:31-39. If it will help you, try memorizing verse 38: "Nothing can ever separate us from God's love." Do not think that your troubles somehow mean the end of his love. You can always feel totally secure that he loves you and will be with you.

A perfunctory "luv ya" is about as convincing as a used-car advertisement. It is easy to pass off and too trivial to be taken seriously. You wouldn't build a relationship on a "luv ya," would you?

Like us, God does not care for or desire a "luv ya." In this reading, Paul tells the Romans that there is more to believing in Jesus than mouthing the words *Jesus is Lord*. There must be a commitment of the heart as well. As you read, consider whether your faith has moved beyond words to the heart.

Also in this reading, note the lesson on God's sovereignty that Paul teaches through the illustration of clay pots. In addition, notice Paul's love for the Jews, despite their inhumane treatment of him. Read about God's mercy toward both Jews and Gentiles.

Read Romans 9:1–11:36

"How do I become a Christian?" That question will receive a wide variety of answers, depending on the religious affiliation or denomination. But Romans 10:8-13 gives the true answer: If we believe in our hearts and say with our mouths that Christ is the risen Lord, we will be saved. Salvation takes no more or less work than that.

Some people try to complicate the process of becoming a Christian with additional requirements, such as belief in a cherished doctrine or certain patterns of behavior, but they should not. God has left it all marvelously simple and plainly outlined in this portion of Scripture.

⁹If you confess with your mouth that Jesus is Lord and believe in your heart that God raised him from the dead, you will be saved. ¹⁰For it is by believing in your heart that you are made right with God, and it is by confessing with your mouth that you are saved. ¹¹As the Scriptures tell us, "Anyone who trusts in him will never be disgraced." ¹²Jew and Gentile are the same in this respect. They have the same Lord, who gives generously to all who call on him. ¹³For "Everyone who calls on the name of the Lord will be saved." ¹⁴But how can they call on him to save them unless they believe in him? And how can they believe in him if they have never heard about him? And how can they hear about him unless someone tells them? . . . ¹⁵That is why the Scriptures say, "How beautiful are the feet of messengers who bring good news!"

ROMANS 10:9-15

Jesus will save those who truly believe in him (10:13). Don't complicate what God has made simple, especially something of such great importance as salvation. Leave doctrinal disputes and differences of opinion out of the salvation equation.

¹Accept other believers who are weak in faith, and don't argue with them about what they think is right or wrong. ²For instance, one person believes it's all right to eat anything. But another believer with a sensitive conscience will eat only vegetables. ³Those who feel free to eat anything must not look down on those who don't. And those who don't eat certain foods must not condemn those who do, for God has accepted them. ⁴Who are you to condemn someone else's servants? They are responsible to the Lord, so let him judge whether they are right or wrong. And with the Lord's help, they will do what is right and will receive his approval. ⁵In the same way, some think one day is more holy than another day, while others think every day is alike. You should each be fully convinced that whichever day you choose is acceptable.

ROMANS 14:1-5

God's Word turns everything topsy-turvy. The firs will be last, the last first. The poor will be blessed the weary given rest. God's academy of life make foolish people wise and worldly-wise people foolish What we call common sense, God sometimes call nonsense.

In this last reading of Romans, Paul's advice on how to treat "believers who are weak in faith" is another one of those lessons. Here Paul tells strong believers to refrain from arguing with weaker believers over issues of right and wrong. As you read, look at your life from God's perspective—upside down.

Read Romans 12:1–16:27

God wants us to welcome "believers who are weak in faith" (Romans 14:1). Exactly what kind of weaknesses do these Christians have? And what does it mean to be a "strong" Christian?

Every believer is weak in some areas and strong in others. Wherever our faith is strong, we can survive contact with sinners without falling into sin ourselves But wherever it is weak, we must avoid contact with those activities, people, or places so we can avoid falling into sin. Thus there are differences among believers and what they regard as right and wrong.

Aside from being gracious to other believers who have different convictions, we need to be aware of our own strengths and weaknesses. Whenever we don't know whether an activity is appropriate for us we should ask, "Can I do that without sinning? Can I influence others for good, rather than being influenced by them?" Let the answers to those questions be your guide.

Take the time to ask those questions of yourself today. Then, in areas of strength, do not fear being defiled by the world. In areas of weakness, be cautious. And in the company of other Christians, be protective of the weaknesses that threaten them.

Long division is a math skill that most students greatly dislike. Those who are really good at math may tolerate it, but few ever love it.

What is tolerable in the field of math is destructive in the body of Christ. No one knows this better than Paul. In this reading, Paul addresses the problem of division in the Corinthian church. What once was one church has now split into four. Paul pleads with them to stop arguing and to start getting along—a relevant message for today's church also. As you read, consider the potential for division in your church, and determine to be one who brings peace and unity in the body.

Read 1 Corinthians 1:1–4:21

The Corinthian church had split because the believers there thought they could judge people's motives. Individuals had rallied around certain "superstar" preachers (Paul, Peter, Apollos, and others) and had formed groups within the church based on who followed whom. The groups argued with each other over whose leader was the best Christian. But all this conflict depended on their ability to judge the hearts and motives of others—which they could not do. Paul urged them to stop judging one another, to rally around Christ, and to let God decide who served him faithfully and who did not (1 Corinthians 4:1-5).

Believers today should learn a lesson from the Corinthians. We should beware of judging others. This does not mean that we should avoid confronting those who sin (5:12-13). But we ought to stay away from judging who is a better servant for Christ. When judgments like this are made, we cast ourselves in God's role, which we do not have a right to play. Only God knows a person's heart, and only he has the right to judge.

[1]Look at Apollos and me as mere servants of Christ who have been put in charge of explaining God's mysteries. [2]Now, a person who is put in charge as a manager must be faithful. [3]As for me, it matters very little how I might be evaluated by you or by any human authority. I don't even trust my own judgment on this point. [4]My conscience is clear, but that doesn't prove I'm right. It is the Lord himself who will examine me and decide. [5]So don't make judgments about anyone ahead of time—before the Lord returns. For he will bring our darkest secrets to light and will reveal our private motives. Then God will give to each one whatever praise is due.

1 CORINTHIANS 4:1-5

¹⁵Don't you realize that your bodies are actually parts of Christ? Should a man take his body, which is part of Christ, and join it to a prostitute? Never! ¹⁶And don't you realize that if a man joins himself to a prostitute, he becomes one body with her? For the Scriptures say, "The two are united into one." ¹⁷But the person who is joined to the Lord is one spirit with him. ¹⁸Run from sexual sin! No other sin so clearly affects the body as this one does. For sexual immorality is a sin against your own body. ¹⁹Don't you realize that your body is the temple of the Holy Spirit, who lives in you and was given to you by God? You do not belong to yourself, ²⁰for God bought you with a high price. So you must honor God with your body.

1 CORINTHIANS 6:15-20

The phrase "damage control" is used frequently in political circles, referring to limiting negative press coverage following a potentially damaging act or statement by a politician. The phrase could, however easily be applied in a number of other areas. Take sex for instance. Sex is a wonderful expression of love between a husband and wife. It is an experience that strengthens and builds the marriage relationship. Why would damage control be needed in this area?

Paul addresses this topic in his first letter to the Corinthians, warning them to avoid sex outside of marriage Ignoring this warning today is not only spiritually harmful, but it can be physically deadly. It is important to stop the damage before it begins. As you read this passage, note the seriousness and intensity of Paul's teaching, and determine not to let sexual sin devastate your life.

Read 1 Corinthians 5:1–6:20

The hissing doubt of the world says that the Bible's restrictions only keep us from harmless pleasures. The world downplays the risks and plays up the pleasures, making exceptions and excuses.

Spare yourself some grief, and keep in mind the damage that sexual sin can do. It hurts God because it defies the guidelines that he so lovingly gave us. It hurts others because it breaks the commitment necessary to a relationship. And it deeply affects our personalities, which respond in anguish when we harm ourselves physically and spiritually. The destruction caused by sexual sin is so great that God urges us to *run* from it (1 Corinthians 6:18).

Sex itself doesn't do any harm—sexual sin does. Preserve God's design for sex in your life, and you'll enjoy the pleasure of his Holy Spirit.

When Lady Diana and Prince Charles were wed, there were high hopes for this romanticized couple. Their wedding was so perfect that it seemed to have been taken out of a storybook; few would have guessed the turmoil and pain their marriage would contain.

Perhaps marriages fail because people do not know how to build good relationships. Enter Paul and his first letter to the Corinthians. Paul knows the difficulty of building a successful marriage. He knows that marriage is rarely "storybook," and people should think twice before they call for the preacher. His cautious approach, however, is part of the Bible's overall celebration of love. The bottom line remains: Marriage is a gift from God.

For singles, Paul assures us that life is full and rich, and perhaps less complicated than being married. In any case, we all belong to God. Learn about marriage and about yourself in this section.

Read 1 Corinthians 7:1-40

Paul said that it was OK to marry, but he advised against it because it would lead to extra problems (1 Corinthians 7:28). Many people naively believe that marriage will solve several of their most pressing problems: loneliness, sexual temptation, deep emotional needs, and purpose in life. But marriage alone solves none of these uncertainties. In addition, it often brings about greater conflicts over finances, sacrificed dreams and ambitions, child rearing, personality differences, TV viewing, and a multitude of other issues.

³¹Those who use the things of the world should not become attached to them. For this world as we know it will soon pass away. ³²I want you to be free from the concerns of this life. An unmarried man can spend his time doing the Lord's work and thinking how to please him. ³³But a married man has to think about his earthly responsibilities and how to please his wife. ³⁴His interests are divided. In the same way, a woman who is no longer married or has never been married can be devoted to the Lord and holy in body and in spirit. But a married woman has to think about her earthly responsibilities and how to please her husband. ³⁵I am saying this for your benefit, not to place restrictions on you. I want you to do whatever will help you serve the Lord best, with as few distractions as possible.

1 CORINTHIANS 7:31-35

Only Christ can satisfy our deepest needs and protect us from temptation. As wonderful as it is, marriage cannot take Christ's place.

Whether you are married or single, find your contentment in Christ. Do not expect loved ones to meet your every need, even if they love you with all their heart.

¹I don't want you to forget, dear brothers and sisters, about our ancestors in the wilderness long ago. All of them were guided by a cloud that moved ahead of them, and all of them walked through the sea on dry ground. ²In the cloud and in the sea, all of them were baptized as followers of Moses. ³All of them ate the same spiritual food, ⁴and all of them drank the same spiritual water. For they drank from the spiritual rock that traveled with them, and that rock was Christ. ⁵Yet God was not pleased with most of them, and their bodies were scattered in the wilderness. ⁶These things happened as a warning to us, so that we would not crave evil things as they did, ⁷or worship idols as some of them did. . . . ¹²If you think you are standing strong, be careful not to fall. ¹³The temptations in your life are no different from what others experience.

1 CORINTHIANS 10:1-7, 12-13

Harry Houdini will always be remembered as a master of escape. No matter what the contraption, he could free himself. Chains, locks, straitjackets, boxes, jails, and trunks could not hold Houdini. It seemed he *always* managed to find a way out.

When it comes to temptation, God wants us to be like Houdini. That's the clear teaching in this section of 1 Corinthians. God wants us to escape temptation's chains, trunks, and straitjackets, but he does not expect us to do this alone. In fact, he has given us an advantage even Houdini did not have—the Holy Spirit showing the way to escape temptation's grasp.

Paul also teaches in this section that we need to be Houdini-like with these other issues as well: false guilt; useless restrictions; silly rules; vain legalism; and the special temptation of religious pride.

Read 1 Corinthians 8:1–11:1

Corinthian society was much like ours today. Immorality was everywhere, and the pressure on Christians to participate in it was tremendous. For believers surrounded and plagued by all this temptation, Paul offered these words of hope: There's *always* a way out (1 Corinthians 10:13).

At times we may feel that temptation is overpowering or impossible to resist, but God never lets that happen. Wrong desires and temptations happen to everyone all the time. In every case, God provides a way out.

There are five steps you can take to avoid unnecessary temptations: (1) learn to recognize tempting circumstances; (2) stay away from every activity you know is wrong; (3) consciously choose to do only what is right; (4) ask God to help you; and (5) ask friends who love God to hold you accountable. Most importantly, whenever you are tempted, take the way out that God provides. Do not think that you have no choice. There's always a way out.

Try to put together a model airplane that's missing a piece, and you will soon give up in frustration. Or if you are resourceful, you might make your own piece. But still, it will probably not fit as well as the original. Missing pieces become the most essential pieces, no matter how insignificant they may seem.

In this passage we learn that the same is true for spiritual gifts. All spiritual gifts are given by God to build up the church. But Christians tend to place more importance on some gifts and less on others. Those that are considered less important, however, are usually missed in one way or another when they are absent. As you read, think about the gifts that God has given you and how well you are using them to serve him.

Read 1 Corinthians 11:2–14:40

Some spiritual gifts are still thought of more highly than others. In fact, some gifts are completely discredited as real gifts. But no spiritual gift given by God should ever be considered useless. Likewise, "acceptable" or "desirable" gifts should not be put on a pedestal above others. As Paul writes, "God works in different ways, but it is the same God who does the work in all of us. A spiritual gift is given to each of us so we can help each other" (1 Corinthians 12:6-7).

Learn to appreciate the variety of spiritual gifts that God uses to build his church. Give people with various gifts an opportunity to serve. See them all as helpers who can do something useful for God. At the same time, use the gifts God has given you to strengthen your church for the glory of Christ. Don't allow yourself or your gifts to be "missing in action."

[1]Now, dear brothers and sisters, regarding your question about the special abilities the Spirit gives us. I don't want you to misunderstand this. [2]You know that when you were still pagans, you were led astray and swept along in worshiping speechless idols. [3]So I want you to know that no one speaking by the Spirit of God will curse Jesus, and no one can say Jesus is Lord, except by the Holy Spirit. [4]There are different kinds of spiritual gifts, but the same Spirit is the source of them all. [5]There are different kinds of service, but we serve the same Lord. [6]God works in different ways, but it is the same God who does the work in all of us. [7]A spiritual gift is given to each of us so we can help each other. . . . [11]It is the one and only Spirit who distributes all these gifts. He alone decides which gift each person should have.

1 CORINTHIANS 12:1-7, 11

⁵⁰What I am saying, dear brothers and sisters, is that our physical bodies cannot inherit the Kingdom of God. These dying bodies cannot inherit what will last forever. ⁵¹But let me reveal to you a wonderful secret. We will not all die, but we will all be transformed! ⁵²It will happen in a moment, in the blink of an eye, when the last trumpet is blown. For when the trumpet sounds, those who have died will be raised to live forever. And we who are living will also be transformed. ⁵³For our dying bodies must be transformed into bodies that will never die; our mortal bodies must be transformed into immortal bodies. ⁵⁴Then, when our dying bodies have been transformed into bodies that will never die, this Scripture will be fulfilled: "Death is swallowed up in victory. ⁵⁵O death, where is your victory? O death, where is your sting?"

1 CORINTHIANS 15:50-55

How do you feel about the future? If you asked your neighbors that question, what do you think they would say?

Floods, earthquakes, and fires have devastated certain parts of our country and the world. Add to that the crumbling economies and civil unrest in the third world, plus increased crime rates and pollution in the West, and you have one big world mess. In light of all this, the future does not look too bright.

For those who do not know Christ, the future looks even more bleak. For Christians, however, the future holds a great deal of hope. In this reading, Paul urges the Corinthian Christians to anchor their lives in the hope of eternal life, promised by God and won by Jesus Christ. Read and be encouraged. Find your hope in Christ.

Read 1 Corinthians 15:1–16:24

Did you know that Christians have great hope for the future? Someday all believers will be given new bodies. Eternal life in heaven with God will cancel out death and give us a joyful, permanent home with God far better than anything we could experience here. Nothing we do for God goes unnoticed—none of it is in vain (1 Corinthians 15:51-58).

No nuclear threat, no biological menace, no political coup, no financial collapse can undo our hope for the future. Despite the worldly problems we face each day, God has a plan for us and is in control of everything.

Do not despair. No matter what the headlines say, keep your eternal future in view and keep on doing the will of God.

"What is your only comfort in life and in death?" The first question of the Heidelberg Catechism—one of the great documents of the church—gets right to the heart of human despair. It is a question few people can face without a frown, for real comfort is hard to come by.

Paul, of all people, knows what it is like to feel despair. After all, he has been persecuted for his faith just about everywhere he has gone. But that is not the sum of Paul's experience—he also knows God's comfort personally. Because Paul knows how good God's comfort is, he wants Christians to rest in it and feel its healing power. So he writes his second letter to the Corinthians. Find comfort as you read this passage.

Read 2 Corinthians 1:1–2:13

Paul had an amazing testimony about God's comfort. In Asia, Paul was near death, but God was faithful to Paul and not only comforted him through his trial but also delivered him from death (2 Corinthians 1:9-10).

Throughout history many people have asked, *Why am I suffering?* At least one of the answers (though not the only one) is this: so that the comfort you receive from God can make you a comforter to others. Being comforted means receiving strength, encouragement, and hope to deal with our troubles. The more we suffer, the more comfort God gives us. The point is that we can then comfort people who hurt. Apart from experiencing God's comfort, we don't really know how to comfort others (1:3-5).

²May God our Father and the Lord Jesus Christ give you grace and peace. ³All praise to God, the Father of our Lord Jesus Christ. God is our merciful Father and the source of all comfort. ⁴He comforts us in all our troubles so that we can comfort others. When they are troubled, we will be able to give them the same comfort God has given us. ⁵For the more we suffer for Christ, the more God will shower us with his comfort through Christ. ⁶Even when we are weighed down with troubles, it is for your comfort and salvation! For when we ourselves are comforted, we will certainly comfort you. Then you can patiently endure the same things we suffer. ⁷We are confident that as you share in our sufferings, you will also share in the comfort God gives us.

2 CORINTHIANS 1:2-7

If you are feeling overwhelmed, allow God to comfort you. Remember that every trial you endure will help you better relate to other people who are suffering. After your trial has passed, look around for other weary souls who need your compassion and God's comfort. Then minister to them by the grace and strength of our Comforter, Jesus Christ.

¹⁴Don't team up with those who are unbelievers. How can righteousness be a partner with wickedness? How can light live with darkness? ¹⁵What harmony can there be between Christ and the devil? How can a believer be a partner with an unbeliever? ¹⁶And what union can there be between God's temple and idols? For we are the temple of the living God. As God said: "I will live in them and walk among them. I will be their God, and they will be my people. ¹⁷Therefore, come out from among unbelievers, and separate yourselves from them, says the Lord. Don't touch their filthy things, and I will welcome you. ¹⁸And I will be your Father, and you will be my sons and daughters, says the Lord Almighty."

2 CORINTHIANS 6:14-18

Charlie Brown and Snoopy, Lois Lane and Clark Kent, Tonto and the Lone Ranger, Captain Kirk and Mr. Spock—all these are examples of relationships that augment and thrive on differences. Opposites attract and differences can be healthy and good.

The one major exception to this rule: differences are not healthy and good in any intimate relationship between a Christian and a non-Christian. In this passage, Paul warns against forming binding relationships with people who don't know Christ. His warning is not merely a prejudice or preference. There is a real hazard in developing strong partnerships with people who have no vested interest in serving and glorifying God, so we need to beware.

Read 2 Corinthians 2:14–7:16

God wants us to avoid binding relationships with non-believers because such bonds can weaken our integrity, standards, or commitment to Christ. A partnership between a believer and a nonbeliever mismatches the values, goals, and desires of the two people involved. This doesn't mean that Christians should always avoid all relationships with non-Christians (see 1 Corinthians 5:9-10). We should definitely care for nonbelievers, showing them Christ's love. Also, a Christian who is married to a nonbelieving spouse should stay with that spouse, and not leave him or her (see 1 Corinthians 7:12-14). The bottom line, however, is that God wants us to be free to live righteous lives. Locking ourselves into personal or business relationships that could cause us to make moral compromises keeps us from doing that.

Protect your freedom to serve Christ. Don't make agreements, enter relationships, or form partnerships that could force you to do something wrong, immoral, or dishonest.

To discover the joy of giving, imagine what it would be like next Christmas if no one in your family gave you anything. Ditto for your birthday.

These examples just go to show how valuable giving really is. Imagine how foolish you would feel for doing any of the above. In a way, this is what the Corinthians were guilty of. They had made a commitment to give an offering, but when it came time to give, they changed their minds. This presented Paul with an opportunity to talk about giving and to hold the Corinthians accountable. As you read, hold *yourself* accountable for your giving habits.

Read 2 Corinthians 8:1–9:15

It is so easy for us to promise to give to the church or other Christian causes. But when it comes time to write out the check, our enthusiasm can quickly dwindle.

To avoid such situations, there are four steps you can take to maintain your enthusiasm when you give. First, realize that *how* you give matters more than *how much* you give. An attitude of cheerful giving is more important than the amount given. Second, budget for giving. Control your spending habits so that after you give to God, you will have enough left over to meet all of your financial obligations. That way you will not have to go back on your word in order to pay your bills. Third, realize that material wealth will not bring eternal satisfaction. Wealth can, however, be used to glorify God and lay up treasures in heaven, both of which will bring you eternal satisfaction. Fourth, give as a service to Christ, not as a way of obligating others to give back to you (otherwise it's not giving at all). If you promise to give, do it. If you can give anything at all, give it. The amount isn't the issue. The motivation and attitude is.

[10]Last year you were the first who wanted to give, and you were the first to begin doing it. [11]Now you should finish what you started. Let the eagerness you showed in the beginning be matched now by your giving. Give in proportion to what you have. [12]Whatever you give is acceptable if you give it eagerly. And give according to what you have, not what you don't have. [13]Of course, I don't mean your giving should make life easy for others and hard for yourselves. I only mean that there should be some equality. [14]Right now you have plenty and can help those who are in need. Later, they will have plenty and can share with you when you need it. In this way, things will be equal. [15]As the Scriptures say, "Those who gathered a lot had nothing left over, and those who gathered only a little had enough."

2 CORINTHIANS 8:10-15

⁶If I wanted to boast, I would be no fool in doing so, because I would be telling the truth. But I won't do it, because I don't want anyone to give me credit beyond what they can see in my life or hear in my message, ⁷even though I have received such wonderful revelations from God. So to keep me from becoming proud, I was given a thorn in my flesh, a messenger from Satan to torment me and keep me from becoming proud. ⁸Three different times I begged the Lord to take it away. ⁹Each time he said, "My grace is all you need. My power works best in weakness." So now I am glad to boast about my weaknesses, so that the power of Christ can work through me. ¹⁰That's why I take pleasure in my weaknesses, and in the insults, hardships, persecutions, and troubles that I suffer for Christ. For when I am weak, then I am strong.

2 CORINTHIANS 12:6-10

The first gunshot heard at many ten-kilometer races and marathons is not for runners but for wheelchair racers. These people have taken what many would consider a disadvantage and turned it into an asset. They have taken one of life's setbacks and have turned it into a major victory.

Like wheelchair racers, Paul, too, has a physical disadvantage. He never really explains what it is, but we can tell from what he says that it is painful and crippling. Paul does not let this condition overcome him, however. Instead, he counts it to his advantage. As you read, think of your "limitations" and how you can turn them into strengths for Christ's sake.

Read 2 Corinthians 10:1–13:13

Today, it is not easy to find someone so willing to boast about a personal weakness as Paul was. That is because weaknesses are seen as liabilities, not assets. But God sees the situation exactly the opposite. When we are strong and confident in our abilities, we may never notice our need for God. However, when we are weak and incapable, we may realize our need for him.

Have you ever felt weak? Your human frailty—whether physical, emotional, mental, or spiritual—gives God an opportunity to display his power in your life. Admit your weaknesses, and rely on God's power to be effective in those areas. Thank him for your talent, but thank him also for your weaknesses (2 Corinthians 12:9). They will help you develop Christian character, accomplish God's work, and deepen your worship.

A child and a new puppy are virtually inseparable. They can spend so much time together that you would think they were a young couple in love or a mother and her newborn. Every time you turn around they are playing together, napping together, or getting in trouble together. They can become best friends.

In a sense, fellowship with Christ is like a marriage or like that relationship between a child and a puppy. It is a relationship so intimate that Christ and the Christian are—or at least should be—inseparable.

In this passage, Paul describes his close relationship with Jesus. Paul reviews his life story to remind readers of the miracles God can perform. Paul even goes so far as to say that he has been crucified with Christ and that Christ now lives in him. How close are you to Christ?

Read Galatians 1:1–2:21

Paul was not one of the people crucified with Christ outside Jerusalem. So what did he mean by claiming to have been "crucified with Christ" (Galatians 2:20)? Paul meant that his sinful nature had been put to death when he accepted Christ as his Savior. In essence, he had exchanged one life for another. He had given up control of his life, as well as his desire to sin, in exchange for Christ's redemption from sin and new life in the Spirit.

This spiritual reality holds true for all Christians. When we trust in Christ as Savior, God looks at us as though we had died on the cross with Jesus. Because we have been crucified with Christ, we will also be raised with him (see Romans 6:5). Now Christ lives in us, and we are spiritually alive by his power. By Christ's power we are also no longer bound by the chains of sin.

The next time you face temptation, remember that you have been crucified with Christ and that he lives in you. Then resist the temptation, confident that Christ will strengthen you and provide a way of escape as well.

[17]Suppose we seek to be made right with God through faith in Christ and then we are found guilty because we have abandoned the law. Would that mean Christ has led us into sin? Absolutely not! [18]Rather, I am a sinner if I rebuild the old system of law I already tore down. [19]For when I tried to keep the law, it condemned me. So I died to the law—I stopped trying to meet all its requirements—so that I might live for God. [20]My old self has been crucified with Christ. It is no longer I who live, but Christ lives in me. So I live in this earthly body by trusting in the Son of God, who loved me and gave himself for me. [21]I do not treat the grace of God as meaningless. For if keeping the law could make us right with God, then there was no need for Christ to die.

Galatians 2:17-21

¹If a father dies and leaves an inheritance for his young children, those children are not much better off than slaves until they grow up, even though they actually own everything their father had. ²They have to obey their guardians until they reach whatever age their father set. ³And that's the way it was with us before Christ came. We were like children; we were slaves to the basic spiritual principles of this world. ⁴But when the right time came, God sent his Son, born of a woman, subject to the law. ⁵God sent him to buy freedom for us who were slaves to the law, so that he could adopt us as his very own children. ⁶And because we are his children, God has sent the Spirit of his Son into our hearts, prompting us to call out, "Abba, Father." ⁷Now you are no longer a slave but God's own child.

GALATIANS 4:1-7

Growing up in the White House would definitely have its perks. Every school day you would get a limo ride to and from school. In the summer you would travel the world on presidential trips with your parents. During campaign years, you would see the entire country with Mom and Dad. When you were at home, you would have more than one hundred rooms to explore. And if these benefits were not enough, you could brag a lot about what your parents did for a living.

Obviously the overwhelming majority of people have never had and never will have such privileges. But as Christians we are really better off than being a son or daughter of the president. That is because we are the children of the almighty God. As Paul reminds us in his letter to the Galatians, there is no greater privilege. What does it mean to you to be a child of the King of kings?

Read Galatians 3:1–4:31

Under Roman law, an adopted child was guaranteed all legal rights to his or her father's property. The child was not second-class, but equal to any other children, biological or adopted, in the father's family.

Before Christ died, we were all slaves to sin. But now that Christ has paid the penalty for our sin, we can accept his sacrifice as payment for our debt. When we do this, we are freed from the bondage of sin and are adopted into God's family. As God's adopted children, we share with Jesus all the rights of an heir.

If you belong to Christ, all he has belongs to you (Galatians 4:7). God is your heavenly Father. You can come boldly into his presence, confident that he will lovingly welcome you as his own child.

Some people are just destined to leave things better off than they found them. Take, for instance, John Chapman—the real-life orchardist who inspired the Johnny Appleseed legend. Chapman spent forty years of his life traveling across western Pennsylvania, Ohio, and Indiana sowing apple seeds. Undoubtedly, many people benefited from the fruits of his labor.

Paul, too, spent much of his adult life sowing seeds. In this reading, he teaches the Galatians about sowing and reaping. He also teaches them how to distinguish between fruit produced by evil and fruit produced by the Holy Spirit. The difference, not surprisingly, is tremendous. As you read, note that all believers are seed-planters, tree-growers, and fruit-pickers. How's your spiritual fruit?

Read Galatians 5:1–6:18

Most people know the eternal consequences of living a life of sin. But we may not be aware of the immediate consequences of our sins. For instance, when we lie or bend the truth, we do not consider how our credibility will be damaged when the truth eventually gets out. A credibility problem is only the beginning of other problems that may result, such as losing others' trust and friendship, losing a job, or damaging family relationships. All of these consequences could be one kind of immoral "crop." Just think about the negative results of other sinful behaviors. They are overwhelming. By contrast, "those who live to please the Spirit will harvest everlasting life from the Spirit" (Galatians 6:8). When we do this, we will not only reap the benefits of eternal life, but we will also give the Holy Spirit the opportunity to produce good fruit in us (5:22-23).

⁴Pay careful attention to your own work, for then you will get the satisfaction of a job well done, and you won't need to compare yourself to anyone else. ⁵For we are each responsible for our own conduct. ⁶Those who are taught the word of God should provide for their teachers, sharing all good things with them. ⁷Don't be misled—you cannot mock the justice of God. You will always harvest what you plant. ⁸Those who live only to satisfy their own sinful nature will harvest decay and death from that sinful nature. But those who live to please the Spirit will harvest everlasting life from the Spirit. ⁹So let's not get tired of doing what is good. At just the right time we will reap a harvest of blessing if we don't give up. ¹⁰Therefore, whenever we have the opportunity, we should do good to everyone—especially to those in the family of faith.

GALATIANS 6:4-10

What kind of seeds are you sowing in your life? Are you sowing to please your own desires? Or are you sowing to please God? If you are planting a selfish crop, try planting one that pleases God. Then have the patience to see how much more bountiful that crop will be in comparison to your own.

¹¹Don't forget that you Gentiles used to be outsiders. You were called "uncircumcised heathens" by the Jews, who were proud of their circumcision, even though it affected only their bodies and not their hearts. ¹²In those days you were living apart from Christ. You were excluded from citizenship among the people of Israel, and you did not know the covenant promises God had made to them. You lived in this world without God and without hope. ¹³But now you have been united with Christ Jesus. Once you were far away from God, but now you have been brought near to him through the blood of Christ. ¹⁴For Christ himself has brought peace to us. He united Jews and Gentiles into one people when, in his own body on the cross, he broke down the wall of hostility that separated us.

EPHESIANS 2:11-14

In November 1989, one of the most significant wall ever erected in history was torn to the ground. Thi barrier—the Berlin Wall—was built to keep the citi zens of East Berlin from fleeing to the West. But with the collapse of Communism, the wall was no longe necessary. This once-divided people was now free to reunite. They did so in October 1990, becoming the Federal Republic of Germany.

Almost two millennia before the Berlin Wall fell, Jesu broke down the greatest barrier that ever existe through his death on the cross. Sin stood between humans and God. This, however, was not the only barrier to fall on the day of Christ's crucifixion.

Read Ephesians 1:1–3:21

Paul wrote that Christ broke down "the wall of hostil ity" between Jews and Gentiles (Ephesians 2:14). The wall refers in one sense to the barrier that separated the Court of the Gentiles from the Court of Israe in the Temple. In another sense, this physical wal represents the societal barrier that existed between Jews and Gentiles. Jesus did not come to affirm these barriers but to offer salvation to anyone who would believe and trust in him, including Gentiles. Thu through his death, Jew and Gentile were saved and became part of one body (2:15).

Although Christ's death should unite all believers many Christians have erected barriers that divide God's family. Differences in doctrine, worship prac tices, and beliefs about acceptable behavior have severed parts of the body from one another. In addi tion, Christians have not been immune to prejudices such as racism.

As followers of Christ, we should not build walls between ourselves. Rather, we should remember that Christ's death served not only to redeem us from our sin but to end discord between believers.

The popularity of conflict resolution has put a damper on old-fashioned, red-eyed anger. Ranting, raving, and name-calling have almost become felonies today.

Despite this recent trend, conflict resolution is really nothing new. It has been around for a long time, even before Paul wrote his letter to the Ephesians. That is why Paul is able to give great advice in his letter for dealing with one of the main ingredients of conflict—anger. What stirs your temper?

In addition to handling anger, Paul also warns the Ephesians against illicit sex and smooth talkers who peddle fancy religious ideas. He also gives family members advice on how to relate to each other.

Read Ephesians 4:1–6:24

Anger is a dangerous emotion, "for anger gives a foothold to the Devil" (Ephesians 4:27). The Bible, however, does not tell us to avoid *being* angry but to avoid nursing our anger (4:26-27). When we respond in anger to a situation, we sin by choosing the destructive alternative to the problem. We also open ourselves up to developing a pattern of sinful behavior that may include physical abuse and verbal attacks. If we nurse our anger into a grudge, we will become bitter, which can negatively affect all our relationships—especially the one we have with God.

Learn to control your anger without letting it rule you. When you are angry, confess your feelings to God, and ask him to help you respond to the situation as Christ would. When you are angry, follow Paul's advice and resolve your conflict before the sun goes down (4:26). Let God, not your anger, determine how you act.

²²Throw off your old sinful nature and your former way of life, which is corrupted by lust and deception. ²³Instead, let the Spirit renew your thoughts and attitudes. ²⁴Put on your new nature, created to be like God—truly righteous and holy. ²⁵So stop telling lies. Let us tell our neighbors the truth, for we are all parts of the same body. ²⁶And "don't sin by letting anger control you." Don't let the sun go down while you are still angry, ²⁷for anger gives a foothold to the devil. ²⁸If you are a thief, quit stealing. Instead, use your hands for good hard work, and then give generously to others in need. ²⁹Don't use foul or abusive language. Let everything you say be good and helpful, so that your words will be an encouragement to those who hear them. ³⁰And do not bring sorrow to God's Holy Spirit by the way you live.

EPHESIANS 4:22-30

⁶I am certain that God, who began the good work within you, will continue his work until it is finally finished on the day when Christ Jesus returns. ⁷So it is right that I should feel as I do about all of you, for you have a special place in my heart. You share with me the special favor of God, both in my imprisonment and in defending and confirming the truth of the Good News. ⁸God knows how much I love you and long for you with the tender compassion of Christ Jesus. ⁹I pray that your love will overflow more and more, and that you will keep on growing in knowledge and understanding. ¹⁰For I want you to understand what really matters, so that you may live pure and blameless lives until the day of Christ's return. ¹¹May you always be filled with the fruit of your salvation—the righteous character produced in your life by Jesus Christ.

PHILIPPIANS 1:6-11

It would be nice to renovate a room or an entire home with the click of a button or a wave of a magic wand. Imagine the time you would save, the hassle and mess you would avoid, and all the money you would have left over because it did not cost you a penny. Despite these great advantages, there is one downside to all this convenience. You would not enjoy the satisfaction that comes from achieving a difficult task through hard labor and perseverance.

The Christian life is like a home-renovation project. It is a long, tiring, and sometimes painful process. There are no buttons to push to become a mature and perfect Christian instantly. But Paul reminds the Philippians that God will see his children through the process to completion and perfection. As you read, be encouraged that God is working in you, conforming you to the likeness of his own Son (see Romans 8:29).

Read Philippians 1:1-30

God begins a process of changing believers as soon as he saves them. Through the Holy Spirit, God works on each Christian's character bit by bit. This process takes a lifetime. Signs of progress come and go, but the work is never finished. Only when Christ returns will all believers be made perfect. Meanwhile, God's work in us continues (Philippians 1:6).

If you belong to Christ, do not let life's setbacks and failures discourage you. God has promised to finish the good work he has begun in you, and in time, he will do just that. In the meantime, keep your relationship with him vital by studying his Word and spending time in prayer. Also, encourage other Christians who may be struggling with failure by reminding them of God's promise.

erhaps no other topic today—except for salvation—more obscured by falsehood than that of rights. Just out everyone thinks that he or she is entitled to a ng list of rights not guaranteed by the Bible or the onstitution. For instance, some people believe they ave the right to do illegal drugs. Others think they ave the right to play their stereos loud any hour of e night. Some even believe they have the right to reak the law and get away with it.

learly, the demand for rights has gotten out of hand America. But Paul has an antidote for Christians ught up in or dismayed by a rights-obsessed soci-y. His advice is to imitate Christ, who sacrificed his ghts as God's own Son to save his people. As you ad, consider how you can become more like Christ, ur humble Lord and Savior.

Read Philippians 2:1-30

sus had the right to be worshiped, obeyed, and hon-red as God. Yet he did not lay claim to that right. istead he lowered himself, gave up his rights, and ied a humiliating death for our sins. He had more ghts than anyone will ever have, and he gave them l up to save his people (Philippians 2:5-11).

ll kinds of evil deeds have been committed in the ame of rights. Selfish attitudes, such as "I deserve it," It's my right," and "You have no right to stop me," ave been used to justify cheating, abortion, material-m, and countless other sins.

hose who follow Christ must not only refuse to lfishly uphold their rights but avoid having selfish attitudes as well. Instead, believers ould allow God to develop an attitude of humility within them.

³Don't be selfish; don't try to impress others. Be humble, thinking of others as better than yourselves. ⁴Don't look out only for your own interests, but take an interest in others, too. ⁵You must have the same attitude that Christ Jesus had. ⁶Though he was God, he did not think of equality with God as something to cling to. ⁷Instead, he gave up his divine privileges; he took the humble position of a slave and was born as a human being. When he appeared in human form, ⁸he humbled himself in obedience to God and died a criminal's death on a cross. ⁹Therefore, God elevated him to the place of highest honor and gave him the name above all other names, ¹⁰that at the name of Jesus every knee should bow, in heaven and on earth and under the earth, ¹¹and every tongue confess that Jesus Christ is Lord, to the glory of God the Father.

PHILIPPIANS 2:3-11

8Everything else is worthless when compared with the infinite value of knowing Christ Jesus my Lord. For his sake I have discarded everything else, counting it all as garbage, so that I could gain Christ 9and become one with him. I no longer count on my own righteousness through obeying the law; rather, I become righteous through faith in Christ. For God's way of making us right with himself depends on faith. 10I want to know Christ and experience the mighty power that raised him from the dead. I want to suffer with him, sharing in his death, 11so that one way or another I will experience the resurrection from the dead! 12I don't mean to say that I have already achieved these things or that I have already reached perfection. But I press on to possess that perfection for which Christ Jesus first possessed me.

PHILIPPIANS 3:8-12

Many people use the word *know* to cover the loosest possible connections. Someone might say, "Sure, I know Joe," when in fact, Joe is a friend of a friend. Or someone might say he knows about a product because he happened to see a commercial for it the other day. Knowing about people and things hardly means anything more than having heard about them.

The meaning of the word *know* was different for Paul. It did not mean having a casual acquaintance or hearing a passing reference. In this passage, Paul explains what it means for him to know someone. And that someone he knows is Christ. As you read, think of how well you know the Savior.

Read Philippians 3:1-21

Paul accomplished a great deal, and most who know anything about him consider him a great man. But he regarded all his accomplishments to be "garbage" when compared with the greatness of knowing Christ (Philippians 3:8). One personal relationship mattered more to Paul than anything else. That's why he endured so much suffering, rejection, physical abuse, and hardship—to stay close to Christ (3:10-11).

Many priorities clamor for our time—family, job, friends, and certain goals and plans. But our relationship with Christ matters more than all of them. To know Christ is the ultimate achievement, the first priority, the best option, the highest goal. A crowded schedule in order to set aside a few minutes each day for prayer and Bible study, a friend's disapproval, sacrifice of plans or pleasures are small prices to pay for such a reward.

Spend time getting to know your Savior. Make "knowing" Christ your highest priority.

In a celebrated Florida murder trial, an adolescent claimed television addiction as his defense for the crime. "The tube made him do it," his attorney argued.

Despite this argument, media programming never "makes" anyone do anything. What we put in our minds, however, does influence our actions. With this in mind, the apostle Paul advises believers in this last chapter of Philippians to meditate on truth and other pure thoughts. This includes our TV shows, movies, videos, and music. What are you doing to keep the garbage out?

Read Philippians 4:1-23

It seems nearly impossible today to think good and pure thoughts when we are constantly bombarded with immoral images, stories, and suggestions. Little entertainment today is free from profanity, "adult sexual themes," or violence. In addition, many books, magazines, and newspapers focus on the those "big three," in one way or another.

Many people defend violent, obscene, and sexually explicit media on the grounds that they do no harm. They say that watching violent television doesn't make people violent. But they miss the point. The evil lies in thinking untrue, bad, wrong, impure, ugly, coarse, and contemptible thoughts. Whether or not we become monsters, we all think monstrous thoughts. Even if all the negative thoughts never corrupt our behavior directly, our minds can still become filled with violent, evil images, and that is an evil in itself.

The situation is not hopeless, however. If you commit yourself to God and follow Paul's advice here, you can find media entertainment that is clean and even glorifying to God.

4Always be full of joy in the Lord. I say it again—rejoice! 5Let everyone see that you are considerate in all you do. Remember, the Lord is coming soon. 6Don't worry about anything; instead, pray about everything. Tell God what you need, and thank him for all he has done. 7Then you will experience God's peace, which exceeds anything we can understand. His peace will guard your hearts and minds as you live in Christ Jesus. 8And now, dear brothers and sisters, one final thing. Fix your thoughts on what is true, and honorable, and right, and pure, and lovely, and admirable. Think about things that are excellent and worthy of praise. 9Keep putting into practice all you learned and received from me—everything you heard from me and saw me doing. Then the God of peace will be with you.

PHILIPPIANS 4:4-9

⁹We have not stopped praying for you since we first heard about you. We ask God to give you complete knowledge of his will and to give you spiritual wisdom and understanding. ¹⁰Then the way you live will always honor and please the Lord, and your lives will produce every kind of good fruit. All the while, you will grow as you learn to know God better and better. ¹¹We also pray that you will be strengthened with all his glorious power so you will have all the endurance and patience you need. May you be filled with joy, ¹²always thanking the Father. He has enabled you to share in the inheritance that belongs to his people, who live in the light. ¹³For he has rescued us from the kingdom of darkness and transferred us into the Kingdom of his dear Son, ¹⁴who purchased our freedom and forgave our sins.

COLOSSIANS 1:9-14

The child away from home is always welcome to call collect, and your spouse's calls are welcome at work even during a busy day. With people you care about, talk is precious and almost never an inconvenience. With strangers, though, it can sometimes be just the opposite.

Prayer should be like talking to a loved one. But the only way that will happen is to talk with God often and about everything. As Paul illustrates with his own example in this letter, intimate prayer even includes praying for those we do not know. As you read, think about your relationship with your heavenly Father. Have you spoken with him lately?

Also notice the other lessons in these chapters on how to have a new life in Christ, and how to stay free of legalism.

Read Colossians 1:1–2:23

Paul had never met the Colossian Christians, but he faithfully prayed for them (Colossians 1:9-14). He did not just pray vaguely; he prayed about specifics, asking God to cause them to grow in their understanding, wisdom, and good works so that they could know God better. Paul didn't feel timid about praying for strangers.

Needs and prayer requests fly at us from all directions. Some of the people we hear about have casual connections to us. Others we know only as names or faces. Still others have no connection to us at all. Whatever their specific needs, all have the same basic need to grow in the knowledge of God. Paul's prayer for the Colossians gives us a good pattern to follow in praying for those we do not know.

The next time you learn of a stranger's needs, do not feel overwhelmed by another prayer request. Instead, pray for that person's needs as well as for his or her growth in understanding, wisdom, and knowledge of God.

In 1944, Allied armies launched a disastrous mission along a narrow corridor through Holland to reach a bridge on the Rhine. The story came to be called "A Bridge Too Far."

Like the Allies' mission to reach this bridge, efforts to bridge gaps between races, social classes, and religious denominations may seem too costly and unattainable. But Paul has the solution for this impossible mission: Jesus Christ. As you read, consider the walls that separate you from others. Determine, through Christ, to tear down those walls and build bridges.

This passage also has a lot to say about successful parenting, loyal employment, and setting life goals. At the end of his letter, Paul sends greetings to friends near and far.

Read Colossians 3:1–4:18

Jesus does not discriminate between people on the basis of race, nationality, ethnic background, level of education, or social position. He ignores all social distinctions and accepts all people who come to him in faith (Colossians 3:11).

Looking around the world, we see that such acceptance is not the norm. People constantly make distinctions between each other on the basis of nationality, race, education level, social standing, wealth, gender, religion, and power. Cultures practice and protect these distinctions. Governments sanction them. People fight over them. But God hates distinctions.

10Put on your new nature, and be renewed as you learn to know your Creator and become like him. 11In this new life, it doesn't matter if you are a Jew or a Gentile, circumcised or uncircumcised, barbaric, uncivilized, slave, or free. Christ is all that matters, and he lives in all of us. 12Since God chose you to be the holy people he loves, you must clothe yourselves with tenderhearted mercy, kindness, humility, gentleness, and patience. 13Make allowance for each other's faults, and forgive anyone who offends you. Remember, the Lord forgave you, so you must forgive others. 14Above all, clothe yourselves with love, which binds us all together in perfect harmony. 15And let the peace that comes from Christ rule in your hearts. For as members of one body you are called to live in peace. And always be thankful.
Colossians 3:10-15

Do not be like the world. Do not discriminate against others because of their race, gender, or socioeconomic status. Instead, pray that God will help you to love all people, and welcome them into your church community. Be like Jesus, befriending and loving those who are different from you. Never treat them as lesser people.

²We always thank God for all of you and pray for you constantly. ³As we pray to our God and Father about you, we think of your faithful work, your loving deeds, and the enduring hope you have because of our Lord Jesus Christ. ⁴We know, dear brothers and sisters, that God loves you and has chosen you to be his own people. ⁵For when we brought you the Good News, it was not only with words but also with power, for the Holy Spirit gave you full assurance that what we said was true. And you know of our concern for you from the way we lived when we were with you. ⁶So you received the message with joy from the Holy Spirit in spite of the severe suffering it brought you. In this way, you imitated both us and the Lord. ⁷As a result, you have become an example to all the believers in Greece—throughout both Macedonia and Achaia.

1 THESSALONIANS 1:2-7

"Monkey see, monkey do" describes the behavior of toddlers—and many grown-ups as well. Those with siblings especially pick up on new tricks and habits that they see brothers or sisters demonstrate. It's cute to see, but it's also scary for parents. They know that their children are watching them.

Paul understands this principle and has seen it applied in a more positive way. In this first letter to the church at Thessalonica, he commends the Thessalonians for their imitation of the one person everyone should strive to be like—Christ. In what ways do you imitate Christ?

Read 1 Thessalonians 1:1–3:13

When the Thessalonian Christians turned to Christ, they were dramatically changed. They gave up their idols, began serving God, and eagerly awaited Christ's return from heaven (1 Thessalonians 1:7-10). People soon noticed how they had changed, and news about them spread. No one could mistake the fact that these people believed in Jesus, because everyone could see their faith in action.

What was true then is also true now: If God is at work in your life, people will notice. Word will spread. People will see you doing "odd" things because you call Jesus Lord, and God's influence will soon be obvious to all. Whether you regard this as a blessing or a curse depends on you.

Do not underestimate the influence your good deeds can have on others. If you serve Christ, others who see the difference in you will be influenced to love and serve Christ too.

At the Academy Awards in Hollywood, award-winning movie stars, producers, and artists say thank-you to other stars, producers, and artists. Normally these people viciously compete with each other, but one night a year, they pause to recognize each other's achievements. Perhaps some express gratitude more often than this. For some, however, this is the only time they take to say thanks.

Saying thanks was not a once-a-year occasion for Paul. Rather it was a lifestyle. In the last chapter of 1 Thessalonians, Paul explains why believers should always maintain an attitude of thankfulness. When did you last thank God for his innumerable blessings?

Paul also gives practical reasons for living holy lives, especially in the area of sexual relations.

Read 1 Thessalonians 4:1–5:28

Paul wrote that believers should "be thankful in all circumstances" (1 Thessalonians 5:18). His statement can be easily misunderstood. Paul was not teaching that Christians should thank God *for* everything that happens in their lives. For instance, they should not thank God for personal sin and for the evil in the world. Evil comes from sin and from Satan, not from God. But they should thank God *in* every situation.

No matter what goes wrong or right, we can still be thankful to God for his presence and help. We have his promise that "God causes everything to work together for the good of those who love God and are called according to his purpose for them" (Romans 8:28), so we have a reason to be thankful.

At all times, keep in mind all that God has done. Then you will have plenty of reasons to be thankful—for God, for the joys he brings, and for the spiritual growth he can bring about through trials.

¹²Dear brothers and sisters, honor those who are your leaders in the Lord's work. They work hard among you and give you spiritual guidance. ¹³Show them great respect and wholehearted love because of their work. And live peacefully with each other. ¹⁴Brothers and sisters, we urge you to warn those who are lazy. Encourage those who are timid. Take tender care of those who are weak. Be patient with everyone. ¹⁵See that no one pays back evil for evil, but always try to do good to each other and to all people. ¹⁶Always be joyful. ¹⁷Never stop praying. ¹⁸Be thankful in all circumstances, for this is God's will for you who belong to Christ Jesus. ¹⁹Do not stifle the Holy Spirit. ²⁰Do not scoff at prophecies, ²¹but test everything that is said. Hold on to what is good. ²²Stay away from every kind of evil.

1 THESSALONIANS 5:12-22

[16]Now may our Lord Jesus Christ himself and God our Father, who loved us and by his grace gave us eternal comfort and a wonderful hope, [17]comfort you and strengthen you in every good thing you do and say. [3:1]Finally, dear brothers and sisters, we ask you to pray for us. Pray that the Lord's message will spread rapidly and be honored wherever it goes, just as when it came to you. [2]Pray, too, that we will be rescued from wicked and evil people, for not everyone is a believer. [3]But the Lord is faithful; he will strengthen you and guard you from the evil one. [4]And we are confident in the Lord that you are doing and will continue to do the things we commanded you. [5]May the Lord lead your hearts into a full understanding and expression of the love of God and the patient endurance that comes from Christ.

2 THESSALONIANS 2:16–3:5

A car accident wipes out a family. Cancer strikes a young wife and mother. A poor managerial decision puts an eager, productive employee out of work. Rebel soldiers slaughter people huddled in a church. Some events in life make no sense at all. That is why we call them tragedies.

In this reading, Paul offers no easy answers for life's hardships. He does, however, offer one piece of advice that, if followed, brings real comfort and encouragement for those who are persecuted. At the same time, he warns us of the evil in this world, in particular, of those who speak falsely for God.

Read 2 Thessalonians 1:1–2:17

God had given gifts of infinite value to the Thessalonians. Paul urged the Thessalonians to thank God for these gifts. Yet Paul also knew that they would face challenges to their belief in Christ. They would have doubts, and certain people and circumstances would encourage those doubts. Unless the Thessalonians had a firm conviction about all they had been taught, their faith would die. So Paul urged them to "stand firm and keep a strong grip on the teaching we passed on to you" (2 Thessalonians 2:15). They had the Scriptures and the letters that Paul had written to keep them on track.

As he did for the Thessalonians, God has given us a great gift—his Word. Yet it is so easy to take this gift for granted and not use it. When we stop using his gift, we make ourselves more susceptible to falsehoods. To strengthen our faith and protect ourselves from falsehoods, we need to spend time in God's Word every day.

If you do not spend time reading your Bible every day, think of things you can cut from your schedule to make time for God. If you faithfully spend time in the Word, challenge yourself to spend even more time with God.

wo work ethics are at odds in our culture today. One ys that people should work hard for a living. The ther says that people deserve the easy life. Why work hen you can play, right?

hese same work ethics were around during Paul's ay. So Paul addresses the real issue behind the bad ork ethic—laziness. He not only condemns the bad thic but gives the Thessalonians an example of what good work ethic looks like. As you read, determine ever to be lazy in the things of God.

lso in this passage, Paul asks for prayer, guarantees ae authenticity of his letter, then says good-bye in is own special way.

Read 2 Thessalonians 3:1-18

ome people in the Thessalonian church were falsely eaching that because Christ's second coming could appen any day, people should set aside their respon- ibilities, quit work, do no future planning, and simply vait for the Lord to appear. But their lack of activity ed them into sin. These people became a burden to he church, which was supporting them. They wasted ime that could have been spent helping others, and hey gossiped (2 Thessalonians 3:6-11). They may ave thought they were being more spiritual by not vorking, but Paul told them to be responsible and et back to work.

3eing ready for Christ means obeying him in every rea of life. Because we know Christ is coming, we nust do everything we can to live in a way that will lease him when he arrives.

⁶Stay away from all believers who live idle lives . . . ⁷For you know that you ought to imitate us. We were not idle when we were with you. . . . ⁸We worked hard day and night so we would not be a burden to any of you. ⁹We certainly had the right to ask you to feed us, but we wanted to give you an example to follow. ¹⁰Even while we were with you, we gave you this command: "Those unwilling to work will not get to eat." ¹¹Yet we hear that some of you are living idle lives, refusing to work and meddling in other people's business. ¹²We command such people and urge them in the name of the Lord Jesus Christ to settle down and work to earn their own living. ¹³As for the rest of you, dear brothers and sisters, never get tired of doing good. ¹⁴Take note of those who refuse to obey what we say in this letter. Stay away from them so they will be ashamed.

2 THESSALONIANS 3:6-14

Make the most of your talent and time. Cut out activities that only distract or make it tarder for you to fulfill your responsibilities.

³When I left for Macedonia, I urged you to stay there in Ephesus and stop those whose teaching is contrary to the truth. ⁴Don't let them waste their time in endless discussion of myths and spiritual pedigrees. These things only lead to meaningless speculations, which don't help people live a life of faith in God. ⁵The purpose of my instruction is that all believers would be filled with love that comes from a pure heart, a clear conscience, and genuine faith. ⁶But some people have missed this whole point. They have turned away from these things and spend their time in meaningless discussions. ⁷They want to be known as teachers of the law of Moses, but they don't know what they are talking about, even though they speak so confidently.

1 TIMOTHY 1:3-7

When in trouble, often a child's favorite trick is to divert a parent from the main issue to something else. A typical conversation may go like this:

"Why were you out so late?"

"Worried about me? You worry too much, Mom. Life would be happier without so much worry. We need a family vacation. What about Disneyland?"

Spiritual speculators in the church are much like children who divert their parents' attention. Paul warns his readers not to get distracted by the false teachers who are more interested in their own reputation than in God's truth. Their religion is complex and confusing. As you read, determine to let nothing cloud God's truth and your view of Christ.

Read 1 Timothy 1:1-20

Speculating about what the Bible may mean can make for interesting conversation, but it can also cause us to muddle the intent of God's message. We need to guard against over-spiritualizing parts of the Bible or falling in love with our own ideas about it. The Good News of salvation in Jesus Christ doesn't need new or additional "improvements" invented by clever thinkers.

The main point of Scripture is that Jesus came to save people from their sins. Let that message hold center stage in your mind and heart. Do not waste your time speculating on minute details of the Bible. You may never know the real meaning behind the detail and, at the same time, only draw attention away from the One who gave his Word to point people to him.

More than a million conversations a day trade news about how to win on the stock market. More than 10 million try to predict the outcome of upcoming sports events. How many conversations relate to politics—100 million? More? Too many, most people would say.

Just when you think you have had enough of politics, Paul throws his hat in the ring. But the good news about Paul's involvement in this arena is that he is not throwing mud but advocating prayer—for leaders. How often do *you* pray for your elected officials?

In addition to promoting prayer for our political leaders, Paul also discusses the standards we should uphold for church leaders.

Read 1 Timothy 2:1–3:16

Paul urged Timothy to pray for civil authorities so that believers could enjoy peace and freedom, thus enabling them to live for Christ and share the gospel with others. And the reason this matters so much is that God desires all people to be saved (1 Timothy 2:4; see 2 Peter 3:9).

God wants us to take the news of Christ to others, but this won't happen if chaos and disorder have us occupied. Not everyone *will* be saved—many refuse to go through Christ's narrow gate (see Matthew 7:13; 25:31-46; John 12:44-50; Hebrews 10:26-29). But the message about Christ matters so much to God that we should pray and work for the freedom to publish it.

God's appointed means for keeping the peace resides in the hallowed halls of our civil governments, at every level. Pray often for the leaders and authorities who govern our land.

¹I urge you, first of all, to pray for all people. Ask God to help them; intercede on their behalf, and give thanks for them. ²Pray this way for kings and all who are in authority so that we can live peaceful and quiet lives marked by godliness and dignity. ³This is good and pleases God our Savior, ⁴who wants everyone to be saved and to understand the truth. ⁵For there is only one God and one Mediator who can reconcile God and humanity—the man Christ Jesus. ⁶He gave his life to purchase freedom for everyone. This is the message God gave to the world at just the right time. ⁷And I have been chosen as a preacher and apostle to teach the Gentiles this message about faith and truth.

1 TIMOTHY 2:1-7

¹²Fight the good fight for the true faith. Hold tightly to the eternal life to which God has called you, which you have confessed so well before many witnesses. . . . ¹⁵For at just the right time Christ will be revealed from heaven by the blessed and only almighty God, the King of all kings and Lord of all lords. . . . ¹⁷Teach those who are rich in this world not to be proud and not to trust in their money, which is so unreliable. Their trust should be in God, who richly gives us all we need for our enjoyment. ¹⁸Tell them to use their money to do good. They should be rich in good works and generous to those in need, always being ready to share with others. ¹⁹By doing this they will be storing up their treasure as a good foundation for the future so that they may experience true life.
1 Timothy 6:12, 15, 17-19

Sharing can be a measure of love. People who lov[e] each other willingly share all they have. Conversel[y] when sharing becomes a chore, love is at low tide.

Just as couples in love share with one another gen[-] erously, so should Christians. In this reading, Pau[l] admonishes believers to share their wealth with thos[e] in need. But he does not stop there. He tells Chris[-] tians to give happily, from the heart, and not merel[y] out of duty to the law. How does your giving com[-] pare to Paul's admonition?

In this section, Paul also advises young leaders on ho[w] to win the respect of older people, and he reveals th[e] source of true contentment.

Read 1 Timothy 4:1–6:21

Timothy lived and ministered in Ephesus, a large an[d] wealthy city. His church probably had many wealth[y] members. Paul's instructions to Timothy include[d] the charge to teach the believers how to manag[e] wealth (1 Timothy 6:17-19). Having a lot of mone[y] he wrote, carries great responsibility. The wealth[y] must be generous, but they should not be arrogan[t] just because they have a lot to give. They must tak[e] care not to hoard their money for security instead o[f] finding their security in God. And they should tak[e] encouragement from the fact that their giving store[s] up "treasure as a good foundation for the future" (6:19).

If you have a surplus of money, the opportunities to do good with it are almost endless. Rather than keeping all of it for yourself, ask God how you can use the resources he ha[s] given you to build up treasures in heaven. If money is scarce, you can still be generou[s] with what you have. Just be sure to ask for direction to help you share what you have wisely.

"I just want to" is a kid's reply

To parents begging for reasons why.

I just want to … experiment with drugs, find out about sex, try bungee jumping, shop till I drop. "Don't ask why," they beg, and parents say no.

For Christians who have a hard time resisting the lure of bad ideas and do not have parents around to stop them, Paul says, "Run!" Do not even give the temptation time to present its case. Just get out of there. Live boldly, Paul writes, but live wisely. A little bit of well-placed fear goes a long way. As you read, consider when you should run and when you should stand and fight.

In addition to his advice for making a hasty retreat, in these chapters Paul also encourages Christians to not be afraid of suffering and to not be ashamed of their work for the gospel.

Read 2 Timothy 1:1–2:26

Paul urged Timothy to run away from anything that tempted him to do wrong (2 Timothy 2:22). Some may consider this to be cowardly, but wise people run from dangers and from enemies they cannot fight. They know their limits and respect their weak spots. When the danger involves temptation, they avoid it altogether. Running from a strong temptation makes more sense than trying to resist it.

What recurring temptation do you have difficulty resisting? Avoid any situation that tempts you in that area. Know when to run and don't be ashamed to do so. There's no point in trying to be tough and falling into sin as a result (see 1 Timothy 6:11).

[20]In a wealthy home some utensils are made of gold and silver, and some are made of wood and clay. The expensive utensils are used for special occasions, and the cheap ones are for everyday use. [21]If you keep yourself pure, you will be a special utensil for honorable use. Your life will be clean, and you will be ready for the Master to use you for every good work. [22]Run from anything that stimulates youthful lusts. Instead, pursue righteous living, faithfulness, love, and peace. Enjoy the companionship of those who call on the Lord with pure hearts. [23]Again I say, don't get involved in foolish, ignorant arguments that only start fights. [24]A servant of the Lord must not quarrel but must be kind to everyone, be able to teach, and be patient with difficult people. [25]Gently instruct those who oppose the truth.

2 TIMOTHY 2:20-25

¹⁴Remain faithful to the things you have been taught. You know they are true, for you know you can trust those who taught you. ¹⁵You have been taught the holy Scriptures from childhood, and they have given you the wisdom to receive the salvation that comes by trusting in Christ Jesus. ¹⁶All Scripture is inspired by God and is useful to teach us what is true and to make us realize what is wrong in our lives. It corrects us when we are wrong and teaches us to do what is right. ¹⁷God uses it to prepare and equip his people to do every good work. . . . ⁴:²Preach the word of God. Be prepared, whether the time is favorable or not. Patiently correct, rebuke, and encourage your people with good teaching. . . . ⁵Don't be afraid of suffering for the Lord. Work at telling others the Good News, and fully carry out the ministry God has given you.

2 TIMOTHY 3:14-17; 4:2, 5

Little League coaches know that very young ballplayers have to use a tee to learn how to bat before they can swing and hit pitches. Surgeons have their interns watch procedures before they let them pick up a scalpel. Parents of budding violinists endure hours of squeaks before enjoying the beautiful notes of a school orchestra. Practice makes perfect—or at least makes things better.

The same principle applies to spiritual growth. Believers cannot get better (become more like Christ) without regularly studying God's Word and applying it to their lives. That is why Paul tells Timothy about the Bible's usefulness in teaching what is true and right. As you read, evaluate your "practice" schedule.

Also in this passage, Paul gives a glimpse of the future. Life on earth does not look good for Christians, but Christ will return soon and take us to a better place.

Read 2 Timothy 3:1–4:22

God gave the Bible so that people could learn to love and serve him (2 Timothy 3:16-17). A lot of the study and learning we do in life aims to make us smarter or more knowledgeable. That will happen when we study the Bible, but it's not the main reason that God gave us his Word. God wants us to change our thoughts, behavior, and character.

Some people use their knowledge of the Bible only to win arguments or to make themselves look clever. Besides missing the aim of having such knowledge, they become worse people, not better, by falling into pride (see 1 Corinthians 8:1-3).

Never flaunt your knowledge of God's Word. Study the Bible to learn how to live, not to win an argument or to show somebody up. Seek to know Christ and learn to do good.

Phonies are not always easy to spot. Some look so real that they could fool the most suspicious and skeptical people. Phony people may even believe their own scams.

In this reading, Paul urges Titus to warn the Christians on Crete to beware of phonies. These false teachers are not concerned with truth. As you read, think of how you can determine truth from error, what is real from what is false.

In this chapter, Paul also outlines what is required of spiritual leaders, and he reminds Titus that God always tells the truth.

Read Titus 1:1-16

Paul warned Titus about people who teach wrong doctrines (Titus 1:10-14). He told this protégé and young pastor to be harsh with these false teachers because they teach from evil motives and lead people away from Christ. Some false teachers simply have misguided opinions or a poor understanding of the Bible. Others *try* to deceive—they pretend to be sincere while hiding their cravings for money or influence over others. Jesus and the apostles repeatedly warned against such false teachers (see Mark 13:22; Acts 20:29; 2 Thessalonians 2:3-12; 2 Peter 3:3-7).

Many people think that false teaching about God makes little difference. But believing falsehoods about God, Christ, or salvation can be more fatal to your faith than drinking poison. False teachings about eternal life meddle with people's eternal destiny.

⁶An elder must live a blameless life. He must be faithful to his wife, and his children must be believers who don't have a reputation for being wild or rebellious. ⁷For an elder must live a blameless life. He must not be arrogant or quick-tempered; he must not be a heavy drinker, violent, or dishonest with money. ⁸Rather, he must enjoy having guests in his home, and he must love what is good. He must live wisely and be just. He must live a devout and disciplined life. ⁹He must have a strong belief in the trustworthy message he was taught; then he will be able to encourage others with wholesome teaching and show those who oppose it where they are wrong.

TITUS 1:6-9

Be on guard against false spiritual teachers, and be careful of any person who claims to have spiritual truth. False teachers betray their motives by pointing people away from the Bible and toward other ideas. Test all teachings by comparing them to God's Word before letting someone teach and lead you.

¹Promote the kind of living that reflects wholesome teaching. ²Teach the older men to exercise self-control, to be worthy of respect, and to live wisely. They must have sound faith and be filled with love and patience. ³Similarly, teach the older women to live in a way that honors God. They must not slander others or be heavy drinkers. Instead, they should teach others what is good. ⁴These older women must train the younger women to love their husbands and their children, ⁵to live wisely and be pure, to work in their homes, to do good, and to be submissive to their husbands. . . . ⁶In the same way, encourage the young men to live wisely. ⁷And you yourself must be an example to them by doing good works of every kind. Let everything you do reflect the integrity and seriousness of your teaching.

TITUS 2:1-7

Effective teaching depends on demonstration. We can find out how to do anything by just reading about it, but usually the directions or concepts do not sink in until we have seen the technique or skill demonstrated. The teacher says, "Watch me," and we learn.

Demonstrations are also useful in Christianity. Like anything else new and different, living the Christian life may be difficult to grasp and understand just by reading the instruction manual. That is why Paul advises Titus to live the Christian life in front of everyone he meets. It is a demonstration on how living for Christ is done. What do people learn about Christ when they watch you?

Read Titus 2:1-15

Paul urged Titus to be a good example to those around him, to let his life be a living demonstration of the truth and doctrine he taught (Titus 2:7). Considering the fact that Titus was a preacher, that was quite a charge—part of his job had nothing to do with talking. As a leader, he needed to *show* the way, not just point in that direction.

Nothing communicates quite like a demonstration. It's one thing for a parent to say, "Floss your teeth," and quite another for that mom or dad to be a flosser. Seeing the living example, children will begin to learn the skill. And it's one thing for a person to say, "Christ is number one in my life," and quite another to see that statement lived out in values, choices, and commitments.

Place a great deal of emphasis on how you live, not just on what you stand for. Give attention to your habits, plans, lifestyle choices, and scheduling priorities. Bring these areas of your life under the jurisdiction of Christ so when people hear about your faith, they will have no problem understanding what you mean.

far-fetched explanations of how things work sometimes turn out to be right. The idea that the earth revolves around the sun was heresy eight hundred years ago! Silly, brainless, and hostile arguments against the truth often oppose and delay common-sense progress.

Using good judgment, we do well when we make smart choices and stay clear of stupidity, Paul writes. Pointless arguments tangle the brain, he insists. Use your best intelligence, with openness to new ideas, but do not get tangled up in nonsense. As you read, consider what you can do to stay focused on the important issues in life.

At the close of this letter, Paul also writes of more important projects that beg for attention.

Read Titus 3:1-15

Paul warned Titus, as he warned Timothy, not to get involved in foolish and futile arguments (Titus 3:9; see 2 Timothy 2:14). Paul knew that Titus would often get into discussions about emotionally charged topics. He knew that this pastor's study of the Scriptures and teachings about them would invite heated discussion. Thus, Paul urged Titus to choose his battles carefully and to avoid arguments that would reach no conclusion.

Some arguments lead nowhere. They concern topics that don't matter or do no one any good, even if someone does "win." We should avoid those kinds of arguments.

¹Remind the believers to submit to the government and its officers. They should be obedient, always ready to do what is good. ²They must not slander anyone and must avoid quarreling. Instead, they should be gentle and show true humility to everyone. ³Once we, too, were foolish and disobedient. We were misled and became slaves to many lusts and pleasures. Our lives were full of evil and envy, and we hated each other. ⁴But—"When God our Savior revealed his kindness and love, ⁵he saved us, not because of the righteous things we had done, but because of his mercy. He washed away our sins, giving us a new birth and new life through the Holy Spirit. ⁶He generously poured out the Spirit upon us through Jesus Christ our Savior. ⁷Because of his grace he declared us righteous and gave us confidence that we will inherit eternal life."

TITUS 3:1-7

If you're in disagreement with someone over an issue, consider what difference it makes who's right. If it's not important, then give up arguing. Change the subject or politely excuse yourself. Make peace a prime goal even when you discuss significant matters (see Romans 12:18).

[10]Show kindness to my child, Onesimus. . . . [11][He] hasn't been of much use to you in the past, but now he is very useful to both of us. [12]I am sending him back to you, and with him comes my own heart. [13]I wanted to keep him here with me while I am in these chains for preaching the Good News, and he would have helped me on your behalf. [14]But I didn't want to do anything without your consent. I wanted you to help because you were willing, not because you were forced. [15]It seems Onesimus ran away for a little while so that you could have him back forever. [16]He is no longer like a slave to you . . . for he is a beloved brother, especially to me. Now he will mean much more to you, both as a man and as a brother in the Lord. [17]So if you consider me your partner, welcome him as you would welcome me.

PHILEMON 1:10-17

Have you ever had the unfortunate experience of being looked down upon? Perhaps you were at a social occasion dressed a little too casually when you were snubbed. Maybe you ventured into "the wrong part of town" and were assaulted with evil stares or racial slurs. Whatever your experience may have been, one thing is certain—it hurt.

Paul's letter to Philemon deals with this issue. Here Paul writes: Respect all people. Give everyone your love, and do not regard social class, economic position, career field, or family background as a basis for judging others. Wage earners and board chairpersons are brothers and sisters in the sight of God. As you read, think of any prejudices that you may harbor.

Read Philemon 1:1-25

Onesimus was a slave who had run away from his master, Philemon. While Onesimus was on the run, he had become a Christian. What a difference his new identity would make in his relationship with Philemon. Now they were no longer just master and servant but brothers in Christ (Philemon 1:16). Because of Christ, both Onesimus and Philemon had equal status in God's family, and Paul wrote Philemon to remind him of this.

A Christian's identity as a member of God's family overrides all other distinctions. Race doesn't matter; social status doesn't matter; ethnic background doesn't matter; political label doesn't matter; gender doesn't matter—all Christians are part of the same family, equals in Christ, equally important, equally loved by God.

Don't look down on any fellow Christians. In Christ, all stand before God as your equal (see Galatians 3:28). Treat your fellow Christians as the equals they are.

The United States of America was established so that people can have a say in how they are governed. But as soon as many of the elected officials take office, it seems that the citizens who elected them can forget about hearing from them until the next election. Perhaps, for most politicians, the will of the people is easier to forget than the power of the press. This confusion of command makes it impossible to know who really is in charge of the country—the people, the politicians, or the media.

Many who spend their time trying to figure out who is in control down here overlook the one who is in control of everything—Jesus. In this reading, the writer of Hebrews reminds readers that just because Jesus is seated in heaven does not mean that he is unaware or uninvolved in the events on earth. As you read and think of current events, remember that your sovereign and all-powerful Lord reigns.

Read Hebrews 1:1–2:18

Sometimes the chaos, violence, immorality, and evil of this world can cloud our vision of Jesus' reign. Yet Christ does rule in heaven, and everything on earth belongs to him. He is King, even if all his subjects do not yet obey him. This is Christ's world. He has control of it.

If you want to affect the world, talk to Jesus about it. Christ's reign on earth has not yet begun, but his rule from heaven is no less real. When you are confused by present events and grow anxious about the future, remember Jesus' true position and authority. He is Lord of all, and one day he will rule on earth as he does now in heaven (see Matthew 6:10).

[1]Long ago God spoke many times and in many ways to our ancestors through the prophets. [2]And now in these final days, he has spoken to us through his Son. God promised everything to the Son as an inheritance, and through the Son he created the universe. [3]The Son radiates God's own glory and expresses the very character of God, and he sustains everything by the mighty power of his command. When he had cleansed us from our sins, he sat down in the place of honor at the right hand of the majestic God in heaven. [4]This shows that the Son is far greater than the angels, just as the name God gave him is greater than their names. [5]For God never said to any angel what he said to Jesus: "You are my Son. Today I have become your Father." God also said, "I will be his Father, and he will be my Son."

HEBREWS 1:1-5

⁹There is a special rest still waiting for the people of God. ¹⁰For all who have entered into God's rest have rested from their labors, just as God did after creating the world. ¹¹So let us do our best to enter that rest. But if we disobey God, as the people of Israel did, we will fall. ¹²For the word of God is alive and powerful. It is sharper than the sharpest two-edged sword, cutting between soul and spirit, between joint and marrow. It exposes our innermost thoughts and desires. ¹³Nothing in all creation is hidden from God. Everything is naked and exposed before his eyes, and he is the one to whom we are accountable.

Hebrews 4:9-13

Anyone who has ever had surgery knows how scary it can be. The fact that surgeons cut and stitch every day does not help, either. We still feel anxious and frightened about having our bodies opened up, even in the simplest procedures. If not for anesthesia, the operation would be indescribably painful, but even with the help of unconsciousness we know that we will be vulnerable and helpless during the procedure. And afterward, some kind of painful recovery will follow. No one can blame anyone for feeling nervous about all that.

As scary as surgery is, there is a nonphysical operation that scares some people even more. The writer of Hebrews clues us in as to who the doctor is, as well as what instrument he will be using to perform this surgery. No anesthesia is needed here, only a humble and willing heart. Are you open to spiritual surgery by the divine Surgeon?

Read Hebrews 3:1–4:13

God uses his Word to work on our lives as a surgeon uses a scalpel (Hebrews 4:12). It cuts through our pretender's skin. It goes after the cancerous sinful growths that infect our character. It attacks our spiritually diseased condition.

For this very reason, many people fear the Bible. They fear the discomfort and pain in confronting and dealing with their spiritual problems. They fear the changes that will take place in their character and life. But changes for good should not be feared, for God removes from our character only what harms us—our sinful attitudes and behaviors.

Do not be afraid to read the Bible. Let God do corrective surgery on your thoughts, attitudes, and behaviors. Although it may be painful now, the end results will be well worth the discomfort you may experience.

It seems as though everything changes. Friendships, jobs, children, marriage relationships, financial security—they all change for better or for worse. Can anything or anyone be counted on to remain the same?

Yes. Today's passage invites us to step onto the solid foundation of God. If we can count on anything, we can count on him. As you read, feel both calmed by finding security in him and energized for all the changes in and around you.

Just as this passage reminds us of God's steadfastness, it also reminds us of our need to change. In addition, it presents Jesus in a new light, as High Priest.

Read Hebrews 4:14–7:28

The original readers of this letter may have wondered, just as Christians sometimes wonder today, *Will God ever revoke his salvation?* They could rest assured, as can we, that the answer is no. God does what he says he will do, and he has promised to save all who call on him (Hebrews 6:18). He does not change his plans just because we do.

If you worry about your salvation, ask yourself whether you sincerely asked God to save you from your sins. If you did, be assured that he has done what you asked. But if you still have doubts every once in a while, remember that God is faithful. He will not abandon you.

[16]When people take an oath, they call on someone greater than themselves to hold them to it. And without any question that oath is binding. [17]God also bound himself with an oath, so that those who received the promise could be perfectly sure that he would never change his mind. [18]So God has given both his promise and his oath. These two things are unchangeable because it is impossible for God to lie. Therefore, we who have fled to him for refuge can have great confidence as we hold to the hope that lies before us. [19]This hope is a strong and trustworthy anchor for our souls. It leads us through the curtain into God's inner sanctuary. [20]Jesus has already gone in there for us. He has become our eternal High Priest in the order of Melchizedek.

HEBREWS 6:16-20

¹¹Christ has now become the High Priest over all the good things that have come. He has entered that greater, more perfect Tabernacle in heaven, which was not made by human hands and is not part of this created world. ¹²With his own blood—not the blood of goats and calves—he entered the Most Holy Place once for all time and secured our redemption forever. ¹³Under the old system, the blood of goats and bulls and the ashes of a young cow could cleanse people's bodies from ceremonial impurity. ¹⁴Just think how much more the blood of Christ will purify our consciences from sinful deeds so that we can worship the living God. For by the power of the eternal Spirit, Christ offered himself to God as a perfect sacrifice for our sins.

HEBREWS 9:11-14

A broken leg usually means a time of walking on crutches. If the break is bad enough, getting around becomes impossible without them. Some may think this novel for a time, but the novelty soon wears off. The patient looks forward to the day when the crutches can be thrown into the closet for good.

Before Jesus came to this earth and died for everyone's sins, people depended on the crutch of animal sacrifice for forgiveness. But Christ's blood heals and frees people from sin and their dependence on spiritual crutches. Are you leaning on a crutch or on Christ?

As you read this passage, notice the comparisons between the old covenant of animal sacrifice and the new covenant with Jesus as your High Priest.

Read Hebrews 8:1–10:18

Animal sacrifices played an important role in Israel's relationship with God. They provided a means for people to cover their sins until the coming of Christ. But these sacrifices only imitated and foreshadowed Jesus' future sacrifice. His offering paid for all sin, once and for all, and did what the animal sacrifices could only point to: *full* payment *forever* for sin.

Today, Jesus serves as our High Priest before God the Father in heaven (Hebrews 8:1-2; 9:24-28). Our hope of eternal life lies in him, and our day-to-day access to God depends on Jesus' loving intercession on our behalf.

Look to Christ for fulfillment of your spiritual needs, because he can meet them all.

Toddlers are notorious for their short attention spans. Older children and especially adults, however, can fix their attention on something for quite some time. Have you ever tried to pull a ten-year-old away from a favorite video game? Or how about trying to pull an avid sports fan away from the game of the week?

It is with this kind of absorption that the writer of Hebrews says we should fix our attention on Jesus. Unlike video games and sporting events, focusing our entire attention on Jesus can benefit us in many ways, the most important of which is a deep relationship with God. As you read this passage, refocus your eyes on Christ.

This reading also teaches us some graduate-level lessons in faith and helps us to understand more about the *D*-word—discipline.

Read Hebrews 10:19–13:25

Jesus suffered tremendous humiliation, injustice, and physical pain to do God's will (Hebrews 12:2-4). Strangers arrested him for crimes he didn't commit, beat him, mocked him, and spat on him. Friends deserted him. His heavenly Father left him to die alone. He died slowly and painfully in the company of common thieves. He became an offering for our sin (see 2 Corinthians 5:21). That is the price Jesus paid to obey his heavenly Father.

The struggles you endure to follow Jesus are real. It takes energy and commitment to say no to sinful desires, to do good deeds that you don't want to do, and to discipline yourself to pray and study God's Word on a regular basis.

[1]Let us strip off every weight that slows us down, especially the sin that so easily trips us up. And let us run with endurance the race God has set before us. [2]We do this by keeping our eyes on Jesus, the champion who initiates and perfects our faith. Because of the joy awaiting him, he endured the cross, disregarding its shame. Now he is seated in the place of honor beside God's throne. [3]Think of all the hostility he endured from sinful people; then you won't become weary and give up. [4]After all, you have not yet given your lives in your struggle against sin. [5]And have you forgotten the encouraging words God spoke to you as his children? He said, "My child, don't make light of the Lord's discipline, and don't give up when he corrects you. [6]For the Lord disciplines those he loves, and he punishes each one he accepts as his child."

HEBREWS 12:1-6

When you feel discouraged in your Christian life, think of Jesus and all he went through to do what God wanted. Then take heart knowing that you can do what God requires of you by his strength and grace. Stay focused on him.

²When troubles come your way, consider it an opportunity for great joy. ³For you know that when your faith is tested, your endurance has a chance to grow. ⁴So let it grow, for when your endurance is fully developed, you will be perfect and complete, needing nothing. ⁵If you need wisdom, ask our generous God, and he will give it to you. He will not rebuke you for asking. ⁶But when you ask him, be sure that your faith is in God alone. Do not waver, for a person with divided loyalty is as unsettled as a wave of the sea that is blown and tossed by the wind. ⁷Such people should not expect to receive anything from the Lord. ⁸Their loyalty is divided . . . and they are unstable in everything they do. . . . ¹²God blesses those who patiently endure testing and temptation. Afterward they will receive the crown of life that God has promised to those who love him.

JAMES 1:2-8, 12

Most people do not welcome the hard lessons of life "Why do I have to learn this the *hard* way?" they fume. "Why couldn't I have just been able to read a good book on the topic?"

James, no stranger to trials himself, urges readers to take the most unexpected attitude when bad times descend. Although his admonishment sounds strange at first, the outcome of doing so is spiritually rewarding. As you read, consider what you are learning from your troubles.

In this passage, James also teaches us how to acquire wisdom; how to handle temptation; and how hearing God's Word and doing good works go together.

Read James 1:1-27

Be glad when you have a bad day—the experience will do you some good, James wrote (James 1:2-4). As uncomfortable as this message is, James is not saying that we should enjoy trials. Rather, he is saying that we should be glad for the good effects that trials can have on us.

A bout of suffering, usually considered a curse, can be a blessing. Suffering through trials teaches many things essential to life—such as how to have patience and endurance. Living through a trial is also the best way to build character.

When troubles come your way, welcome them as teachers, however unpleasant they may be. Take advantage of your bad circumstances by depending on God to get you through hard times. He will not only take care of you, but he will also make you a better person through it.

Imagine yourself in a coffee shop with a bunch of your friends, having a good time laughing and talking. Suddenly, you see a disheveled person approach the table. *Oh no,* you think, *he's coming over here. What if he asks to join us?*

In this passage, James confronts the Jerusalem churchgoers for having this kind of attitude toward the poor. He reminds them that showing favoritism to the rich while neglecting or slighting the poor is wrong. As James says in a roundabout way, you cannot judge a book by its cover. When have you played favorites?

A famous passage on a chicken-and-egg question also appears: what comes first, faith or works? Get ready as well for some giant-sized lessons on one of the smallest, yet most powerful, parts of the human body.

Read James 2:1–3:12

People of the ancient world had just as much concern for wealth and status as people do today. They wanted to be associated with rich people and undisturbed by the problems of the poor. Even some Christians would flatter the rich and dote on their needs while pushing aside poor people who came to church. James made it clear that Christians who understand their Lord live by a different standard: They dispense with the favor-the-rich custom and treat all people alike, regardless of how wealthy or impoverished they happen to be (James 2:1-4).

Jesus never showed favoritism toward rich people, and neither should we. Attempts to associate only with the financially secure betray a selfish, faithless, and uncaring attitude.

Make a point to show proper respect to all people regardless of the cut of their clothes or the size of their bank accounts.

¹My dear brothers and sisters, how can you claim to have faith in our glorious Lord Jesus Christ if you favor some people over others? ²For example, suppose someone comes into your meeting dressed in fancy clothes and expensive jewelry, and another comes in who is poor and dressed in dirty clothes. ³If you give special attention and a good seat to the rich person, but you say to the poor one, "You can stand over there, or else sit on the floor"—well, ⁴doesn't this discrimination show that your judgments are guided by evil motives? ⁵Listen to me, dear brothers and sisters. Hasn't God chosen the poor in this world to be rich in faith? Aren't they the ones who will inherit the Kingdom he promised to those who love him? ⁶But you dishonor the poor! . . . ⁹If you favor some people over others, you are committing a sin.

JAMES 2:1-6, 9

¹What is causing the quarrels and fights among you? Don't they come from the evil desires at war within you? ²You want what you don't have, so you scheme and kill to get it. You are jealous of what others have, but you can't get it, so you fight and wage war to take it away from them. Yet you don't have what you want because you don't ask God for it. ³And even when you ask, you don't get it because your motives are all wrong—you want only what will give you pleasure. ⁴You adulterers! Don't you realize that friendship with the world makes you an enemy of God? I say it again: If you want to be a friend of the world, you make yourself an enemy of God. ⁵What do you think the Scriptures mean when they say that the spirit God has placed within us is filled with envy? ⁶But he gives us even more grace to stand against such evil desires.

JAMES 4:1-6

The Wild West brought about new kinds of heroes: the lone wolf, the independent pioneer, and the classic rugged individualist. No one could tame the untamed frontier like they could. They did not obey rules—they made them.

The Christian life is not an untamed frontier demanding Wild West heroes. Rather, it is a sanctuary for settlers who respect the boundaries. As you read this passage, look for the boundaries in which believers are to live.

Here James also discusses the nature of true wisdom; getting along with other people; faith and what it can do; and having the right perspective on the future. If you want to blaze a trail to God, this is a good spot from which to start.

Read James 3:13–5:20

Getting close to God requires a transfer of ownership—a humble submission of our lives to him (James 4:7-10). Once that transaction takes place, we must continue the fight against the forces that draw us away from Christ. We must resist the devil and flee from him. We must embrace God's will and let go of our own evil desires. We must grieve our sinfulness rather than celebrate it. And we must purify ourselves.

To sign away your life won't mark you as a distinctly heroic person in most people's eyes. But it will lead to intimacy with God, and it will allow God to "lift you up" (4:10)—something he does not do for lone wolves.

Few things are more frustrating than buying "quality" merchandise that falls apart as soon as you take it out of the box. Then you look inside the box and find a small slip of paper that reads: "Inspected by Number 45." Apparently, your merchandise had not been inspected closely enough. A few seconds of mild abuse by Number 45 probably would have shown this merchandise for what it was, and spared you the disappointment.

In Peter's first letter, he warns and encourages us about disappointments—how we can approach them, live through them, and be strengthened by them. They are tests or, if you will, inspections of God's merchandise—us.

Notice also in this passage a living hope, hints at what angels long to see, and the high standards for those whose faith has been tested and strengthened.

Read 1 Peter 1:1–2:10

Peter wrote of suffering several times in this letter (1 Peter 1:6-7; 3:13-17; 4:12-19; 5:9). His readers needed this discussion of trials because non-Christians misunderstood, harassed, and even physically abused Christians. Some of the opposition came from government officials, some from non-Christian individuals, and some from family members. To those abused and aching Christians, Peter wrote: "Be truly glad. There is wonderful joy ahead, even though you have to endure many trials for a little while" (1:6).

Christians are not of this world—our goals, values, and allegiance contrast and clash with society's. Thus, eventually, all believers will face trials of rejection because of their choice to follow Christ.

Accept rejection and suffering for your faith as a test. God will purify and refine you through your trials.

⁴We have a priceless inheritance—an inheritance that is kept in heaven for you, pure and undefiled, beyond the reach of change and decay. ⁵And through your faith, God is protecting you by his power until you receive this salvation, which is ready to be revealed on the last day for all to see. ⁶So be truly glad. There is wonderful joy ahead, even though you have to endure many trials for a little while. ⁷These trials will show that your faith is genuine. It is being tested as fire tests and purifies gold—though your faith is far more precious than mere gold. So when your faith remains strong through many trials, it will bring you much praise and glory and honor on the day when Jesus Christ is revealed to the whole world.

1 PETER 1:4-7

¹³Now, who will want to harm you if you are eager to do good? ¹⁴But even if you suffer for doing what is right, God will reward you for it. So don't worry or be afraid of their threats. ¹⁵Instead, you must worship Christ as Lord of your life. And if someone asks about your Christian hope, always be ready to explain it. ¹⁶But do this in a gentle and respectful way. Keep your conscience clear. Then if people speak against you, they will be ashamed when they see what a good life you live because you belong to Christ. ¹⁷Remember, it is better to suffer for doing good, if that is what God wants, than to suffer for doing wrong! ¹⁸Christ suffered for our sins once for all time. He never sinned, but he died for sinners to bring you safely home to God. He suffered physical death, but he was raised to life in the Spirit.

1 PETER 3:13-18

A good explanation goes a long way. Think of a time when someone completely misunderstood something you did, and perhaps even asked, "Why did you do that?" Your answer made perfect sense to you. All you needed to do was enlighten the other person to your way of thinking.

Be ready to do that, Peter says in this passage. For you as a Christian, misunderstanding (but also plain curiosity) will bring questions as surely as you breathe. A good explanation will go a long way.

Other important lessons in this reading deal with obeying authority; the husband–wife relationship; and suffering for doing good.

Read 1 Peter 2:11–4:19

The idea of following Christ strikes some people as a new and radical notion. To them any Christian's faith will seem odd or curious. That is why Peter told his readers to be ready to answer questions about their faith (1 Peter 3:15).

Unfortunately, many believers feel constrained by popular assumptions that tell us to stay off the topic of religion. But we do not have to avoid the subject altogether just to stay civil. We can explain our faith to a questioner without causing conflict, especially if we are invited to do so, by conversing "in a gentle and respectful way" (3:16).

Think about why you follow Christ—why you believe and how you might explain your faith and your reasons to someone. Then the next time someone asks you why you believe, feel free to answer, gently and respectfully. Be prepared because the subject will come up eventually, especially if people catch you doing good (3:13).

"You're so old-fashioned you just don't understand!" "Well, let me tell you what it was like when *I* was your age." On which side of the generation gap do you stand?

A key word in the last chapter of Peter's first epistle is *humble*. Yet it is not a word that often describes relationships between young people and their elders. Whether you are old or young, take an attitude check as you read.

Haughty leaders beware, for Peter has strong words in this passage for those who abuse their positions and responsibilities. Suffering again sets the tone, but so does the certainty of God's grace and power to carry his people through.

Read 1 Peter 5:1-14

The variety of ages among Christians in the early church posed a challenge. The older believers had wisdom to share; the younger ones did not always want to listen to them and follow their lead. Peter told his readers that they could solve their problem by letting the older ones humbly lead the way (1 Peter 5:3). It would take humility from *both* sides—the young would have to submit to the old, and the old would have to respect the young (5:5).

The lines of communication between older and younger generations have always had a bit of static. Humility toward each other clears up the signal. Pride breaks communication between generations, while humility opens the lines.

[1]And now, a word to you who are elders in the churches. I, too, am an elder and a witness to the sufferings of Christ. And I, too, will share in his glory when he is revealed to the whole world. As a fellow elder, I appeal to you: [2]Care for the flock that God has entrusted to you. Watch over it willingly, not grudgingly—not for what you will get out of it, but because you are eager to serve God. [3]Don't lord it over the people assigned to your care, but lead them by your own good example. [4]And when the Great Shepherd appears, you will receive a crown of never-ending glory and honor. [5]In the same way, you younger men must accept the authority of the elders. And all of you, serve each other in humility, for "God opposes the proud but favors the humble." [6]So humble yourselves under the mighty power of God, and . . . he will lift you up.

1 PETER 5:1-6

Look to those who are older than you for leadership and guidance. Ask them for advice. Consider their input, and when appropriate, let them lead. At the same time, never look down on the young just because they may lack the wisdom that you once lacked yourself.

¹²Therefore, I will always remind you about these things—even though you already know them and are standing firm in the truth you have been taught. ¹³And it is only right that I should keep on reminding you as long as I live. ¹⁴For our Lord Jesus Christ has shown me that I must soon leave this earthly life, ¹⁵so I will work hard to make sure you always remember these things after I am gone. ¹⁶For we were not making up clever stories when we told you about the powerful coming of our Lord Jesus Christ. We saw his majestic splendor with our own eyes ¹⁷when he received honor and glory from God the Father. The voice from the majestic glory of God said to him, "This is my dearly loved Son, who brings me great joy." ¹⁸We ourselves heard that voice from heaven when we were with him on the holy mountain.

2 PETER 1:12-18

Championship teams build their success upon the basics of their sport. The coaches routinely review the basics with the players. Good athletes practice them again and again. Great athletes strive to perfect them in their technique. Winners never forget the basics and build their game upon them like a house on a foundation.

In his second letter, Peter plays the part of the coach. He does not want Christians to forget the basics of their faith, so he reviews them in this passage. The key word here is *remember*. How's your practice schedule?

As you read, watch also for God's escape hatch and an amazing chain or fortification for your faith. And pay attention to a call to pay attention.

Read 2 Peter 1:1-21

Peter was concerned about his readers' faith surviving over the long run. Because Peter knew that he would die soon, he reviewed the basics of the faith to etch them into their memory (2 Peter 1:12-15). Peter wanted his readers to firmly grasp the gospel's basic message, a goal that would take repetition to achieve. He wanted them to hear again and again that Jesus had come to die for their sins, had risen on the third day, had given them eternal life, and would one day return to judge the earth. Knowing and believing those simple basics would uphold their faith and keep them strong.

From time to time, it is good to review the basics of our faith in Christ. Doing this will refresh our memory, strengthen our faith, and dispel any spiritual falsehoods we may have begun to believe.

Do you remember the basics of the faith? Whether you do or not, be sure to review the Gospels and Epistles regularly to stay spiritually sharp.

"When I grow up," says many a child, "I'll do whatever I please." When they grow up, some actually try. Freedom to do anything they want looks heavenly.

Peter knows that appearances can be deceiving. In this second epistle, Peter warns his readers about the trade-off of "totally free" living. This concern that Peter addresses comes from heretics who advocate a do-what-you-like philosophy. But Peter says their teachings are really more binding than freeing. With guidance as perfect for our century as for the first, Peter provides insight into the slave-master relationship. Who is your master?

Read 2 Peter 2:1-22

Peter's second letter dealt with a heresy that urged Christians to sin. The heretics argued that we may as well do whatever we like because God will forgive us. They called this freedom. But Peter pointed out that freedom to do whatever we like is actually *slavery* to our sinful desires (1 Peter 2:19). He also wrote that God frees us from sin so that we can obey him rather than our sinful desires. God does not free us from the restraint to do good but from the rule of our appetites and desires.

Some people say that they want to be totally free. By this they usually mean that they do not want moral convictions or laws restraining them from doing whatever they like. In reality their desire to be totally free requires them to obey their appetites. Thus they are not totally free. Whether they realize it or not, they obey a master, too.

¹²These false teachers are like unthinking animals. . . . They scoff at things they do not understand, and like animals, they will be destroyed. ¹³Their destruction is their reward for the harm they have done. They love to indulge in evil pleasures in broad daylight. They are a disgrace and a stain among you. They delight in deception even as they eat with you in your fellowship meals. ¹⁴They commit adultery with their eyes, and their desire for sin is never satisfied. They lure unstable people into sin, and they are well trained in greed. They live under God's curse. ¹⁵They have wandered off the right road and followed the footsteps of Balaam son of Beor, who loved to earn money by doing wrong. . . . ¹⁹They promise freedom, but they themselves are slaves of sin and corruption. For you are a slave to whatever controls you.

2 PETER 2:12-15, 19

What or whom will you call your master? Will you follow your fleshly desires and be a slave to sin? Or will you obey God's commands and be free from sin? It is your choice. Choose wisely.

⁹The Lord isn't really being slow about his promise, as some people think. No, he is being patient for your sake. He does not want anyone to be destroyed, but wants everyone to repent. ¹⁰But the day of the Lord will come as unexpectedly as a thief. Then the heavens will pass away with a terrible noise, and the very elements themselves will disappear in fire, and the earth and everything on it will be found to deserve judgment. ¹¹Since everything around us is going to be destroyed like this, what holy and godly lives you should live, ¹²looking forward to the day of God and hurrying it along. On that day, he will set the heavens on fire, and the elements will melt away in the flames. ¹³But we are looking forward to the new heavens and new earth he has promised, a world filled with God's righteousness.

2 PETER 3:9-13

When visiting another country or culture, we may discover that the sense of time is quite different from our own. What does it mean to be on time? How long should something take? Another country, another timetable. It behooves us to adjust if we want to get along.

God's sense of time is the focus of this reading. Here Peter explains that God's timing is different from that of humans. Despite the differences, however, Peter encourages readers to have patience. God is in control and has not forgotten his people. As you read, consider how you can be both watchful and relaxed.

Note that hope is held up in abundance in this reading, as is the example of Jesus.

Read 2 Peter 3:1-18

Some of the Christians to whom Peter wrote faced harassment and suffering for their faith. They knew that God planned an eventual judgment of the earth, when all would be put right. But they wondered, *Why was he waiting?* and *Why not do it now?* Peter told them: God has a different timetable than we do (2 Peter 3:8-9; see Psalm 90:4).

While we anxiously await God's gavel of justice to fall, God patiently waits for more people to repent. He moves with perfect timing, not slowness.

Keep waiting with Jesus for more people to repent and turn to him. Each day he delays is another opportunity for us to have compassion as he does and to give a few more people an opportunity to accept him. Use the time God's given you to spread the Good News.

You have to develop a taste for certain foods. Though some people love it, liver, for example, gags many people on the first try. It takes a commitment to continue eating this "delicacy" before you can get over the initial taste shock.

Being a Christian involves an adjustment of appetites, John writes. Love of the right things is an acquired taste, but worth every bit of effort.

John's goal in this reading is to enlighten his readers. He does this through a message about light and dark that tells a simple truth: You can see where you are going when you walk in God's light. Otherwise you are stumbling in the dark.

Read 1 John 1:1–2:29

John instructed his readers to neither "love this world nor the things it offers you" (1 John 2:15). He listed three appeals that would drag believers down: "a craving for physical pleasure, a craving for everything we see, and pride in our achievements and possessions" (2:16). These pursuits would offer nothing of importance, and they would all fade away. Only doing God's will would have any kind of lasting effect.

To love the world and its treasures takes no effort at all—we do it naturally. That is why God tells us *not* to love it. This means that we must wean ourselves from it. We must set our sights on doing God's will, and let the world's appeals fall away in importance.

All the acts you do for Christ's sake will have lasting value—a changed life, an eternal reward, God's greater glory. Learn to love and do what God loves.

[15]Do not love this world nor the things it offers you, for when you love the world, you do not have the love of the Father in you. [16]For the world offers only a craving for physical pleasure, a craving for everything we see, and pride in our achievements and possessions. These are not from the Father, but are from this world. [17]And this world is fading away, along with everything that people crave. But anyone who does what pleases God will live forever. . . . [24]So you must remain faithful to what you have been taught from the beginning. If you do, you will remain in fellowship with the Son and with the Father. [25]And in this fellowship we enjoy the eternal life he promised us.

1 JOHN 2:15-17, 24-25

¹¹This is the message you have heard from the beginning: We should love one another. ¹²We must not be like Cain, who belonged to the evil one and killed his brother. And why did he kill him? Because Cain had been doing what was evil, and his brother had been doing what was righteous. ¹³So don't be surprised, dear brothers and sisters, if the world hates you. ¹⁴If we love our Christian brothers and sisters, it proves that we have passed from death to life. But a person who has no love is still dead. ¹⁵Anyone who hates another brother or sister is really a murderer at heart. And you know that murderers don't have eternal life within them. ¹⁶We know what real love is because Jesus gave up his life for us. So we also ought to give up our lives for our brothers and sisters.

1 JOHN 3:11-16

Suppose you had a friend who was in serious financial trouble. What would you do for that person? Would you help bail him or her out or give financial counseling? What if your friend's problem was health related? Or worse, what if your friend was in trouble with the law? How far would you go out of your way to help this friend?

In this reading, John illustrates how far Jesus went to save us from our serious spiritual trouble—sin. Through Jesus' sacrifice, we see what true love really is. As John points out, we now have a standard against which to compare our love for others.

Read 1 John 3:1–4:21

Jesus loved us so much that he gave his life for us. His death on the cross to pay the penalty for our sins came as a result of his love. His selfless, sacrificial gift models how we should show love to one another (1 John 3:16).

To love someone means to be like Jesus to that person—to be selfless and to give sacrificially. Loving this way ignores all the enticements that normally compel us to be nice to people, such as the personal benefits we may gain from doing so. Also, loving others as Jesus did may not feel good all the time. This kind of love regards others' welfare above our own, and it may cost an awful lot (pride, possessions, time, money). It may cost everything.

If you truly want to reach out to others, extend to them what God extended to you: unconditional love.

The news occasionally features a story that seems too incredible to be true. A construction worker has a nail driven into his skull and does not suffer any ill effects. A woman is shot six times during a robbery and lives. How can you know if these stories are really true? For the most part you cannot. You just have to trust the source.

In this reading John covers a story that some Christians sometimes doubt—their salvation. He explains to his readers how to know if they are truly saved or not. Read this passage and gain assurance.

As an added feature, John reviews Jesus' mission in coming to earth and in dying. He also throws in a sidebar on what to do if a fellow Christian is sinning.

Read 1 John 5:1-21

John wrote this letter to reassure Christians in their faith; some false teachers had given them cause to doubt that their salvation was secure.

How can we *know* we have eternal life? John tells us: trust in Jesus Christ (1 John 5:13). Jesus is God's own Son, the one who came as a human being, died to pay the penalty for our sins, and rose again. His work alone gives him the power and right to forgive all who confess their sins to him (1 John 1:9). Anyone who believes in Christ has eternal life (see John 3:16).

The next time you feel insecure about your salvation, reaffirm your trust in Christ. Then you can *know* you have eternal life, whether you feel close to God or far away.

¹Everyone who believes that Jesus is the Christ has become a child of God. And everyone who loves the Father loves his children, too. ²We know we love God's children if we love God and obey his commandments. ³Loving God means keeping his commandments, and his commandments are not burdensome. ⁴For every child of God defeats this evil world, and we achieve this victory through our faith. ⁵And who can win this battle against the world? Only those who believe that Jesus is the Son of God. ⁶And Jesus Christ was revealed as God's Son by his baptism in water and by shedding his blood on the cross—not by water only, but by water and blood. And the Spirit, who is truth, confirms it with his testimony. ⁷So we have these three witnesses— ⁸the Spirit, the water, and the blood—and all three agree.

1 JOHN 5:1-8

²Dear friend, I hope all is well with you and that you are as healthy in body as you are strong in spirit. ³Some of the traveling teachers recently returned and made me very happy by telling me about your faithfulness and that you are living according to the truth. ⁴I could have no greater joy than to hear that my children are following the truth. ⁵Dear friend, you are being faithful to God when you care for the traveling teachers who pass through, even though they are strangers to you. ⁶They have told the church here of your loving friendship. Please continue providing for such teachers in a manner that pleases God. ⁷For they are traveling for the Lord, and they accept nothing from people who are not believers. ⁸So we ourselves should support them so that we can be their partners as they teach the truth.

3 JOHN 1:2-8

Do you remember the first time someone put you up for the night? You were away from home and a friend or relative gave you a place to sleep and the promise of a good breakfast the next morning. The bed felt different. The walls looked different from the ones in your room. You made sure that you knew where the bathroom was, just in case. Was that a sense of adventure . . . or homesickness?

In the apostle John's day, traveling teachers and missionaries spent many nights away from home. Their travels created a need for hospitality. Gaius, the person to whom John wrote this third letter, was one believer who extended hospitality to these teachers. Unfortunately, however, not all the believers back then did the same. In addition, not all of the traveling teachers preached the truth about Jesus. So John, in his second letter, warns the believers about these false teachers.

Read 2 John 1:1–3 John 1:15

John commended Gaius for "being faithful to God when you care for the traveling teachers who pass through, even though they are strangers to you" (3 John 1:5). Traveling preachers would travel from place to place, presenting the good news about Christ to unbelievers and helping new churches get started. These ministers depended on fellow Christians to house and feed them. Believers like Gaius therefore provided a valuable ministry to ministers (1:5-8).

Today, ministers still have many needs, and like Gaius, you can help meet some of those needs. By helping ministers, you enable them to do what God has called them to do and therefore participate in their work (1:8). Don't underestimate the importance of your ministry to ministers. Anything you can do to support them through hospitality, gifts, or even words of encouragement will be welcome.

Margaret can hardly wait to get her driver's license. As soon as Margaret turns sixteen, Mom will drive her to the Department of Motor Vehicles where she will take the test and, if all goes well, get official permission to drive a Class A motor vehicle. It will mean new freedom and new responsibility.

Just as driving is a privilege, so is freedom in Christ. In this letter, Jude tells of Christians who have taken their freedom too far. He has no patience with their abuse of this privilege because they know the rules of the road and have deliberately disobeyed them.

Also in this reading you will find strong fight language for the spiritual battles we face. And our duties to one another conclude the letter.

Read Jude 1:1-25

Jude wrote this brief letter to rebuke false teachers. These false teachers taught that Christians can live "immoral lives" because God has forgiven them (Jude 1:4). Such false teachers were wrong, and God's severe judgment awaited them (1:5-11, 14-16).

The same heresy taught back in Jude's day still flourishes today. Many people try to justify immorality and wrongdoing by appealing to God's forgiveness. But God never forgave us so that we could sin without consequence. Jesus died to free us *from* sin. He did not die to free us *to* sin.

Take care of how you use your freedom in Christ. Do not freely sin and cheapen God's forgiveness after you have indulged your appetites. Having this freedom is a privilege that comes with great responsibility. Live wisely and reverently before God.

[20]Build each other up in your most holy faith, pray in the power of the Holy Spirit, [21]and await the mercy of our Lord Jesus Christ, who will bring you eternal life. In this way, you will keep yourselves safe in God's love. [22]And you must show mercy to those whose faith is wavering. [23]Rescue others by snatching them from the flames of judgment. Show mercy to still others, but do so with great caution, hating the sins that contaminate their lives. [24]Now all glory to God, who is able to keep you from falling away and will bring you with great joy into his glorious presence without a single fault. [25]All glory to him who alone is God, our Savior through Jesus Christ our Lord. All glory, majesty, power, and authority are his before all time, and in the present, and beyond all time! Amen.

JUDE 1:20-25

[18]"Write this letter to the angel of the church in Thyatira. This is the message from the Son of God, whose eyes are like flames of fire, whose feet are like polished bronze: [19]I know all the things you do. I have seen your love, your faith, your service, and your patient endurance. And I can see your constant improvement in all these things. [20]But I have this complaint against you. You are permitting that woman—that Jezebel who calls herself a prophet—to lead my servants astray. She teaches them to commit sexual sin and to eat food offered to idols. [21]I gave her time to repent, but she does not want to turn away from her immorality. [22]Therefore, I will throw her on a bed of suffering, and those who commit adultery with her will suffer greatly unless they repent and turn away from her evil deeds.

REVELATION 2:18-22

Some things in life just seem too good to pass up. For instance, a 30 percent-off sale at the mall always seems to happen when we have no money. At a time like this it is easy to justify spending more than we should with our credit cards. Or what about indulging in foods that are not healthy for us? Opportunities to do so always seem to come right after we have made a commitment to healthier living.

The same rule applies to sin. Just because people have made a commitment to Jesus Christ does not mean that the temptations stop. In this reading, Jesus has strong words for those who think that God's moral law has been suspended for them. He especially condemns those who have taught others the same.

Not every word in this reading is one of condemnation, however. Jesus has some encouraging words for the persecuted church as well as for the obedient church.

Read Revelation 1:1–3:22

In this portion of Revelation, John rebuked the Thyatiran believers for tolerating sexual immorality in their church (Revelation 2:20). The false prophetess Jezebel taught them to regard it lightly, but it was not a light matter at all.

The temptation to minimize the problems of sexual immorality has never been greater. Virtually *everyone* regards sexual choice as a freedom and right of adulthood. If "two consenting adults" can't be free to decide to have sex, then who can? Or so the reasoning goes. Yet God invented sex to be an intimate bond between husband and wife *only* (see Genesis 2:24). The fact that we can easily corrupt it gives us all the more reason to guard its purity closely.

Cherish your sexuality as you would a precious gem. How you express it matters a great deal. Keep yourself pure for the sake of Christ and the purpose for which he created you.

Suppose you won a Nobel or a Pulitzer prize, or some equally prestigious honor. Would you feel worthy to receive such an award? What would you do with all the praise and acclaim? Suppose then, after the shock wore off, you had it revoked. "Not worthy of it after all," the committee decided. How *then* would you feel?

In this reading, the award winners do something that would be considered unusual in our culture. They willingly give back their awards without anyone asking them to do so.

Read Revelation 4:1–5:14

In his vision of heaven around God's throne, John saw the twenty-four elders cast their crowns before God and worship him, proclaiming the Lord to be "worthy . . . to receive glory and honor and power" (Revelation 4:11). God's awesome greatness compelled them to cast their crowns at the feet of Jesus. And why shouldn't they? Jesus has done more to be worthy of the glory, honor, and power he claims than human beings can ever comprehend. Is not Jesus' birth proof enough of that?

Those who find it difficult to accept God's authority or claim of glory have the wrong god in mind. They have forgotten the total sacrifice he made when Jesus, the Creator of all, came down to earth as a tiny baby in the home of a simple Jewish couple. Their concept of God does not match the reality of his victory over sin and death, either.

²I saw a throne in heaven and someone sitting on it. ³The one sitting on the throne was as brilliant as gemstones—like jasper and carnelian. And the glow of an emerald circled his throne like a rainbow. ⁴Twenty-four thrones surrounded him, and twenty-four elders sat on them. They were all clothed in white and had gold crowns on their heads. ⁵From the throne came flashes of lightning and the rumble of thunder. And in front of the throne were seven torches with burning flames. This is the sevenfold Spirit of God. ⁶In front of the throne was a shiny sea of glass, sparkling like crystal. In the center and around the throne were four living beings, each covered with eyes, front and back. . . . ⁸Day after day and night after night they keep on saying, "Holy, holy, holy is the Lord God, the Almighty."

REVELATION 4:2-6, 8

Give God the glory and honor he deserves. Take your "crown"—your claim to fame, or whatever your "glory" may be—and cast it at Jesus' feet by praising him. Fall down and worship, as the twenty-four elders did. What could make more sense at such a time as this?

⁹When the Lamb broke the fifth seal, I saw under the altar the souls of all who had been martyred for the word of God and for being faithful in their testimony. ¹⁰They shouted to the Lord and said, "O Sovereign Lord, holy and true, how long before you judge the people who belong to this world and avenge our blood for what they have done to us?" ¹¹Then a white robe was given to each of them. And they were told to rest a little longer until the full number of their brothers and sisters—their fellow servants of Jesus who were to be martyred—had joined them. ¹²I watched as the Lamb broke the sixth seal, and there was a great earthquake. The sun became as dark as black cloth, and the moon became as red as blood. ¹³Then the stars of the sky fell to the earth like green figs falling from a tree shaken by a strong wind.

REVELATION 6:9-13

It is easy to get caught up in the grimy details of our lives. We can become so mired in our problems that we fall in with the complainers. Then something convicting happens. We hear that someone else has suffered or died for believing in Christ. Suddenly our suffering seems paltry by comparison, and we ponder the question: What would *we* do in a situation like that?

This reading provides a vivid picture of those who have suffered for Christ and are patiently waiting in heaven for God to bring about justice. The news they receive is both good and bad—more will die for their faith. But God will judge the earth justly, and their deaths will be avenged.

Read Revelation 6:1–8:5

After the Lamb (Christ) broke the fifth seal, John saw the souls of martyrs who had died for telling others about Christ. These martyrs had been killed "for the word of God and for being faithful in their witness." They cried out to God for justice, asking when God would avenge their blood. Jesus told them to wait a little while longer, until they were joined by the others who had yet to be killed for their faith (Revelation 6:9-11).

In contrast to these saints, we seem to care more about getting justice for the petty inequities we suffer. A traffic ticket, a snide remark, or an accusation of bad motives can set us off on a holy crusade. How poorly those causes compare to the cause of these men and women who had entrusted themselves to Jesus.

Rest assured that God is perfectly just and good. He does not forget when a child of his suffers for doing right. He keeps accounts and will one day settle them. Wait for God to bring about justice instead of taking it into your own hands.

News programs occasionally report about a person who took a stand for right against a tremendous injustice or wrong. Although the person's crusade may seem hopeless, he or she continues to stand on conviction. And sometimes this person even wins.

In this reading, two prophets stand up against the world for God's message. Their mission is life-and-death, for themselves and for those to whom they preach.

Read Revelation 8:6–11:19

The two witnesses were opposed for telling everyone about sin, repentance, and the coming judgment. The opposition came from everyone, not just a large majority or a powerful few. The opposition included violence. As soon as God withdrew his protection from the two witnesses, the people killed them and then celebrated their death (Revelation 11:10). Even though the witnesses were right, no one listened.

Being the only spokesperson for God's point of view doesn't make that point of view wrong. The majority may very well be wrong, every single one of them. If so, it doesn't do you any good to be wrong right along with them. And if you try, the most you can hope for is to have some company in your failure, but what consolation is that? In the case of the two witnesses, virtually the entire *world* was wrong.

Stand up for what is right no matter how few people share your convictions. Those who have closed their minds to God's Word will have to answer for themselves. God's truth will stand on its own, even if you're the only one defending it.

3"And I will give power to my two witnesses, and they will be clothed in burlap and will prophesy during those 1,260 days." 4These two prophets are the two olive trees and the two lampstands that stand before the Lord of all the earth. 5If anyone tries to harm them, fire flashes from their mouths and consumes their enemies. This is how anyone who tries to harm them must die. 6They have power to shut the sky so that no rain will fall for as long as they prophesy. And they have the power to turn the rivers and oceans into blood, and to strike the earth with every kind of plague as often as they wish. 7When they complete their testimony, the beast that comes up out of the bottomless pit will declare war against them, and he will conquer them and kill them. 8And their bodies will lie in the main street of Jerusalem.

REVELATION 11:3-8

[9]A third angel followed them, shouting, "Anyone who worships the beast and his statue or who accepts his mark on the forehead or on the hand [10]must drink the wine of God's anger. It has been poured full strength into God's cup of wrath. And they will be tormented with fire and burning sulfur in the presence of the holy angels and the Lamb. [11]The smoke of their torment will rise forever and ever, and they will have no relief day or night, for they have worshiped the beast and his statue and have accepted the mark of his name." [12]This means that God's holy people must endure persecution patiently, obeying his commands and maintaining their faith in Jesus. [13]And I heard a voice from heaven saying, "Write this down: Blessed are those who die in the Lord from now on. Yes, says the Spirit, they are blessed indeed."

REVELATION 14:9-13

"No money down! No payments for a year! Zero percent financing!" Sound familiar? You know the deal. You also know that they are not going to give you something for nothing, so you had better find out what the catch is. Somewhere down the line, you will pay for that too-good-to-be-true offer.

In this passage, John tells of a bad deal that many will make with the beast from the sea in the end times. At first the deal looks good, but that is because the real payment—the eternal consequences—has not yet come due. As you read, determine not to fall for Satan's sales pitch.

The rest of this reading contains a retelling of the Christmas story and a heavenly war. Michael and the other angels fight for God, while Satan enlists the help of a strange beast. The battle is on.

Read Revelation 12:1–14:20

Those who worshiped the beast suffered the consequences (Revelation 14:9-12). At first it appeared that Satan had offered a better way—just take this mark, worship the beast, and all will be well; you'll be able to buy food for your family. But the price was eternal punishment.

Satan often comes along to deceive us, and the only way to avoid falling into his trap is to trust and obey God. Satan will try to make his way seem more attractive, easier, less painful, and more pleasurable than God's. But just beyond Satan's attractive, painless solution lies a more painful consequence.

When God's way seems to exact a price, trust in his plans for your future. Though you may pay a short-term price for obeying God, trust that he will reward you greatly for your obedience. You can be sure that the reward will be well worth the sacrifice.

Nothing seems more certain than death and taxes. Everyone knows that he or she will die someday. It is a given, a nasty fact of life, although not everyone will admit or think about that for too long. Another fact every adult U.S. citizen knows is that on April 15, they have to have their income-tax forms completed and in the mail. Despite the fact that they have had significant sums of money taken from each of their paychecks throughout the year, they may owe more. So they have to pay up.

One thing is more certain than death and taxes—Christ's return. In this reading John tells his readers to be prepared today for Christ's second coming because preparing tomorrow may be too late. For those who heed John's warning, there is a wonderful blessing. As you read, consider what you must do to be prepared.

Read Revelation 15:1–16:21

Christ will return "as unexpectedly as a thief!" (Revelation 16:15; see 1 Thessalonians 5:1-6). His return will take everyone completely by surprise, and it will mark the beginning of the final judgment (Revelation 16:1-21). There will be no more opportunities to turn to God.

The certainty of tomorrow's sunrise falls somewhat shy of 100 percent. When God's plan calls for it, tomorrow will not come—Christ will. Many people will have planned to get their act together that day, to stop their indulgences and start living prudently on that day, to do what they knew they ought to have done before that day. Their one more chance will not materialize. Christ will have returned to judge the earth, and only those who awaited his return—only those who *already* submitted their lives to him—will be prepared.

Be ready when Christ returns. If you have not accepted him as your Savior and Lord, today may be your last opportunity to respond to the invitation he has been holding out for two thousand years.

[12]Then the sixth angel poured out his bowl on the great Euphrates River, and it dried up so that the kings from the east could march their armies toward the west without hindrance. [13]And I saw three evil spirits that looked like frogs leap from the mouths of the dragon, the beast, and the false prophet. [14]They are demonic spirits who work miracles and go out to all the rulers of the world to gather them for battle against the Lord on that great judgment day of God the Almighty. [15]"Look, I will come as unexpectedly as a thief! Blessed are all who are watching for me, who keep their clothing ready so they will not have to walk around naked and ashamed." [16]And the demonic spirits gathered all the rulers and their armies to a place with the Hebrew name Armageddon.

REVELATION 16:12-16

[1]I saw another angel come down from heaven with great authority, and the earth grew bright with his splendor. [2]He gave a mighty shout: "Babylon is fallen—that great city is fallen! She has become a home for demons. She is a hideout for every foul spirit, a hideout for every foul vulture and every foul and dreadful animal. [3]For all the nations have fallen because of the wine of her passionate immorality. The kings of the world have committed adultery with her. Because of her desires for extravagant luxury, the merchants of the world have grown rich." [4]Then I heard another voice calling from heaven, "Come away from her, my people. Do not take part in her sins, or you will be punished with her. [5]For her sins are piled as high as heaven, and God remembers her evil deeds. [6]Do to her as she has done to others. Double her penalty for all her evil deeds."

REVELATION 18:1-6

Books on business management sell quite well, and for good reason: all businesses—large, medium, and small—compete in a brutal marketplace where nice guys really do finish last. Every competitive edge makes a difference. Every competitive edge soon becomes obsolete, too, which only quickens the pace, raises the stakes, and deepens the businessperson's commitment to finding a sure way to make more money.

John's vision in this passage is disheartening to anyone who is greedy for wealth. Here, the mother of all material wealth, Babylon, is destroyed. But the bad news for businesspeople, or merchants, is good news for those who love God more than wealth. As you read, determine to focus on God and his plan, not on money.

Read Revelation 17:1–20:15

The greed demonstrated by the merchants in John's vision is nothing new. People have always exploited sinful human desires, such as greed, lust, and pride, for money. They view human vices as opportunities to make a living or even to get rich. They reason, "As long as people want this, why not give it to them?" But those who love God hate evil. They do not want to encourage it in others any more than they want it ruling their own lives. They don't see people's greed and evil desires as opportunities to exploit, but as sad facts of human nature that need to be brought under the lordship of Christ.

Honor God in your business dealings. Avoid the temptation to take advantage of people's vices to enrich yourself. If you make or sell goods or services, uphold God's glory in it all. No one can undermine your business ethics if you care most about their effects on other people.

There are not too many things in this world that feel better than reaping the fruits of your long, hard labor. For parents, their labor is rewarded when their children grow up and become good, productive members of society. For college students, this is receiving a diploma on graduation day. For sports teams, this is winning the championship.

One day our labor to believe in and follow Christ will also come to fruition. In this reading, John describes the reward God will give his followers for their faithfulness. He will take us to our heavenly home—the new Jerusalem. Living here for eternity will be worth every sacrifice made, every prayer offered, every trial endured, and every persecution suffered. As you read, rejoice in Christ's victory and determine to remain faithful to him.

Read Revelation 21:1–22:21

At the end of history, God will destroy the old heaven and earth and create new and perfect ones. Those who died in their sins will be cast into the "fiery lake of burning sulfur," separated from God forever (Revelation 21:8). In sharp contrast, those who have been covered with Christ's blood will enter God's Holy City to live with him in eternal joy. Inside that city the people will hear Jesus say, "[God] will wipe every tear from their eyes, and there will be no more death or sorrow or crying or pain. All these things are gone forever" (21:4). Actually, the end of history is also a beginning—the beginning of God's perfect world.

Everyone longs for a perfect world, one that is without suffering, death, or sadness. In this perfect world, we also long for fulfilling love and justice. All of this seems like an impossible fantasy. But here it is—God's promised future for all who love him.

¹Then I saw a new heaven and a new earth, for the old heaven and the old earth had disappeared. And the sea was also gone. ²And I saw the holy city, the new Jerusalem, coming down from God out of heaven like a bride beautifully dressed for her husband. ³I heard a loud shout from the throne, saying, "Look, God's home is now among his people! He will live with them, and they will be his people. God himself will be with them. ⁴He will wipe every tear from their eyes, and there will be no more death or sorrow or crying or pain. All these things are gone forever." ⁵And the one sitting on the throne said, "Look, I am making everything new!" And then he said to me, "Write this down, for what I tell you is trustworthy and true." ⁶And he also said, "It is finished! I am the Alpha and the Omega— the Beginning and the End."

REVELATION 21:1-6

TOPICAL INDEX

THE ONE YEAR WAY

Do-able. Daily. Devotions.

START ANY DAY THE ONE YEAR WAY.

Do-able.
Every One Year book is designed for people who live busy, active lives. Just pick one up and start on today's date.

Daily.
Daily routine doesn't have to be drudgery. One Year devotionals help you form positive habits that connect you to what's most important.

Devotions.
Discover a natural rhythm for drawing near to God in an extremely personal way. One Year devotionals provide daily focus essential to your spiritual growth.

For Women

The One Year®
Devotions for
Women on
the Go

The One Year®
Devotions for
Women

The One Year®
Devotions for
Moms

The One Year®
Women of the
Bible

For Men

The One Year®
Devotions for
Men on the Go

The One Year®
Devotions for
Men

For Couples

The One Year®
Book of Devotions
for Couples

For Families

The One Year®
Family
Devotions

For Teens

The One Year®
Devos for Teens

The One Year®
Devos for Sports
Fans

For Bible Study

The One Year®
Praying through
the Bible

The One Year®
through the
Bible Devotional

For Personal Growth

The One Year®
Walk with God
Devotional

The One Year®
Daily Grind

The One Year®
Great Songs of
Faith

The One Year®
Life Verse
Devotional

It's convenient and easy to grow with
God the One Year way.

CP0145

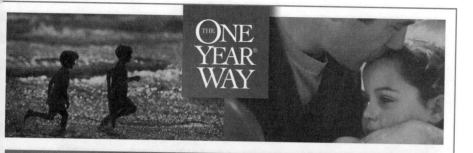

THE ONE YEAR® WAY

Teach Truth.

MEET JESUS EVERY DAY THE ONE YEAR WAY.

For Kids

The One Year®
Devotions for
Girls

The One Year®
Devotions for
Boys

The One Year®
Devotions for
Preschoolers

The One Year®
Devotions for
Kids

The One Year®
Make-It-Stick
Devotions

The One Year®
Bible for Kids:
Challenge
Edition

The One Year®
Children's Bible

The One Year®
Book of Josh
McDowell's
Youth Devotions